The Life and Work of Jane Ellen Harrison

Frontispiece: Portrait of Jane Harrison by Augustus John, 1909, now hanging in the Senior Combination Room, Newnham College, Cambridge. The painting in the background is *The Yachts* by Wilson Steer

The Life and Work of Jane Ellen Harrison

Annabel Robinson

OXFORD
UNIVERSITY PRESS

OXFORD

UNIVERSITY PRESS

Great Clarendon Street, Oxford OX2 6DP

Oxford University Press is a department of the University of Oxford.
It furthers the University's objective of excellence in research, scholarship,
and education by publishing worldwide in

Oxford New York

Auckland Bangkok Buenos Aires Cape Town Chennai
Dar es Salaam Delhi Hong Kong Istanbul Karachi Kolkata
Kuala Lumpur Madrid Melbourne Mexico City Mumbai Nairobi
São Paulo Shanghai Singapore Taipei Tokyo Toronto

and an associated company in Berlin

Oxford is a registered trade mark of Oxford University Press
in the UK and in certain other countries

Published in the United States
By Oxford University Press Inc., New York

© Annabel Robinson 2002

The moral rights of the author have been asserted
Database right Oxford University Press (maker)

First published 2002

All rights reserved. No part of this publication may be reproduced,
stored in a retrieval system, or transmitted, in any form or by any means,
without the prior permission in writing of Oxford University Press,
or as expressly permitted by law, or under terms agreed with the appropriate
reprographics rights organization. Enquiries concerning reproduction
outside the scope of the above should be sent to the Rights Department,
Oxford University Press, at the address above

You must not circulate this book in any other binding or cover
and you must impose this same condition on any acquirer

British Library Cataloguing in Publication Data

Data available

Library of Congress Cataloging in Publication Data
Robinson, Annabel.
The life and work of Jane Ellen Harrison.
p.   cm.
Includes bibliographical references (p.) and index.
ISBN 0-19-924233-X (acid-free paper)
1. Harrison, Jane Ellen, 1850–1928.   2. Classicists—Great Britain—Biography.
3. Archaeologists—Great Britain—Biography.   4. Civilization, Ancient—Historiography.
5. Newnham College—Biography.   6. Mythology—Historiography.
7. Ritual—Historiography.   I. Title.
PA85 .H33 R63 2002   938.007202—dc21   [B]   2001055731

ISBN 0-19-924233-X

1 3 5 7 9 10 8 6 4 2

Typeset in Dante MT by SNP Best-set Typesetter Ltd., Hong Kong
Printed in Great Britain on acid-free paper by
T. J. International Padstow, Cornwall.

To Chris Stray

χαριστήριον

Preface

THIS book owes its existence to the coincidence of two events in 1981, a conversation and an article. The conversation was a casual, coffee-break exchange of ideas in which Joan Givner was talking about her life of Katherine Anne Porter. I was looking for a research project at the time, and knew at that moment that what I most wanted to do was a biography. That same week I came across an article in *Classical World* by William M. Calder III entitled 'Research Opportunities in the Modern History of Classical Scholarship', in which he suggested that a 'woman might write the life or edit the letters of Jane Ellen Harrison, a passionate scholar working in an important field and a pioneer in her struggle to find a place in a man's world'. It was important, Calder urged, that the history of classical scholarship be written by classicists. I immediately sensed that I had found an ideal subject.

Although academic research into the work of Harrison and her colleagues was a new departure for me, in a sense I have been conversant with their ideas all my life. When my father died in 1980 I discovered her *Ancient Art and Ritual* on his shelves. A science teacher, he was in many ways a self-educated man. I remember from childhood his interest in the ideas of J. G. Frazer, totem and tabu, and sympathetic magic. He was irrationally hostile to Christianity and all organized religion, but seemed to revere some unifying life force in a way he could never articulate. It was only as I worked on this biography that I understood why he had so often impressed on me that in his youth he had read Pausanias. To him, that epitomized what it meant to be truly educated. I have reflected that he may be typical of the kind of reader on whom Jane Harrison had so much influence. These are the ordinary people, hungry for education, that Harrison sought to reach. They never published. They are mute now, and their debt to Harrison must remain undocumented. Through her influence on many other like my father, Harrison contributed to the great change of outlook that marked the transition from Victorian to Edwardian England.

A.R.

Acknowledgements

UNWITTINGLY and posthumously, Jane Harrison has introduced me to many new friends. My thanks go first and foremost to Chris Stray, whose unfailing encouragement and practical help have sustained me throughout. Chris is the most generous of colleagues, feeding me with references and quotations wherever he came across them, critiquing my work with friendly insight, always ready to answer my e-mailed questions. Chris put me in touch with Douglas Wood, who was working on a biography of Francis Cornford at the time of his death.

The idea for this book was prompted by a conversation with Joan Givner, who helped me in the initial stages, as did Joan Stubbs, Nigel Nicolson, Frances Partridge, Barbara Strachey, Hugh Lloyd-Jones, Robert Ackerman, and William M. Calder III, whose Oldfather Conference on the Cambridge Ritualists was invaluable for the understanding of the intellectual background of Harrison's work. Jean Pace, the daughter of Harrison's student and biographer Jessie Stewart, shared with me material in her possession and passed on helpful personal memories of both Jane Harrison and Hope Mirrlees. I am sorry that her death has prevented me from thanking her personally now that the book is complete.

It has been a great pleasure to stay at Newnham College for periods of research. Ann Phillips, formerly archivist at Newnham, went out of her way to show me kindness. To her successor, Anne Thomson, I likewise owe much. My friendship with the Principal of Newnham, Onora O'Neill, goes back to our days together at St Paul's Girls' School, and it has been a special delight to engage once again in stimulating conversation.

Kenneth and Jean Nelson provided me with what no library could: a connection with Harrison's own family. They also put me in touch with Elizabeth Lane, Harrison's great-niece, who sent me various material from the family archives. I am saddened that she did not live to see my book come to light. Kenneth Nelson accompanied me on a memorable day of visiting places in Yorkshire and Lincolnshire that were significant in Harrison's life, notably the beautiful house at Great Limber where Harrison's mother (his grandfather's sister), Elizabeth Nelson, had grown up. Thank you, Sue Woods, for your kindness to me on a more recent visit to your house.

Classical colleagues in Canada, the United States, Britain, and Germany have encouraged me by their interest in my work in progress as I have presented it at conferences or discussed it by e-mail. I am especially grateful to Bob Todd, Harry Edinger, Eric Csapo, Anthony Podlecki, Catherine Rubincam, John Humphrey, Martin Cropp, Sarah Pomeroy, Martha Carpentier, Robert Fowler, Mary Beard, Matthew Leigh, Claire Breay, and Renate Schlesier. From many of these people I have received not only academic stimulus but warm hospitality.

Kate Deasington at the University of Glasgow library sought out valuable material. My thanks also go to Carl Spadoni and Kenneth Blackwell at the Bertrand Russell archives at McMaster University and to Janet Johnstone at Cheltenham Ladies' College. My thanks to Shelley Sweeney, formerly archivist at the University of Regina library, and to Marion Lake and Susan Robertson-Krezel at Inter-Library Loans for superb service.

I am grateful to the University of Regina for travel grants and three sabbaticals since I embarked on this project. I have been helped by so many of my colleagues in so many ways that it would be invidious to mention names. But it is significant that those who have shown interest in Jane Harrison come from a variety of disciplines: English, French, history, women's studies, and music. I owe especial thanks to Brian Rainey for much collegial help with French and German, and to Barbara Kaltz and the President, David Barnard, who took the time to read the manuscript and discuss it with me. My thanks also go to Corrine Gogal for unfailing administrative support. The mistakes that remain are all my own.

To Hilary O'Shea and Oxford University Press, many thanks for all your kindness and helpfulness.

This book has been prepared using Nota Bene's suite of academic software: Lingua, Ibidem, and Orbis. These tools have been a pleasure to use and quite indispensable. I greatly appreciate the prompt and personal assistance I have received from their technical support.

Thank you, Reid, for your lifelong love of biography and your sustained interest in my work all these years, for ferreting in libraries and bookstores and for reading the manuscript when it was finally complete. Thank you, Stephanie and Nigel, Muriel, Jennie, and Christa Rose for your welcomes when I needed a place to stay. Heather and Knut Olav, thank you for doing the Christmas baking this year, and jeg vil også rette en takk til deg, Andreas, fordi du minner meg på at livet består av mer enn det å skrive bøker.

Contents

List of Illustrations

A Note on the Text

As Harrison herself observed, what to call people is a problem. 'Miss Harrison' is dated, and she herself hated being addressed that way, while 'Jane' is over-familiar, especially when writing of her scholarship. I like the full name, 'Jane Harrison', as avoiding both these pitfalls, but it is too cumbersome to sustain, and so I have generally followed the North American practice of referring to her by her last name alone. However, I have referred to her as 'Jane' during her childhood and whenever I mention her in the context of her family or (occasionally) close friends. In a few instances I have departed from this procedure and used her full name to avoid monotony or when the rhythm of the sentence seemed to me to demand it.

The marriage of Francis Cornford to Frances Darwin (daughter of Francis Darwin) caused problems for everyone. (A family member wrote a charade entitled 'The Importance of Being Frank'.) I have tended to use whatever name is least confusing in the context.

In the case of maiden and married names, I give the right name for the particular moment in time, but where confusion could arise, the alternative name is provided in brackets, maiden name before married name.

The words 'primitive' and 'savage' present a special problem. Where it is necessary to use them, in reference to sources, I have placed them within inverted commas on their first occurrence to signal that they are now loaded terms, though in their historical context their cultural bias was not recognized. The inverted commas are dropped thereafter.

Archive abbreviations

JHA   Jane Harrison archives, Newnham College, Cambridge
BRA   Bertrand Russell archives, William Ready Division of Archives and Research Collections, McMaster University Library, Hamilton, Canada

Unless specified otherwise, all letters are held in the Jane Harrison archives.
MS MacColl are held by the Glasgow University Archives.
MS Gilbert Murray are held by the Bodleian Library, Oxford.

Introduction

JANE ELLEN HARRISON (1850–1928), scholar, lecturer, and writer on ancient Greek art and religion, deserves to be better known than she is. She occupies a genuinely unique place in the history of women, a pioneer as a woman academic whose success lay in her research rather than her teaching, one of the first women to receive an honorary degree, whose calibre as a scholar made her comfortable in the masculine milieu of Cambridge University at the beginning of the twentieth century, and who regarded the pursuit of knowledge as more important than fulfilling any societal expectations of a woman's role. Harrison's life, both academic and personal, was not easy. The loss of her mother at birth overshadowed her, she suffered the handicap of an early education at the hands of unschooled governesses, and her chosen field of ancient Greek religion embroiled her in some of the most contentious academic disputes of the time. But she had a brilliant mind and strength of character which ultimately enabled her to transcend these difficulties and make a mark on her generation. Part of her genius was to set her academic research in the wider context of human life, in the belief that what we think about Greek religion affects what we think about everything else. Harrison's work was important to her because, she believed, it touched the experience of every human being. She was read, and continues to be read, not only by academics but by writers, poets, and thinkers.

The originality of her vision comes to many of her readers as an epiphany. She was not afraid to be unconventional, in either her private or her scholarly life. Her students claimed that she changed the way they viewed the world. At a time when classics at Cambridge was bogged down in minutiae of textual and grammatical analysis, her student, friend, and biographer Jessie (Crum) Stewart observed that she held the creation of beauty higher even than research and scholarship, she saw meaning in the pattern rather than the detail, she loved the brilliant generalization, and drawing a conclusion from masses of data gave her an aesthetic satisfaction. The test of truth was whether the theory resonated with life as a whole. She was, admittedly, wrong in some of her conclusions, but then so were her male contemporaries.

After her death Jane Harrison's memory was eclipsed for several reasons. One was the failure of her companion Hope Mirrlees to complete the biography which her academic friends had hoped would defend her work and preserve her personality. Sexism and gender bias played a part. I would argue that the main reason is that her work lay in an area rife with unsolved problems of history and ethnography which was abandoned by most for lack of a reliable basis.

Within the last-decade there is a resurgence of interest. Her passionate commitment to the importance of what we *feel* in religion, as opposed to what we *believe*, and elevation of the irrational over the rational is of increasing relevance in a post-modern world. Jane Harrison confronts all those interested in gender studies as a human being who defies all simplistic categorization.

To write a biography is to take in one's hands the life and reputation of another human being. When the subject is no longer living, defenceless in the face of unjust or biased accounts, the biographer has a particular responsibility to stand back and to take as much care as possible that his or her own preconceived notions do not get in the way.

In the case of Jane Ellen Harrison, however, it is notoriously difficult to arrive at any undistorted account. Apart from the public record of schools attended, lectures given, employment held and distinctions received, and Harrison's own published books and articles, the evidence available to her biographers consists of a small book of memoirs written at the end of her life entitled *Reminiscences of a Student's Life*,[1] various letters, including over 800 addressed to Gilbert Murray, a collection of testimonials and various memories of friends and family, assembled for a memoir soon after her death, and the notes and a rough draft of the first part of this memoir, written by the woman who was Harrison's companion for the last eight years of her life, Hope Mirrlees. Jessie Stewart published *Jane Ellen Harrison: A Portrait from Letters* in 1959,[2] and more recently, Sandra Peacock has written *Jane Ellen Harrison: The Mask and the Self*.[3] In his introduction to a recent reprint of her *Prolegomena to the Study of Greek Religion*, Robert Ackerman

---

[1] Jane Ellen Harrison, *Reminiscences of a Student's Life* (London: Hogarth Press, 1925).

[2] Jessie G. Stewart, *Jane Ellen Harrison: a Portrait from Letters* (London: Merlin Press, 1959).

[3] Sandra J. Peacock, *Jane Ellen Harrison: the Mask and the Self* (New Haven: Yale University Press, 1988).

has set her work in its intellectual context.[4] Harry Payne, in an unpublished article, offers some interesting insights into her life and work.[5] Mary Beard's *The Invention of Jane Harrison*[6] covers a decade of Harrison's life and explores the problem of tendentious archives.

All of the primary material is problematic, for two reasons, both of which have to do with Harrison's own personality. First, she, more than most people, cultivated an outward persona that was quite different from her natural (one is tempted to say 'true') self. Just to read *Reminiscences* in conjunction with the letters she wrote to Gilbert Murray is to be brought face to face with what deconstructionists might call an *aporia*: a paradox of self-contradictions. Secondly, the image she succeeded in conveying had the effect of making her, a scholar remembered for her work on Greek myth, a 'myth' herself. The legend of Jane Harrison was already powerful when Virginia Woolf referred to her elliptically ('could it be the famous scholar, could it be J—H—herself?').[7] Others who knew her personally constructed their own myths: Dora Carrington speculated amongst her Bloomsbury friends whether she was a lesbian, Jessie Stewart set her on a pedestal, and Hope Mirrlees, whose personal relationship to Harrison was complicated by her own emotional dependence, further compounded the myth with obsessive and Freudian overlay.

Reminiscences consists of an assembly of anecdotes that give the impression of a satisfying life of scholarly achievement and warm friendships. The reader perceives Harrison as serene in her later years, a woman with a sense of humour and a quick eye for the absurd, who does not take life too seriously. Her only regret, it would seem, was that she had not devoted more time to learning languages (never mind that she could, by the end of her life, read fluently not only Greek and Latin, French and German, but also to a lesser extent Italian, Spanish, and Russian, and had worked hard at acquiring a knowledge of Sanskrit, Cuneiform, Hebrew and Persian, Swedish and Icelandic). The memoirs make no mention of any of the people whom she

---

[4] Jane Ellen Harrison, *Prolegomena to the Study of Greek Religion*, Mythos edn. (Princeton: Princeton University Press, 1991). See also Ackerman, 'The Cambridge Group: Origins and Composition' in William M. Calder III (ed.), *The Cambridge Ritualists Reconsidered* (Atlanta: Scholars Press, 1991), 1–19. For a slightly different view, see Annabel Robinson, 'A New Light our Elders had not Seen: Deconstructing the "Cambridge Ritualists"', *Échos du Monde Classique/Classical Views*, 42, NS 17.3 (1998), 471–87.

[5] Harry Payne, 'Jane Harrison: Lady of the Wild Things' (unpublished).

[6] Mary Beard, The Invention of Jane Harrison (Cambridge, Mass.: Harvard University Press, 2000).

[7] Virginia Woolf, *A Room of One's Own* (London: Hogarth Press, 1929; repr. Toronto: Clarke, Irwin & Co., 1978), 26.

had known best and who had most influenced her (Henry Butcher, D. S. MacColl, Gilbert Murray, Francis Cornford, and Prince Mirsky), on the grounds that they were still living. She says nothing of the major disappointments of her life or of the deep depression and physical pain that overshadowed many years and is evident from her letters. *Reminiscences* raises a number of questions: Why did she publish it? Was it a deliberate attempt to nuance the record? Did she believe it herself? If so, was the writing of it a sort of spiritual exercise, undertaken in an attempt to bring satisfactory closure to a troubled and turbulent life? Or was it no more than an ornamental show-piece, the writer's equivalent of a needlework sampler?

Harrison herself was all too conscious that the face she presented to the world was a persona of her own construction. She wrote in *Reminiscences* 'Until I met Aunt Glegg in the *Mill on the Floss*, I never knew myself. I am Aunt Glegg; with all reverence I say it. I wear before the world a mask of bland cosmopolitan courtesy and culture',[8] but these self-conscious words are themselves part of the mask.

In her scholarly writing there is the same awareness of the nature of self, albeit covert. The extent to which she was conscious of the complex interrelationship between research and researcher is exceptional for the time at which she wrote. Following the publication of Charles Darwin's *Origin of Species* in 1859, the great impulse in anthropological research at the beginning of the twentieth century was the search for 'origins' (in Harrison's case the origins of religion), in the belief, first, that origins exist and can be recovered, and secondly, that the original form of anything is the 'real' thing, the 'thing-in-itself', which, if we could only gaze at it, would reveal 'the truth' and illuminate all subsequent history. Harrison's language is revealing: she writes of the 'contaminatio' of a myth as it developed, of 'stripping off the layers of cult', of 'getting behind' the appearances. In all of this she was aware that her search for the origins of Greek religion (and of religion in general) was a search for the meaning of her own life—and indeed of life itself. If she wrote *Reminiscences* to conceal, she can hardly have written her academic books with the same purpose.

The myth-making of her own person, begun by Harrison, was vigorously taken up after her death by her companion Hope Mirrlees. Written records are not kind to Mirrlees. Virginia Woolf once described her as 'over-dressed, over-elaborate, scented, extravagant' with 'a greed, like a greed for almond paste, for fame'.[9] I cannot help suspecting that her friendship with Harrison

[8] Harrison, *Reminiscences*, 11–12.
[9] *The Diary of Virginia Woolf*, ed. Anne Olivier Bell (Harmondsworth: Penguin Books, 1981), 75 (Tuesday, 23 November 1920).

was fuelled by a craving for fame-by-association, as it were, since there is little else to explain their close relationship. Mirrlees, despite her poetic ability, had few of Harrison's intellectual gifts. They did, however, share the same sense of humour, frequently degenerating to a level of puerile silliness, much of it centring on Harrison's stuffed teddy-bear which had become her mascot. The First World War devastated Harrison with the collapse of academic life at Cambridge and the debates over the moral justification of the war, in which she found herself separated by a wide gulf from her closest friend, Gilbert Murray. Mirrlees offered her what she most needed: companionship and emotional (and probably financial) support. She also undertook to relieve Harrison, whose health was failing, by managing her practical affairs.

But there was a darker side to this arrangement. In 1921 Mirrlees made efforts to sever Harrison from all earlier relationships and become her exclusive friend. She persuaded Harrison to leave Cambridge to live in Paris, ostensibly so that both women could study languages at the École des Études Orientales. Before they left, Mirrlees supervised a great bonfire of Harrison's personal papers. This process of isolating Harrison culminated when Harrison was on her death bed and Mirrlees attempted, unsuccessfully, to bar the door to all Harrison's earlier friends who came to see her. One could read these acts as well-meant efforts to protect Harrison, but the obsessive–possessive side of Mirrlees's character keeps reasserting itself in the record.

After Harrison's death Mirrlees set out to write her biography, encouraged by various of Harrison's friends and colleagues who agreed that a life was called for. She began by writing to a number of people who had known Harrison in her earlier years, and received replies from Harrison's two elder sisters, friends from her days as a student at Newnham College, Cambridge, and friends and colleagues from her time in London. Mirrlees copied material from these replies into a notebook, now in the Newnham College archives. Without all the original letters there is no way of knowing how much of the material has been edited or suppressed. In a terse account of Harrison's emotional life after her return to Cambridge at the age of 50, names have either been replaced by a blank (———), or scratched out (but in such a way that they can still be deciphered). It is difficult to know what of this material is transcribed from the letters and how much is Mirrlees's own comment. From these notes Mirrlees proceeded to undertake the biography itself, a scrawl that covers both sides of about fifty huge sheets of paper, progressing to some point in the years between 1880 and 1895 when Harrison was in London. Realizing that there were serious gaps in the story and many details that Harrison had chosen not to reveal, Mirrlees attempted to fill the narrative with her own account of the intellectual tradition in which Harrison had worked. Mirrlees, who fancied herself as a novelist and a poet, writes in an effusive, cloying style, with little understanding of her subject matter. There is not much here for the biographer. Sandra Peacock's Freudian reading of Harrison's life fails to question Mirrlees's bias while purporting to have extricated Harrison's 'self' from her self-constructed 'mask'.

Another problem emerges when one analyses Harrison's published work. All attempts to establish her position on academic issues confront the reader with paradox. Whether she is writing about evolution, matriarchy, anthropomorphism, asceticism, ecstasy—whatever the topic—the diligent reader will be able to cite contradictory positions. Frequently she simply changed her mind on an issue. At other times a change of focus led her to brush away previously held beliefs, and their supporting arguments with them. She claimed not to worry about having been wrong in the past, but put forward new ideas boldly, consoling herself with the thought that 'there will always be an army of sound scholars coming along behind to clean up'. (However, Renate Schlesier in a very perceptive article argues cogently that it was only in its nuances that her position changed, while her whole life's work was informed by a coherent model of the history of ancient Greek religion, with consistent underlying notions and conceptions.)[10] Many of her conclusions, though buttressed by 'evidence', were reached by intuition as much as by logical argument.

In her recent book, *The Invention of Jane Harrison*, Mary Beard explores in detail the problems that the biased nature of archives presents to the would-be biographer. While her main point, that sources must never be used uncritically, is both well made and well taken, Beard exaggerates the biographer's dilemma. Post-modernist disclaimers notwithstanding, a coherent—and interesting—life can be reconstructed from the public record and illustrated by excerpts from letters and diaries (other people's diaries in the case of Harrison). The impression she made on other people is another facet of the record. Choices made and opportunities declined reveal something of her character. Her letter-writing style is, as Gilbert Murray observed, brilliant, displaying what she was able to do with words, frequently giving vivid expression to her emotions of the moment. From all this disparate material, together with her published work, a coherent person does indeed emerge. For, although each of us is the sum total of all the diverse faces we present to

---

[10] Renate Schlesier, 'Prolegomena to Jane Harrison's Interpretation of Ancient Greek Religion' in Calder (ed.), *The Cambridge Ritualists Reconsidered*, 185–226, esp. 195.

the world and to ourselves, there can nevertheless be discerned what Leon Edel has so aptly described as 'the inner myth we all create in order to live, the myth that tells us we have some being, some selfhood, some goal, something to strive for beyond the fulfillments of food or sex or creature comforts'.[11] Such an 'inner myth', like all myth, is nothing static, but kaleidoscopic and constantly evolving. Justin Kaplan writes,

The irreducible reality of literary lives may not be the naked self at all but the sum of a writer's public verbal acts and ecstasies with language. And as a corollary to this, the drama of literary biography may have less to do with stalking the naked self to its burrow than with the tensions between the familiar, shared life of human beings—making it, making out, making a go of it, making waves, making a name—and a vision so singular it deserves to be regarded with awe.[12]

The genius of Jane Harrison lies not in any of the myths she or anyone else wove around her name, but in the extraordinary vision with which she crafted her inner myth. From her early days at Cheltenham Ladies' College to her death in 1928 she made a lasting impression on all she met. Some of her genius died with her: the genius of her conversation, her flair for style, her innovative teaching are preserved only in the testimony of those who knew her in the flesh. But their testimony squares with the evidence of her writing. She was by temperament a passionate supporter of the underdog, whether a hapless foreign student who appeared before her when she was a Justice of the Peace or a pre-patriarchal goddess of her researches. She loved to give voice to the inarticulate, to help an embryonic idea to birth. She had an amazing capacity for searching out and understanding material in her own field, but was never satisfied to amass facts. She had contempt for those of her contemporaries who simply 'grubbed up' the facts without relating them to the living world, dismissing them as 'sound scholars' whose minds were in bits. Facts had no meaning for her in themselves; it was their power to shed light on larger issues that mattered. Her own research followed a career path of ever-widening circles, starting in Greek art (a burgeoning field in the 1880s as archaeology was providing a steady stream of new finds), extending through Greek mythology to ancient Greek religion until she wrote *Themis* in 1912, offering a vista through Greek anthropological material to the possibilities of what she believed was a new religion for humankind. Along the way she read a prodigious quantity of contemporary

[11] Leon Edel, 'The Figure Under the Carpet' in *Telling Lives: the Biographer's Art*, ed. Marc Pachter (Washington DC: New Republic Books, 1979), 30.

[12] Justin Kaplan, 'The Naked Self and Other Problems', ibid. 55.

writing in other fields: anthropology, psychology, sociology, and literature, and this not only in English, but in French and German, and, to a lesser extent, various other European languages. She was able to weave a number of different strands into one thread: her conviction that religion consists primarily in what people do rather than what they believe and that art is no 'handmaid' of literature but develops independently. She embraced Nietzsche's opposition of Dionysos to Apollo, the study of the religious practices of peasants as described by Wilhelm Mannhardt and J. G. Frazer, J. J. Bachofen's speculations about matriarchy, the breathtaking finds of Minoan and Mycenaean archaeology, the latest in psychology, sociology, and anthropology. New ways of thinking were everywhere in the air and she inhaled them all. She often confessed that her head was seething with ideas. She cleared it by writing, and the result each time was the statement of a coherent position that was nevertheless riddled with paradox.

But she was no recluse in her study; on the contrary she was immensely sociable, participating in and contributing to the stimulating artistic and academic environment of London and Cambridge, hating to work alone, passionate in debate, a friend to her students. She despised all affectation of status, she hated all orthodoxy and dogma, she loved the young.

On her own discipline, classics, she left an indelible mark. Ferreting out from literary and artistic sources a mass of material about what the ordinary person in ancient Greece actually *did* in connection with his religion, she demonstrated that the Olympian gods played a far lesser role than anyone in Britain had hitherto dreamed. The ordinary Greek, she claimed, was far more concerned with a multitude of spirits. With a thorough knowledge of German and French she kept abreast of intellectual developments on the Continent, and was particularly influenced by Nietzsche, who first questioned the supremacy of the Homeric Olympian gods in Greek religion and drew attention to primitive superstitions. Following his lead, Harrison discerned in Greek art and literature earlier, darker forms, which continued to live in the imagination and practices of the Greeks for centuries after Homer. She drew attention to rituals of 'aversion', designed to bid spirits depart, as contrasting with the more familiar rituals of 'tendance'. She separated religion from mythology, taking the myths as later theological elaboration of ritual. What people *do*, she argued, is far more telling than what they *say*. Hence ritual is 'real' (a favourite word with her) in a way in which myth is not. Her pioneering work in this field was taken up (among others) by E. R. Dodds (*The Greeks and the Irrational*, 1951)—though he nowhere acknowledged her—and by Walter Burkert (*Greek Religion*, 1983). From the years spent in studying vases at the British Museum and at museums on the

Continent she learned to see with an artist's eye and all her life looked to artistic as well as literary sources for her understanding of Greek religion. Her interest in what we would now term 'material culture' (then 'archaeology') immediately became an integral part of the classical Tripos at Cambridge. Under her influence classics was transformed from a closed field of textual study to an open inquiry into every aspect of the ancient Greek and Roman world, amenable to the questions and insights of other disciplines, especially anthropology and sociology.

She wrote with a passion that came from seeing her research as intensely practical. She believed that to study the origins of Greek religion was to discover the essence of the nature of religion—something as relevant to the existential anxieties of men and women today as then. By temperament she observed no boundaries between academic study and everyday life, and worked on the assumption that the experience of the ordinary Greek spoke directly to the ordinary person of today. In reading about Greek religion, she wrote, one cannot help feeling that the ancients were writing about oneself (*mutatis mutandis de te,* as she put it). This, and the vivid style of her writing, carried her message far beyond academe. She offered to her readers a 'real' religion, a credible alternative to Christianity (credible because of its grounding in the practices of the highly esteemed ancient Greeks), built not on dogma but on the celebration of shared emotion. She thereby undermined the Victorian patriarchy and hierarchy that surrounded her. Her *eniautos-daimon,* or 'year spirit', gave expression to the eternal cycle of birth and death, ever renewed.

Among her young friends was Virginia Woolf, who looked to Harrison as her mentor. Harrison had achieved what eluded Woolf, a university education and an academic career. They shared a commitment to the education of women, Harrison having the opportunity to live it out in the environment of a women's college. When (as for example in *A Room of One's Own*) Woolf invites the reader into a community of readers, she is following Harrison's academic practice (she always sought to work in collaboration), her lifestyle (the community of Newnham College was her home), and her teaching methods (her students always felt that they were in a joint pursuit of some goal). Likewise, Harrison's books take the reader on a voyage of joint discovery: she gathers the evidence and invites us to join her as she draws her conclusions. Woolf was also influenced by Harrison's ideas: her rejection of patriarchal Christianity, the primacy of the female principle in pre-Olympian religion, the importance and prevalence of ritual, and her understanding of life as a continual process. Harrison wrote that art must arise from 'a keen emotion felt towards things and people living to-day, in modern conditions, including, among other and deeper forms of life, the haste and hurry of the modern street, the whirr of motor cars and aeroplanes',[13] which is surely the impulse behind the narratives of Virginia Woolf.

In an essay entitled 'Scientiae Sacra Fames' she endorsed the belief that 'women are more *resonant* than men, *more subject to induction from the social current*'.[14] It was certainly true of Harrison herself that she was influenced by every social wind. Feeling the needs and anxieties of a wide range of her contemporaries she wrote for a wide audience. It was not only classicists who read her work, but writers and poets, who may have had more of a disposition to 'resonate' than to argue, notably T. S. Eliot and James Joyce.[15] The plot of John Buchan's *The Dancing Floor* (1926) centres on the re-enactment of a pagan rite on a Greek island and the book is so infused with notions of 'primitive' thinking to be found in Harrison's *Themis* that one must assume he knew her work.[16]

Jane Harrison was a woman *sui generis*, with a powerful influence. In her own day, when only a handful of women had had the benefit of a university education, she was renowned for her public lectures on Greek art, for her books on Greek religion and mythology, for her unconventional and outspoken views. She went on to earn an international reputation as a scholar. In all of this she redefined the possibilities for academically gifted women. Her research into aspects of ancient Greece hitherto overlooked trans-

---

[13] Jane Ellen Harrison, *Ancient Art and Ritual*, Home University Library of Modern Knowledge (London: Williams and Norgate, 1913), 237.

[14] Jane Ellen Harrison, 'Sacra Scientiae Fames' in *Alpha and Omega* (London: Sidgwick and Jackson, 1915), 126 (italics hers).

[15] The most detailed treatment is in Martha Celeste Carpentier, *Ritual, Myth, and the Modernist Text: the Influence of Jane Ellen Harrison on Joyce, Eliot, and Woolf* (Amsterdam: Gordon and Breach, 1998). See also Melba Cuddy-Keane, 'The Politics of Comic Modes in Virginia Woolf's *Between the Acts*', *Publications of the Modern Language Association of America*, 105/2 (Mar. 1990), 273–85; Patricia Maika, *Virginia Woolf's Between the Acts and Jane Harrison's Con/spiracy* (Ann Arbor: UMI Research Press, *c.* 1987), K. J. Phillips, 'Jane Harrison and Modernism', *Journal of Modern Literature*, 17/4 (Spring 1991), 465–76; Annabel Robinson, 'Something Odd at Work: the Presence of Jane Harrison in *A Room of One's Own*' in Eleanor McNees (ed.), *Virgina Woolf: Critical Assessments* (Mountfield: Helm Information Ltd, 1994) 2/63, 215–20; Sandra Shattuck, 'The Stage of Scholarship: Crossing the Bridge from Harrison to Woolf' in Jane Marcus (ed.), *Virginia Woolf and Bloomsbury: a Centenary Celebration* (London: Macmillan, 1987), 278–98; Marianna Torgovnick, 'Discovering Jane Harrison' in Carola M. Kaplan and Anne. B. Simpson (eds.), *Seeing Double: Revisioning Edwardian and Modern Literature* (New York: St. Martin's Press, 1996), 131–48. For her influence on T. S. Eliot, see William Skaff, *The Philosophy of T. S. Eliot from Skepticism to a Surrealist Poetic, 1909–1927* (Philadelphia: University of Pennsylvania Press, 1986), 80–2, and Carpentier, *Ritual, Myth and the Modernist Text*, 101–32. For Joyce see ibid. 69–99.

[16] John Buchan, *The Dancing Floor*, ed. Marilyn Deegan, (Oxford: Oxford University Press, 1997).

formed the discipline of classics at Cambridge. Unlike all her contemporaries at Newnham she succeeded in negotiating for herself an academic position in which she was able to devote herself to research rather than teaching, and wrote as a woman in a field almost exclusively occupied by men. Her writing addressed, and continues to address, issues which are central to the women's movement, yet she wrote as she did, not because she was championing any cause, but out of a passionate desire to share with the world what she believed to be important and true.

1. Origins: Yorkshire and Cheltenham 1850–1874

THE gardens of Fernham lay before me in the spring twilight, wild and open, and in the long grass, sprinkled and carelessly flung, were daffodils and bluebells, not orderly perhaps at the best of times, and now wind-blown and waving as they tugged at their roots. The windows of the building, curved like ships' windows among generous waves of red brick, changed from lemon to silver under the flight of the quick spring clouds. Somebody was in a hammock, somebody, but in this light they were phantoms only, half guessed, half seen, raced across the grass—would no one stop her?—and then on the terrace, as if popping out to breathe the air, to glance at the garden, came a bent figure, formidable yet humble, with her great forehead and her shabby dress—could it be the famous scholar, could it be J—H—herself? All was dim, yet intense too, as if the scarf which the dusk had flung over the garden were torn asunder by star or sword—the flash of some terrible reality leaping, as its way is, out of the heart of the spring. For youth—[1]

So Virginia Woolf, with a heart 'like a singing bird' under the magic of Christina Rossetti, takes us in imagination to the garden of Newnham College (Fig. 1), lovely in its wildness, where 'the beauty of the world which is so soon to perish, has two edges, one of laugher, one of anguish, cutting the heart asunder'. There she is still, the spirit of Jane Harrison, in the setting she most loved, still a reality, still 'leaping . . . out of the heart of spring'. For even though she died at the age of 78, like the 'year spirit' of her own writings which died and was reborn every spring, she had never grown old.

On Saturday 27 October 1928, friends gathered at Newnham to salute her memory and hear the inaugural Jane Harrison Lecture, given by her friend and colleague, Professor Gilbert Murray.[2] The Principal reminded the audience how often within these walls he and Miss Harrison had 'tired the sun with talking, and sent him down the sky' and went on to speak of the

---

[1] Woolf, *A Room of One's Own*, 25–6. For the influence of Harrison in *A Room of One's Own*, see Robinson, 'Something Odd at Work', ii. 215–20.

[2] Just one week after Virginia Woolf had read at Newnham the paper on women and knowledge that was later published as *A Room of One's Own*.

1. Newnham Garden, 1930

interplay of age and youth felt in a college like Newnham, a young college in an ancient university.[3] The past, for Jane Harrison, had been an impulse for the present. She had loved, inspired, and invigorated the young, and would be remembered not only for her monumental intellect but also for her captivating human character.

Gilbert Murray took the podium. 'The Year Spirit, born young again every spring, has entered into your soul, and taught us all alike to feel ourselves the companions and sharers of your youthfulness' he began, quoting Walter Leaf's farewell address given when Jane Harrison had left Cambridge six years previously. It would have pleased her to have known she was being remembered first for her youthful spirit.

Jane Ellen Harrison was born at Cottingham, Yorkshire, on 9 September 1850, the third daughter of Charles Harrison, a timber merchant, and

[3] This account is taken from the *Newnham College Letter*, Jan. 1929, 51. The quotation is from William Cory's 'Heraclitus' in *The Oxford Book of Greek Verse in Translation*, ed. T. F. Higham and C. M. Bowra (Oxford: Clarendon Press, 1938), p. 584.

Elizabeth Hawksley Nelson. Although she left Yorkshire at the age of 17 and never lived there again for any length of time, she was, by her own confession, intensely proud of being a Yorkshire woman. She claims that she 'first met herself' in a Yorkshire woman of fiction:

Until I met Aunt Glegg in the *Mill on the Floss*, I never knew myself. I *am* Aunt Glegg; with all reverence I say it. I wear before the world a mask of bland cosmopolitan courtesy and culture; I am advanced in my views, eager to be in touch with all modern movements, but beneath all that lies Aunt Glegg, rigidly, irrationally conservative, fibrous with prejudice, deep-rooted in her native soil.[4]

The remark quoted here is, of course, ironic; she is much more to be found in the central character of this novel, Maggie Tulliver, who craves the education that is reserved for her less gifted brother, Tom. Yet it catches a facet of Harrison's temperament, and coming from her own pen hints at one way in which she wished to be remembered. The scrapbook of memories handed down in the family on her father's (Yorkshire) side certainly reveals 'Aunt Glegg' attitudes.

Her family, like many of the families of the East Riding, was descended from Danish immigrants. By the seventeenth century they had settled as farmers near Rudstone, a village in the York wolds, not far from Bridlington. A gift for languages ran in the family. Jane's great-aunt was apparently a good linguist, and taught two of her nephews, Richard and John Harrison, French and German, and possibly other languages also. Both brothers knew Russian, and went to Russia, returning in 1811 to settle in Hull and open a business as timber merchants. The business maintained its links with Russia, so that Jane Harrison could write nostalgically: 'In view of my present cult for Russia . . . I like to think that my first childish memory is of the word "Moscow". Moscow to me was a dog. . . . When I later learned that to some people Moscow was a cathedral city, not a dog, my universe rocked with Einsteinian relativity.'[5] Other childhood memories included a box of bricks and soldiers, called 'The Siege of Sevastopol', caviare, cranberries, and reindeers' tongues sent by business friends every Christmas, and a little Russian sledge in which her father took her for rides. Though it was Greece that inspired her life's work, her life began and ended with ties with Russia.

---

[4] Harrison, *Reminiscences*, 11–12. Aunt Glegg was the aunt of Maggie Tulliver in George Eliot's *The Mill on the Floss* (1860), a strong-minded woman of rigid habits, thrift, and old-fashioned values. See 'Enter the aunts and uncles' in *The Mill on the Floss* (Harmondsworth: Penguin Books, 1979), 50–73. George Eliot's novels were first published during Harrison's adolescence and she devoured them.

[5] *Reminiscences*, 9.

Jane's paternal grandmother, Harriet Metcalfe, was remembered as a martinet. She married John Harrison in her habit and rode all the way from Leeds to Hull. John died 'through the Harrison obstinacy', they said in Hull, as the result of being thrown from his horse when trying to make him pass a carrier's cart. His seven daughters were left to be ruled by their brothers and their mother until she died at the age of 96, having never been ill, she claimed, in all her life. Each daughter that married was temporarily ostracized by the brothers, who were convinced that their husbands were rascals who only wanted their money. The two who did not marry young were kept on an allowance, reluctant spinsters, 'dressed in black satin gowns, sitting drearily hour after hour in the Hull house, gazing out of separate windows'. When one of them married at the age of 51 Jane remembered her father's fury. The bride had the sense and fortitude to ignore her family's outrage, being very happy with her new life and enjoying a trip to Italy. That in itself was scandal. Travel to Europe was particularly taboo, perhaps because of a rigid low-church prejudice which forswore contact of any kind with the Roman Catholic church. In writing of her governesses Harrison notes that they were all British. 'My father's creed was a simple one: All foreigners were Papists, all Papists were liars, and he "wouldn't have one in his house".'[6]

It is curious which personal traits make an impression on others. The family records how proud their grandmother was of her legs and feet, and those of her sons, being heard to exclaim, 'I have five of the straightest legged sons in Yorkshire', and gazing at her own feet in rapture (a trait, we are told, that was inherited by Jane). Old age sharpened her eccentricities. Jane remembered her grandmother muttering to herself over and over again, 'Three vegetables for lunch and ruin staring us in the face.' She had always been frugal, but in her last years this turned into a quite irrational fear of poverty and debt, another 'Aunt Glegg' trait that Jane likewise was to display all her life. But in other ways Mrs Harrison's wits remained clear to the end. Jane's cousin Marian relates that the day before she died she insisted that one of her sons see about some shares—at once. The next day she told the maid that 'the fringes of the towels need combing'. The maid went to look at them, and came back to find the old lady sitting bolt upright,—and dead. Hope Mirrlees observes that Aunt Glegg herself could not have found more suitable words for her last.[7]

Of her sons, the eldest, Crowther, entered the family business, but was better known for his avocation, breeding horses, one of which won the Derby. Crowther was a good classical scholar, with a passion for acquiring

---

2. Pimlico House, Great Limber, the home of Jane Harrison's mother, Elizabeth Nelson

new languages, to the extent that he went and lived with the Gypsies to study Romany, and published an article on Romany. His first wife died after being capsized from a pony carriage that he was driving. From the shock and guilt he became temporarily insane and was locked up for a while. His younger brother, Joe, suffered from similar nerves. He began his career as a doctor, but when his first patient died, he was so upset that he refused ever to practise again and he too went into the family business. Two other brothers, Edward and Arthur, started a business of their own, though Edward had originally wanted to be an architect. Almost every member of the family showed artistic ability in some way. The youngest daughter, Jessie, was interested in photography. There is a stipple engraving of Jane's two elder sisters when they were small; it may have been the work of their aunt Jessie.[8]

Jane's father, Charles Harrison, at six-foot four and very thin, was known as 'the lamp-post'. He inherited the sensitive, artistic nature that ran in the family, and what was taken for unsociability was perhaps just painful

---

[8] The engraving is in the possession of Rev. Kenneth Nelson, a grandson of Thomas Sherlock Nelson, brother to Elizabeth Hawksley Nelson.

self-consciousness. He followed his brothers in the timber business, and in 1846 married Elizabeth Hawksley Nelson, of Great Limber, Lincolnshire.

Legend (probably apocryphal) has it that the Nelsons had blue blood in their veins, but there is no doubt of the Hawksley family's Tory blue connections. In 1715 Thomas Hawksley, who was mayor of Nottingham, was imprisoned for supporting the Pretender. In the year of his office he had drunk the health of 'The Old Pretender' on his knees, in his own house. For this he was deposed from the mayoralty, and fined one thousand pounds in addition to being imprisoned for one year. His appeal failed, and resulted in the loss of a further two thousand pounds. The story goes that while in prison he held regular dinner parties, and his blue satin bed-curtains were carried as the Tory flag on political occasions, (blue being recognized as the badge of the Covenanters as opposed to the red of royalty).[9]

Thomas Hawksley's grand-daughter Sarah married George Nelson of Limber, and the family prospered. Their grandson, also George, was noted as 'a man of consequence'. As a tenant farmer with 865 acres under the Earl of Yarborough in the 1840s, he pioneered turnip husbandry in Lincolnshire. When the advent of the railway made it possible for fertilizer to be transported, he realized there were other new opportunities; from the bones which were used he also built a soap factory on his property. He retired with a fortune of £80,000.[10] Elizabeth, who married Charles Harrison, was the seventh of his eight children. She loved poetry, which was considered odd by her family, but would have been appreciated by Charles, who was known to read Dickens with sentimental tears pouring down his cheeks. 'My father was the shyest man I ever knew', Jane recalls, 'and terribly absent-minded.'[11] Indeed he was: two years after his marriage he is reputed to have ridden to Limber Grange and to have asked to see Miss Elizabeth Nelson.

Jane Ellen was their third child, a younger sister to Elizabeth and Lucy. After her birth her mother developed puerperal fever. The doctor bled her but, either in spite of or as a result of his attentions, Elizabeth died. All her life Jane bore the burden of believing that she had caused her mother's death. She naturally developed a tendency to idealize her mother's memory and her emotions on the subject of motherhood remained forever intense as she could never come to terms with what had happened. It left an indelible mark on the lens through which she viewed life, whether her personal

---

[9] See Keppel Creswell, letter to the *Daily Mail*, 4 March 1910. A similar letter of an earlier date was found in the pocket book of Charles Harrison.

[10] Samuel Sidney, *Railways and Agriculture in North Lincolnshire* (London: W. Pickering, 1848), 72. The turnips were shipped to London as fodder for horses.

[11] *Reminiscences*, 39.

3. Charles Harrison, Elizabeth Harrison, and Jane (aged 5)

relationships with other people and their families, her decision not to marry and have children of her own, or her heightened awareness of the significance of mother–child relationships in the academic arena of anthropology.

To a sensitive man like Charles Harrison the illness and death of his wife after childbirth brought abnormally intense suffering. He arranged for Elizabeth to be buried not at Cottingham but at Kirkella, near Hull (where her sister lived). After her mother's death, Jane and her sisters were looked after by their 'Auntie' Harriet, who came to live with them, and for a while the girls were happy. Her cousin Marian remembers Jane as a 'pretty, plump little blue-eyed girl with fair complexion and hair', who spoke nicely and used long words which she had picked up from her elders and applied correctly.[12] She learned to read at so early an age that she had no memory of not knowing how.

The children knew that their father, 'in his silent way', was fond of them, helping them with their garden plots, and taking them on Sundays for a walk to their Uncle Crowther's to see the horses. Later on Jane was to develop an interest in collecting birds' eggs, a hobby encouraged by her father. In 1862 the three girls were taken by their father to London to see the International Exhibition, an experience that made a lasting impression on Jane. Though less well-known than the Great Exhibition of 1851, the 1862 exhibition was far more significant in its contribution to a public awareness of good taste, reflecting the advance in design during the intervening eleven years. Here Jane would perhaps have seen the furniture and embroideries of William Morris, exhibited publicly for the first time, and have been introduced to the work of the Pre-Raphaelites of which she later became such a devotee.

Their father took them on another occasion to see York Minster. Jane, filled with awe at the interior, wrote in her diary that 'the music seemed to run up and down along the roof'. Her sister Lucy was much struck later when she came across William Wordsworth's Sonnet 'Inside of King's College Chapel, Cambridge' and noted the similar description of 'lofty pillars' and 'branching roof | Self-poised, . . . where music dwells | Lingering'.[13] She testified that neither she nor Jane had read it at the time of their visit.

Auntie was sensitive and wise in her role as surrogate mother, doing what she could to fill their mother's place. Their mother had dressed them beautifully, with much greater daintiness and taste than was usual in their circle. It is to Auntie's credit that she continued this tradition, though she herself was

---

[12] 'Marian Harrison', Mirrlees's notebook.
[13] Wordsworth, Sonnet XLIII, *Ecclesiastical Sonnets* (1822).

thoroughly old-fashioned and doubtless thought pretty clothes vanity and a waste of money, but she felt their mother would wish it. Jane, an affectionate child, loved her, and Lucy remembers her sitting on Auntie's lap with her head on her shoulder—she called this 'dudding' (loving). This and other anecdotes about Jane preserve the difficulty she had as a small child with her consonants. On being introduced to a new little cousin, she is said to have remarked (precociously): 'Poor itty thing! All its itty troubles 'et to come!'

This regime came to an abrupt end when Auntie commissioned a friend in London to find a suitable governess for the children and a 'very pretty little black singletted and pleasant-mannered Welshwoman' arrived on the scene. Her beauty soon attracted the attention of all the men in the neighbour-hood, including their father. In 1855 he and Gemimi Meredith were married.[14]

Jane liked her at first. But with her change in status a great change came over Gemimi's attitude to the three little girls. No longer were the children prettily dressed, but now their dowdy and old-fashioned appearance became a byword. Their stepmother had a horror of 'mannishness' in women's dress, insisting, for example, that their raincoats be trimmed with a fringe to make them look feminine. No longer were they allowed to walk to Uncle Crowther's on a Sunday, ostensibly because to do so was to break the Sabbath. Their father became more of a recluse than ever, dividing his time between carpentry and gardening. The contrast between their voluble stepmother and silent father is illustrated by a marvellous anecdote in Jane Harrison's *Reminiscences*:

I heard her voice once in an adjoining room passionately haranguing my father. From him not a sound. But when we met for dinner, we saw with some embarrassment that a portrait of my mother, long consigned to an attic, was hanging on the wall opposite my father's seat. He had himself brought it down and hung it up. Such was his dumb reprisal.[15]

The new Mrs Harrison set about to isolate her three stepdaughters from their own relatives, instigating a move first to Wales, where they stayed only a short time, then back to Yorkshire, to Filey for a year, and from there to Scalby. When they were at Filey their cousins saw them during the summer holidays, but noticed how they were now kept strictly under their gov-erness's tight control and were not allowed to play on the sands and rocks with the other children.

[14] 'Meredith' pronounced with the stress on the second syllable. Some years later she was described by Caroline (Birch Dutton) Mitchell as 'very odd-looking, just like a gypsy, with jet-black corkscrew curls' ('Mrs Charles Mitchell', Mirrlees's notebook).   [15] *Reminiscences*, 28.

The emotional scars never healed. Fifty years later Harrison was to write about the trauma which a daughter suffers when a widowed father remarries. All her life she was to regard marriage as a selfish relationship between two people too blinded by their love for each other to perceive the desolation that their marriage causes others. The child was more observant, astute, and sensitive than her elders realized.

Her consolation was the schoolroom, which at first was a haunt of peace. But as the family gradually grew to twelve children, it must have become pandemonium. Charles Harrison's eccentricities compounded the chaos. Marian remembered the governess complaining that no sooner had she with infinite difficulty succeeded in chivvying all the children into the schoolroom for their lessons than the bell would go for prayers, which were whenever Mr Harrison felt inclined to read them; and the hour varied. No wonder the governesses came and left in rapid succession. Jane remembered them with affection and in later years did not hold them responsible for the standard Victorian curriculum for girls: meaningless memorization of names and dates, needlework, and deportment. In Jane's case the hours spent memorizing Scripture and poetry were formative in inculcating a love of language. One governess stood out in her memory:

a woman of real intelligence, ignorant but willing and eager to learn anything and everything I wanted. Together we learnt to read German, Latin badly, and with the quantities of course all wrong, the Greek Testament and even a little Hebrew. Unfortunately, having no guide, we began with the Psalms which are hard nuts to crack. I wanted to find out the meaning of such obscure and exciting verses as 'Or ever your pots be made hot with thorns, so let indignation vex him even as a thing that is raw'. Alas! my kind governess was shortly removed to a lunatic asylum. What share I may have had in her mental downfall I do not care to inquire.[16]

We do not know whether the governess recovered sufficiently to realize the value of the time she had devoted to Jane; we do know that the poor soul was reprimanded for neglecting all the other children!

Books were a serious problem; Jane saved up her pocket money to buy a copy of Vergil, and a friend, Peveril Turnbull, taught her to her delight how to scan it. She managed to acquire for herself a Greek grammar, only to have it confiscated with the 'chill, cutting words: "I do not see how Greek grammar is to help little Jane to keep house when she has a home of her own."'[17] Her anger at her stepmother was further fuelled by the preferential treatment given to her stepbrothers. Whereas the boys in the family were sent to Harrow, the girls were consigned to an education whose sole

---

[16] *Reminiscences*, 26–7.   [17] Harrison, 'Scientiae Sacra Fames' 116–17.

purpose was to prepare them to be good wives. They were taught languages so that they might be able to entertain foreign guests; general knowledge enabled a woman to admire men's conversation. Appearances and deportment were what mattered, while 'the dear delight of learning for learning's sake a "dead" language for sheer love of the beauty of its words and the delicacy of its syntactical relations, . . . the rapture of reconstructing for the first time in imagination a bit of the historical past' was considered 'unwomanly'.[18]

Apart from languages, Jane's other interest in childhood was botany; it was not the pressing of the specimens that she enjoyed, but the classifying. All her life she loved to discover patterns in seemingly disparate material, and when she was engaged in her major life's work on ancient Greek religion and held Athenian ritual practice under scrutiny, the underlying impulse was the same.

One aspect of her upbringing caused more scars than any other. Jane Harrison described her stepmother as a Celt 'of the fervent semi-revivalist type' who indoctrinated the children by an appeal to terror. She writes in a light-hearted vein of the religious training she received:

She was a conscientious woman and tried to do her duty, I am sure, to the three rather dour little girls who had been her pupils and were later presented to her as stepdaughters. She gave us Scripture lessons every Sunday. Her main doctrines were that we must be 'born again' and that 'God would have our whole hearts or nothing'. I think I early felt that this was not quite fair. Why, if we were to care for Him only, had He made this delightful world full of enchanting foreign languages? Anyhow, the holocaust I honestly attempted was a complete failure. I was from the outset a hopeless worldling.[19]

Her father did not share his new wife's views, being apparently incapable of forming a conviction. He attended church, and approved of religion as long as it did not interfere with a man's private life. Jane Harrison remembered his fury when an Evangelical clergyman once came to say goodbye to them and asked if, before parting, they would all kneel down and 'ask a blessing' on their journey.[20]

The three stepdaughters reacted differently to their religious upbringing. Although Elizabeth and Lucy grew up to marry clergymen and remained within the Anglican fold, Jane repudiated her stepmother's fundamentalism with an antipathy of astonishing force. Her friends later in life remarked that this was the only area in which she was totally irrational.

However, Jane was not averse to what she called the 'apparatus' of

[18] Ibid.   [19] Reminiscences, 19.   [20] Ibid. 18

religion, describing Sunday as an 'exciting if laborious day' on which at the age of 12 she taught twice in the Sunday school, played the organ for two services, followed 'the prayers in Latin, and the lesson in German and the Gospel in Greek'.[21] When they got home the girls were required to write out one of the sermons from memory, memorize the Collect for the day and either the Epistle or the Gospel. Every day the children were required to memorize Bible verses. The effect of this regime was curious. If it failed in its intent as spiritual formation, it succeeded in imprinting on Jane's memory the language and thought forms of the Prayer Book and Authorized Version. The music of their rhythm and cadences formed her writing style, and even their thought forms can be traced, subverted, in all her work.

As she progressed through her teenage years, Jane chafed increasingly at the social, educational, and religious restrictions imposed on her at home. Perhaps her father perceived this and was sympathetic; perhaps Gemimi felt her to be too much of a trouble-maker and was ready to relinquish parental responsibility. It so happened that the local curate had sent his daughter to a recently founded boarding school in Cheltenham, and suggested that this might be a solution for Jane. There was, however, a problem. Charles Harrison had promised his first wife that none of her girls would be sent away to school. The difficulty was adroitly solved when Mrs Cox pointed out that Cheltenham Ladies' College was a college, not a school, which was not at all the same thing. The immediate events that purportedly led up to her being sent away to school at the age of 17 are recounted in her *Reminiscences*, doubtless embellished in the telling, but worth recounting:

A keen impulse was given to my study of the Greek Testament by the arrival of a new curate. He was fresh from Oxford and not, I think, averse to showing off. Rashly in one of his sermons he drew attention to a mistranslation. This filled me with excitement and alarm. I saw in a flash that the whole question of the 'verbal inspiration of the Bible' was at issue. That afternoon I took my Greek Testament down to the Sunday School and, eager for further elucidation, waylaid the hapless curate. I soon found that his knowledge of Greek was, if possible, more slender than my own. But, if embarrassed, he was friendly. Alas! that curate did not confine his attentions to the Greek text. I was summarily despatched in dire disgrace to Cheltenham. My step-mother said I was behaving 'like a kitchen-maid'. Considering the subject of my converse with the curate, I fail to see the analogy.[22]

Lucy embellished the story with more details. Jane was 'madly in love with him'. There were clandestine meetings halfway between the house and the church, 'but their chief opportunity for flirting was choir practices

<hr />

[21] *Reminiscences*, 19.   [22] Ibid. 27.

where Jane played the organ. It began to be noticeable that Mr Houseman seemed to have a great deal to say to the organist, and was for ever popping behind the red curtains'. Lucy warned Jane to be careful, reminding her that there were several 'old cats' in the village who lived on gossip. Sure enough, the flirtation was discovered and there was a terrible scene—Jane in hysterics and Mr Houseman forbidden the house. For safety's sake Jane was sent away to Normanton to stay with her oldest sister. From there she wrote to Lucy, in German; their stepmother discovered the letter and insisted that Lucy tell her its contents. As a result Lucy too was in disgrace. It was imperative to get Jane away from Scalby.[23]

Gossip aside, Charles Harrison may have decided, recognizing Jane's scholastic ability, to send her away to school for solid academic reasons. Cheltenham Ladies' College had been founded in 1853 on the experimental principle that a girl should receive education in the same subjects as a boy.[24] The aim was to provide first rate education at a reasonable cost. In 1854 the school opened in Cambray House, with S. Anne Procter as Principal and a staff of ten.[25] Curriculum was perforce *ad hoc*, since it was necessary to rely on the availability of visiting teachers for many subjects. At first Latin was taught, but was soon replaced by German, not for any ideological reason, but because Annie Procter could teach German and save the school some expense. But the intention was that instruction in German might be made 'equally instrumental with the Latin language for conveying accurate, exact and logical knowledge of the principles of general Grammar'. In 1858 Dorothea Beale was appointed as Principal.[26]

It was a stroke of good fortune that Cheltenham was the school to which

---

[23] 'Lucy' in Mirrlees's notebook.

[24] It is hard now to understand the fears felt by opponents to this principle. There was a strong sentiment felt by many that to give a girl the same education as a boy would be to make her into a boy, or, even worse, to unsex her and to create some kind of inhuman monster. See A. K. Clarke, *A History of the Cheltenham Ladies' College, 1853–1979* (3rd edn. London: Faber and Faber, 1979; 1st pub. 1953), 88, and Martha Vicinus, *Independent Women*: Work and Community for Single Women, 1850–1920 (London: Virago, 1985), 134.

[25] The building has since been torn down and the Cambray Court Flats built on the site. The school moved to its present buildings in 1873.

[26] Beale had been educated by governesses and then sent away to school, where she developed an antipathy to the rote learning that was the order of the day. After attending Queen's College, Harley Street, she took up a position for a year as headteacher of Casterton, Westmorland, the model for Charlotte Bronte's 'Lowood'. She wrote, as a resource for history teachers, and with the optimism of a Casaubon, a 'History of the Whole World since the Beginning of the Christian Era'. See Elizabeth Raikes, *Dorothea Beale of Cheltenham* (London: Archibald Constable and Co., 1908).

Jane was sent in 1868. Dorothea Beale, while still subscribing to the Victorian ideal of educating a woman to be a submissive wife, had nevertheless initiated some significant change. She was opposed to teaching mere accomplishments, which were more useful for attracting husbands than living as wives, and believed that girls should be given a thorough foundation, not a veneer of education. One of her fundamental aims was to develop moral character, and to this end she encouraged studies that would brace the mind. In languages, for instance, she maintained that girls as well as boys should be required to master the grammar. She believed that the teaching of history was of fundamental importance. She insisted on meticulous correction of written work, and on examinations every year by external examiners. For Harrison the experience of Cheltenham itself was valuable, and even more valuable was the vista that it offered of further studies at Newnham College, Cambridge. This, of course, was not foreseen by her stepmother when she first enrolled Jane as a pupil.

For Jane, leaving home held out hopes of a merciful release. Her years at Cheltenham show her in the turmoils of adolescence: academically she welcomed the challenge and recognition, and the opportunity to study the sciences, newly introduced into the curriculum, but if she had expected release from the pettiness of Victorian attitude towards young women she was disappointed; emotionally there were storms ahead in her relationships not only with boys but with her school friends and also with Miss Beale.

Accommodation was provided at 24 Lansdown Place, under the supervision of a certain Miss Caines. In the early days of the school it was a brave woman who would run a boarding house, such was the opprobrium of the school in Cheltenham society. There was constant tension between Miss Caines and the girls. From Miss Caines's point of view it was important to demonstrate that education made a woman no less feminine by ensuring that the girls in her charge were always models of deportment. Lucy remembered the effect on Miss Caines one Sunday morning when she overheard one lady saying to another as they came out of church, 'Oh, these are college girls. They aren't ladies.' One can also understand how unnecessary and irritating this constant vigilance would seem to youth, unconcerned with the wider cause, seeing only their own lives.

In the sensitive matter of dress Jane started out inauspiciously. The way to Miss Caines's heart was to be well dressed. Yet Jane's stepmother had always begrudged any of their father's money being spent on clothes, and packed Jane off to Cheltenham with a wardrobe that Lucy said was a 'disgrace—nothing but plain alpaca skirts, without a bow, without a flounce, and without a tuck, made up by the village dressmaker'. The one concession which Mrs Harrison made to her wardrobe turned out in disaster: she did give her a nice piece of material with instructions for Miss Caines to have it made up in Cheltenham for her 'Sunday dress'. Miss Caines accordingly took it to a dressmaker who turned it into a most stylish gown trimmed with green satin. When Jane returned home for the holidays and presented the bill there was a scene. Whereas Mrs Harrison was accustomed to paying five shillings, the dressmaker in Cheltenham had charged two pounds. Jane cried bitterly. 'A strange greeting', observed Lucy, 'for a girl who had so brilliantly distinguished herself.' There was not a word of praise for her academic achievements.[27]

Academically, when she started at Cheltenham she was already far ahead of all her contemporaries. One of them recalled how on their walks (taken for exercise before games were sanctioned) Jane would recite Greek poetry. The friend did not understand a word, but always remembered how beautiful and significant it was, 'spouted' in Jane's incomparable voice. Jane was the only pupil who came with some previous knowledge of Greek. It was most unfortunate that no tutor could be found for her to build on the knowledge she had acquired piecemeal and mostly by her own efforts. A few years after her time Greek was taught at the college.

Sixty years later she could recapture the emotional quickening she experienced in the study of arithmetic ('it was a rapture to me to understand at last why you turned fractions upside down in division. When I first got possession of an x I felt I had a new mastery of the world.') and chemistry, for which selected pupils were allowed to make use of the laboratories at the boys' college ('things are never the same to you again. You know they are not what they seem; you picture hidden terrific forces, you can even imagine that the whole solid earth is only such forces held in momentous balance').[28]

Here is an instance of Jane's genius, the ability to reorganize her universe when some discovery flashed on her consciousness. It was a dangerous gift, which needed dispassionate rigour as a counterpoise, and that she lacked. Years later Gilbert Murray observed that to her all facts were not equal. 'If the fact had a living message she embraced it and loved it; if it had not, it was entirely unimportant to her.'[29] What gave a fact a 'living message' was primarily an emotional or intuitive consideration; here lies one of her great

---

[27] All the information here about Harrison's years at Cheltenham are taken from 'Lucy' Mirrlees's notebook. Unfortunately the school has no archival records of Jane Harrison as a student.

[28] *Reminiscences*, 37.

[29] Gilbert Murray, *Jane Ellen Harrison: an Address Delivered at Newnham College, October 27th, 1928* (Cambridge: W. Heffer and Sons Ltd, 1928).

strengths of personality—and one of her great weaknesses as a researcher. Of the excitement of learning she was later to write, 'Anyone who makes even a very small mental discovery can note how, at the moment of the making, there is a sudden sense of warmth, an uprush of emotion, often a hot blush, and sometimes tears in the eyes.'[30] Anyone? Not Aunt Glegg, for one. Jane Harrison, all her life, found real learning exciting to the point of physical sensation—a rare enthusiasm—and uniquely combined her down-to-earth temperament with a flair for conveying her emotions.

In 1869 the college began to issue its own certificates, with examinations marked by external examiners, mostly from the University of London, but also from Oxford, and, in the case of Holy Scripture, the Principal of the Gloucester Theological College. Jane obtained a first-class certificate (Fig. 4) in Holy Scripture, modern history, English literature, geology or physical geography, chemistry, natural philosophy (physics), mathematics, arithmetic, French and German, with an average mark of 80.6 per cent. She excelled in arithmetic, with a mark of 95 per cent, and did well in everything else except natural philosophy, in which her mark was 47 per cent. Miss Beale's comment reads, 'She has been an earnest and zealous student, her work excellent, and her conduct exemplary.'[31]

Lucy, who later joined Jane at Cheltenham as a 'bye' student, testified that it was Miss Beale's Scripture lessons that thrilled Jane the most. Miss Beale was known to be something of a mystic, with High Church sympathies and an interest in theosophy. Her esoteric interpretation of the Scriptures sent Jane 'nearly crazy with excitement', and Jane used to share them with her former governess, Miss Cook, in a confidential correspondence. Miss Cook became concerned when Jane started quoting Dr Plumtre, brother-in-law of F. D. Maurice,[32] 'whose heretical views on Hell he was suspected of sharing', especially as Dr Plumtre was external examiner to the college. Feeling that Jane's parents ought to know what was going on, but fearing the consequences if she told them, Miss Cook compromised by informing William Lane, a clergyman who was married to Jane's oldest sister. He calmed her down and put the veto on telling her parents. In spite of this, Miss Beale received a letter from Mr and Mrs Harrison, and summoned Jane to her

---

[30] 'Scientiae Sacra Fames', 141–2.

[31] I am grateful to the late Elizabeth Lane, great-niece of Jane Harrison, for showing me her school certificate.

[32] These students were not enrolled in the regular course of study, but had a special status—presumably a concession to the continuing demand of parents that their girls be 'finished' in such subjects as French, German, music, and drawing. The account of Jane's relationship with Miss Beale is taken from 'Lucy' in Mirrlees's notebook.

Ladies' College, Cheltenham.

ESTABLISHED 1854.

VISITOR:
THE LORD BISHOP OF GLOUCESTER AND BRISTOL.

COUNCIL:
THE REV. EDWARD WALKER, INCUMBENT OF CHELTENHAM, *President.*
THE REV. HENRY WALFORD BELLAIRS, H.M. INSPECTOR OF SCHOOLS.
THE REV. ALFRED BARRY, PRINCIPAL OF KING'S COLLEGE, LONDON.
THE REV. T. W. JEX BLAKE, PRINCIPAL OF THE CHELTENHAM COLLEGE.

J. HOUGHTON BRANCKER, ESQ., *Hon. Registrar.*
J. FENRICE BELL, ESQ., *Hon. Secretary.*
W. DUNN, ESQ.
JOHN GALE, ESQ.
JOHNSON BROWN, ESQ.

PRINCIPAL:—MISS BEALE.

First CLASS CERTIFICATE.

Miss Jane Harrison Has attended this College for *Two* years, and has been for two years in Class I. She has obtained *806.5* marks out of a maximum of *1.000* in the Final Annual Examination. She is entitled, therefore, to a *First* Class Certificate. The Subjects of Examination were as follows:—

SUBJECTS	Percentage of Marks	SIGNATURES OF EXAMINERS
Holy Scripture	80	*Rob Girdlestone, Principal of the Gloucester Theological College*
Modern History	86	*S. J. Owen M.A. Lee's Reader in Law & History at Ch. Ch. Oxford*
English Literature	85	*J. J. Toph M.A. Examiner in the University of London, & of the*
Geology or Physical Geography	84	*Arch. Geikie F.R.S. Civil Service of India. Examiner in the University of London*
Chemistry	85	*H. Debus Ph. D. F.R.S. Examiner in the University of London*
Natural Philosophy	47	*G. Griffith M.A. Secretary of the British Association*
~~Euclid~~ *Mathematics*	83	*D. R. Fearon M.A. H. M. Inspector of Schools,*
Arithmetic	95	*and Ass't Commissioner, S. I. C.*
~~Algebra~~		
French	76.5	*P. H. Ernest Brette, L.D. Head master of the French School, Christ Hospital, London; Examiner in the University of London; for the Civil service of India; &c. &c. &c.*
German	85	*I. Althaus Ph. D. Examiner in the University of London &c*
Total	80.65	

She has been an earnest and zealous student; her work excellent, and her conduct exemplary.

Dorothea Beale Lady Principal.
Signed   *J. Fenric Bell* Hon. Secretary.
June 1869   *J. Houghton Brancker* Hon. Registrar.

4. Cheltenham Ladies' College Certificate

study to inform her that her family had written to say they felt Jane had been long enough at Cheltenham and that they planned to remove her. Miss Beale wrote back offering to waive the fees if they would allow Jane to stay on, craftily suggesting that 'no doubt they would find an advantage with the younger children if Jane stayed on another year', there being an automatic assumption that she would go home to be governess to her own brothers and sisters. The argument won the day.

Jane was an outstanding student and a credit to the college, but there are undercurrents in Miss Beale's generosity of more than a teacher's desire to promote the academic interests of a pupil. Between Jane and Miss Beale had developed an intense emotional friendship. As was so often the case, this was sublimated by the older woman into a spiritual mentorship, to which the younger responded as a disciple, expressing her devotion by acts of personal attention. (Jane knitted for Miss Beale a shawl in which was enclosed a poem.) Every girls' school of the period was rife with such relationships, fed by the desire on the part of the school authorities to deny any sort of heterosexual experiences to the girls in their charge (though by all accounts Jane was not short of boyfriends either), and by the ambivalent position of the teachers, who purportedly devoted themselves to preparing adolescent girls for marriage, yet themselves were resigned to a life of celibacy.[33] When Jane heard that her parents were planning to separate her from Miss Beale she fainted, and we can assume that Miss Beale's desire to keep her on was not entirely altruistic. When eventually Jane did leave, Miss Beale continued to write to her. At this time Jane read David Friedrich Strauss's *Life of Jesus*,[34] and rejected Christianity once and for all. Miss Beale wrote long imploring letters. Jane refused to reply, refused to go and see her, and Miss Beale was deeply wounded. The *grande passion* ended in the typical way.

Jane coped with the trauma by acting in a way that was to become for her a pattern in her relationships with both women and men: by consciously or unconsciously eradicating the whole episode from her memory. The account in *Reminiscences* of the famous headmistress is stark in its omission of everything with emotional implications and its distortion of fact that discredits Miss Beale:

I carried away from Cheltenham College a dislike for history which has lasted all my life. Our history lessons consisted mainly in moralisings on the doings and misdoings

---

[33] See Vicinus, *Independent Women*, 187–210, for a sensitive and insightful discussion of this issue.

[34] David Friedrich Strauss, *The Life of Jesus, Critically Examined*, trans. Marian Evans (New York: C. Blanchard, 1860). 'Marian Evans' is the autonym of George Eliot.

of kings and nobles. We did the Stuart period in tedious detail, and as Miss Beale was Cromwellian and I, like all children, a passionate Royalist, I was in a constant state of irritation. There was an odd rule throughout the College that no girl might buy a book. It sprang from Miss Beale's horror of what she called 'undigested knowledge'. She need not have feared with most of us that the amount of knowledge absorbed, digested or undigested, would have been excessive. I broke the rule and secretly bought a small life of Archbishop Laud. This I read, learned, marked and inwardly digested. Later, I again broke the rule and bought Bryce's Holy Roman Empire. Mr. Bryce was coming to examine us and I scored handsomely by my perfidy. Normally, what we had to feed on were the notes we took of lectures; these notes were carefully corrected and severely commented on. It was a wretched starvation system, but gave constant practice in composition.[35]

It appears that Jane's memory also played her false in the matter of buying books: none of her contemporaries could remember such a rule, and seriously doubted whether Miss Beale would ever have imposed such a restriction.

Lucy records something of Jane's friendships in the sentimental manner of her era. Amongst her peers Jane had an adoring circle of friends, according to Lucy, who often spoke of the magnetic quality of her personality. Initially she had found it difficult to make friends. On first acquaintance people found her aloof, or perhaps it was rather that they felt themselves inferior in the presence of her giftedness. But when they discovered her sense of humour, her originality, playfulness, and wit, and her affectionate, generous nature, they grew to love her, but always with a sense that she was the leader. She never realized her own power of attracting devotion, and always had difficulty coping with the consequences in relationships with friends of either sex. There were people who thought she had been much more intimate with them than she had. She could not tolerate clinging admirers, yet did not know how to discourage them gently. The result of this was that all her life she was to be accused of being brutal to her friends, dropping them mercilessly when they came too close. Physically she could not stand anyone putting their face too close to hers, and emotionally too she took care to preserve distance—paradoxically, because at the same time she craved intimacy. In later days many of her former friends were rather bitter when they talked about her, accusing her of being ruthless and fickle in her dealings with them. What they may not have appreciated was her peculiar combination of sensitivity, pride, and affection. Flight was her only escape, but it left a trail of misunderstandings.[36]

[35] *Reminiscences*, 35–6.
[36] This account is derived from 'Lucy' in Mirrlees's notebook.

In 1870, at the end of her last year at Cheltenham, she took the London matriculation examination. This required special preparation, requiring as it did knowledge of Latin, chemistry, geometry, algebra, and natural philosophy (optics, statics, dynamics, hydrostatics). Here was an opportunity for women to prove that they were academically as capable as men, yet it was difficult to persuade most girls to stay on at school past the age of 18. Some were needed at home, some wanted to 'come out', some felt they should be earning their living as teachers. The examination had been opened to women just the previous year, when eight women had taken it; only two passed. This time three students from Cheltenham, including Jane, passed.

She then proceeded to do what was expected of her and returned home to teach her younger brothers and sisters. The family moved back to Wales that year, and then back again to Scalby. Life was not comfortable for the older girls, the house having become 'rather sordid' (Lucy's description) as the result of being overrun by children. In the old days they had dined late, and the older sisters had come down for dessert and a sip of port. Now there was a meagre bread and butter and tea at six o'clock and supper at nine. The silence which Lucy remembers at mealtimes suggests strained relationships. Jane herself never spoke about these years.

Her first open break with her family was made when she came of age in 1871, and inherited from her mother an annuity of about £300.[37] Claiming that the craving to see a foreign country was too insistent to be resisted, she used this money to travel abroad. Her stepmother considered such a course of action undutiful, and reminded her of the horrors of selfishness and the necessity of sharing with her younger brothers and sisters, but her desire to go abroad was, in her own words, 'neither to hold nor to bind'. She offended her parents by indicating that teaching the little ones was not enough to fill her life completely. She first visited Holland under the chaperonage of a retired governess from Scarborough. The following year she travelled with a Cheltenham friend, Caroline Birch Dutton, joining a party to the Engadine,[38] and in 1873 to Pontresina. After these initial acts of self-assertion she travelled frequently, one of her great pleasures being, she said, to wake up in some strange place.

Her days at home she made bearable by cultivating the two things she said made life worth living: friendship and learning. In place of Miss Beale Jane

---

[37]   I have not been able to trace any legal document pertaining to the annuity that Elizabeth Harrison left Jane.

[38]   The party included Tom Verrall and his sister, cousins to the classical scholar A. W. Verrall who was to play an important role in Harrison's life at Cambridge. See 'Mrs Charles Mitchell' (Caroline Birch Dutton) in Mirrlees's notebook.

found a new confidante in the Greek wife of the new rector, Zoe Bruce, sister-in-law to the Archbishop of York.[39] Since she, like Jane, was unhappy in her home life (her husband being 'a man of excellent family but selfish and brutal and intensely philoprogenitive') they consoled each other with their confidences. Mrs Bruce worshipped Jane and 'mothered' her. Although, like the relationship with Miss Beale, this type of friendship was by no means uncommon, it has in Jane's case a peculiar poignancy. Learning brought satisfaction of another sort. During these years she studied on her own natural philosophy and chemistry for the University of London Examination for women, earning the 'special certificate of higher proficiency' in 1871. Then, Mary Paley, who had grown up in Scarborough and had known Jane from childhood, paid her a significant visit. Mary was one of the original five students who went to Newnham in 1871, and, considering Jane Harrison to be 'the cleverest woman in England', encouraged her to consider doing the same.[40] Jane decided to take 'for fun' (to use her own expression) the Cambridge University Examination for Women. Her success won her the scholarship offered by Newnham College to the best candidate in this examination, and her father, to everyone's surprise, but betraying his deep admiration for his daughter's ability, did not stand in the way of her accepting it.

[39] 'Mrs Herbert Paul' in Mirrlees's notebook.
[40] See J. M. Keynes, 'Mary Paley Marshall' in Edward Shils and Carmen Blacker (eds.), *Cambridge Women: Twelve Portraits* (Cambridge: Cambridge University Press, 1996), 73–92.

2. A Room of Her Own: Newnham College 1874–1879

W H E N Jane Harrison arrived in Cambridge in 1874 she found herself among a group of twenty women students from a variety of backgrounds, who were there for a variety of reasons. Of the thirteen in her year, most were, like Harrison, from the North of England or Scotland.[1] The majority were intending to become teachers or governesses, and went to Cambridge to take advantage of a new series of lectures which would enhance their qualifications. A few, more ambitious, were, like Jane, interested in following a course of studies similar to that taken by the men undergraduates. The women were not considered in any sense members of the university, nor was their presence even noticed by the university at large. With no access to libraries, laboratories, or examinations and not even a college of their own, permitted to attend only certain university lectures, no right to read for a degree, and barred by propriety from participating in the rich social life of the university, they had every reason to feel, as Harrison said, 'like a peri outside Paradise'. Nevertheless, some significant privileges had recently been won for women; the door was open just a chink, and the hope of future gains buoyed their spirits. When Harrison went up she had the benefit of a scholarship (without which she could not even have considered the possibility of going to Cambridge), a place to live, and access to some lectures— either those offered specially for women or those that women were permitted to attend, chaperoned. Above all she had the counsel and encouragement of Henry Sidgwick.

Henry Sidgwick had achieved a double first in classics and mathematics at Cambridge in 1859, and had been elected a Fellow of Trinity College. He was tormented all his life with religious doubt; Maynard Keynes has written of him that 'he never did anything but wonder whether Christianity was true

---

[1] *Contra* Sandra Peacock, who argues in *Mask and Self passim*, that as a northerner Harrison always felt marginalized by her provincial background. This is simply not true. The first principal of Newnham, Anne Jemima Clough, herself came from the North of England.

and prove that it wasn't and hope that it was'.[2] It is not fair to Sidgwick to allege that he never did anything else, since after resigning his Trinity Fellowship when he no longer felt able to subscribe to the Apostles' Creed he remained as a lecturer in moral sciences and devoted his life to university reform. He worked for the abolition of celibacy and religious requirements for dons and of compulsory Latin and Greek for admission to the university. He campaigned to abolish the Poll, or Ordinary, degree, and was determined to see the range of degree subjects, which had hitherto consisted of classics, mathematics, and, more recently, law, history, theology, and moral sciences (philosophy), extended to include the natural sciences and English literature. With equal dedication he worked to make education accessible to all who could benefit from it, including women. His foremost achievement was the foundation of Newnham College.

The reforms that opened Cambridge to women had twin roots in the beginnings of extension education and in the Schools Inquiry Commission of 1864. Extension education had originally been conceived of as early as 1850 in order to bring lectures to the blue-collar worker of the day.[3] To this end university lecturers had been sent to give courses in various cities, particularly in the disadvantaged North of England, but in the event those who attended the lectures were mainly women. What had begun as a philanthropic venture aimed at benefiting the poor had revealed a new category of social need—women, in particular those of the upper classes, hungry for education and academic challenge, and eager to escape from the drawing room. The Schools Inquiry Commission, which had included in its report a consideration of the educational needs of girls, had urged that in large towns a series of lectures should be given to older pupils both at school and from private families. Out of this step grew the North of England Council for the Higher Education of Women, whose purpose was to send university dons to give lectures in the provinces. Anne Jemima Clough, who was later to become the first principal of Newnham College, had played a part in these developments, first in securing that the terms of reference of the Schools Inquiry Commission be extended to include girls' schools, and later in serving as secretary to the North of England Council.[4]

Miss Clough knew from experience what it was to benefit from distance

[2] See Robert Skidelsky, *Henry Sidgwick: Between Reason and Duty*, an address given at the University of Warwick on 31 May 1988 and published by Newnham College, Cambridge.

[3] See W. Sewell, 'Suggestions for the Extension of the University' (1850), 8–11, quoted in J. F. C. Harrison, *Learning and Living': a Study in the History of the English Adult Education Movement* (London: Routledge & Kegan Paul, 1961).

[4] See Blanche Athena Clough, *A Memoir of Anne Jemima Clough*. (London: Arnold, 1897).

education, for her family had moved from Liverpool to South Carolina when she was a child, leaving the boys in England to attend school at Rugby. She had been encouraged during her years in America by letters from her brother, the poet Arthur Hugh Clough, in which he had shared with her something of what he was learning at school. It was the only education she ever received.

In 1869 the question had been raised as to whether Cambridge should not go further than offering isolated lectures in the provincial towns. It was felt that an examination for women was needed in order to provide the extension students with some objective. Since the extension lectures were clearly meeting a very real need amongst women of the upper classes, could not a whole course of lectures be offered in Cambridge itself to prepare women for the examination? In December, 1869, a pivotal meeting took place in Cambridge in the drawing room of Millicent Garrett Fawcett, (sister of the doctor Elizabeth Garrett Anderson), a pioneer of women's rights. Those present included Henry Sidgwick, James Stuart (the pioneer of extension education), Mr Markby (a member of the North of England Council), Prof. Benjamin Hall Kennedy (Regius Professor of Greek) together with his daughters Marion and Julia, and Prof. Maurice. They set up a committee and arranged a course of special lectures for women.[5] The classes could not, of course, be held in university buildings, but were given in a rented room in Trumpington Street. In addition to this, various university professors had for some time been willing to have women attend their lectures. Henry Sidgwick built on this foundation to persuade others to extend the same welcome to women, and by 1873 twenty-two out of a total of thirty-four professors consented, and a few years later the number grew to twenty-nine. St John's College offered the use of its chemistry laboratory outside of regular hours. Mrs Fawcett launched an appeal for scholarship funds; John Stuart Mill and Helen Taylor were among the first benefactors, contributing £40 a year for two years. A longer-term goal was the provision of a residence for students from outside Cambridge.[6]

The scheme was not without its critics. Most strenuously opposed to the whole venture was Emily Davies, later Mistress of Girton. While sharing with Henry Sidgwick a passionate commitment to making higher education available for women, she was determined from the outset not to settle for anything less than total equality with men, and to her the very idea of a

---

[5] For the Lent term of 1870 the lectures comprised English history (Prof. Maurice), English language and literature (Dr Skeat), algebra and arithmetic (Prof. Cayley), Latin (Prof. Mayor), and economics (Prof. Marshall). See Rita McWilliams-Tullberg, *Women at Cambridge*, 56.

[6] See Alice Gardner, *A Short History of Newnham College* (Cambridge: Bowes & Bowes, 1921).

special examination for women was anathema, for she felt it would consign women eternally to a lower status than men. On the opposite side it was argued that the situation of women was different from men and that the existing examinations were unsuitable; the Cambridge Local Examination, to which women had recently been admitted, was of too low a standard for those intending to become teachers; on the other hand the Previous Examination, taken by all undergraduates, included compulsory papers in Latin and Greek. It seemed to Henry Sidgwick both unnecessary and impractical to impose such a requirement on all women desiring a Cambridge education. Moreover, Sidgwick was already involved in a campaign for the total reform of university education at Cambridge, part of which involved the abolition of compulsory Latin and Greek. Emily Davies conceded that it was unrealistic to expect women to read for the Honours degree, and proposed instead the Poll, or Ordinary degree—a degree which Sidgwick was campaigning to abolish altogether. A great deal of contention and bitterness arose over strategy, which finally led to the separate foundation of two women's colleges. Miss Clough (like Miss Beale) did not share Miss Davies's passionate conviction that the whole attitude of society towards women needed to be changed. Emily Davies held out for the principle that women must demand nothing less than complete equality of opportunity, and so must fight for the right to enter the same degree courses as men, and comply with all regulations (such as the stipulation concerning how much time may be taken in studying for the Tripos examinations). Henry Sidgwick felt that to take that position was to risk the failure of the whole venture, and that to seize whatever gains could be made, step by step, by a series of compromises, was more likely to succeed in the long run. In the end each position was vindicated in its own way. Both Emily Davies's college at Hitchin, which later became Girton College, and Newnham College were a success, and with the gradual change in social attitudes the root of the conflict lessened in importance.

The lectures for women in Cambridge were an immediate success, with an attendance of between seventy and eighty the first year. Accommodation was now needed for women travelling from a distance. So it was that in 1871 Henry Sidgwick took a house at 74 Regent Street, furnished it at his own expense, and persuaded Anne Jemima Clough to preside. The communal life was not always easy: the five original students lived frugally in close quarters with Miss Clough, and there was a great deal of friction.[7]

---

[7] Mary Paley Marshall, *What I Remember* (Cambridge: Cambridge University Press, 1947), 11f.

The housing scheme and the lecture scheme began as separate ventures, the housing initially being almost entirely the private venture of Henry Sidgwick. For its management Miss Clough had at her side a steering committee, composed mainly of wives of Cambridge dons. Their support was essential to the success of the project as they were able to mediate between Miss Clough and the students on the one hand, and traditional Cambridge society on the other. The demand for housing rapidly exceeded the available space, and for the first few years the Cambridge women students lived under difficult circumstances. By 1874, after two moves, it was clear that the women needed a hall of residence. The committee set about to raise funds. Miss Clough explained the need in a leaflet she wrote for distribution among friends, referring to the lectures as 'a free-will offering of higher culture made to women by members of the University, to enable them to pass with credit the examination for women over eighteen'. The appeal found support, land was leased from St John's College, Sir Basil Champneys was appointed as architect, and plans were drawn up for Newnham Hall. In the mean time temporary accommodation was found in two adjacent houses in Bateman Street.

Most of the women who came to Newnham arrived in Cambridge with no clear idea of what they wanted to study. By far the majority of them, rather than attempting a degree course, came with the intention of picking up what education they could, most of them governesses or teachers seeking to improve their credentials. Many of these stayed for only one or two terms, returning to their positions. Miss Clough would work out a course of study for each student on an individual basis. Henry Sidgwick's personal interest in each student and his influence in the university at large made it possible to set up a curriculum of lectures and tutorials that were tailored to individual needs. Such a makeshift system had its advantages and disadvantages, the chief advantage being the flexibility that such an arrangement offered to women, very few of whom had the educational background to undertake the same course of studies as their male counterparts.

Of the first 221 students at Newnham in the 1870s, only about forty read for the degree examinations—the Tripos.[8] Unlike the students at Girton, the Newnham students were not tied to any timeframe in which to complete their studies. Henry Sidgwick had reservations about this 'irregularity', but Miss Clough, determined to prove that young women were capable of mas-

---

[8] Information taken from the Newnham College Register. The incomplete information about the early students makes it impossible to compile exact figures.

tering academic studies, felt that they would be most likely to succeed if they were allowed to work in their own time. Women embarked on the degree course with no certainty that they would be able to take the Tripos examinations at all. (Indeed, one may wonder why an issue should have been made about 'irregularities' in fulfilling the requirements, since they were not awarded a degree in any case.)[9] Until 1881, when they gained the right to be examined for a certificate (not a degree), they were admitted to examinations only unofficially and by private arrangement with university lecturers who were willing to read their papers. Students thus had no guarantee that their achievements would ever be recognized in any way. The difficulties that the early women students faced were considerable. While Emily Davies's insistence that her students complete exactly the same course as the men, under the same conditions, was vindicated in the success of her first students, she did not take into account the enormous emotional strain involved. One early Girton student groaned that very little allowance was made for their colossal ignorance of the subjects they were expected to know. Under the less stringent regime at Newnham, Jane Harrison, although in advance of nearly all her female contemporaries in her knowledge of Latin and Greek, still fell far behind the male undergraduates who had studied these subjects intensively in public schools from the age of 8, under teachers who themselves had a thorough grasp of the languages. Although by extra study and tutorials she caught up sufficiently to be able to read Greek and Latin fluently and with ease, and to do well in the Tripos examinations when she took them, she never felt confident when it came to philology, even in later years. At times she was overwhelmed with paralysing self-doubt.[10]

Harrison was among the minority at that time who decided from the first to read for the Tripos. Alfred Marshall had tried to interest her in the moral sciences, but she was persuaded by Henry Sidgwick to read for the classical Tripos instead.[11] Classics, considered until the middle of the nineteenth century to be the core of a liberal education, was being challenged at this period by the introduction of the sciences and modern

---

[9] Women were not awarded degrees at Cambridge until 1948.

[10] In matters of philology she deferred to the judgement of others all her life. Perhaps this is what Sir Hugh Lloyd-Jones means when he writes, 'She did not know Greek well'—a comment that is apt to be misunderstood if read in the context of present-day competence (*Blood for the Ghosts*: Classical Influences in the Nineteenth and Twentieth Centuries (London: Duckworth, 1982), 202).

[11] After this incident Mary Paley Marshall recalls that Jane afterwards called him 'the camel', for she said that she trembled at the sight of him 'as a horse does at the sight of a camel'.

languages; nevertheless a disproportionate number of women still opted for classics. The focus was heavily on language (especially composition, including, optionally, verse composition)[12] and literature (mainly translation), with compulsory papers in philosophy, philology, and history. She was just too early to benefit from the 'divided Tripos' that was introduced in 1879, in which Part I was devoted to language and literature, with Part II offering a choice of subjects: philosophy, history, archaeology, and philology. Even after this reform, the linguistic requirements of Part I were a formidable hurdle for women.[13]

To bring her students up to the necessary level of competence, Miss Clough also arranged for them to have individual tutorials. Harrison's 'coach' was S. H. Butcher, Fellow of Trinity College (best remembered for his translation, with Andrew Lang, of Homer's *Odyssey*).[14] She fell in love with him and was led to believe that he loved her in return and had intentions of proposing to her. However, she was called home in 1875 to nurse one of her younger sisters, Jessie, who had fallen ill with peritonitis. Jessie's condition itself placed Jane under all the stress felt by a close relative during a terminal illness. The nursing was not pleasant: baths in oil and enemas were prescribed and Jane, who hated a sickroom and never had any stomach for the unsavoury aspects of nursing, had to cope. Jessie died on 23 April 1875, and for Jane the consequences were devastating. To the exhaustion of caring she now added bereavement. Jane had felt closer to Jessie than to any other of her sisters; in fact Jessie was the only one of her siblings for whom Jane had felt anything like sisterly love and had shown this by promising to pay the fees for her to attend Newnham. Desolate, Jane returned to Cambridge having missed a whole term. There she discovered that Henry Butcher was

---

[12] Dora Ivens (Pym) observed in 1913 that few women took the verse paper so that they could concentrate on the rest of the syllabus, but that without the verse it was almost impossible to attain a first.

[13] See Claire Breay, 'Women and the Classical Tripos 1869–1914' in *Curriculum, Culture and Community*, suppl. 24 (Cambridge: Cambridge Philological Society, suppl. 1999), 49–70.

[14] Mirrlees records an amusing anecdote in her draft biography: 'In spite of, (or perhaps, because of) the relentless chaperonage, Cupid was busy in those early Newnham days. A group of brilliant, one or two of them splendidly handsome, young Fellows used to "coach" the students—& when the "coachings" took place in May evenings with the nightingales singing loudly in the garden, they were apt to become sentimental. The lighter side of these discreet flirtations is shown by the following anecdote. Miss Clough had started a book, so runs the story, in which one was to jot down any interesting observation from Nature made in the Newnham garden. The contribution of Mr H. Butcher, at that time a young and brilliant Fellow of Trinity, was as follows: "Observed two lady birds." The next entry . . . was "Observed the Butcher bird observing two lady birds" ' ['butcher bird' being another name for the shrike].

already engaged to Rose Trench. They were married and in 1876 moved to Oxford.[15]

These events, enough to overwhelm anyone, brought Jane to an emotional breakdown. She turned to the arts for solace. Unable to study she poured out her emotions on the piano for hours on end, playing duets whenever possible, and finding an outlet in the romantic music of Chopin and Brahms, notably his Hungarian Dances. One of her contemporaries vowed she had never known anyone who so completely abandoned herself to music and beauty in every way, with tears pouring down her cheeks. Near the end of Harrison's life, Hope Mirrlees expostulated at the 'barbarous sacrifice', angry at an ethic which regarded it as shocking for anyone with a mother or sisters to be nursed by a professional. Harrison spurned the criticism. 'Of course I went', she retorted. 'Jessie needed me.' Near the end of her life she told Mirrlees that she had learned that one never regrets having made a sacrifice. But it took her many years to recover from the disappointment.

While at Newnham Harrison formed some life-long friendships. Foremost among them was Ellen Crofts, cousin to Henry Sidgwick. Like Jane, Ellen came from Yorkshire and shared Jane's sense of humour. She was appointed to the Newnham Staff in 1878, though she resigned on her marriage to Frank Darwin (third son of Charles Darwin and himself a botanist) in 1883. Ellen introduced Jane to the Darwin family, with whom she remained close friends all her life. Mary Paley, Harrison's Scarborough friend, was just one month younger than Harrison and joined the staff a year after Harrison arrived, having come to Newnham straight from school. In 1877 Mary Paley married the economist Alfred Marshall, merged her life in his, and collaborated with his work. She taught first at Newnham, then went on with her husband to lecture in economics at Bristol (where she eventually received an honorary D. Litt. in 1928), and at Oxford. When he returned to Cambridge as Professor of Political Economy in 1885, she resumed her teaching at Newnham until 1908. Academically she pioneered, but socially, unlike Harrison, she had no desire to break with tradition by participating in serious discussion outside the lecture hall. When the question of degrees for women came up, Alfred Marshall was opposed.[16]

In 1875 the students moved into a college of their own (Fig. 5). They now

[15] By 1876 three colleges at Oxford countenanced married dons. Butcher may have been helped by his connections: G. G. Bradley, Master of University College, was a well-known member of the academic liberal group to which Sidgwick also belonged.

[16] Ellen (Crofts) Darwin and Mary (Paley) Marshall maintained their formal associations with Newnham College, both as Associates and as Council members.

5. Newnham College, 1875 (now Old Hall)

could enjoy their own rooms, a good dining-hall, and a library as well as additional common rooms. Wide passages, lit by windows at each end, ran the length of the house on each of the four floors, and made it light and airy. There were pleasant views, over the garden and to the country beyond in one direction, and to the spires of Cambridge in the other.[17] The women must have felt now for the first time that they had passed beyond the stage of being an 'experiment'. The buildings and their grounds conferred an identity. To Harrison they were a haven. Here she enjoyed peace and solitude for the first time in her life, and the opportunity to shut herself away to study in a room of her own. At the end of her life she could write,

I like to live spaciously, but rather plainly, in large halls with great spaces and quiet libraries. I like to wake in the morning with the sense of a great, silent garden round

[17] Marshall, *What I Remember*, 21.

me. . . . If I had been rich I should have founded a learned community for women; . . . as it is, I am content to have lived many years of my life in a college.[18]

The students were given the freedom to express themselves by choosing the wallpaper for their rooms. Mary Paley remembered how both she and Jane were carried away by the Pre-Raphaelite wave. They bought Edward Burne-Jones photographs and dressed accordingly. 'We had our rooms papered with Morris papers (I remember hers was a dark jessamine and mine a light).'[19] Similarly, another student reminisced how 'a good many students wore aesthetic green gowns & the harmony of colours against the green and blue walls was quite delightful. Miss Harrison had a new dress much the colour of mine only even a better colour, so really she & Miss Richmond & Miss Wimbush should never be apart, their dresses harmonize so beautifully.'[20] In a much-quoted incident the Pre-Raphaelite décor of Harrison's room led on one occasion to a fainting fit when George Eliot came to the college, and visiting Harrison for a few minutes in her room, 'she said in her shy, impressive way, "Your paper makes a beautiful background for your face." The ecstasy was too much, and I knew no more.' George Eliot spoke like a true aesthete; one of the principles of the movement was that a person should harmonize with the décor.[21]

By breaking away from traditional forms of dress aesthetic women were proclaiming their liberation from traditional roles. At a time when ladies of society still laced themselves into stiff dresses for the drawing room, those who took up careers began to think of dress in terms of convenience and comfort. Burne-Jones's limp ladies, who look so old-fashioned to us more than a hundred years later, were making an important social statement. We forget that simply not to wear a crinoline was to be liberated. The 'tennis frock' was a similar innovation. Recognizing that 'tight stays and sleeves and tied-back skirts are incompatible with success in rowing or tennis' women were demanding less constricting clothes for sports. It was fashionable to embroider them with the emblems of the movement. In the summer of 1880, one Cicely, a reader of *The Queen*, was advised that she 'might embroider her bluish green art dress with peacock's feathers, the pattern carried from the shoulder down both sides of the front of the dress over the side darts as in the newest style of tennis aprons'.[22] Mary Paley remembered how

[18] *Reminiscences*, 88–9.   [19] 'Mary Paley Marshall' in Mirrlees's notebook.
[20] Mirrlees's draft biography.
[21] *Reminiscences*, 45–6. Similarly, at Oxford in 1874 Oscar Wilde's rooms at Magdalen were popularly considered to be one of the showpieces of the college. See Elizabeth Aslin, *The Aesthetic Movement* (New York: Excalibur Books, 1981), 98.
[22] From *The Queen*, 1881, quoted in Aslin, *The Aesthetic Movement*, 145–6.

she and Jane were caught up in it all, sitting together in the evenings embroi-
dering their tennis frocks, 'hers with pomegranates and mine with Virginia
Creeper' as they talked freely on all subjects.[23] The aesthetic movement was
more than a fashion: it was a new attitude to life.

House rules imposed strict limitations on the students' life outside of the
college.[24] During the Michaelmas and Lent terms the students were required
to be in college at half-past six each evening; this was extended to half-past
eight on Sundays and throughout the Easter term. It was natural that under
such circumstances the secluded community of women soon developed
its own social structure. At the tea parties and cocoa parties they held in
their rooms intimacy grew as they talked on all subjects—'Morris, both as
a decorator & poet, & Deronda & the Mill on the Floss & Lord Lytton's
books & Thackeray and Jane Eyre & Dickens & all sorts of things'.[25]
Mary Paley remembered visits to the town gymnasium once a week with
Mrs Fawcett as a chaperon.[26] The letters written to her parents by one
student, Mabel Malleson, provide a vignette of their social life: lawn tennis
in the summer, with a Devonshire cream tea to celebrate a tournament;
music (a Brahms quartet and a Schumann trio given by Mr Stanford and
some amateurs of the musical society); a Shakespeare reading with Harrison
taking the part of Viola (delighted to obtain an unbowdlerized version);
ghost stories in Ellen Crofts's room. Debates were held 'on rather dreary
subjects, for instance "That the greatness of the nation is due, rather to the
perfect development of the individual than to that of state organization"',
and on less dreary topics, such as dress. In one of these debates the topic of
wearing bloomers came up, and her friend Margaret Merrifield was startled
to find that the issue could be considered from the point of view of convenience ('they must be so delightful in muddy weather') rather than morals.
Mrs Bateson, the wife of the Master of St John's, gave dances in the Hall of
the Lodge. They danced quadrilles, gallops, the Lancers—all the latest
vogue—though 'Miss Clough was not keen on dances'. Sometimes the lecturers invited them to Sunday evening parties in their rooms. On other
evenings Mr Sidgwick read aloud to them from Eliot's *The Mill on the Floss*.
There were distinguished visitors: Turgenev, Ruskin (who, on being shown
around the library by Harrison is reported to have made the condescending
remark, 'Each book that a young girl touches should be bound in white

---

[23] 'Mary Paley Marshall' in Mirrlees's notebook.

[24] Except where otherwise noted, the following material about social life at Newnham
College in this period is taken from Mirrlees's draft biography.

[25] Mirrlees attributes this memory to Margaret (Merrifield) Verrall.

[26] Marshall, *What I Remember*, 15.

vellum'), and Burne-Jones. There were 'endless' tea-parties given by Miss Clough to introduce the students to distinguished members of town and gown.

Throughout her student days Harrison was in conflict with Miss Clough. On the surface it was the old issue of 'hats and bonnets' again. Like Miss Caines at Cheltenham, Miss Clough lived in constant fear that she would forfeit the approval of 'the Cambridge ladies' through some social indiscretion of one of her charges. Harrison thought the whole issue was ridiculous and all the attention to tact and prudence futile, and attributed Miss Clough's fussiness to a need in her personality to 'energize'. Most of Miss Clough's energy was directed towards matters of dress. She disliked the long narrow flannel skirts worn for tennis ('I suppose she would have liked us to play in bustles!' was one angry protest); aesthetic and 'mannish' clothes were her particular bugaboo. Harrison wore both. She appeared one term with a yellow plaid ulster, described by her friend Eleanor Ritchie as 'a frightful object, with very loud yellow checks'. (A few years later the ulster—a long, loose overcoat of a rough fabric—was immortalized in the pages of *Punch*. On the occasion of an exhibition of George Frederick Watts portraits at the Grosvenor, a poem was printed in the media that contained the lines: 'Here's Sir Frederick robed in scarlet, here's Dean Stanley's thoughtful face | And the lady in the Ulster has a certain kind of grace.') Even the height of the two students was a problem. Miss Clough is reputed to have approached them as they were going out for a walk with the plea, 'M'dears, don't you think you could try to look a little less tall?' There can be no doubt that Harrison, emancipated, unconventional, influential, and popular, was a threat to Miss Clough, who still saw Newnham College as an experiment, *her* experiment, and primarily a philanthropic venture as 'a means of enabling penniless young women to earn their living', whereas to Harrison it was a haven of learning for learning's sake. Harrison never doubted for a moment that the cause of women's education was bound to succeed, and considered the whole issue silly, pointing to the success of Girton. Emily Davies had never cared about the opinion of the Cambridge ladies.

In 1877 Harrison and two other students decided to put on a Greek play. The idea was novel though not unprecedented: there had been a production of Antigone at Edinburgh in the 1840s. Apart from this production Greek tragedy in performance was unheard of. The very idea bears testimony for Harrison's gift of originality, perhaps also to her sense of the wholeness of things, that Greek tragedies were not texts but dramas, and would come to life only on the stage. Euripides was the natural choice, with his penchant for representing his characters as if they were his contemporaries, and for bringing the mythological past into the present, for which he was parodied in Aristophanes' *Frogs*. He was irreverent, sceptical, iconoclastic. The Victorians were divided in their attitude towards him, strong in their praise or condemnation, and the choice of Euripides would have been seen as 'naughty'. This attitude is well captured in the vignette Harrison records of her encounter with Gladstone when he visited the college:

His daughter Helen was a college friend of mine, or rather, more exactly, a friendly enemy. . . . I was a rigid Tory in those days, and I resolutely refused to join the mob of students in cheering and clapping the Grand Old Man on his arrival. I shut myself up in my room. Thither—to tease me—she brought him. He sat down and asked me who was my favourite Greek author. Tact counselled Homer, but I was perverse and not quite truthful, so I said 'Euripides'. Aeschylus would have been creditable, Sophocles respectable, but the sceptic Euripides! It was too much, and with a few words of warning he withdrew.[27]

Reading this, one wonders if Harrison, at the age of 76, was still 'perverse and not quite truthful'. Euripides was her favourite Greek author and remained so all her life.

At first they considered the *Medea*, but in the end they decided on the *Electra*. Harrison took the parts of the messenger and the paidagogos, and taught the chorus their dances. The costumes were made up to the students' own designs by a local dressmaker. Harrison had a white costume with a border of gold and crimson, Margaret Merrifield a knee-length blue tunic with a border of gold and blue, and blue sandals, Eleanor Ritchie a similar costume in saffron with a white chlamys.

However, when Miss Clough found out that they were intending to act with bare arms and legs before the Cambridge ladies, she put a stop to the proceedings, adding that she disapproved of theatricals and would not hear of women acting as men. Margaret Merrifield remembered with indignation that earlier 'she had given full consent to our acting and had said she would be very pleased if her niece acted in the Chorus; it was entirely her own idea asking people from the town, we did not wish them to come at all—as to the arms, they are no more 'bare' than in every ball dress;—as to the legs we certainly had no stockings, but our legs were encased in sandals from the sole of the foot to the knee'.[28] Miss Clough proposed that Mrs Sidgwick inspect their costumes, at which point the women lost interest in the whole production and called it off.

They were just a few years before their time and hampered by their

---

[27] *Reminiscences*, 44 f.

[28] Mirrlees's draft biography, drawing on the memory of Margaret (Merrifield) Verrall.

gender. The *Agamemnon* was produced in Oxford in 1880, *Oedipus Tyrannus* at Harvard in 1881, and *Alcestis* at Bradfield College in 1882. The first Cambridge Greek play, the *Ajax*, was produced later that year, and was so successful that special trains were run from King's Cross. That a man should play the part of a woman shocked no-one; in fact A. R. Macklin's performance as Tecmessa was acclaimed. In 1883 Girton staged Sophocles' *Electra* (with the leading role played by Janet Case, who two years later took the part of Athena in a university production of the *Eumenides*, albeit in flowing robes).

It was through their common interest in the Greek play that Harrison became close friends with Margaret de Gaudrion Merrifield, who later married the classicist Arthur Woollgar Verrall (notorious for his daring emendations of texts), and with whom Harrison was to collaborate in one of her most successful books.[29] From her French mother Margaret Merrifield inherited 'an alertness, a clarity, a dexterity which left some of us with a feeling that we were half-baked and wholly unfinished'; she was 'punctiliously law-abiding', and 'never an ardent or even very active Suffragist', yet held startlingly strong views on the importance of women's independence. Hearing a speaker extol the virtue of a woman who had given up her whole life to the furthering of her husband's career, she expostulated, 'Wonderful? I call it simply squalid; fancy giving up your whole life to your husband!' and added, reflectively, 'how it would bore Arthur if I did!'.[30]

By her second year Harrison had begun to surround herself with the aura that developed into 'the myth of Jane Harrison'.[31] This is how Alice (Lloyd) Dew-Smith, who became one of Harrison's life-long friends, remembered her:

The earliest impression that remains in my mind of Jane Harrison is as the central figure of a group of students seated round a dining table in the S.E. corner of the Old Hall, Newnham College. . . . Central, in that she was the dominating figure of a little set of friends that in those days dined at that particular table during term time. . . . Like a Rembrandt picture the rest of the dining hall is shrouded in darkness. I cannot even with an effort call up an image of what it was like, or a memory of who was in it. Only a shadowy picture of that table in the corner, with a high light on Harrison's imposing and vital figure. Nor can I in the least remember what threw me, a 'fresher' of no 'parts,' into that interesting group. But there I was, and fortunately for myself I was equipped with an appreciation for the exceptional.

---

[29] *Mythology and Monuments of Ancient Athens: Being a Translation of a Portion of the 'Attica' of Pausanias, wih an Introductory Essay and Archaeological Commentary* (London: Macmillan, 1890). Margaret Verrall did the translation.

[30] Jane Harrison, 'In Memoriam Margaret Verrall', *Newnham College Letter*, 1916, 53.

[31] See Beard, *Invention*, *passim*.

Certainly, even at that time, Jane Harrison was exceptional; exceptional in appearance, character and intellect. I can see her now, her tall willowy figure clad in a tight-fitting olive green 'art serge' such as used to be supplied to Newnham students by Messrs Boyd-Burnett in the days of the aesthetic craze; her long neck and well-set head, with brown hair in a Greek coil at the back; her fine deeply-fringed eyes—all made an ineffaceable picture. Moreover I can hear her delightful voice and her amusing talk. Looking back over many years I can think of no one else who could pour forth such a continuous stream of delightful nonsense as Jane entertained us with, evening after evening. . . . It was like a felicitous flow of well chosen words adapted with ludicrous effect to whatever was the subject under discussion, and poured forth in the unconscious, heedless, lavish way that a spring bubbles from a rock and tumbles over the surrounding area.[32]

Only one letter survives from this period of her life. It illustrates just the light banter and the gift with language that Alice Lloyd recognized.

Dear Miss Wilson,
I have been meditating a letter of condolence ever since I heard you were so smitten and afflicted, and now I can no longer forbear, since M. tells me (but the thought is intolerable) that the Doctor has forbidden you to take cold baths. You with your crest a fish rampant, your motto 'never pass a good pool.' Don't believe him. Defy him. Read the snark all night and splash all day and you will come right. Indeed I speak from experience. Seriously though, I am sorry you are not to come back yet, we miss you horribly at our table, though I do quote Tennyson with more ease and complacency. However, you will be sure to come up next term. . . .
So you may only work a quarter of an hour. It really is quite enough. The best coach I ever had told me (at scattered intervals) that it was 'absurd to work in the afternoon', 'a great mistake in the evening' and 'almost impossible in the morning'; and I have gathered from other sources that the best men only do ten minutes a day. When one thinks of it seriously it is difficult to excuse oneself doing any work at all. I am sure tennis is a plain leading to better paths. Now I must stop. I've got some bricks to make and no straw, i.e. Iambics and no ideas. If you have time and inclination do let me know how you fare.[33]

She had all her life learned to be independent, from the death of her mother, through childhood to the years at Cheltenham, where even among her peers she was set apart by her quick intellect, forming more of a bond with Miss Beale than with any of her own contemporaries. To some, however, she appeared not so much brilliant as snobbish. Mary (Paley) Marshall pointed out that among the criteria for acceptance in Jane's set was

[32]   Alice Dew-Smith in 'Jane Ellen Harrison', *Newnham College Letter*, Jan. 1929, 62–3.
[33]   Letter to Edith Wilson, 26 Nov. 1876, quoted in Stewart, *Jane Ellen Harrison*, 8.

6. Newnham Hall, 1878. Jane Harrison is looking out through the window, on the right

that one 'had to be amusing'.[34] With north of England self-deprecation, Harrison was intolerant of others who took themselves too seriously. Older than most of the students, she carried herself with a poise that had twin roots in her own intellectual competence and social refinement. She was irritated by anyone who was not sensitive to the social code. Alice Dew-Smith remembered that 'she was so easily bored: people bored her if they talked too much; or if they had a vivacious manner, or if they were egoists. And if they put their faces too close to hers they completely alienated her. She was the most fastidious person I have ever known.'[35]

At Newnham she had discovered her own social style, as she began to live out the inner freedom she was now experiencing, for which the life style of the Pre-Raphaelites offered just the right outward code. She became popular with those, who, like her, were sick of Victorian pretentiousness. She had no patience with others, less sure of themselves, who chose to conform. Perhaps she was right in associating her hatred of hypocrisy with her Yorkshire roots; she certainly inherited this trait from her father and found it lacking in her Welsh stepmother.

Books played a significant part in her emancipation. Like her mother, she loved poetry. As a child she had read anything she could get her hands on, as did all girls of her time who loved to read, and memorized quantities of verse. Later she was to laugh at herself for her youthful love of the sentimental, quoting with glee, 'My hair is white | But not with years' and other such verse. During her Newnham years she discovered Dante Gabriel Rossetti, and *The Stream's Secret* became her favourite poem.

Above all, perhaps influenced by the enthusiasm of Henry Sidgwick, she read Swinburne. She loved the stuff of his early poetry: 'passion and rebellion and liberty and the sea'.[36] It was Swinburne's avowed aim to subordinate all his own gifts to the ideal of re-creating Hellenism. Harrison's response was on two levels. She 'resonated' (to use her own word) to the classical ideas and imagery, but she also fell under the hypnotic spell of the Swinburnian rhythms, which were not classical at all, but derived from romantic English poetry.[37] Like his heroes and models, Byron and Shelley, Swinburne ideal-

---

[34] 'Mary Paley Marshall' in Mirrlees's notebook.

[35] 'Alice Dew-Smith' in Mirrlees's notebook.

[36] Grierson, H. J. C., *Swinburne* (rev. edn. London: Longmans, Green and Co., 1959), 6.

[37] Later, Gilbert Murray was to render the choruses in his translations of Euripides in similar metres, with the same hypnotic effect on Harrison. (She wrote to him of his translation of the *Troades*, when he appeared to her to have failed to live up to his usual magic: 'I always want the rhythm of anything—as I want the words—to seem inevitable. . . . I don't think one shld attempt to echo a metre unless it can be quite unstrained in English' (JEH to GM 184, n.d.).

ized the Greeks, but he wrote for an audience that had seen Greece reborn in two ways. In the 1820s Greece had once again become a free nation, and now in the 1870s the archaeological discoveries of Heinrich Schliemann at Troy and Mycenae, together with the earlier German excavations at Olympia, brought back to life the ancient myths. The romantic fantasy began to take on a Pygmalion-like reality. Swinburne translated it into a Victorian idiom. At the same time he was an iconoclast, and as he turned for inspiration to the pagan Greeks, he spoke honestly if irreverently of his feelings about Victorian religion. He wrote of 'the supreme evil, God' that

> Because thou are cruel and men are piteous . . .
> At least we witness of thee ere we die
> That these things are not otherwise, but thus;
> That each man in his heart sigheth, and saith,
>   That all men even as I,
> All we are against thee, against thee, O God most high.[38]

More than anything else at this period of her life Harrison sought an emotional release from the weight of her religious upbringing. Poems like Swinburne's 'Hymn to Proserpine', gave a voice to her experiment with unbelief and excited her to ecstasy by its rhythms. 'Thou hast conquer'd, O pale Galilean; the world has grown grey from thy breath | We have drunken of things Lethean, and fed on the fulness of death', leads to the conclusion, 'For there is no God found stronger than death; and death is a sleep'; although her perspective on religion was to change with the years this remained her philosophy to the end.

The very name of Swinburne blazed emancipation. 'Atalanta in Calydon' tells of the destructive power of love, and of a fate which plays havoc with natural family ties. In other poems Swinburne wrote of homosexual and lesbian love—just as the great classical authors, long looked to as models, had done without embarrassment. His volume *Poems and Ballads* was condemned for its 'depravity' and 'feculent corruption', and he was castigated for his 'passionate zest and long-drawn elaboration of enjoyment' of vice.[39] Yet boys in school were given the poems of Sappho and plays such as Sophocles' *Oedipus the King* as required reading. The satires of Martial and Juvenal abound in obscenity.[40] Such a curriculum was defended on the

---

[38] Algernon Charles Swinburne, *Atalanta in Calydon*.

[39] Unsigned review in *London Review*, 4 August 1866, xiii, 130–1, quoted in Clyde K. Hyder, *Swinburne, the Critical Heritage* (London: Routledge & Kegan Paul, 1970), 36 f.

[40] Donald Thomas, *Swinburne, the Poet in His World*, (London: Weidenfeld and Nicolson, 1979), 132, gives some nice examples.

grounds of its moral value—by those who had inherited unthinkingly a tradition that believed that it was more important to construe and scan the lines than to understand their message. Now the meaning of the texts excited Harrison. As a student she read Aristophanes for the first time and discovered that the pagan Greeks were 'real people'.

But it was Aristotle's *Ethics*, one of the set books for her year at Cambridge, that made a real change in her thinking. She records the effect:

To realise the release that Aristotle brought, you must have been reared as I was in a narrow school of Evangelicalism—reared with sin always present, with death and judgement before you, Hell and heaven to either hand. It was like coming out of a madhouse into a quiet college quadrangle where all was liberty and sanity, and you became a law to yourself. The doctrine of virtue as the Mean—what an uplift and revelation to one 'born in sin'! The notion of the *summum bonum* as an 'energy', as an exercise of personal faculty, to one who had been taught that God claimed all, and the notion of the 'perfect life' that was to include as a matter of course friendship. I remember walking up and down in the College garden, thinking could it possibly be true, were the chains really broken and the prison doors open.[41]

She wrote these words, however, fifty years after the event, when the conversion of her attitudes could be seen as complete. Rarely does the impact of an encounter bring about such instantaneous change.

In March 1879 Harrison wrote her Tripos examinations. The preceding months were filled with the agony of apprehension known as 'Trip fever', even more paralysing to the early students than it is today. The students carried the extra burden of realizing that their own performance would contribute to the success or failure of 'the cause'. In Harrison's case further anxiety was caused by the refusal of two out of the six classical examiners to examine women, and Miss Clough's fretting over how to handle the situation. When the day came a great fuss was made over the candidates. Each one had her 'bridesmaid'. One student described their duties (and rewards):

at the end of the morning paper I took up my stand outside the door of the room where Nellie was working [until] she came out. I had to order lunch, then take her in the garden & make her rest in the one hour's interval. Lunch & dinner are served up separately for Tripos students & consist of choice food, so the reward of the bridesmaids is that they are allowed to share the dainties. At five o'clock I again waited for Nellie & then we had a nice little dinner together in one of the lecture rooms. Only

---

[41] *Reminiscences*, 80–1.

think of having fish and lamb & jelly & dessert & Champagne at Newnham! I could hardly believe my eyes.[42]

The Tripos lasted for eight days. Harrison's stress was compounded by toothache. The results were read out in the Senate House. Margaret Merrifield and Helen Gladstone went with Miss Clough to hear the list read out, Harrison staying in bed for nervousness. The news was brought back: she was top of the second class.

It was small comfort to be told that the examiners had in fact been divided over whether or not to place her in the first class, or that she achieved the highest marks of all the candidates in philosophy. The news of her results, 'so much better than anyone expected since the examination', was greeted by Newnham with 'loud clapping as a token of congratulation', but for Harrison it was a bitter, bitter disappointment.

Harrison had probably never seriously considered the possibility of having to leave Newnham. She had hoped, even assumed, that after taking her Tripos she would be invited to join the Newnham staff as the first lecturer in classics, and had often talked about what she would do in this capacity. To her disappointment no offer was made, and in the summer of 1879 she was faced with the problem of what she was to do. Returning home was unthinkable. She had severed her connections with her family. Her thoughts naturally turned to teaching, not because she had any desire to teach, but simply because it was still assumed that students went to Newnham to prepare to be teachers, and her gifts and training were not suited to anything else. She joined the staff of the Oxford High School for Girls. She liked the pupils and they loved her, 'booking' the privilege of taking one of her arms during the morning's break in the playground. But she stayed only one term. She was out of place in a school. She did not subscribe to the Victorian ideal of education as progress; the Christian basis for education, observed in morning prayers, grace at meals, and compulsory Scripture lessons, she repudiated. Her own philosophy was unorthodox:

let children early speak at least three foreign languages, let them browse freely in a good library, see all they can of the first-rate in nature, art, and literature—above all, give them a chance of knowing what science and scientific method means, and then leave them to sink or swim. Above all things, do not cultivate in them a taste for literature.[43]

[42] Mirrlees's draft biography. Based on a letter from Hope Malleson.
[43] This quotation, and the substance of the following paragraph is taken from *Reminiscences*, 37–8.

She deplored the belief that it was part of the responsibility of the teacher to 'develop a child's mind' or to exercise any kind of influence beyond the teaching of the subject itself; character training she believed was best left to one's contemporaries. For the teacher to interfere in this she thought very dangerous, and bad for the teacher. This attitude to schooling was not altogether rational, owing as much to her own experience at Cheltenham as to any considered philosophy of education. The intensity with which she articulated these ideas at the end of her life is an indication that her infatuation for Miss Beale, followed by its reversal and the repudiation of all that Miss Beale represented, left her with a personal conflict that she was never able to resolve. No wonder she decided that teaching within the system of the day was not for her. Moreover, in Oxford she could not avoid the occasional social encounter with Henry Butcher. The stress was too much. With her small but adequate private income she could afford to resign her teaching post and in January 1880 she moved to London.

Meanwhile, Miss Clough had offered a lectureship in classics to Margaret Merrifield. It is not hard to see why she was preferred over Harrison. Miss Clough wanted a 'safe' candidate and Miss Merrifield was the natural choice. As a teacher she proved to be clear, confident, and scholarly; she became valued as an examiner for scholarship examinations, for she was meticulous and reliable, 'trenchant, clear-eyed and discriminating'. When, two years later, she married Arthur Woollgar Verrall, Fellow of Trinity, she kept up her work at Newnham, lecturing in Greek as well as giving private tutorials and superintending the classical students. She continued to dine at college once or twice a week, and to participate in meetings and social functions. Years later Harrison knew her as a colleague, 'business-like, unselfish and convenient. There was never anyone less fussy.'[44]

However, Margaret Merrifield did not accept the appointment without protest at the injustice done to Harrison, who never forgot her 'generous rage' and irrational insistence that Jane, not she, should have the position. Margaret 'came immediately up to London to see me, and literally stamped about the room, healing thereby her friend's hurt vanity'. It was far into the night before Jane could persuade her that 'refusal would be as useless as Quixotic'. Harrison had realized that she had no chance of being appointed to the staff at this stage. Instead, she decided to settle in London, taking a part-time teaching position at Notting Hill High School to supplement her income.

She must have been a good teacher. She loved her subject for its own sake

---

[44] 'In Memoriam Margaret Verrall'.

and appreciated that its difficulties served to brace the mind, but was not content with teaching a class to parse, construe, and translate. Equally important was that her pupils should understand—see, feel, and enter into—the literature they were reading. She was fortunate at Notting Hill that the British Museum was only a few miles away. Teaching the passage from Ovid's *Metamorphoses* about the rape of Proserpina she would not tell them but show them the goddess Demeter 'with the corn-blades in her hair, and the fishes of the Sicilian sea playing around her, on the coins of that very Syracuse of which we have just read'. She would show them Demeter Thesmophoros—the 'lawgiver' of Ovid—goddess of fixed homes *because* of agriculture, of marriage and women's rights, worshipped by women in strange mystic ceremonies. She showed them the tablets with the curses ('mis-spelt too often, for the ladies of those days were more vengeful than literate'), and the sculpture of Proserpina bearing in her hand the fateful pomegranate. Reading of the Sirens she would convince them that *doctae Sirenes* were not to be translated 'learned' but rather 'skilful' Sirens by showing them the vase in which a bird-maiden touches her lyre with a skilled hand.[45] But the teaching was 'still just drudgery, a dreary *pis aller*, the dull residuum of golden dreams—poetry which had turned into prose'.[46] Two years later, writing to her Newnham friend Hope Malleson who had seemed sad, she confessed, 'I have so many doleful thoughts hidden away in my own soul that sometimes they betake themselves to other people's faces'.[47] For the next twenty years she was restless (though not unproductive, and certainly not without friends), until her dreams materialized and she was invited to return to Newnham in 1898.

---

[45] Jane Ellen Harrison, 'Archaeology and School Teaching', *Journal of Education*, 2 (1880), 105–6.

[46] Mirrlees's draft biography.   [47] JEH to Hope Malleson, Apr. 14 1882.

3. 'Salvationist for Greek Art': London 1879–1886

T H E very air . . . breathed antiquity. There was a fine photograph of the Parthenon on the wall; over an etching of one of Burne-Jones' pictures a piece of mummy cloth was hung; there were strange vases and pots; and books and pamphlets innumerable concerning the ancient Greeks stood on the shelves and in the quaint eighteenth-century book-case. It was an occasion 'when Greek meets Greek'. Two ladies bent together over a book of daintily coloured plates, lost in admiration of something which I was presently called upon to admire. The two ladies were Miss Jane Harrison, the lady to whose lectures during the last ten years the revival of popular interest in ancient Greece is almost solely due, and Miss Millington Lathbury, one of the three of Miss Harrison's pupils who have made Greek life and art their 'professional' study, who has just been appointed Lecturer to the Oxford Society for the Extension of University Teaching. 'Isn't it beautiful?' I was asked as the picture of a yellowish, noseless, and otherwise rather decrepit old Greek was handed to me. 'Very,' I replied, emphatically, and thought of the beauty of ugliness.[1]

'Looking back over my own life, I see with what halting steps I made my way to my own special subject.'[2] Twenty years were to pass before Harrison felt that she had found her own proper field of research in religion; meanwhile, the time she spent in England and on the Continent studying archaeology and anthropology laid an invaluable foundation. During this period of her life she studied and travelled, visiting archaeological sites in Greece and museums all over Europe. She supplemented her small private income by lecturing. She tasted fame; she experienced failure. She published several books and numerous articles, and coped with the concomitant hostile criticism, recanting when she recognized that her critics were sometimes right. She plunged herself into the social life of London, with its new vogue of 'dining out'; she made new friends; she fell in love. As she embraced these

---

[1] ' "A Woman's View of the Greek Question": an Interview with Miss Jane Harrison', *Pall Mall Gazette*, 3 Nov. 1891. The other two pupils were Eugénie Sellers Strong and Katherine Raleigh (sister to Sir Walter Raleigh). The last sentence echoes a biblical quotation (Psalm 96: 9).
[2] *Reminiscences*, 82.

experiences and allowed herself to be moulded by them, she began, falteringly, to find direction for her life. Harrison attributed her initial interest in art and archaeology to a lecture on Olympia which she attended with Hope Malleson's sister Mabel, just after sitting the Tripos examinations in the spring of 1879. It was given by Sidney Colvin, who had visited Greece four years previously with Sir Charles Newton of the British Museum. They were particularly interested in Olympia, where excavations were just being begun by a German team, and 'fragments of sculpture and architecture were coming up as thick as potatoes under the spade', raising 'a hundred absorbing problems' to the trained mind.[3] Colvin's systematic classification of mythography, of types of statues and reliefs, monumental artwork and vase paintings, and the typology of the myth as represented in each medium would have appealed to Harrison. Unlike many of his contemporaries, Colvin placed a high value on art and archaeology 'not merely for the new life and light that [they] might give to the old classical training,' Harrison later wrote, 'but as an independent field for serious study—a field in which the harvest is plentiful, but, alas! the labourers few; and the reward he looked to was that these should be more'.[4] She took these words as an invitation.

Colvin's dream of inserting archaeology into the classical Tripos at Cambridge was on the brink of realization,[5] but for Harrison in 1880 the only way to study archaeology in Britain was at the British Museum, under Charles Newton, supplemented by visits to Germany where the universities of Berlin and Munich, supported by their museums, taught classical art and archaeology. Newton had begun his career as an assistant at the British Museum on his graduation from Oxford, a time when there was one undivided Department of Antiquities. In 1852 he had been appointed vice-consul at Mytilene, where his duties included protecting the interests of the British Museum. During this period he excavated the mausoleum at Halicarnassus and brought the remains to the museum.[6] He became Harrison's mentor. At the British Museum she would also have met Wilhelm Klein, who spent the year 1880–1 at the British Museum, and who later became Professor Ordinarius of Classical Archaeology in Prague. Through Klein she was introduced to the work of Karl Otfried Müller (1797–1840), who had pioneered the

---

[3] Sidney Colvin, *Memories and Notes of Persons and Places* (London: Arnold, 1921), 219.

[4] Jane Ellen Harrison, 'Hellas at Cambridge', *Magazine of Art*, 7 (1884), 510–11.

[5] The first examinations of the new divided Tripos were held in 1882.

[6] He was also instrumental in the foundation of the Society for the Promotion of Hellenic Studies (1879), the Egypt Exploration Fund (1882), and the British School at Athens (1885). See also 'Sir Charles Newton, KCB (1816–1894)' in Ian Jenkins and Geoffrey B. Waywell (eds.), *Sculptors and Sculpture of Caria and the Dodecanese* (London: British Museum Press, 1997), 10–23.

study of myth as a source for history. She must surely have also met Lewis
Farnell, who went to the British Museum to study archaeology in 1880, and
whose early career, studying at the museums in Germany, closely parallels
Harrison's. But she and Farnell were temperamentally poles apart and were
much later to become arch-enemies. She never mentions meeting Farnell at
this time, nor he her.[7]

Her adjustment to London was smoothed by the kindness of the Malleson family, at whose home she appears to have stayed while she looked for a
place to live. In 1864 Mrs Elizabeth Malleson had founded the College for
Working Women as a counterpart to the Working Men's College, which had
been opened ten years previously under the leadership of Frederick Denison
Maurice. Harrison was invited to teach Greek art. It is not clear whether
all instruction was offered on a volunteer basis, but she surely must have
loved the atmosphere, which doubtless reflected something of Elizabeth
Malleson's ethos. Unsectarian in religion and heedless of social class, it
became a community devoted to knowledge for its own sake, and fostered
genuine companionship and friendship among women whose lives outside
the college were widely segregated by social distinctions. At the college isolated and lonely women discovered a larger life.

Elizabeth Malleson's philanthropy was not limited to the public sphere.
She was 'courageously unconventional' in her practice of inviting people of
widely different standing in society to meet one another in her drawing-
room. Elizabeth Malleson was, by all accounts, a most attractive person, a
remarkable woman of great energy as well as great compassion (her crest,
Harrison said, should be 'an express train rampant'). Courteous, poised,
open-minded, she delighted in good conversation. She became a good friend
to Marian Evans (George Eliot), who lived with George Lewes at the Priory
nearby, and who must have appreciated her lack of censure.[8] Her spacious
house at Wimbledon included three tennis courts in the garden, and it
became a regular institution for her to invite guests for tennis during Saturday afternoon and Sunday. Among those who frequented the house were the
many acquaintances she had made in London over her philanthopic work,

---

[7]   See Lewis R. Farnell, *An Oxonian Looks Back* (London: Martin Hopkinson, Ltd, 1934), 79–80.
Part of the reason for their ignoring each other may have been his chauvinistic attitude to
women.

[8]   See Elizabeth Malleson, *Autobiographical Notes and Letters, with a memoir by Hope Malleson*
(Guildford, privately printed, 1926). Impressed by the needs of working-class women, Malleson
had secured the support of 'many leaders of liberal thought' including Mme Bodichon, John
Stuart Mill, George Eliot, Harriet Martineau, Vernon and Godfrey Lushington, and Anna
Swanwick.

together with 'many young men from Oxford and young women from Cambridge'. The Arabic scholar Stanley Lane-Poole reflected how he and other 'homeless bachelor youths' used to come and stay unconscionable hours. 'I often think of those happy good days and evenings of music with Hope and sometimes with Rachael's fiddle and Reggie's 'cello. How good you were to us, and how little we thought of the tax we must have been to you when you wanted peace and quiet.'[9] It may indeed have been Mrs Malleson who first introduced Harrison to Sir Charles Newton, who was a regular visitor to the house, having been widowed in 1866. Another frequent guest was Stanley Lane-Poole's brother Reginald. Both worked at the British Museum, Reginald as an assistant in the department of manuscripts, and Stanley in the department of coins under his uncle Reginald Stuart Poole. In 1881 Reginald Lane Poole married the Mallesons' second daughter Rachael.

At the British Museum, Charles Newton brought to classical scholarship a new appreciation of the value of art and archaeology in understanding the past.[10] The nineteenth century was an era in which many, like Miss Beale, naïvely undertook to write a 'history of the whole world', thinking of historiography as a scissors and paste affair relying on written records for its data and broad moral judgements for its themes. Newton, perceiving like Colvin that 'the record of the Human Past is not all contained in printed books', recognized that oral tradition, manners and customs, songs and myths, art, and rituals offer important evidence for an understanding of the past, and that this understanding is continually revised and updated. Fresh archaeological discoveries and new insight into the connections and significance of interrelated material continue to provide data for the historian. 'Hence', he wrote, 'it is obviously necessary for the Archaeologist to study customs', directing his attention 'less to those customs which form a part of the established religion and legal code of a race than to those which, being the result of ideas once generally prevalent, still survive among the peasantry in remote districts, or of which dim traces may be still discerned in the institutions of modern society.'[11] To understand the beliefs of an 'uncivilized' people, he recognized the necessity of studying their rituals and their art, since

---

[9] Ibid. 95.

[10] Whereas a museum had hitherto been regarded as a collection of aesthetic masterpieces, Newton saw the British Museum as being to archaeologists what a botanical garden is to botanists: a collection of specimens so arranged that the student is able to learn by comparison of one exhibit with another. See C. T. Newton, 'On the arrangement of the collections of art and antiquities in the British Museum', in *Essays on Art and Archaeology* (London: Macmillan and Co., 1880), 39–72.

[11] *Essays on Art and Archaeology*, 5.

dramatic and pictorial representations are older than literary formulations of belief.

Of these other branches of Greek antiquities it was vase paintings that particularly interested Harrison. Her approach to them, tutored by Newton's appreciation of their historical value, was at the same time stamped with her own individuality. Although she was yet to publish two books extolling 'ideality' in Greek art, her sympathies all her life lay with the ordinary, which to her was real, rather than the ideal. Newton did not think highly of the artistic merit of the Greek vase painting in the British Museum, describing it as a 'faint reflection' of the higher art (now lost) of wall painting. His disparagement may well explain the appeal the vase paintings had to Harrison. He did appreciate, however, the importance of their subject matter. Many of the vases in the collection depicted mythical subjects, sometimes myths not recounted elsewhere in art or literature. Vase paintings do not 'illustrate' literature; they stand as an independent expression of a myth, which literature or sculpture may subsequently explain. Since many of the figures were identified in lettering by the artist, it was now possible to use the paintings to interpret and restore isolated fragments of sculpture. The vases could be set out in a chronological sequence, the development of styles traced, and with them the evolution of the myth, for the artist might abandon one method of portrayal for another which was more aesthetically satisfying. Thus the form of the myth as we know it from literature may sometimes have been determined by artistic considerations. Studying under Newton and adopting his methodology Harrison devoted her attention to the mythology portrayed on the vases, using the chronological dating of the vases to trace the development of a myth. Plans formed in her mind for her first book, to be devoted to the iconographic tradition of the *Odyssey*, and although there was much in *Myths of the Odyssey in Art and Literature*[12] that Harrison later repudiated, Newton's chronological approach to the study of mythology in Greek art became the foundation for her life's work.

In August 1881 Harrison set out for Europe to extend her study of Greek vases to other museums, accompanied by Mabel Malleson. Mabel was eight years younger than Jane, 'a tall, graceful young woman with great practical simplicity'.[13] At Newnham she had read history and written the Tripos examinations.

They crossed to Hamburg, travelling from there to Berlin, where they

---

[12] Jane Ellen Harrison, *Myths of the Odyssey in Art and Literature* (London: Rivingtons, 1882).
[13] Mirrlees's draft biography.

stayed in a somewhat Spartan pension. Harrison, with her only means of support the small annuity from her mother, was constrained to be economical. (A remark in *Baedeker's* caused her considerable amusement and she never tired of quoting it: 'Mit Damen zu reisen ist sehr köstlich' ('It is very expensive to travel with women').) They gained access to the museum collections through letters of introduction furnished by Reginald Stuart Poole.

In the Pergamum museum she met the archaeologist Ernst Curtius, a pioneer in Mediterranean archaeology. In 1874 he had persuaded the German government to sign an agreement with Greece that would permit German archaeologists to excavate Olympia on the understanding that the Germans would erect a museum on the site for the permanent display of the finds. (Prior to this, archaeologists such as Schliemann had financed their work out of their own pockets, and without any formal agreement as to the disposition of the finds, had become embroiled in rancorous disputes with the Greeks.) Curtius's arrangement put an end to predatory expeditions, secured good relationships between Greece and archaeologists from other countries and has become the model for archaeologists ever since. When Harrison first met him in 1881 he had just completed the first excavations and had returned to Berlin to write up his account.

Ernst Curtius was also among the first to forsake the romantic infatuation with Greece and its aesthetic ideals for a professional study of antiquity, above all through archaeology. He had been turned from philology to the study of geography, history, and culture by Karl Otfried Müller, his professor of philosophy at Bonn, and his career was further influenced in this direction when he travelled around Greece in 1837 as a tutor to Müller's children. In 1840 he returned to Greece with Müller, who tragically died of heatstroke. The sad task fell to Curtius of burying his friend, mentor, and fellow-traveller at Colonus, the very place where Oedipus had been taken to heaven. Curtius became in turn a mentor to Harrison, who espoused his 'scientific' approach to the study of archaeology.[14] His love of the Greek landscape and appreciation of monuments *in situ* may have confirmed her in her resolve to experience these things for herself. Certainly it was Harrison's first-hand experience of the Greek countryside and its people that set her work apart from that of many of her less adventurous contemporaries.

The museums at Berlin caught Harrison's attention both for the collections themselves and also for the method of their display. The Old Museum had been built in 1830 to house the collection of sculptures that had been

---

[14] Mortimer Chambers, 'Ernst Curtius' in Ward W. Briggs, and William M. Calder, (eds.) *Classical Scholarship: a Biographical Encyclopedia* (New York: Garland Publishing, 1990), 37.

acquired over the previous hundred years. The first archaeologist to be appointed by the museum, Eduard Gerhard, had resolved that the collection should serve research and teaching rather than stand as a collection of master works, and supplemented originals with drawings and casts. The result was a complete overview of the history of ancient art. Soon the building became too small, and the 'neue Museum' was added in 1843–55 by Friedrich August Stüler. He had had the imaginative idea of setting the artefacts in an authentic décor, but despite moving the collections around, the acquisition of so much material from excavations in Greece and Turkey rendered this impossible.[15]

Harrison was particularly struck by the educational value of the use of plaster casts to supplement the museum's own originals. She wrote to Elizabeth Malleson:

I cannot tell you at all how keenly I have felt (since I have been here) what a museum *may* be and what alas! ours in England is not—with the single exception of the Pergamos [sic] marbles these Germans here have not one important original to stimulate them and yet they have gathered together casts of every single thing a student can need to set the whole subject in its historical aspect clearly before his eyes and the arrangement is so wonderful. Wherever comparison is needed duplicate casts or replicas or even photographs are placed side by side, and the very walls of the galleries are decorated with designs and sketches and plans of the sites of temples etc. and scenes from ancient life. Thanks of course to Mr Newton we have been received with more than kindness—and it is an immense pleasure to me to see how at the least mention of his name all eyes lighten—we have the free use of a splendid archaeological library, books brought at a moment's notice and still better I am allowed to take books to any part of the Museum I wish and read them there before the very statues and vases themselves—this is a privilege I do not get at home except with the constant [genie?] of an attendant behind me—then in the vase department, as Prof Curtius is away, I have the use of his room to work in when I like. The vases are brought in and left with me for hours with no sort of surveillance. It really amazed me that they should have such confidence. Mabel has been so good, spending so much of her time when she might have been enjoying herself tracing and drawing for me, and it has been an immense advantage to me being able to compare the drawing with the actual objects before me—the plates of my next book (if ever it sees the light) will be very superior to those of my last. I think with practice she will soon be very skilful.[16]

[15]   By 1930 continuing acquisitions made a further new building inevitable and the present Pergamon museum was erected on Museum Island. A new wing added in 1982. See Max Kunze, *Die Antikensammlung im Pergamonmuseum und in Charlottenburg* (Mainz: Philipp von Zabern, 1992), 9–20.

[16]   JEH to Elizabeth Malleson, 9 Sept. 1881.

Mabel Malleson took tracings from Greek vases which Harrison was able to use for her research and as illustrations in *Myths of the Odyssey*, published later that year. 'All my archaeology was taught me by the Germans', Harrison wrote in her *Reminiscences* with some exaggeration, considering the influence on her of Colvin and Newton.[17]

From Berlin they travelled to Munich, where they met the eminent Heinrich Brunn. Harrison remembered how 'Heinrich Brunn came to see me in my lodgings at Munich, where I was thriftily living on four marks a day. I remember his visit—a knock, a huge figure looming in the doorway, a benevolent, bearded spectacled face, and he presented himself with the words, "Brunn bin Ich".' Brunn had established his scholarly reputation with his *Geschichte der griechischen Künstler* in the 1850s, a work which 'feeble readers of German will do well to let . . . alone'[18] but which Harrison had cited in *Myths of the Odyssey*.[19] In his doctoral thesis he had maintained that he 'would rather err methodically than hit upon truth without method'; later scholars have observed that his mistakes are more instructive than the right guesses of others. Since 1865 he had held the Chair of Archaeology at Munich, where he devoted his time to scholarly cataloguing of the antiquities in the Glypotek and arranging in one straight line his personal collection of 730 plaster casts. In 1870 he had published the results of the study of Etruscan grave reliefs he had made while in Italy.[20] After that he was reluctant to revisit Italy, so disquieting were the new impressions made by travel. He never went to Greece, afraid that a visit to Olympia and Athens would disturb his history of Greek art altogether. But for all his intellectual ferocity, Brunn was known for his affection for the young, and it was no doubt he who encouraged Harrison to see the Etruscan reliefs for herself.[21]

In September they left Munich for Florence, where they stayed in a pension kept by two English ladies. Florence 'simply swarmed with elderly English spinsters', to whom Harrison made herself charming, with the result that they 'gave us no end of help as to our future travels in Italy'. Sightseeing was not neglected. They spent one morning in the Uffizzi. Harrison later told Hope Mirrlees that she 'had no natural affinity with pictures—they were (unlike literature) an acquired taste'.[22]

---

[17] *Reminiscences*, 64.

[18] Alfred Emerson, 'Heinrich von Brunn', *American Journal of Archaeology*, 9/3 (1894), 367.

[19] *Myths of the Odyssey*, 215.

[20] Heinrich von Brunn, *I relievi delle urne etrusche*, i (Berlin: Deutsches archäologisches Institut, 1870).

[21] Emerson, 'Brunn', 366–71.

[22] Mirrlees's draft biography, quoting Mabel Malleson's letters.

After a month in Florence they left for Rome, stopping en route to visit the Etruscan tombs at Volterra. Mabel Malleson wrote home describing the scenery as 'rather desolate and grey-looking but with a great beauty of its own'—words which Mirrlees was sure echoed Harrison, for 'Miss Malleson was obviously—and so naturally—very much under the influence of her brilliant senior; nor would she, a young and rather timid girl, have dared on her own initiative to admire such strange beauty—but it was of the kind to which Harrison instantly and passionately responded.' The inn they stayed in was an old palace, built around an arched courtyard; rough accommodation, and primitive, but clean. Mabel writes of how they saw at Corneto the 'strange Etruscan tombs' with their urn burials which Colvin had described in his lecture on the Amazons, and a secret garden. To see the most interesting tomb, left exactly as it had been found and full of urns, they had to find its custodian, an old gardener—and this took them into a perfect Italian garden, enclosed in painted walls, with orange and lemon trees in fruit and masses of flowers. Harrison was delighted by its hidden, modest beauty. Moreover, the bas-reliefs from the Etruscan sarcophagi afforded her what she had come to search for, depictions of scenes from the *Odyssey*. Drawings were made and more material collected for *Myths of the Odyssey*. From Etruria they left for Rome, with some trepidation, as they had made arrangements to stay in a hostel kept for girls studying art in Rome by an English lady with strong evangelical leanings, Mary Anna Mayor (sister to the Cambridge scholar J. E. B. Mayor[23]). However, the 'prayers and hymns before meals' were the only drawback to the place.[24]

I think we are *most* fortunate to be installed here—the house is really *sumptuous* and all the arrangements are comfortable, almost too English—and, oh rapture unspeakable! I have discovered a large marble bath! a thing which in no form or shape has met our eyes since we left England. Our hostess is . . . *deeply* religious. We read a Psalm in alternate verses seated in a circle round the room at 8 a.m. and then the good lady prays fervently for a short space of time while breakfast is cooling. I get so hungry that it costs her an extra piece of bread and butter but that is the only harm done—the same happens I believe before dinner. We are very nervous about Sunday and should be very grateful if you would send us by post any spare prayer books you happen to have in the house.[25]

---

[23] For all you ever wanted to know about Mayor, see John Henderson, *Jurenal's Mayor: The Professor who Lived on 2ᵈ a Day*, Suppl. 20 (Cambridge: Cambridge Philological Society, 1988).

[24] Christopher Stray notes, 'She fought the good fight for protestantism there. And where better to choose as a *pays de mission*?' in a letter to the author, 3 Sept. 1999.

[25] JEH to Elizabeth Malleson, 20 Oct. 1881.

While they were in Rome *The Myths of the Odyssey in Art and Literature* was published. Harrison, anxious for her reputation to stand or fall on its own merits, was annoyed with Rivingtons for giving her full name rather than her initials. However, the reception of the book must have allayed her fears. We never hear again of her wishing to conceal her gender.

Myths of the Odyssey was a pioneer attempt to use vases and other forms of art to throw light on the development of the myths. It proceeds from narrative taken from Butcher and Lang's translation of the *Odyssey*, through analyses of various depictions of the same scenes in art—sarcophagi, wall paintings, gem engravings and vase paintings, taken from different periods of Greek, Etruscan, and Roman art. The illustrations are culled from various sources, including some reproductions of works in the British Museum published for the first time. Her method is mainly descriptive, alternating quotation or paraphrase of Homer with an account of the features presented by the artist and noting the similarities and differences from the Homeric version.

In the preface she justifies such a juxtaposition of mythology and mythography. The ancient artist was no illustrator in the modern sense, but rather represented a visual tradition that had developed parallel to the literary tradition. She argues that the real value of such a study lies in 'the discipline of taste and feeling which it affords':

Greek art does, it is true, occasionally elucidate obscure passages in Greek literature, but such verbal intelligence is but the small coin she deals out to the hirelings who clamour for payment, not the treasure she lays up as guerdon for her true servants. Such verbal intelligence may be gained in a moment, but . . . the trained eye, quick instinct, pure taste, well-balanced emotion—these we may be thankful if we gain in a lifetime.[26]

Although she says in the preface that she will not venture, except incidentally, into comparative mythology, she does in fact introduce many parallels to several of the Homeric narratives and proceeds to make comparisons. The stories, she reminds us at the outset, were not invented by Homer, but are 'the common property of both Aryan and non-Aryan peoples'. The crudity of the raw material revolted her, so that she was 'glad that Homer did not invent it' and glad that the Greek artists likewise toned down the original story.[27] Her attitude towards the Greeks was at this stage unreflective; they were naturally refined and genteel like the Victorians themselves.

---

[26] *Myths of the Odyssey*, xii–xiii.   [27] Ibid. 1.

At some points in the narrative (such as, for example, the descent into Hades), comparative mythology is introduced, though without any conclusions being drawn, except the periodic assertion that beside the Greek version other renderings are crude.

Her treatment of the story of Circe[28] and that of the Sirens[29] will serve to illustrate. After comparing Circe with the witch-woman of Eastern, Celtic, and medieval folk tale Harrison notes how in these versions we are never allowed to forget that she is repulsive, but Homer,

in his simple reverence for the goddess, in his tender admiration for the beautiful woman, scarcely raises the question of good or bad. The Greeks were less anxious than either easterns or moderns to point a moral; their praise or blame is, as we so often see, adapted to an ethical standard which is aesthetic rather than judicial. A fatal dualism had not yet sundered for them the divine wedlock of the good and the beautiful; so in their large human sympathy, they grant to the fair-haired Circe a meed of praise for her loveliness born only of a gentle nature.[30]

The 'beautiful myth' soon became degraded, however, into a moral tale. In the hands of Socrates the beast-form becomes a symbol of greediness; under the influence of Plato Etruscan sarcophagi depict souls in the underworld in animal form and 'the spell of Circe becomes part of the mysteries of Hades'. 'We are ashamed for philosophy when she lays her hand upon poetry', comments Harrison. The chapter on Circe concludes with an invitation to the reader to 'turn our eyes away from this "sight too fearful for the feel of fear"', and, looking back at the old-world picture, quiet our vision by its restful outline'. The account of the Sirens notes in a similar vein:

With the good fame of our Sirens at heart, we are glad to leave this spectacle of unseemly rout, and view the goddesses fulfilling a function more orderly, such as links them the closer to the muses, yet nowise dissevers them from Dionysos, the function of Inspiration. Never, perhaps, so keenly as in the conception of the Sirens are we made to feel how fluctuating, how almost antithetic, are the elements which go to form a Greek myth: the sinister daemon of one moment is the gracious goddess of the next, the boundary between good and evil is a soft shadow land to a people whose moral standard was in the main aesthetic.[31]

She soon abandoned such priggishness, stung by the criticism of D. S. MacColl, who attacked all her views on art as second-hand. It is easy to agree with him and to shrug off all her efforts at inculcating taste as Victorian cliché. Certainly, when she dropped this approach she took a significant step towards finding her own 'voice'. In *Myths of the Odyssey* she has already taken

[28] *Myths of the Odyssey*, 63–92.   [29] Ibid. 146–82.   [30] Ibid. 88.   [31] Ibid. 165.

her first steps. Just as reading Aristotle's *Ethics* had opened up to her a whole new world of rationality as a basis for right living, so in Homer's *Odyssey* she found a world wider than that of her stepmother. She sees the treatment of the stories by pagans and Christians alike as tainted by pernicious moral indoctrination. Hence the sting with which she denounces moralizing. In Hellenism, as opposed to Hebraism, she could 'see things as they are' without the taint of sin.[32] To Harrison, brought up under rigid Hebraism, with its heavy emphasis on sin, the discovery of Hellenism was the first stage of liberation. Later she was to shift her ground when she abandoned 'ideal-ism' and in reaction preferred the ugly manifestations of superstition over the aesthetic beauty of Classical art, but her attitude to moralizing remained constant to the end.

Myths of the Odyssey was unfavourably reviewed by Andrew Lang in the *Saturday Review*. Harrison professed not to care, but the incident rankled suf-ficiently that she recalled it many years later, when she described meeting

with 'Andrew of the brindled hair', at a dinner party. Our hostess brought him up to me and, with a misguided desire to be pleasant, said, 'You know Miss Harrison, and I am sure you have read her delightful books.' 'Don't know Miss Harrison,' muttered Andrew, 'never read her delightful books, don't want to,' etc. (Oh, Andrew, and you had reviewed those 'delightful books' not too delightedly!) 'Come, Mr. Lang,' I said, 'we're both hungry, and I promise not to say a single word to you. Be a man.' Alas! I broke my word. It was an enchanting dinner.[33]

Style, prudery, and literary taste aside, *Myths of the Odyssey* is significant for the new ground it breaks in the reading of visual art as myth. In this she was indebted to a scientific methodology developed in Germany following the work of Karl Otfried Müller, who had pioneered this approach as early as 1817 in his doctoral dissertation at Berlin. An appendix of authorities which she describes as 'a tolerably complete list' cites over a hundred scholarly works. A few are in English, several in French and in Italian, but the majority are German. Harrison's command of modern languages gave her access to scholarship on the Continent, an advantage denied to her male col-leagues whose early education had been strictly classical. Wilhelm Klein had directed her to these sources while he was in London.

---

[32] Matthew Arnold, 'Hebraism and Hellenism' in *Culture and Anarchy* (London: Macmillan, 1903), 127: 'To see things as they are, and . . . to see them in their beauty, is the simple and attrac-tive ideal which Hellenism holds out before human nature; and from the simplicity and charm of this ideal, Hellenism . . . is invested with a kind of aerial ease, clearness, and radiancy; they are full of what we call sweetness and light.'

[33] *Reminiscences*, 62.

From Rome Jane and Mabel continued to Naples and Palermo, studying the art in their museums. At Palermo they stayed with their Newnham friend Mary Paley (now married to the economist Alfred Marshall). Jane and Mary scandalized the Sicilians by going for a six-mile walk with no thought for the danger of bandits.[34]

Elizabeth Malleson had arranged to have a camera sent out to them. The following letter reminds one with a jolt of the practical difficulties of taking photographs at the time:

I am so grateful to both you and Mr Malleson for taking all this trouble—the whole seemed to me a very moderate cost and I should by this time have been the happiest of amateur photographers but alas! my faithless Oxford friends [the Butchers] were frightened at the size of Negretti's large wooden box and said it could never be got thro' the customs as it was nailed up, so they left it behind with their sisters with orders to send it by ship. I telegraphed to stop this and fortunately in time—we are always so uncertain as to the time we stop any where that I did not wish to have it following me about from port to port always arriving too late—it is very vexatious and if they were not the nicest people in the world I should certainly never forgive them, but as we sail on Monday in the same boat and shall go with them to Olympia I cannot maintain my wrath—by the by as the husband is the son of a bishop and the wife the daughter of an archbishop Mabel's theology is likely to be well seen to—I know this will be a relief to your mind!

Her bantering style covers up any emotion she may have felt at the prospect of travelling with Henry Butcher and his wife. Stoicism and a stream of wit, as always, were her defence. The letter continues with a 'comical archaeological experience':

Today we have just come back from a lovely drive to Pompeii. How you would delight in those charming graceful frescoes whose fresh colouring is all lost in the photographs of which I am bearing sheaves. I often think not the least delight of our journeyings will be to fight these battles over again with you, in front of a blazing fire. . . .—oh dear how tired I am of Hotels and table d'hôtes tho' we have only had 3 weeks of it. Mabel laughs at me—she says I am like you because I cannot bear living anywhere if I cannot establish *personal relations*—it is quite true.[35]

They sailed from Italy to Athens, where they met William and Agnes Ramsay. William Ramsay was travelling on an Oxford studentship and embarking on his life's work: the exploration of Anatolia for a study of its antiquities. Ramsay seems to have been more sympathetic to *Myths of the Odyssey*, and later on was doubtless influential in her nomination for an hon-

---

[34] Marshall, *What I Remember*, 33–4.   [35] JEH to Elizabeth Malleson, 17 Dec. 1881.

orary degree at the University of Aberdeen in 1895, where he held the position of Regius Professor of Humanity. When she was invited to give a guest lecture at Aberdeen in 1899, the student newsletter remarked that *Myths of the Odyssey* exhibits 'a point of view which is distinctive of her writing', effected by a 'delicate discrimination of the development of a myth in art from the development of the same myth in poetical legend; or by revealing the hidden springs of thought and feeling which can be traced through various manifestations of the Greek spirit'.[36]

Of this first visit to Greece she records only one anecdote in her *Reminiscences*, her memory perhaps coloured by her weakness for anything connected with bears:

the first time I went to Athens I had the luck to make a small archaeological discovery. I was turning over the fragments in the Acropolis Museum, then little more than a lumber-room. In a rubbish pile in the corner, to my great happiness, I lighted on the small stone figure of a bear. The furry hind paw was sticking out and caught my eye. I immediately had her—it was manifestly a she-bear—brought out and honourably placed. She must have been set up originally in the precinct of Artemis Brauronia. Within this precinct, year by year, went on the arkteia or bear-service. No well-born Athenian would marry a girl unless she had accomplished her bear-service, unless she was, in a word, confirmed to Artemis. . . . All these well-born, well-bred little Athenian girls must, to the end of their days, have thought reverently of the Great She-Bear.[37]

The two young women returned from their travels, some time in early 1882, to discover that Mabel's parents were planning to leave Wimbledon, a move that was to have long-lasting repercussions for Harrison. Both Elizabeth and her husband Frank were in poor health; Elizabeth having suffered some kind of major breakdown in 1877 had retired from public life, although, as her daughter noted, she 'never faltered in her sympathy with and interest in all that passed'.[38] Frank had always longed to live in the country, and in 1882 bought a house in Gloucestershire. In June of that year, with great regret at leaving London, they moved.

Their move raised practical difficulties about whether the house in Wimbledon should be kept and who should occupy it. First, there was a young woman named 'Get' living at the house on the Mallesons' charity. Get's real name was Jane Wilson. She was a sister of Stanley Lane-Poole's wife,

---

[36] *The Student*, 1899, 153.

[37] *Reminiscences*, 71. For more on the 'bear-service', see Hugh Lloyd-Jones, 'Artemis and Iphigenia', *Journal of Hellenic Studies*, 103 (1983), 92–3.

[38] Malleson, *Autobiographical Notes and Letters*, 141.

Charlotte, and thus a distant relative of the Mallesons, and a great-niece of Francis Rawdon Chesney, who had explored the Euphrates. Perhaps his wife's name, Georgette, which was inherited by other members of the family, is a clue to the unusual name of 'Get', probably pronounced with a soft 'g' as acquaintances occasionally spelled it 'Jet'. Get had been working for the previous two years with the philanthropist Louisa Twining, acting as 'assistant honorary secretary' in her efforts to provide trained nurses for the workhouses. For those two years she had lived in some sort of communal housing provided by Miss Twining. In 1882 Miss Twining retired, and Get had gone to live with the Mallesons.

Moreover, on her return Mabel needed a place to live in London. It appears that Elizabeth Malleson made the suggestion that Jane Harrison might wish to live with Mabel and Get, along with some other (unidentified) people, presumably in the Wimbledon house. Harrison found this proposal problematic. Without Elizabeth Malleson there to 'oil intricate wheels' she feared that the 'four sets of people in the house' would run into conflict (the details—who the 'four sets of people' were, and why they could not get along—are obscure).

There was the issue of propriety, too. Sarah Prideaux,[39] one of Harrison's Newnham contemporaries (a 'poisonous cat' according to Alice (Lloyd) Dew-Smith), spread rumours which necessitated Harrison to be more than ordinarily cautious about her living arrangements. 'As to my own personal difficulty', Harrison wrote,

I took counsel with my friends and they think that the malicious (not the merely conventional) . . . would at once if they found out you were not always in town think that the chaperonage I pretended to was merely specious and would be more inclined to gossip afresh than if I faced them independently—I feel the justice of this knowing as I do the sort of tongues I have to dread but I do not expect you will understand it for you are so far removed from these villanies. At present then Get and I think of looking about for unfurnished quarters of a very modest kind and as she is obliged to be very oeconomical [sic] I shall be so too and try to get a good deal of time abroad for a few years at least so that my constant presence in London living alone may not keep me too much before the public eye. I feel as if I had given you a great deal of trouble and worry for no purpose but I think it is Fate who has altered plans not I. . . .[40]

The reference to chaperonage suggests that the substance of the rumours concerned some sexual impropriety in connection with the other 'sets of

[39] Sarah Prideaux (1853–1933), artist and bookbinder.
[40] JEH to Elizabeth Malleson, 30 April 1882.

people' in the house, but without knowing who they might have been it is difficult to ascertain anything more. Sarah Prideaux, many years later, dropped the name of Lionel Robinson.[41] Hope Mirrlees claimed to know of some scandal involving Harrison and Henry Butcher, and with all the allusiveness of the possessor of inside knowledge covered up with the words, 'Her Newnham love-affair was not a tragedy of unrequited passion. The particular plot of the drama I do not feel at liberty to divulge. Suffice it to say, it nearly broke her heart.'[42] Presumably Mirrlees is correct in her reference to Henry Butcher. Although he was not living in London at this time, but in Oxford, whence he moved to Edinburgh later in 1882, events such as meetings of the newly founded Society for Hellenic Studies in London would have brought them together. In her relationships with other men who lived in London and were her friends, there is no evidence of any scandal. If the impropriety involved her relationship with a man, Henry Butcher seems the most likely candidate, but we do not know what happened.

However, there were other reasons, which could not be divulged to Elizabeth Malleson, why Harrison might not have wished to live at the Wimbledon house. She returned from her travels in Europe exasperated with the 'leech-like attachment' of Mabel Malleson, unable to shake her off without being brutally direct.[43] Whatever the cryptic allusions in the letter to Elizabeth Malleson may mean, it is clear that part of Jane's motive in deciding to look for accommodation with Get was to create some distance between herself and Mabel.

A compromise was reached. The Mallesons, needing a *pied-à-terre* in London, rented a set of rooms at 42 Powis Square, Notting Hill Gate, and Jane and Get finally settled in the upper two storeys where they lived for about three years with the Mallesons occupying the ground floor. Soon after they began living together Get became an invalid. No one who remembered her in later years seemed to know exactly what her illness was, except that she had several operations, required a great deal of nursing, was unable to do her share of the housekeeping, and that it was suspected in retrospect that she was something of a hypochondriac and that the problem was more emotional than physical. Jane spent a good deal of time over the next fifteen years looking after her, a burden which added to the stress of her London years. Her relationship with Get puzzled even those who knew her well. Alice (Lloyd) Dew-Smith referred to Get as her 'rather queer Irish friend', while Hope Mirrlees claimed that they 'had nothing whatever in common' besides

---

[41] Letter from Lionel Robinson to DSM, 15 May 1922, MS MacColl R123.
[42] Mirrlees's draft biography.   [43] Ibid.

7. Jane Harrison (aged 33)

a shared sense of humour. (Mirrlees, however, consistently played down the strength of Harrison's friendships with anyone but herself.)

Harrison meanwhile developed a wide circle of friends and acquaintances and dined out continually. In her *Reminiscences* she mentions Robert Browning ('only to me a cheerful, amusing gossip')[44] Herbert Spencer, who invited her to dinner on one occasion ('but he would discuss the Athenaeum cook, and on that subject he found me ill-informed'); Walter Pater and his sisters ('I always think of him as a soft, kind cat; he purred so persuasively that I lost the sense of what he was saying'). At Pater's house she often met Henry James, and liked to watch 'that ingenious spider' weaving his webs. At the time Henry James's writing held no appeal for her; it was only years afterwards that she realized what she had missed. She frequently dined with Walter Raleigh and his family ('the best talker I ever knew, and a quite inspired lecturer. The views he tenaciously held were reactionary, and, to my mind, preposterous. We wrangled ceaselessly'). In her *Reminiscences* Harri-

---

[44] *Reminiscences*, 46.

son scrupulously avoids mentioning any living person, but from Hope Mir-rlees we learn that she particularly enjoyed the intellectual dinner-parties at the homes of a number of prominent women,[45] and the innovative lun-cheon parties given by a certain Mrs Crackenthorpe for women only. She met the explorer Mary Kingsley, and developed a great admiration for her. Although Kingsley did not embark on her travels in Africa until the death of her father, George Kingsley, in 1892, she was passionately interested in his travels and anthropological work.[46] With a temperament and outlook similar to Harrison, she may have been formative in Harrison's career. Milli-cent Fawcett attended her classes and invited her to dine with her and her sister, Elizabeth Garrett Anderson, in Gower Street.[47] She enjoyed the wit of the two Garrett sisters and delighted in their common sense, but did not share their devotion to 'the cause'. Later on Harrison was persuaded to speak out on women's issues (though she disdained political involvement), but neither in the 1880s nor later did she take any interest in the question of suffrage. At a time when many women were plunging into philanthropy of all sorts she preserved a condescending aloofness from all their causes. She wrote in her *Reminiscences*:

In those days I met many specimens of a class of Victorian who, if not exactly distin-guished, were at least distinctive and are, I think, all but extinct—British Lions and Lionesses. The Lionesses first—that was the name we gave them at Newnham. They were all spinsters, well-born, well-bred, well-educated and well off. They attended my lectures on Greek Art. Greek Art was at that time booming and was eminently respectable. At home they gardened a great deal; they, most of them, had country houses. Their gardens were a terror to me, for I never could remember the names of the plants with slips attached to them, and to blunder over a plant's name was as bad to a Lioness as a false quantity [mispronunciation of Latin]. They kept diaries in which they entered accurately the state of the weather on each day. If they lived in London they promoted Friendly Girls and Workhouse Nursing. Above all, they kept a vigilant eye on the shortcomings of local officials; they frequently wrote to the Times, heading their letters: 'Re Mud and Slush'. . . . They were a fine upstanding

---

[45] Mirrlees mentions 'the Greenes in Kensington Square' and 'Lady Audrey Buller's informal luncheons'.

[46] Mary Kingsley (1862–1900) was the niece of Charles Kingsley. Her father explored West Africa, studying cannibal tribes and collecting fish. On his death in 1892, she took up his work. Mary Slessor wrote of her: 'She had an individuality as pronounced as it was unique, with charm of manner and conversation, while the interplay of wit and mild satire, of pure spontaneous mirth and of profoundly deep seriousness' (www.spartacus.schoolnet.co.uk/Wkingsley.htm, p. 4).

[47] Millicent Garrett Fawcett (1847–1829) was a leading campaigner for women's suffrage. Elizabeth Garrett Anderson (1836–1913) became a doctor and feminist pioneer.

breed, and I miss them. They had no unsatisfied longings, had never heard of 'suppressed complexes', and lived happily their vigorous, if somewhat angular, lives.[48]

She liked to quote a remark made by D. S. MacColl in an English church service in Gibraltar when he contemplated the tight coils in which these women wore their hair: 'All of England is in these buns.'[49]

Harrison's absorption in an intellectual career stands out in contrast to the activities of other women in London at the time. The people with whom she mixed most comfortably tended to be 'advanced' in their views, iconoclastic, espousing a 'muscular paganism',[50] in contrast to the traditional pietism of many of the philanthropic women.

Of her closer friendships with Mrs Greene, Bella (Mrs Mark) Napier, and Eleanor (Mrs Lionel) Tennyson (daughter-in-law of the poet), nothing but the names and a few inconsequential anecdotes survive. Her closest friendships were with Alice Lloyd (Dew-Smith) who had been at Newnham 1878–80, taught at Wimbledon High School, then gave up teaching to devote herself to journalism; and with the sisters of Henry Butcher: Fanny (Prothero), Augusta (Crawley), and Eleanore. Like their brother, they were witty and vivacious. Eleanore went through the anguish of a broken engagement and Jane's similar experience drew the two women together. The group of friends would spend hours in keen introspective conversation. Alice showed them how to distinguish personality types by colour in a psychological game she called 'Soul Shapes'.[51] There were frequent opportunities for weekends away from London, staying with the families of various friends. Eleanor Tennyson took her on one occasion to stay with the great poet.

He met us at the station, grunting fiercely that he 'was not going to dress for dinner because I had come'. It was rather frightening, but absurd. The vain old thing (he was the most openly vain man I ever met) knew quite well that he looked his best in his ample poet's cloak. It is a rare and austere charm that gains by evening dress. He was very kind to me according to his rather fierce lights; he took me a long, memorable Sunday morning walk, recited 'Maud' to me, and countless other things. It was an anxious joy; he often forgot his own poems and was obviously annoyed if I could not supply the words. He would stop suddenly and ask angrily: 'Do you think

---

[48] Reminiscences, 51–2.   [49] 'D. S. MacColl' in Mirrlees's notebook.

[50] Ibid. A deliberate corruption of the phrase 'muscular Christianity'. It is not clear whether the phrase is MacColl's or Mirrlees's: the pithiness of it suggests MacColl, or indeed Harrison herself.

[51] The game led eventually to a book of the same name, published by Cambridge University Press in 1890.

Browning could have written that line? Do you think Swinburne could?' I could truthfully answer, 'Impossible.' If he posed a good deal, he was scarcely to blame; the house was so charged with an atmosphere of hero-worship that free breathing was difficult.[52]

Her favourite refuge was the Derbyshire home of her childhood friend Peveril Turnbull and his wife, who encouraged her to come and go whenever she pleased. Peveril was closer to her than her own brothers. Various 'Peverilisms' became enshrined in her own private slang, such as 'Slaa firra, slaa firra' for 'that will do'. She used to delight in his idiosyncracies: 'the cheerful way he had of laying down the law to Bishops and other dignitaries; & his passion for explaining to all & sundry such boring matters as the principle of the barometer.'[53] She went with the Turnbulls when they took a shooting lodge at Aros Moor in Mull in 1884, and decided that 'bonny Scotland' was hideous and that the Scottish moors were but a vulgar copy of the Yorkshire ones. The Pre-Raphaelite artist Walter Crane had been another guest on this occasion.[54]

She also kept in touch with all her friends in Cambridge, particularly Ellen Crofts, now married to Francis Darwin, and Margaret (May) Merrifield, now Mrs Verrall. Margaret, though younger than Jane, became a sort of mentor to her, listening with cool cynicism to the latest passionate episode. Jane, she remembered, was always in love and always captivated by someone fresh, and also the continual victim of Platonic attachments misunderstood.[55]

On her return to England in the spring of 1882, Harrison began supporting herself by lecturing on Greek subjects, both in London and in other parts of the country. The lectures began almost accidentally. She was studying at the British Museum when Charles Newton asked her one day if she would take some parties of ladies round. 'He could not ask me officially', she apologized to an interviewer from the Pall Mall Gazette, 'but he thought I might explain some things to the ladies.'[56] The classes in the British Museum gained in popularity, until she was obliged to limit the numbers to thirty for the 'perambulating lectures'. These lectures 'were of the nature of object lessons in Greek Art. She would guide her little party of students round the galleries, taking up her stand before the various objects and pointing out the

---

[52] *Reminiscences*, 46–7.   [53] Mirrlees's draft biography.

[54] Walter Crane (1845–1915), best known for his illustrations of children's books. He was much influenced by Burne-Jones.

[55] One of her admirers mentioned by Hope Mirrlees in this connection was R. G. Tatton, who after a position of Fellow and Tutor of Balliol College, Oxford, became a member of the Council of the London Society for the Extension of University Teaching.

[56] Interview, *Pall Mall Gazette*.

beauties of the sculpture, or the myth depicted on a vase.'[57] Some idea of the content of these lectures can be gleaned from the book she published in 1885, entitled *Introductory Studies in Greek Art*.[58] She would draw the parallel between Plato's doctrine of the 'ideal'—that perfect form that none of us has experienced in this world but each of us 'recollects' from our previous existence—and the work of the artist. Whereas mere imitation of reality is vulgar and crude, and abstract symbolism is 'a confession of weakness and incapacity',[59] the glory of Greek art is to portray the transcendental form that lies behind the multiplicity of individual manifestations. The photographer, who is an imitator, seeks to catch the passing expression of a man, be it anger, joy, pity, or despair; the true artist, on the other hand, succeeds in portraying the 'ethos' of the man, his genuine, permanent character. This is what gives to Classical Greek art its serenity. Ideality sums up the achievement of Pheidias: 'his majesty, the grandeur of his art, his dignity, his largeness and beauty, his fineness and delicacy, his divine element, also his repose, his self-containedness, his tranquil air, the peace he brings to the troubled heart of the beholder.'[60] Part of the appeal of these guided tours was the sense of drama that Harrison conveyed. She drew attention to the 'personal love and conviction of the artist that gives his work its freshness and charm',[61] while displaying that same 'personal love and conviction' in her own person.

   These tours continued for five years, after which she gave a series of lectures to much larger and mixed (though predominantly female) audiences at the South Kensington Museum for a period of seven years. In later life she attributed the success of these early classes to two things: lectures were in fashion, and so was Greek art. The modesty of this statement obscures the fact that she helped to make it so. That the lecturer was a woman was a novelty, and doubtless drew the curious. However, the audiences were predominantly well-to-do women with time on their hands, though not as scholarly as Harrison would perhaps have wished. 'What people want who attend lectures on Greek subjects is not a deep insight into these subjects. They want to know something, not very much, of the life and manners of a highly-cultured and intellectual race of olden times', she told an interviewer. Others were mothers of young children who wanted to be able to 'talk to the boys, during the school holidays, about these things' or to help them in their studies. She was demoralized by the 'squalor' (her word) of her attitude

[57]   Alice Dew-Smith, *Newnham College Letter*, 1929, 64.
[58]   Jane Ellen Harrison, *Introductory Studies in Greek Art* (London: T. Fisher Unwin, 1885).
[59]   Ibid. 51.   [60]   Ibid. 248.   [61]   Ibid. 169.

towards her audiences, and the need to generalize for their sake. One of her students described how she could come across as 'desperately patronizing'; among her favourite phrases was 'Sufficient is it for *you* to know . . .'.[62]

Harrison gave another reason why her lectures appealed to women, revealing for the light it sheds on the predicament of the Victorian society woman, who was expected to drop whatever she was doing at any time to play the role of hostess.[63] Greek art, she argued, was of great benefit, creating as it did an interest that was non-personal. 'You want to be a woman to know what the rest of that is. People talk of the good that lectures do by bringing people and classes together. I should like to talk of the good they do—for women, at least—by sending them away from each other into a desert place, to think where you only can think—alone; and the more remote the subject, the more averse from modern association—as Greek art is—the better.'[64]

Harrison also received invitations to speak at public schools. Archdeacon Wilson first asked her to Clifton College, Bristol; she was nervous at first, but forgot her nervousness as soon as she knew the boys were with her. Mr Wilson told her afterwards that he had had a rather nervous quarter of an hour just before the lecture, having not dared to tell his Council that the lecturer was a woman, 'But they bore it very well.'[65] Schoolboys, in fact, proved to be Harrison's most appreciative and enthusiastic audiences.

Harrison found out later that on that occasion 'no less people' than John M'Taggart Ellis (who later became a Hegelian scholar) and the artist Roger Fry had been in the audience, and 'they had deigned to discuss my lecture'. Mr Warre Cornish, 'always the kindest of friends', invited her to Eton, where 'a young prig, who bore an honoured name' was introduced to her; 'he wrote me next day a patronizing letter of thanks, in which he said he hoped to go on with archaeology, as he was going up to Oxford to "do Grates". Alas! he never did anything half so useful.' Jane's youngest brother was at Harrow; 'he wrote to me to say he had heard I was lecturing at Eton. It didn't matter, apparently, what I did at that benighted place, but he "did hope I wasn't coming lecturing at Harrow, as it would make it very awkward for him with the other fellows". I saw his position and respected it.'[66]

The success of the classes at the South Kensington Museum (some of them attended by as many as 250 people) led to the opportunity to give courses under the auspices of the London Society for Extension of

[62] Violet Buxton to Eugénie Sellers, 2? Mar. 1892, Strong Papers, Girton College, box 2.

[63] This observation foreshadows an important motif of Harrison's writing twenty years later, when she pleaded for women to be allowed a room of their own.

[64] Interview, *Pall Mall Gazette*.   [65] Ibid.   [66] *Reminiscences*, 54–5.

University Teaching. This organization had been founded in 1876 and was enjoying its heyday in the 1880s.

Synopses of the courses reveal that these lectures were not as insubstantial as some of her comments in the *Pall Mall Gazette* might suggest. She began one course in 1888 with a questionnaire that included such questions as 'Do you know Greek? If not, you are strongly advised to spend a few hours in learning the letters in order to make out easy inscriptions' and 'Do you read German easily?'. Students were advised from the beginning 'to attempt the careful training of the eye. Never consider that you can form an adequate judgment of a work of art unless you have seen the original.' They were urged *from the first* to 'be careful to distinguish between what is a matter of fact and matter of opinion' and to distance themselves from matters of opinion for as long a time as they could. 'Be specially careful to distinguish between the two in reading as an author often misleads in this matter. From the first, when you deal with opinion do not reproduce it as fact and get into the habit of asking yourself whether you agree and why.' For a course on 'Athens, its Mythology and Art', Maxime Collingwood's *Manual of Mythology* 'should be thoroughly mastered; throughout his book abundant reference to other authorities will be found.' The student who wishes to go further should take as his basis L. Preller's "Griechische Mythologie", but is warned that Preller 'admirable as he is in respect to fact, is full of fanciful and baseless theory'; 'the student who cannot read German' should read Thomas Keightley's *Mythology of Ancient Greece and Italy*; all should read the chapters on Greek gods and goddesses in Andrew Lang's *Myth, Ritual, and Religion*; and 'special monographs on mythological points are for the most part to be found scattered about in foreign archaeological journals'. She stressed the importance of reading ahead, since the lectures would deal with information that could not be found in books on the subject, and which could only be grasped by those who knew the facts beforehand. Preparation for the first three lectures consisted in gaining 'thorough familiarity' with the current stories about the mythological characters mentioned in the syllabus; for the next four lectures 'the student should continue his mythological work, and also get thoroughly familiar with the topography of Athens, studying the position of the Agora, Kerameikos, and all the various temples and shrines of the several gods'. For the last three lectures Pierre Paris's *Manual of Ancient Sculpture* 'should be most carefully studied',[67] and for those with leisure for detail a further bibliography was given. Finally, students who

---

[67] This work was originally written in French. Harrison herself translated the book, editing it to include all the most recent finds (Pierre Paris, *Manual of Ancient Sculpture*, ed. and augmented by Jane Harrison (London: Grevel, 1890)).

intended to proceed to professional work in the field were referred to a complete bibliography (in German) and another German compendium. The classes proceeded by means of 'problem photographs', distributed on loan to the students for analysis. In describing a work of art the students were asked 'always to state whether they have studied the original, a cast, a photograph, or woodcut'.[68] Students were required to submit weekly essays, and the series concluded with an examination. Certificates were awarded to successful students.

The lectures themselves were illustrated by magic-lantern photographs, shown by means of an oxy-hydrogen light,[69] and which were sufficiently difficult to prepare that Harrison prevailed upon her friends Alice Lloyd (Dew-Smith), Alice's sister Ethel (Sykes), and Augusta Butcher (Crawley), for help: services which Harrison referred to as 'skilled charring'. Alice Dew-Smith remembered how 'she lectured in a high strained voice, quite different to the voice her friends were accustomed to in her less formal moments, and had numerous affectations of speech about which we, her none the less devoted and admiring pupils, did not fail to chaff her afterwards. But the points she hammered in went deep and became the very bones of one's creed.'[70]

A sense of the drama of her presentation may be gained from *Introductory Studies in Greek Art*. The book preserves for us in written form what must have been not only the content but also the style of her lectures. For example:

It is time we left the hill of Athene to pass into a presence even greater than hers. The festival we may fancy is over, she has crowned the happy victor, the hymn has been chanted, the dance is ended, the peplos has been offered, the victim slain, the youths and maidens and old men, the chariots and horsemen are gone home till another year comes round. The gates are shut and sealed, what for a few hours had been a hall of solemn worship is once more but a treasure-house. The golden Victory is taken down from the hand of Athene, she is stripped of her golden drapery, closely covered, and all is silent. Only outside, the stone gods are still above in the pediments; Athene is born anew each morning; every day is renewed her triumph over Poseidon. In the metopes all day long, Greek struggles with barbarian; along the frieze from morning till night the panorama of worship is unrolled.[71]

No one who heard her could forget the way in which she would enlarge upon the 'unconsciousness' in the pose of some ancient stone man, who stood in unembarrassed nudity with his arms hanging at his side; or on the

---

[68]   Syllabus published by The University Extension Society, 1890.
[69]   Or 'Drummond light', invented in 1825. The intense light was obtained by playing an oxygen/hydrogen flame on a piece of lime (as in the original 'lime-lights').
[70]   Alice Dew-Smith, *Newnham College Letter*, 1929, 64.   [71]   *Introductory Studies*, 215–16.

promise of greatness to come in the grotesque profile on an old Greek coin, compared with the finished perfection of another that had reached the limit of its possibilities. Many shared the recollection of one of Harrison's favourite devices. She loved to begin a sentence with the phrase, 'This beautiful figure which I will now place before you' and then produce some stiff archaic figure or grinning Gorgon to the discomfiture of the audience. Alice (Lloyd) Dew-Smith also recollected writing for one of Harrison's classes 'a frightfully gushing effusion' about some archaic head which she didn't really admire very much. Harrison, however, was delighted, and read it to the class. One wonders if she was only half serious. Did she already in her London days, despite the traditional position taken in *Introductory Studies*, prefer the love of the archaic, what she called 'the beauty of ugliness' to the traditionally beautiful? She paid careful attention to theatrical effect, her low voice vibrating with excitement at the beginning, drawing the audience into her anticipation of some mystery to be disclosed. 'Every lecture was a drama in which the spectators were to share in the emotions of "recognition" at the moment of epiphany.'[72] Another student, Victoria (Buxton) de Bunsen, remembered how

she was exceedingly striking to look at in those days—tall, a little swaying, graceful, massive in build, a wonderful mixture of grace and ruggedness. She held herself finely, but she did not walk well. She dressed with individuality and sometimes very elaborately. I remember her lecturing to crowded audiences at Cambridge, using her hands a great deal, very white hands with delicate wrists and rather square finger tips. She wore long lace cuffs, and there was usually a touch of some spangly stuff and of blue about the black she wore. On one occasion . . . I remember she was quite regally attired with feathers in her hair and a train, and her speech about 'that gracious lady', the Classics at whose shrine she would offer all the treasure of the sister arts and sciences, anthropology, archaeology, comparative religion—was a fitting and memorable creation.[73]

After a lecture at Winchester, one of the boys was asked if he liked the lecture. 'Not the lecture,' he replied, 'but I liked the lady; she was like a beautiful green beetle.'[74] Harrison had been wearing a spangled evening gown that had caught the light of the magic lantern.

The success of the University Extension lectures was beyond anything imaginable in the current age of mass media. The largest audience Harrison recalled was at Dundee, 'where an audience of 1600 came to hear a lecture

---

[72] Francis Cornford, *Newnham College Letter*, 1929, 74.
[73] Victoria (Buxton) de Bunsen, *Newnham College Letter*, 1929, 66.
[74] *Reminiscences*, 54.

on grave reliefs'. She commented wryly: 'The Scotch are said to be unable to appreciate a joke, but if in one town in Scotland 1600 men and women assemble to hear a lecture on a Greek subject, and on a particularly gloomy one to boot, that certainly shows that they appreciate other things.'[75] She got through the lecture with difficulty, after initial fears that she would not be able to make herself heard.

All this lecturing brought her deserved acclaim, yet it wearied and depressed her. In order to support herself in London and abroad, she was obliged to undertake a heavy schedule of lecturing and marking, with long and tiring journeys in dirty and poorly heated trains. She hated the travel, and was never comfortable adapting her scholarship for the mass audience. Public speaking always made her sick with nerves which added to her exhaustion.

In addition to the popular lectures, she frequently addressed more scholarly audiences at the Society for Hellenic Studies. The subject matter of her lectures was material for articles, and during the 1880s she published prolifically, mainly in the *Magazine of Art*, *Journal of Hellenic Studies* and *Classical Review*. The articles in the *Magazine of Art* appeared as a series entitled 'Greek Myths in Greek Art' and can be read with profit today, notably her article on the Judgement of Paris.

If Harrison claimed that she owed her fame to two things that were popular in London in the 1880s, ancient Greece and lectures, she might have mentioned a third factor, acting. Dressing-up, fancy-dress balls, amateur theatricals were all the rage in the 1880s. Dressed in another's part, one might legitimately act in ways not normally sanctioned.[76] The Pre-Raphaelites had favoured medieval costume and dramas; now the fashion was turning to the Greeks. In 1883 Professor Warr of King's College organised a series of private theatricals to raise money for the King's College Lectures for Ladies. 'The Tale of Troy' consisted of scenes from the *Iliad* and *Odyssey* linked together by tableaux. The first of these attempts consisted of performances on two successive nights with two separate casts, the first night in English, the second in Greek. Harrison and her Newnham friend Elinor Ritchie (Paul) were given parts in the Greek cast. The performances were staged in the home of a Mrs Freake, whose interest in the Greek revival ran to the extent of her having built in her house a Greek theatre. Hope Mirrlees describes

---

[75] Interview, *Pall Mall Gazette*.

[76] Richard Jenkyns wryly observes that these amateur theatricals 'brought together two fashionable worlds, the aristocratic and philistine circle of the Prince of Wales, who came to the first performance, and that raffish milieu whose most spectacular member was Oscar Wilde'. Richard Jenkyns, *The Victorians and Ancient Greece* (Oxford: Blackwell, 1980), 303.

Mrs Freake as 'a lady of great wealth but little culture', as evidenced by her pronunciation of Homer as ' 'Omer', and her penchant for declaring that the 'demi-monde' would be there. She meant 'half the world', though some would have said she was right in both senses of the word. 'Bohemia', observed Mirrlees, 'was still an exciting and romantic world, from which occasionally fascinating creatures like Ellen Terry would emerge for a luncheon party', (the Dowagers preferring this not to be on a Sunday—'What would the servants think?'). The scenery was designed by Lord Leighton.[77]

Years later Elinor Paul, in response to an enquiry from Hope Mirrlees, recovered from her diary some further details: that although the absurdities of the whole affair caused constant amusement they took great care about their dresses. Frederic Leighton and Edward Poynter were prominent in advising them about their draperies. 'The Tale of Troy' was a very amateur affair and rather laughed at as giving society ladies an opportunity for dressing up and displaying their beauty, she recalled.[78] Harrison was given the part of Penelope, while Lionel Tennyson was Ulysses. Elinor Ritchie was Andromache. Helen herself was played by Eugénie Sellers. The American classicist Charles Waldstein[79] helped coach them in learning their parts, 'and Jane never forgot the dramatic gifts he disclosed in doing so. . . . At one rehearsal, dissatisfied with the acting of Helen of Troy, he showed her how it ought to be done. "And that ugly little man", she used to say, "BECAME Helen of Troy." ' Mrs Beerbohm Tree 'remarked how the young ladies, coached in their Greek by Professor Warr, each and all became the willing slave of Watts and Millais, Tadema, Poynter and Burne Jones, who flung themselves into the task of supervising the scenery and the costume'.[80] 'It must have been a charming example', wrote Mirrlees, 'of what was known in the 'eighties as "five o'clock antiquity".'[81]

Perhaps it was the fame she acquired through 'The Tale of Troy' that led to her next public appearance on the stage, this time at Oxford. The choice of play was Euripides' Alcestis, done in the original Greek[82] and a woman was

[77]   For a detailed description of 'The Tale of Troy', see Beard, Invention, ch. 4, passim.

[78]   Letter from Elinor (Ritchie) Paul to Hope Mirrlees, 13 June 1934.

[79]   Waldstein, later Sir Charles Walston, came to Cambridge in 1880 to teach classical archaeology. He was responsible for the institution of the Cambridge Greek plays. In 1889 he became Director of the American School at Athens.

[80]   Gladys Scott Thomson, Mrs Arthur Strong: a Memoir (London: Cohen & West, 1949).

[81]   Mirrlees's draft biography.

[82]   Earlier injunctions that OUDS perform only Shakespeare, and that nothing be acted in drag, seem to have been forgotten. Or perhaps a Greek play was deemed to satisfy the requirements for decency. See Humphrey Carpenter, OUDS: a Centenary History of the Oxford University Drama Society, 1885–1985 (Oxford: Oxford University Press, 1985).

8. Jane Harrison as Alcestis, Oxford University Dramatic Society, 1887

needed for the title role. Harrison had recently given a series of lectures on Greek sculpture at Oxford, and was given the part (Fig. 8).

The production made much use of special effects, which had their problems. The steam jets, which were supposed to produce a death-like mist to enshroud Thanatos, were apt to scald; Apollo nearly strangled himself on the flying wires which let him down; and Harrison as Alcestis, sensing that it was indecorous to be carted around by the Boat Club 'heavies', refused to be carried offstage on a bier, and a double had to be found. One reviewer considered Harrison 'a hopeless actress', her performance 'by turns hysterical and stony'. The whole thing 'verged on the ridiculous', but was nevertheless deemed a great success. 'The newspapers reported that in the weeks leading up to the first night copies of the Alcestis could even be seen in punts on the Cherwell.' Other reviews were less flattering.[83]

By this time Greek vases and their restoration were becoming her speciality, and so in September 1886 she paid her one and only visit to Russia with her cousin, Marian Harrison, and visited the Hermitage Museum at St Petersburg to study the rich find of Greek vases excavated at Kertsch. So single-minded was her pursuit of her scholarly interests that she devoted all of her attention to the vases and saw nothing of the country or its people. At the end of her life, when her focus had changed and when she loved everything Russian with a passion, all she could think of were the lost opportunities:

what a fool, what an idiot I was to leave Russia without knowing it! I might so easily have made the pilgrimage to Tolstoy; I might even have seen Dostoevsky. It has been all my life my besetting sin that I could only see one thing at a time. I was blinded by over-focus. . . . Never now shall I see Moscow and Kiev, cities of my dreams.[84]

[83] Carpenter, *OUDS*, 44–5.   [84] *Reminiscences*, 77.

4. Mythology and Monuments: Greece and London 1886–1898

IN the winter of 1886 Harrison was staying with the Turnbulls at their home in Derbyshire when she met a man nine years her junior whose influence was to change the course of her life. Dugald Sutherland MacColl (fig. 9) was at the time visiting his married sister who lived nearby and the Turnbulls entertained the family for luncheon. MacColl had recently graduated from Lincoln College, Oxford, where he had read Greats and also won the coveted Newdigate prize for poetry. Later he was to become an outspoken art critic with a particular interest in modern art and was appointed Keeper of the Tate Gallery and, subsequently, of the Wallace Collection.[1] On returning to London, Harrison invited him to attend one of her lectures on Greek art; he attended, and disagreed vehemently with her opinions, derived from her mentor, Charles Newton, on ideality in art. A correspondence ensued and the association began to flourish.

The previous year she had preached her doctrine of ideality in *Introductory Studies in Greek Art*. 'I shall be satisfied', she wrote in the preface, 'if, by the help of the wisdom of Plato, I can show any of the citizens of our state why, eschewing the dry bones of symbolism and still more warily shunning the rank, unwholesome pastures of modern realism, they may nurture their souls on the fair sights and pure visions of Ideal art.'[2] She argued that if we want to understand Greek art it is essential to know something about the earlier art of Egypt, Assyria, and Phoenicia. We can only appreciate what is original in any style of art once we can eliminate what has been borrowed. This philosophy was the same as had guided Charles Newton in his arrangement of the artefacts at the British Museum. In *Introductory Studies* she first

Readers of Mary Beard's *The Invention of Jane Harrison* may notice that Beard and I have both chosen to name chapter titles after titles of Harrison's works. This is coincidental, and testimony to the intertextuality of her life and work.

[1] See Maureen Borland, *D. S. MacColl: Painter, Poet, Art Critic* (Harpenden: Lennard Publishing, 1995). [2] Harrison, *Introductory Studies*, p. vii.

9. Dugald Suther-
land MacColl, *c.* 1884

described the society that gave rise to each of these artistic styles and then
tried to show how their art was influenced by social and religious factors.
The Egyptians' intense convictions about the afterlife gave rise to Egyptian
realism as they sought by means of art to preserve the exact likeness of the
dead for the soul to inhabit after the flesh had decayed. The Assyrians, desiccated by religious dogmatism, thought in symbols (such as a disk for their
sun-god). The Greeks, with their fine instinct, learned realism from the
Egyptians, but transcended it to create an ideal form; they learned symbolism from the Assyrians and relegated it to decoration. Phoenician art, by

contrast, was eclectic, a mixture of Egyptian and Assyrian. The Phoenicians, merchant seamen, were a practically-minded people who gave Greece the alphabet, weights and measures, and skilled handicrafts, but nothing original in art—providentially, for Greek art learned from the Phoenician much technically, but little expressively. 'A Phoenician symbol misunderstood begets for the Greek a beautiful myth,' she concluded. 'The very sterility of Phoenician art acted as a stimulus to the home-grown creativity of the Greeks.'

MacColl criticized her on two counts: on her ideas on art, which he declared were all second-hand, and wrong at that; and on her showy style of lecturing. He was not the first to make this criticism: Vernon Lee had written in a letter to Eugénie Sellers the previous year that 'she had no instinct for art of any kind and a want of knowledge of other art besides that of antiquity';[3] discussion of her criticism ensued among the circle that included Lee, Sellers, and MacColl, but it was MacColl who confronted her with it.[4] She tore up his letter, but from her reply it is not hard to see that he had taken her own words and quoted them back at her.

She wrote to him on 6 February 1887, after he had attended one of her lectures:

Dear Mr MacColl

I think I had better tell you the real reason your presence was so unwelcome last night, as I do not want you to credit it with any form of personal rudeness.

A month ago I would simply have been a good deal gratified by your coming but then you had not written me that—to me—fatal letter. I daresay you have forgotten its—rather strongly worded—contents, which have been rankling in my mind ever since. I tore it up in the fury of first reading but unhappily that only made me remember every word of it. I knew from the first that my rage against you was caused by the simple fact that you were right & I was wrong, but it was not till I began my work again that it was borne in upon me how wrong—how much more wrong than you could possibly divine. The worst is that all the success I have had has been based on that wrongness. I could always hold an audience—any fanatic can—not by the proper & legitimate virtue of my subject or its treatment but by the harmful force of an intense personal conviction. I had grown into a sort of Salvationist for Greek art—probably a sort of educated decency withheld me from the constant obtrusion of my gospel or someone would before now have told me less politely—not more pointedly—that I was a fool, but none the less the faith in my gospel was the secret of my strength.

The practical proof of this is that I feel now that all virtue is gone out of me;

---

[3] For Vernon Lee, see Beard's summary in *Invention*, 87–8.

[4] For a full discussion of these events, see Beard, *Invention*, 90–4.

lecturing this term has been nothing but a dreary mechanical struggle & if my hearers have not found it out as they soon will it is only that something of the manner of conviction clings.

Last night to this depression your coming added a hitherto unknown sensation, that of absolutely paralysing nervousness. I can only recall that I went on for an hour doggedly determined to make audible sounds—however one failure more or less matters very little & the term's work has to be got thro'—somehow.

It will seem to you—with your sane mind—as absurd that the shattering of a theory should depress as that the building of one should inspire—& indeed it is not the shattering of any particular theory but the giving up of the habit of mind that demands a creed. I know by experience that one gets on much better in practice without a religious creed than with one, but it was none the less desolate at first to live without God in the world—art has to me taken & more than taken the place of religion & my work for it was I see only another form of an old & I thought long dead personal fanaticism—which is, it seems, hydra-headed.

I have added to this personal misery the depressing reflection that I have done a great deal of harm tho'—as you pleasantly point out—'not as much harm as I might'—*littera scripta manet* [the written word is permanent] is a bitter reflection to me just now & it has come only just in time to prevent its own repetition. At the present moment I feel that I shall never teach & certainly not preach any more after this term. I tried a mild plunge from theory into practice but with no relief.

I see I have written two sheets of unpardonable egotism—please forgive me. I really wanted to explain why it is that I fail—as I feel sure I do—in making up my manner to you into a good semblance of cordiality—a right minded person would be grateful to you & perhaps I should have been but that some of your arrows were dipped in a peculiarly irritating poison.

Truly yours,
Jane E. Harrison[5]

It was characteristic of her to respond in this way, in what she herself termed 'an ecstasy of humility', especially when the criticism came from someone to whom she was emotionally attached. Her whole career was to be marked by such epiphanies. And yet her break with the past was not as complete as she herself believed at this point. One can detect in *Introductory Studies* the seeds of ideas and approaches that did develop later in her mature work and in fact she did not abandon her 'creed' entirely: for example, she had already come to the belief that the Greek myths often developed out of something else misunderstood (in one case a Phoenician symbol)[6]—an idea developed a few years later in *Mythology and Monuments of Ancient Athens*. But she felt for several years after absorbing MacColl's criticism that everything she had ever taught or written was all wrong. MacColl for his part had not

[5] JEH to DSM, 6 Feb. 1887, MS MacColl H157.   [6] *Introductory Studies*, 148.

intended to be destructive; he felt responsible for restoring her confidence, as he put it, 'on wider lines'. He immediately wrote another letter, to which she replied,

Dear Mr MacColl,

Thank you more than I can say—you gave me a sort of hope not that I have not been intensely wrong but that I may work right again, & not give everything up—my work is so absolutely my life that the horror of feeling it go as I felt on Saturday utterly unnerved me. The sting of your first letter was that you understood me & the helpfulness of your last is the same—I am generally so well supplied with αὐτάρκεια [self-sufficiency] that I must own in self defence that I cannot sleep now except under drugs; but commit this secret to the grave as I would not have it known for worlds. I know in this state one cannot—if one ever can—distinguish between the moral & mental & the physical so I shall commit myself to nothing desperate till I can sleep—I wish I could think that all the remorse I feel would be resolved into sleeplessness but I cannot. Probably your letter only lighted a long laid train of discontent, but it seemed to cast a sudden flash of light on every foolish thing I had said or written.

I am horribly ashamed of the trouble I have given you—thank you again.

Truly yours,

Jane E. Harrison[7]

There was further correspondence, and as the association deepened, MacColl began to turn her attention to the field of folk religion, introducing her to such books as Wilhelm Mannhardt's *Wald- und Feldkulte*[8] and sharing with her his own interest in the connection of such worship with mimetic dance. Many years later he wrote, 'She embarked on this with renewed enthusiasm—her life, to the very last, was the story of such new impulses—and we studied together the bearing of such dances on Greek vase designs, & the fitting together of fragments. The Germans, I believe, had a name for this departure, the "Harrison programme".'[9]

MacColl felt some responsibility for the disruption to her career, and sought to find her some employment and a source of income while she made plans for her future. Since he was planning to leave for a visit to India early in 1888 he invited her to take over the balance of his University Extension lectures at Oxford. She hesitatingly agreed, though not without protesting that, for the next year at least, she was financially independent.[10]

---

[7] JEH to DSM, n.d., MS MacColl 158

[8] Wilhelm Mannhardt, *Wald- und Feldkulte*, 2 vols. (Berlin: Gebrüder Borntraeger, 1875–7).

[9] D. S. MacColl, 'Jane Harrison', MS MacColl H193, Glasgow University Archives.

[10] She had the £300 annuity from her mother, plus whatever she earned from lecturing. This was sufficient to support her modest lifestyle in London; it was comparable to fellowship

Harrison introduced MacColl to her 'delightful circle' of friends, the Butcher sisters in particular, and Alice Lloyd, who, 'quiet as a dormouse joined in the keen analysis of character that was unceasing in that circle'. That summer she went with Eleanor Butcher to stay at the inn on the beach at Robin Hood's Bay. Lewis Nettleship[11] made up the third member of the party, a 'sad aspirant for Eleanor's affection'. Alfred and Violet Hunt[12] were also staying in the inn. MacColl and his mother, who were there to paint, stayed in a house up the hill. They spent the time in many walks along the coast and over the moors, or lying about on the beach or cliff. The Yorkshire sea and moors were home to Harrison, nourishing her spirit. She had an almost physical need for them. She often referred in Swinburne's words to her 'grey sea-mother', consciously or subconsciously linking her own orphan state to archetypal images of a cosmic mother.

Through MacColl she began to look with an artist's eye. He taught her to see 'the pictorial value of washing hung out to dry' (a motif of the impressionist painter Berthe Morisot). One day she found MacColl enraptured by the beauty of a very fat man who struck her as merely hideous. 'Oh if only I might lie under his paunch', he cried, 'and draw its opulent curves!'[13]

Back in London she saw MacColl frequently, always carefully and properly chaperoned, usually by one Lionel Robinson. (Many years later, after Harrison's death, MacColl corresponded with Lionel Robinson, who mentions his close alliance with her. There is nothing at all in her correspondence that makes reference to Robinson, other than as her 'playfellow' or 'yokefellow', so he remains in the shadows of this period of her life.) She and MacColl were avid theatre-goers, with a love for the avant-garde. She was among the minority that idolized Ibsen, though occasionally his melodrama was too much for her: she disgraced herself on one occasion by being violently sick during a performance. She also invited MacColl to meet Eugénie Sellers ('I think her the most beautiful woman in all London', she wrote). Eugénie's physical beauty seems to have played some part in the attraction that she had for Jane. She came to live with her for a period while Get was away, nearly drove Jane mad with her devotion, and the relationship ended

dividends at Oxford and Cambridge. Only when travelling abroad was she financially constrained. She was sufficiently well off to contribute £100 to Dörpfeld's excavations around the year 1890.

[11] D. S. MacColl, 'Dates and Places', JHA.

[12] Probably the same Violet Hunt as the mistress of Christina Rossetti's nephew. See Violet Hunt, *The Wife of Rossetti: Her Life and Death* (London: John Lane, The Bodley Head, 1932).

[13] 'D. S. MacColl' in Mirrlees's notebook.

with a stormy parting of the ways.[14] The incident illustrates some of the problematic aspects of Harrison's relationships with other women.

Meanwhile she was plunging into her newly found field of folk religion, applying what she had learned from MacColl to her knowledge of Greek vase painting. Using the vases as a source for understanding material culture threw light on rituals and festivals. Following an interest of MacColl's she explored the connection between modern Greek folklore and the ancient Greek festival of the Aiora, with its ritual swinging and swing songs.[15]

With MacColl's encouragement she lectured again that November, at Eton, with trepidation. She Confessed to him,

I was wretched, almost desperate, about that Eton lecture, and all the demons of last spring were camping about my bed. But I was resolved come what might to try your plan and trust the subject to its own value and rid myself of my hateful habit of trying to force upon it meretricious effects, and you were absolutely right. I felt directly I began to speak it all went ever so much better (except the Oxygen Gas which went out half way utterly). I wonder why you so often say just the right thing to me. I acquit you of all intention. You must be an instrument of the gods. I certainly won't call you any more a 'messenger of Satan' and happily I don't now mind the least being your debtor. κοινὰ γὰρ τὰ τῶν φίλων ['friends have all things in common'][16] is spiritually at least my belief and I have begun lately—only quite lately and perhaps too soon—to think of you as friend not foe. I think you must promise (as the candid friend) if you ever see me falling into the old, or any new form of lunacy to write me a thoroughly unpleasant letter and that won't give you much trouble.

Of course I feel all the more keenly what a knave or a fool (I am not sure which) I was last year and what dishonour I did to a particularly self-sufficing subject, but no remorse can mar the holy calm that has set in—a peace better even than that born of whiskey and soda.

    Truly yours,

    JEH

Do not answer this and do not laugh immoderately—you may laugh a little but at yourself cast for the double role of Paraclete or Convincer of sin and Consoler in my Miracle play.[17]

As MacColl continued to search for ways to further Harrison's career, his thoughts turned to the work in progress at Athens, where Wilhelm Dörpfeld

[14] See Gladys S. Thomson, *Mrs. Arthur Strong, a Memoir* (London: Cohen & West, 1949), 24–5. Chapter 2 of Beard's *Invention* explores the relationship between the two women, though there is very little evidence for Beard's thesis that they were close friends.

[15] This led to an article, 'The Festival of the Aiora', *Classical Review*, 3 (1889), 378–9.

[16] Plato, *Phaedrus* 279c.   [17] JEH to DSM, 13 Nov. 1887, MS MacColl H163.

was excavating the Acropolis under the German Archaeological Institute. Dörpfeld's theories had not yet found acceptance among English scholars, and the results of his excavations were as yet unpublished. MacColl saw an opportunity for Harrison to put to use her wide knowledge of archaeology and mythology in formulating Dörpfeld's theories for English readers. Margaret (Merrifield) Verrall, meanwhile, was preparing a new translation of Pausanias, the second-century traveller whose *Description of Greece* had become a primary source for identifying topography and monuments.[18] They conceived the idea of a joint publication, Verrall doing the translation and Harrison an introduction and commentary. MacColl proposed a visit to Greece. Peveril Turnbull was commissioned to 'charter a black ship' in which to visit the islands in order to 'see all the places Pausanias pretended he had visited' and a party consisting of Harrison, MacColl, the Turnbulls, and Arthur Sidgwick and his wife made plans to visit Greece in the spring of 1888.

They began by visiting Athens. The first day of their stay was a fiesta day commemorating Greek independence and the Acropolis was shut, so after a stroll round the Pnyx and Theseion, Arthur Sidgwick persuaded MacColl and Harrison to climb Lycabettus to get a general view, taking what MacColl thought 'a mad delight' in identifying points of topography. In the afternoon they drove to Hymettus. After a stiff climb to the top they 'saw all round— Euboea and the Cyclades—Parnes, Salamis, etc., Sidgwick with his umbrella shouting "that's Acharnae, that's Colonus, that's Aegina" '. The party chartered a small steam launch to take them to Aegina and climbed the hill to see the great Doric temple. 'Then we had a splendid passage home, plunging through the lapis lazuli . . . of the seas.'[19]

Harrison wrote from the Hôtel des Étrangers on 3 April: 'the Gardners came back last night and I am going this afternoon to hear their Cyprus experiences, which I gather have been favourable. . . . We hope next week to start for Delphi. As yet Athens has absorbed all my energies.'[20] She was, of course, gathering material for her proposed book on Pausanias. In everything Dörpfeld was her authority. In particular, she learned from him the importance of topography in archaeology. She wrote many years later,

---

[18]   See Mary Beard, 'Pausanias in Petticoats or *The Blue Jane*', in *Pausanias: Travel and Memory in Roman Greece*, ed. Susan E. Alcock, John F. Cherry, and Jás Elsner (New York: Oxford University Press, 2001), 224–39.

[19]   D. S. MacColl, 'Diary of a Greek Journey', transcript of letters to his sister Lizzie and to his mother, Janet Scott MacColl, made by Jessie Stewart, JHA.

[20]   JEH to Mr Macmillan, 15 Mar. 1888, Macmillan archives, University of Reading, 201/ 284.

Dörpfeld was my most honoured master—we always called him 'Avtos'.[21] He let me go with him on his Peloponnesos Reise and his Insel Reise. They were marvels of organization, and the man himself was a miracle. He would hold us spellbound for a six hours' peripatetic lecture, only broken by an interval of ten minutes to partake of a goat's-flesh sandwich and 'etwas frisches Bier'. Once I saw, to my sorrow, three Englishmen tailing away after the *frisches Bier*. I was more grieved than surprised. They were Oxford men—the (then) Provost of Oriel, the Principal of Brasenose and an eminent Fellow of Balliol. It was worth many hardships to see forty German professors try to mount forty recalcitrant mules. My own horsemanship . . . is nothing to 'write home about', but compared to those German professors I am a centaur.[22]

MacColl saw things from a different angle: 'This afternoon [I listened] to a peripatetic lecture in German on the theatre of Dionysus etc. for four mortal hours. The lecturer Dörpfeld is head of the German school here and quite inexhaustible.'

In 1888 much of the Acropolis was still lying under soil and debris to a depth of ten metres. Excavation was slow, simply because there was so much earth to be moved. At the time of Harrison's visit the Erechtheum was uncovered, with 'the rock laid bare as far as the Belvidere', and excavation between the Parthenon and the museum was still in progress. The foundations of a Mycenaean megaron had been discovered, like those at Tiryns and Mycenae, with a rock staircase similar to that at Tiryns. Of the sculpture that had been unearthed the most interesting recent finds were the head of a Triton, 'a bearded male head, more than life-size, brilliantly coloured'; another head which bore a superficial resemblance to the Apollo found at Olympia, of which the colour was fading fast now that it was exposed to the air; a plinth inscribed with a dedicatory inscription which was tentatively identified as belonging to the Moschophoros; and an archaic painted plaque 'of remarkable beauty' and which Harrison concluded must serve 'as the nearest approach we have or perhaps are likely to have to the wall paintings of Polygnotos'.[23] Harrison made a pointed comment about the fragments of sculpture in the Acropolis Museum:

I cannot leave this question of the identification of fragments without entering a protest against the practice of hasty and hypothetical restoration that obtains in this Museum. It is one thing to publish a hypothesis and illustrate it by a drawing embodying the proposed restoration; it is another to have the fragments actually plastered

---

[21] Literally 'himself'; the Greeks use this term to mean 'the master'.

[22] *Reminiscences*, 65.

[23] Jane Harrison, 'Archaeology in Greece, 1887–1888', *Journal of Hellenic Studies*, 9 (1888), 118–33, esp. 125–6.

together. Nothing short of absolute demonstration can, it seems to me, justify this concrete dogmatism, involving as it does compulsory prejudice to the eye.[24]

A visit to the private collection of the Prime Minister, Tricoupis, revealed a vase which she believed to be by Douris, and which she published in *Journal of Hellenic Studies* the following year, explaining how she was 'specially anxious to secure its immediate publication as, though the vase is at present in such safe hands, the security of antiquities in private collections is always precarious'.[25]

They visited Eleusis, where they saw the recent excavations being undertaken by a Dr Philios. 'The diggings there are very complete, showing the . . . various periods in ground plan and the rock cut theatre in which the spectators saw the mysteries.'[26] They then set out for Delphi, via Itea where they spent a night in a 'bug-infested house'. Delphi was disappointing inasmuch as excavations had been delayed while the Greek government continued to negotiate with the inhabitants of the village of Kastri which occupied the site.[27] Then to Thebes, an uncomfortable journey. MacColl wrote to his sister Lizzie:

And now you must think of Mr Turnbull and me sitting up at night bargaining with a carriage driver through the hotel keeper—a solemn farce which the two went through quite gravely, being probably brothers. . . . In the end a bargain was struck and by 5:00 the next morning we were up and the four of us took our place in the [cab] and set out for Boeotia. It is a sleepy life. First the early start in the coolness before anyone is quite awake. Then the long day gets hotter. The carriage creeps up and down the hills. You climb up and down the mule track on foot sometimes for a short cut, or get out to look at some ground plan. Then comes about midday the long halt for lunch and rest. At Khandura, on the way to Thebes we found a little pine grove on the hill and ate our chicken and drank our wine in great content. Then some slept. . . . Then comes a long space of afternoon broken by halts at road khans where you get cups of coffee and oranges.

Towards sunset we wound down into the Boeotian plain; which is a real plain. Quite flat, with hills rising distinctly all round, not in the usual gradual way, but as one would naturally have made them if told to do so.

---

[24] Jane Harrison, 124. See also Ian Jenkins, *Archaeologists & Aesthetes in the Sculpture Galleries of the British Museum 1800–1939* (London: British Museum Press, 1992).

[25] Jane Harrison, 'Two Cyclices Relating to the Exploits of Theseus', *Journal of Hellenic Studies*, 10 (1889), 231–42.

[26] DSM to Lizzie MacColl, 5 Apr. 1888, MS MacColl M107.

[27] Karl Otfried Müller and Ernst Curtius had begun excavation. Later two Frenchmen, Wescher and Foucart, excavated the polygonal wall. In 1880 the French had continued, uncovering part of the Stoa of the Athenians. Permission was finally given in 1891 to the French team under Théophile Homolle and systematic excavations began in 1892. See Photios Petsas, *Delphi: Monuments and Museum* (Athens: Krene Editions, 1981).

The sun was setting—as never—over Helicon and the snow of Parnassus when we got into Thebes. We strolled about the up and down streets of the town which stands on a little hill. At one turn we had got separated for a few minutes and Turnbull and I were attracted by a large crowd of people in one of the streets. On going up we found the centre of it was Mrs T. and Miss H. A chorus of the women of Thebes were standing round and questioning them. How old were they? Were they married? How often? Had they children? If not married, why not? They pressed Miss Harrison. Why did she not marry the other *kurios*? On her announcing that she objected to being married she was greeted with screams of laughter and followed the rest of the time by an excited and incredulous crowd.[28]

Later in the same day they went to look for the fountain of Dirce. They didn't find it, but did find 'white-clothed women, their faces half bound in Eastern fashion', and pots on their heads. 'One of them gave us a drink from the fountain of Oedipus.'

The Ephor of Thebes helped them with arrangements to visit the next day (15 April) the excavations of a temple dedicated to the worship of the obscure fertility-gods called 'Kabeiroi'.[29] He obtained for them 'a cheap little painted car without springs or cushions, but with two wheels and a canopy and a mule bedecked with gorgeous caparisons and charms'. Dörpfeld had been alerted to the site the previous year when it had been drawn to his attention that bronze votive animals and inscriptions to the Kabeiroi had been uncovered by grave-robbers and were being sold in Athens. There were hopes that the archaeology of the temple might throw some light on the subject of their worship. An open-air precinct had been discovered that contained the bones of many animal sacrifices. She was shown all over the excavations by Paul Wolters of the German Archaeological Institute. From Thebes the party went by boat to Zante and thence to Olympia. The Turnbulls left at this point, while MacColl and Harrison returned to Athens via Corinth. The original scheme had been to visit the Cyclades, but since Turnbull's 'black ship' had not materialized and the rest of the party had deserted them, Harrison and MacColl boarded an ordinary steamer bound for Constantinople.

The ship was intolerably overcrowded with a party of American tourists 'with their awful helmets and bonnets'. After setting sail they ran into a storm that lasted twelve hours, forcing the captain to put in at Mitylene.

---

[28] 'D. S. MacColl' in Mirrlees's notebook.

[29] See Harrison, 'Archaeology in Greece', 118–33, esp. 128–9. Later, arguing from iconographic evidence, she associated the Kabeiroi with the worship of Dionysos. Noting their grotesque features she comments: 'This gives us a curious glimpse into that blending of the cosmic and the mystic, that concealing of the sacred by the profane that seems inherent in the anxious primitive mind' (*Prolegomena*, 653).

'Then one by one a wretched company crept out of their holes and cursed their day.' When eventually things began to improve 'Miss Harrison came up on the bridge and forgot her sorrows in the sight of Troy.' She nearly got no further, having forgotten her passport, but overcame the difficulty by passing herself off as MacColl's wife. In Constantinople their pleasantest experience was the Egyptian bazaar 'where they sell the most lovely smells. I sat down to sketch in the stall of one old Turk & he politely brought us the most delightful coffee and a live coal to light Miss Harrison's cigarette. . . . The trams by the way are each provided with a little hareem for the women in which Miss Harrison has to sit to her great disgust.'

Archaeologically, the visit to Constantinople was disappointing. 'Statuettes and reliefs of Aphrodite, of small lions, and of the Metroon type' had been found in large numbers in Asia Minor, and had been placed in the museum. 'I visited the museum there in the hopes of finding them', Harrison wrote, but the director was absent and the museum was closed.[30]

They landed back in the Piraeus on 6 May, Greek Easter Sunday:

All the flags were up in the harbour and everyone was firing pistols and ancient guns and squibs because Christ was risen. When people met you they said, 'Christos aneste', and the reply was, 'And we with him.' I am bound to say that when I tried the greeting upon the guardian of the Well of Aesculapius he replied 'Cigaretten?' Everywhere families were roasting the Paschal lamb in the streets and open places. At the hotel they gave us red eggs for breakfast and a little bunch of flowers. On Easter Tuesday they went to Megara to see the folk dancing there, and were nearly mobbed when MacColl attempted to sketch a dancer whose brother was fiercely suspicious of the evil eye.[31]

They then 'scandalously determined' to see Sparta and Arcadia; without chaperon or the cost of a dragoman. Harrison's unfailing pluck and good humour with her useful smattering of modern Greek faced all emergencies, and a spirit-kettle with cakes of compressed tea was a treasure at resting points in the thirsty heat.[32] On their visit to Olympia they had missed Bassae; they also wanted to see some of the more out-of-the-way parts of Arcadia. One suspects that the mountainous terrain of that part of the Peloponnese had daunted all the others, and now that the two were left alone Harrison was determined to make the journey. On 13 May MacColl wrote to Lizzie:

The programme is to spend a second night there and make the Demarch get us mules for about a week. On Tuesday we shall 'conceal these mules about our person' as an

[30] 'Archaeology in Greece', 133.
[31] DSM to Lizzie MacColl, 13 May 1888, MS MacColl E59.
[32] MacColl, 'Jane Harrison'.

American Archaeologist we met expressed it and travel to Mistra and Trypi. . . . From Trypi we shall have a long day's march over the pass from Taygetus to Kalamata. Next day we hope to get to the site of Messene and claim hospitality of the monks of Vurkano. This monastery is perched on a precipice of Ithome. It breaks Miss Harrison's heart that we have not been able to go to some other rock monasteries in Thessaly[33] where the only way is to be pulled up by a rope in a basket.

The mules and the driver—a 'wretched, grinning boy'—were one constant cause for grief. Another was food. However, at about two o'clock in the morning they 'rolled into the broad squalid streets of Sparta and up to the shut up inn', where their perseverance finally secured them cutlets, eggs, and retsina. 'Then we lay down and were bitten.' The next day there was the museum to be done and arrangements to be made for the following day's start on mules, so, armed with a letter of recommendation from the Prime Minister, they went in search of the demarch or mayor of the place. They located

a lean and whiskered person who is thought in Sparta to know French. He told me he had been Professor of the French tongue in Patras but was now in retreat [*en retraite* or retired]. The four of us went through an immense amount of howdying. . . . You have no notion what frightful effects it involves to have a Demarch about your person once your small stock of complimentary Greek is exhausted,—plus a Professor in retreat the situation is intolerable.

By five o'clock the next morning they were in the saddle.

A mule goes at a slower pace than is possible to walk at, MacColl wrote, and you see the country in the most contemplative way. . . . They are wonderfully clever beasts. They seem to prefer going up and down the side of a house to anything less arduous. The mule track on the hillsides is always rough and rocky and it is beautiful to see them smell at a rock and then plant their flexible hoofs in the crevices. At the first steep places Miss Harrison could not believe in the safety of the proceeding and begged to be taken down, but she soon got to look on it as a matter of course. As the day went on we had plenty of experience of what mules can do. In some places there was just a ledge broad enough for one to pass with a wall of rock on one side and a precipice on the other and most of the way was a succession of up and down rocky staircases. There is a beautiful nonchalance about the beast. He always takes the very edge of the path and will leave you hanging over a sheer hundred feet while he stops to crop a sprout between his hind legs.

The monastery at Vurkano was a well-known resting place, consisting of partly ruined buildings with a church in the middle. The monks were quite

---

[33] The reference is to Meteora.

willing to offer hospitality, blaming the government for the condition of the buildings. They were very proud, however, of such improvements as had been made (fresh paint in hideous scarlet, green, and blue). Other visitors reported being unable to sleep at night for the sounds of lamentation ('Crucify me, O Lord and make me suffer a thousand deaths to attain my salvation') coming from neighbouring cells. 'Ithome', wrote one traveller, '—the site of human sacrifices to Zeus Ithomatas—is it not strange that still upon the same height men offer to their God these human sacrifices, changed, indeed, in appearance, but in real substance the same?'[34] MacColl's description of their stay there is worth quoting in full:

we sat on the steps of the church till something should happen. After some time a servant came and led us up a rickety wooden staircase to the gallery running round the cloister and through into a large room with two windows opening on small outside balconies . . . on the chief chair was seated the Hegoumenos [prior]. . . . He rose and beckoned us to places on one of the sofas. We got through some preliminary sentences in Greek but there was something working in his mind. He took up a little paper book from the table beside him, studied it diligently for some time and then gravely and with un-natural slowness and distinctness said 'I pray thou be thee seated.' He then chuckled. We were already seated but he could not get quite up to time. This little book is a most amusing work. It gives what it supposes to be the phonetic equivalent in Greek letters of words and sentences in various European tongues, e.g. French *homme* and *femme* become $\dot{o}\mu\mu$ and $\varphi\alpha\mu\mu$, and wife $o\dot{v}\alpha\iota\varphi$—most of the equivalents were ridiculously wrong so that the monk's laborious English phrases were not very easy to understand. However he and Miss Harrison taught one another a good deal of Greek and English. He kept her hard at it most of the time. Coffee was served and we gave him cigarettes. We were getting anxious about our dinner but after consulting his book in several places he announced 'We—hev—littel—ro-ast—mee-eet'. I asked him if I might $\zeta\dot{\omega}\gamma\rho\alpha\varphi\epsilon\iota\nu$ [sketch] the cloisters and he graciously gave me permission, so I sketched while the English lesson went on. It was approaching the hour of nine and we had not seen anything of our bedroom nor sign of dinner so I gently asked if we might wash before dinner. He said yes and softly led us to the balcony where there was a basin and a towel. He conducted our washing and then took us to a little room next the other where the dinner was cooked and served. . . . The three of us sat down at a tiny table covered with a shepherd's check cloth. He gave us first some rice soup and then some plates of lamb. It was a fast day with him so he only had artichokes etc. for himself and the choicest of these he transferred with a fork to our plates. . . . He gave us fresh goat milk cheese to eat with our meat and there were paschal eggs to follow with which he played a game of soldiers trying whose eggshell would break the other's first.

[34]   John Pentland Mahaffy, *Greek Pictures Drawn with Pen and Pencil* (London: Religious Tract Society, 1890), 182–3.

After dinner we returned to the other room—had coffee and smoked. We delicately approached him as to whether we might stop another night as we wanted to see the ruins of Messene before going on. He at once invited Miss Harrison to stay three months and carry on the Greek and English lessons. For the head of a monastery his conduct was really outrageous. He softly stroked her hands at times and said they were whiter than snow (which was not the case after a night spent in the monastery).

Her view was different. 'The Greek clergy, even the monks who may not marry, are quite simple and friendly to women. After the Roman attitude, it is refreshing to be accepted as a man and a brother—if a weaker one—and not looked at with sour eyes as an incarnate snare.'[35] She gave him a lan-guishing photograph of herself in a ball dress which he stuck up in the room next to his icon of the virgin and said he would look at it every day. MacColl continues,

He then asked the cost of the dress. He agreed with her that it may be better to be ἐλευθερα [free]—that was his state. As night went on we became anxious about our chances of sleep. After ten the problem was solved by the entrance of the boy with some sheets which he spread on the two sofas. The old boss then signified that there were our beds for the night and we thought he was about to stay and conduct our undressing, but in the end he softly withdrew.[36]

Harrison had additional recollections:

After supper he said he had a question to ask me. He had heard that rich Englishmen had in their mouths 'stranger' (or 'guest') teeth made of gold, and which moved. Was it true? It was. Had I in my mouth by any chance a stranger tooth? I had, I owned, one, but in the best Oriental fashion I deprecated any mention of it. It was but a poor thing, made not of gold, but of an elephant's tusk. Did I ever take it out? Yes. When? 'Oh,' nervously, 'only very early in the morning.' After a short sleep—sleep in a Greek monastery is rarely for long—I woke. The Hegoumenos was seated at my bed-head telling his beads and . . . watching. Oh, why, why did I not take out that 'stranger' tooth? I might so easily have made a good man happy. The Graiae them-selves pointed the way . . . But he politely withdrew himself, slowly and sadly.[37]

They left Ithome to tackle the journey to Bassae, to visit the Temple of Apollo, whose sculpture Harrison was familiar with since the marbles had been removed in 1811–12 and sold to the British Museum. The way through the mountains was precipitous, cut by ravines, and even today is 'not for those nervous of unprotected drops'.[38] The muleteer made all kind of diffi-culties and said that 'Charones' and other devils haunted the route:

---

[35] *Reminiscences*, 66.   [36] MacColl, 'Diary'.   [37] *Reminiscences*, 66–8.
[38] Stuart Rossiter, *Blue Guide, Greece*, 4th edn. (London: Ernest Benn, 1981), 325.

I had to prod him on with threats . . . Then the muleteer confessed he did not know the way. I told him it was his business to know the way, and if he did not he must take a guide himself. This in the end he was compelled by threats to do and we set off led by a young fellow in a white hooded cloak. . . . At last on the summit we saw the pillars of the temple against the sky. We cast an anxious glance to see whether Apollo the Helper still had a roof to his house, but no, it was all gone. It was a wildish night in the moonlight and rain, under which we lay in mackintoshes. Against the assault of wolf-like dogs, a plague throughout, as well as evil spirits, the guide lit a fire, and consumed in the watches of the night the scraps of our provisions. It was without bite or sup that we started in the dreary dawn for the distant Andritsaina: eggs and dried figs there were ambrosia.[39]

And so, by means of threats and bribes, they made their way to Katakolo, where they found a steamer bound for Trieste. They continued via Munich and Cologne, where they parted company, MacColl to visit Belgium and Holland while Harrison returned home.

Back in England she began work on the mythology of Athens, to accompany Margaret Verrall's translation of the first book of Pausanias, On Attica. Since they had first mooted plans for the book Harrison had learned from Dörpfeld the importance of topography, which she had come to see as a vital source of evidence rather than a 'weary and most distasteful necessity'.[40] The result was that the book acquired a second purpose, that of making Dörpfeld's interpretation of the archaeological finds known to the English public. As such it would serve as a handbook to the students in her University Extension classes. In July 1888 she and Margaret Verrall spent a working holiday together at the inn at Robin Hood's Bay on the Yorkshire coast. She never forgot the feverish rate at which they worked, and Margaret's skill at sorting out a tangled mass of material. MacColl had agreed to do some translations for her from Greek poetry, rendering it into English verse, as prose is 'so flattening to the spirit'.[41]

Macmillan agreed to publish Mythology and Monuments of Ancient Athens[42] and by August Harrison had all of the material for the book ready prepared. The illustrations gave endless trouble. Her sensitivity on this issue was no doubt heightened by the criticisms of Introductory Studies; the Saturday Review had complained that 'the student needs to have the objects before his

[39] MacColl, 'Diary'. This page is missing in the original in the MacColl archives.
[40] See Jessie Stewart, Newnham College Letter, 1929, 54.   [41] JEH to GM [61], n.d.
[42] Jane Ellen Harrison and Margaret de G. Verrall, Mythology and Monuments of Ancient Athens: Being a Translation of a Portion of the 'Attica' of Pausanias (London: Macmillan, 1890).

eyes, and for this purpose the illustrations are not sufficient'[43] and the review in the *Athenaeum* had written that the illustrations were 'not merely inadequate, but actually repulsive' in a book about art, thrusting 'deformity and ugliness' upon the reader.'[44] But more than this, Harrison had derived from Heinrich Brunn a conviction about the paramount importance of good illustrations for a book on archaeology. If the reader is to be able to see for himself, it follows that the illustrations must be treated as an integral part of the text. Harrison's material was in the form of drawings, squeezes of inscriptions, and photographic negatives. The negatives, being glass, were difficult to transport, and she invited Mr Macmillan to come and examine them at her lodgings at his earliest convenience. 'I am anxious to get the matter arranged', she wrote, 'as I fear it will involve going to Athens again as they will go on digging up new things.'[45] Macmillan wrote back asking her to reduce the number of illustrations, and she replied with a promise to try to get the number down to 200, with a view to leaving a margin for such new discoveries as may be made within the year. The process by which the illustrations were to be reproduced gave rise to a great deal of wrangling. Engraving was expensive; a process described as 'hypo-etching' she declared to be perfect. But the engravers Boutall and Walker suggested another process to which she strongly objected as it gave a 'veiled' appearance. Four months later she was still troubled by the illustrations:

I saw Mr Walker at the Museum. I am distressed to find from him that the clearness of the pictures suffers far more by reduction than I had any idea of. In fact he says most of the inscriptions disappear altogether (e.g. from vases) if we reduce them as proposed to half page—& of course to have many full page wld increase the bulk of the book too much. Had I the slightest idea of this I should have chosen a much larger size of page. I fear the illustrations will be rather disastrous.[46]

Before the book was published there were other difficulties with the illustrations: a negative was lost and then the printer wrote to say that three blocks were missing. 'I have had proof long ago of all of them', she complained to Macmillan. 'Cannot the matter be finished off—I am really wearied out with these queries about plates—which I have settled long ago?'[47]

As well as working on *Mythology and Monuments* she spent 1888 and 1889

---

[43] *Saturday Review*, 27 Feb. 1886, 311.

[44] Anonymous review, *Athenaeum*, 2 Aug. 1890, 166–7.

[45] JEH to Macmillan, 17 Aug. 1888, Macmillan archives, 201/284.

[46] JEH to Macmillan, 4 Feb. 1889, Macmillan archives, 7/5.

[47] JEH to Macmillan, 10 Jan. 1890, Macmillan archives, 4/105.

writing a number of articles for publication in the *Classical Review* and the *Journal of Hellenic Studies*. Some of these deal with art, but two are worth noting for their concern with ritual and foreshadowing of her later work: 'The Festival of the Aiora'[48] and 'On the Meaning of the Term Arrephoroi'.[49] In the first of these the influence of MacColl is not far to seek. He had been drawn to Greece in the first place by the 'survivals under disguise of ancient cults; "gods still in exile"; swing Festivals',[50] which he had read of in Theodore Bent's *The Cyclades*.[51] Like Newton, he was interested in the survival of ancient ritual in present-day rites amongst the rural people of Greece. Bent had described one such rite, the 'swing-festival', still practised in the Cyclades as a purportedly Christian ritual on Good Friday. Pausanias, in his description of the frescoes on the Lesche at Delphi, tells how Polygnotus painted Phaedra on a swing, thus indicating the manner of her death. Harrison had observed in *Myths of the Odyssey* that 'vase paintings with female figures swinging occur not infrequently' and noted the parallel with the women who swung themselves at the festival of the Aiora in Athens to the accompaniment of a song called 'Aletis'.[52] In this article she now explained the name of the song as meaning 'the guilty one', and the ritual as expiatory. In the second article she interprets the 'Arrephoroi', whose ritual was observed in Athens, not as 'dew-carriers' but as 'pig-carriers', and links the festival of the Arrephoria with the account of the scholiast of Lucian (mentioned by Andrew Lang in his *Myth, Ritual, and Religion*), who describes the throwing of pigs into chasms and the taking up again of the putrid remains to ensure the fertility of crops.[53] Both these articles found their way in more or less unaltered form into *Mythology and Monuments*.

The material she had collected for *Mythology and Monuments* was also used for further University Extension lectures. The personal interest she took in gifted students is illustrated by a collection of letters to one Miss Marshall, who had been constrained to drop out of an earlier series of lectures by ill health. Some seventeen letters to Miss Marshall have been preserved, giving encouragement, advice, and help. She generously invited Miss Marshall to visit her in her flat ('I think an hour's talk would do more to set your work going than much writing').[54] On 11 July 1889 she wrote to Miss Marshall that

---

[48] *Classical Review*, 3 (1889), 378.   [49] Ibid. 187.   [50] MacColl, 'Jane Harrison'.

[51] James Theodore Bent, *The Cyclades: or, Life Among the Insular Greeks* (London: Longmans, Green and Co., 1885). His collection of artefacts which he donated to the British Museum now form the nucleus of their Cycladic collection.   [52] *Myths of the Odyssey*, 122.

[53] See Andrew Lang, *Myth, Ritual and Religion*, 2 vols. (London: Longmans, Green and Co., 1913; 1st pub. 1887), ii. 288.

[54] JEH to Miss Marshall, 31 Dec. 1888, box 8.

she would probably be away for most of the winter in the Engadine. She had delegated the task of returning to Athens for further photographs for *Mythology and Monuments* to Walter Leaf, formerly senior classic and Fellow of Trinity College, Cambridge.[55] The strain of lecturing and the intensity of her work on the current book, especially all the stress caused by the illustrations, was bringing her to breaking point. A major disappointment at the end of 1888 had also added to her difficulties.

In October 1888 she had applied for the Yates Professorship of Classical Archaeology[56] at the University of London, which became vacant on the resignation of Sir Charles Newton. Her application was supported by testimonials from a wide variety of eminent academics.[57] Arthur Sidgwick, who had attended a course of lectures she had given at Oxford 'some few years ago', praised her 'fluency, clearness and good taste', and the lucid arrangement of material, 'full of matter and instruction'. He noted above all that

she has that combination of qualities so rare and so difficult to analyse, which attracts and stimulates, and detains the interest and attention of her hearers. . . . She has great enthusiasm for her subject and much force of presentment; and at the same time successfully avoids that common danger of lecturers who have the gift of speech—especially lecturers on art—a tendency, namely, to high-flown and overloaded phrases: her style is at once forcible, stimulating and unpretentious.[58]

Of her other referees, Arthur Verrall was obviously aware of one of the obstacles that stood in the way of her election. While acknowledging that in the Tripos examinations she had merited a place only at the top of the

---

[55] Walter Leaf (1852–1927) is best known for his edition of the *Iliad*, published in 1886–8. He collaborated with Jane Harrison in her lecturing in London in 1890.

[56] It is worth pointing out that in 1888 the word 'archaeology' was used in a slightly different sense than it is today. Whereas we think of archaeology as excavation, in the nineteenth century it was closer to its etymological meaning and included much that we would subsume under the category of 'classical studies' e.g. art history, religion, mythology.

[57] Testimonials were submitted by Ernest Babelon, Director of the Bibliothèque Nationale, Paris; Otto Benndorf, Professor of Archaeology, University of Vienna; Henry Craik, Secretary to the Scotch Education Department; Ernst Curtius, Professor of Archaeology, University of Berlin; Richard Garnett, Keeper of the Printed Books, British Museum; Henry Jackson, Fellow and Praelector in Ancient Philosophy, Trinity College, Cambridge; Wilhelm Klein, Professor of Archaeology, University of Prague; Walter Leaf, Trinity College, Cambridge; E. Maunde Thompson, Principal Librarian, British Museum; Luigi Milani, Director of the Archaeological Museum, Florence; Arthur Sidgwick, Fellow and Tutor of Corpus Christi College, Oxford; Henry Sidgwick, Praelector in Moral Philosophy, Trinity College, Cambridge; A. W. Verrall, Fellow of Trinity College, Cambridge; and Paul Wolters of the Kaiserlich Deutsches Archäologisches Institut in Athens. Copies are preserved in the Newnham College Archives.

[58] Arthur Sidgwick, testimonial, JHA.

second class, he noted that her early training had been 'necessarily unsuitable' and that the examination gave no scope to her special faculties. Realizing that her command of the classical languages was liable to be questioned, he testified to her 'prudence in dealing with evidence' and 'clearness of perception', which he avowed would keep her from avoidable error, 'even if her linguistic knowledge were far less' than in fact it was, adding that 'if her work had been liable to injury from inaccuracy or insufficient knowledge of the language concerned, I could not have failed to discover the fact; and I can warrant that, in this respect, she is well-equipped for her work.' On the other hand, her candidature for a professorship of archaeology was weakened by her lack of formal training in archaeology. The testimonials of European archaeologists sought to dispel any such concern. They praised her books and acknowledged her as a colleague in their field.

Harrison was one of two candidates who reached the short list. The committee had no hesitation in placing her ahead of Lewis Farnell and others, noting Harrison's 'large attainments, her enthusiasm in the study to which she has given herself, her unselfish devotion to the pursuit of knowledge and her singular success in imparting that knowledge to her hearers' and recognized that 'her claims were of the very highest order, and would indeed have been irresistible (the question of her sex being supposed to be set aside) but for the competition of a candidate of European reputation in the person of R[eginald] S[tuart] Poole'. Poole, Keeper of Coins in the British Museum, had a wider knowledge of archaeology than Harrison, being an Egyptologist and an expert in Oriental archaeology as well as that of Greece and Rome. He was also an authority in numismatics. They had therefore no hesitation in recommending Poole. It was unfortunate for Harrison that in the last stages of the competition her rival was also her friend and senior colleague at the British Museum, since the situation involved some of her strongest supporters in a conflict of interest: Sir Charles Newton, for example, was bound to support Poole. None the less, they recommended that Harrison's gifts as a teacher should be recognized, and that she should occasionally give lectures for the appointed professor.

However, a minority report was also tabled:

The undersigned disagree with that part of the report which recommends that the Professor of Archaeology should be assisted by Miss Harrison. They think it undesirable that any teaching in University College be conducted by a woman.

E. S. Beesly

G. D. Thane[59]

---

[59]   See Minutes of the Committee, held in the archives of the Library of University College, London (AM/C/216 and AM/D/52). William Calder III discusses this election and the subse-

It has been argued that herein lies the real reason for Harrison's failure.[60] The *Women's Penny Paper*, in an interview with Harrison, reported the rumour that 'it was said at the time by those who knew that her only disqualification was that she was a woman.'[61] Any such discrimination may have been indirect. The terms of the professorship included the possibility of leave being granted for the purpose of 'archaeological research'. Though Harrison protested that her greatest desire was to engage in practical excavation, the regulations of the British School at Athens did not permit women either to reside at the school or to work on the excavations.[62] In other words, any objection to her appointment may have been based on practical difficulties rather than outright gender discrimination. But, as William M. Calder cogently argues, the reason that the committee selected Poole was simply that he was the better candidate.[63] Harrison's disappointment was intense. That the successful candidate was a personal friend must have made the situation doubly difficult.

The severe breathlessness she was experiencing at this time was the recurrence of an ailment she had first known as a student at Cheltenham, when she had been troubled by a cough and had to wear a respirator. The physician who had treated her when younger believed the root problem to be nervousness. Now it was suspected that she suffered from a weakness in her lungs, and a rest cure in Switzerland was prescribed. In retrospect, the evidence seems to point to childhood rheumatic fever, which may have left her with a leaky heart valve.[64] Certainly, later in life her heart was to give her a great deal of trouble. However, the continuing problems with the illustrations kept her in England through the summer of 1889, although she did manage to leave London, where the air was suspected of being especially bad, and retired with her work to Broadstairs. Finally, at the end of September, she was able to leave for Switzerland.

quent one in 1896 in detail in William M. Calder III (ed.), 'Jane Harrison's Failed Candidacies for the Yates Professorship (1888, 1896): What Did Her Colleagues Think of Her?' in *The Cambridge Ritualists Reconsidered*, 37–59. Although I find Calder's arguments for the superiority of the successful candidates convincing, he downplays the role of gender discrimination as a contributing factor.

[60] See Peacock, *Mask and Self*, 90: 'her expertise could not conquer the fears of those who questioned the wisdom of granting the distinguished professorship to a woman. In addition, the hidebound world of classical scholarship had no room for innovative thinking.'

[61] *Women's Penny Paper*, 44 / 1 (24 Aug. 1889).

[62] JEH to Henry Babington Smith, 31 Oct. 1889, Trinity College Archives, Cambridge, HBS 73 93; Helen Waterhouse, *The British School at Athens*, 132.

[63] Calder, 'Jane Harrison's Failed Candidacies', 37–59.

[64] For assistance in evaluating Harrison's medical history, I am grateful to Dr Arnold Andersen of the University of Iowa.

Whether or not her ailment was correctly diagnosed, the treatment agreed with her, and she looked back with considerable pleasure on her three months at St Moritz, skiing, tobogganing, and dancing. Hope Mirrlees tells us coyly that 'she also kept a warm memory of a . . . Mr Macnaughton, who was there for his lungs (he died) & was in love with her'. She returned to England in January of 1890, unexpectedly, for reasons unspecified. As for her health, she could write to Macmillan, 'I have come back like a lion!'[65]

She immediately resumed her lecturing, offering a course of ten lectures on 'Athens: its Mythology and Art' with her own forthcoming *Mythology and Monuments of Athens* serving as a primary text. She also recommended for 'thorough mastery' *A Manual of Mythology* by Maxime Collignon, a book she herself had just finished translating and enlarging. Collignon's book, strictly devoted to mythology as seen in art, deals with an area of study 'so new in England that we have not yet invented for it so much as a convenient name. French writers use the happy and expressive term *"mythologie figurée"*; Germans have adopted the more convenient word *Mythography*'.[66] Harrison concludes the preface with the prophecy that not many years would elapse before 'mythography' became part of the discipline of every classical scholar. It was in fact nearly a hundred years before the subject was to be taken up again. In fact, the methodology currently being articulated as a new approach is exactly that expounded and practised by Harrison.[67]

This series of lectures was followed by one in the autumn, which she taught jointly with Andrew Lang, on 'Homeric Greece and the Myths of the Homeric Cycle'.[68] The division of the course may well have been occasioned by an invitation from the University of Cambridge which was to bear some import for the future.

With the publication of *Mythology and Monuments* she had finally made her mark as a classical scholar. In the summer of 1890 some of the members

<hr/>

[65] JEH to Macmillan, 4 Jan. 1890, Macmillan archives, 204/192.

[66] Maxime Collignon, *A Manual of Mythology in Relation to Greek Art*, translated and enlarged by Jane E. Harrison (London: Grevel, 1890), p. iii. The topic was pioneered by G. E. Lessing in *Laokoon: oder über die Grenzen der Malerei und Poesie* ('On the Limits of Painting and Poetry') in 1766.

[67] See Lowell Edmunds (ed.), Approaches to Greek Myth (Baltimore: Johns Hopkins University Press, 1990) and Schlesier, 'Prolegomena to Jane Harrison's Interpretation of Ancient Greek Religion', 192–4. For a recent treatment of this topic see Anthony M. Snodgrass, *Homer and the Artists: Text and Picture in Early Greek Art* (Cambridge: Cambridge University Press, 1998). Andrew Stewart, reviewing this book (*TLS*, 28 May 1999) cites Harrison and notes that Snodgrass omits any reference to her or Lessing.

[68] Walter Leaf and Jane Harrison, Syllabus for lecture series on Homeric Greece and the Myths of the Homeric Cycle: [London] University Extension Lectures, JHA.

of Newnham College raised the possibility of inviting her to Cambridge to give a course of lectures, and furthermore to have these lectures recognized by the Classical Board and delivered not at Newnham, but in the Archaeology Lecture Room (fondly known as the 'Ark'). It was agreed that Harrison should be paid five guineas per lecture and that a fee of half a guinea should be charged for tickets. The plan met with approval and in October she delivered a course of lectures on classical archaeology, especially in connection with vase painting. They were largely attended by members of the university as well as by students of Newnham and Girton. It was duly noted that Miss Harrison was the first woman to have lectured in the university buildings.

Then in the summer of 1891 a turn of events brought her, emotionally, to a complete halt. The details are clouded by the reserve and innuendo with which the other players in the drama referred to the episode after Harrison's death. She herself never spoke of it, not even to Hope Mirrlees, despite her friend's assiduous attempts to coax out the truth. A correspondence between D. S. MacColl and Alice (Lloyd) Dew-Smith in the 1940s indicates that something memorable happened, without being explicit. A published poem by MacColl would in addition seem to fit the circumstances exactly and can be read as further evidence.

The scene was the seaside town of Camber, where it appears MacColl, his sisters, and his mother had rented a house for the summer, while Jane Harrison and Alice Lloyd stayed at the William the Conqueror Inn across the inlet at Rye Harbour. Reconstructing the events from the scanty evidence would suggest perhaps two incidents. The first is that MacColl became ill. A poem entitled 'Ex Voto: Camber, June 1891' evokes the terror of delirium, followed by a rebirth to health and the tenderness of ministrations of women.[69] Secondly, according to Hope Mirrlees, at some time he proposed marriage to Harrison, and she turned him down. This is probably the occasion. Like Harrison herself, MacColl was not given to speaking of these things in later years, admitting only that his friendship with Jane Harrison, 'a woman of so rich a nature and fine a culture . . . entailed desperate sentimental misunderstanding.'[70] Alongside this we may well place his little poem, 'Twain':

> Two hearts! They had the world at will
> But one of them mistook:

[69]   See 'Ex Voto: Camber, 1891' in D. S. MacColl, *Poems* (Oxford: Blackwell, 1940), 43–8.
[70]   MacColl, 'Jane Harrison'.

> So her's [*sic*] is somewhere in her still,
> And mine is in a book.[71]

Why, if he proposed to her, did she turn down his offer of marriage? When one reflects that until the era of contraceptives marriage included the bearing and raising of a family, one can discern various reasons for her decision. Her own experience of family life had left her with a violent distaste for domesticity, and a somewhat irrational dislike of children in general (though of particular children she could be delightfully fond). Her work must have been a major consideration. Although it is true that married women could, and did, continue teaching at Newnham (one thinks of Margaret Verrall and Mary Paley), Harrison's work was her research, and she needed to be free to travel. But there was a deeper reason. Soon after she had first gone to London a doctor had told her that she could never bear a child without endangering her own life (presumably because of the problems she was experiencing with her heart and lungs).[72] This reminder of how her own birth had led to the death of her mother must have been peculiarly poignant. Apparently on hearing this news she vowed she would never marry. Moreover, she may still have nursed feelings for Henry Butcher, who seems to have reciprocated her affection, despite the fact that he was married to another. Mirrlees quotes Harrison as saying that in fact, after Butcher's marriage, she never seriously contemplated marriage to anyone else. Instead she decided that for the future she must eliminate passion from her life and be satisfied with close friendships based on work. This decision, according to Mirrlees, was to shape the whole future of her life.

Alice (Lloyd) Dew-Smith's correspondence with MacColl corroborates such an interpretation of their relationship. She wrote to him,

As for Jane, my memory tells me (perhaps wrongly) that her passionate friendships were for S. H. Butcher; you; Gilbert Murray; & F. Cornford—all of whom were brilliant intellectuals. One can't imagine Jane liking a fool—even if he were as beautiful as Apollo. And I still feel brains played a major part in your attractions. But thinking it over I think I realised that she 'fell in love' with you all—but that she was more in love with her work than with any of you—& that she would not have married any of you (that were available) as it w. have interfered with her work. It was a case of:

> I cannot love you, dear, so well
> Loved I not stone men more—[73]

---

[71] MacColl, *Poems*, 29.

[72] Mirrlees's draft biography mentions the diagnosis of a fibrous tumour as the cause of this warning.

[73] Alice Dew-Smith to DSM, 2 May 1944 MS MacColl S218.

Her own account is similar. Rationalizing at the age of 76 she wrote:

By what miracle I escaped marriage I do not know, for all my life long I fell in love. But on the whole, I am glad. I do not doubt that I lost much, but I am quite sure I gained more. Marriage, for a woman at least, hampers the two things that made life glorious to me—friendship and learning. In man it was always the friend, not the husband, that I wanted.[74]

There is probably some genuine self-knowledge here. Her attachment to her male friends was passionate, and if she had disavowed marriage she nevertheless somehow expected these friendships with men to be exclusive. She presumed (without foundation) that each of these friends would share her single-minded, over-focused concentration on her research. Then there was an enthusiasm, an energy, an élan in her personality that was contagious and provocatively attractive. But if her vow of sublimation was a noble one, it was one that her male friends were not likely to understand.

Whatever the details of events that summer, exhausted and depressed she gave up lecturing. Perhaps for a second time MacColl was moved by compassion to ease her pain by supporting her academic career, and agreed (if it was not his idea in the first place) to collaborate on a book which would bring together 'choice examples of Greek vase painting which hitherto have been accessible in no handy form and at no moderate cost'. It was difficult for art historians to study Greek vases because they were currently scattered in different periodicals. Edward Burne-Jones had been urging her to produce a book to meet this need. She wrote to Macmillan on 13 December proposing a large folio, containing about a hundred plates, five in colour, ten from original photographs, and the remaining from existing plates, accompanied by a very brief explanatory text.

Macmillan accepted, and *Greek Vase Paintings* was published in 1894, subtitled 'A Selection of Examples with Preface, Introduction and Descriptions by J. E. Harrison & D. S. MacColl'.[75] Despite the conjunction of her name with MacColl's, the book is Harrison's, at least in content. MacColl contributed the four pages of preface, and was also responsible for the cover design and binding. As he explained,

Burne Jones was to have written a preface, but by that time he was disaffected by what they called my 'impressionism', & W. B. Richmond was wrathful over my cover design, based on vase material, but an anticipation also of later 'abstract' & other departures. Beardsley modified his art on seeing the broad blacks, as well as firm lines

[74] *Reminiscences*, 88.
[75] *Greek Vase Paintings: a Selection of Examples* (London: T. Fisher Unwin, 1894).

of the vases, and it may be that the cover entitles me to count among the many grand-fathers of Picasso.[76]

A lavish volume, it was greeted as 'a happy idea'.[77] 'Such a work was needed', wrote the reviewer in the *Athenaeum*, since many of the finest vases are housed throughout the public and private collections of Europe, 'and the artist, therefore, possesses in this volume such a representation of Greek vase painting as he could only acquire by much travelling or very costly bookbuying'.[78] The reviewer was sensitive to Harrison's concerns, for he noted that

perhaps the most interesting pages relate to the interpretation of mythology on vases, where she discusses the artists' treatment of the myths of Odysseus and the ram, the sirens, and the judgment of Paris, with familiar insight, and shows how widely apart the Odyssey stories are from the corresponding representations on the vases. The vase painter was no mere illustrator: "he did not sit down and get some one to recite the Odyssey passage to him, and then translate it into a picture" but worked from independent traditions, and manipulated his materials in accordance with his sense of fitness and harmony.

To the reviewer in the *Nation*, 'it seems to sum up in a brief, comprehensive way, all the latest knowledge in this controverted branch of the history of ancient art'.[79] As to the reproduction of the plates, Harrison seems at last to have satisfied her reviewers. The large format of the book, though cumbersome, allowed the representation of the vases in all their clearness and beauty, said the *Athenaeum*. The *Illustrated London News* praised the 'sumptuous folio' which recalled the publications of the Dilettante Society, and declared the illustrations 'admirable'.[80]

The next few years brought loss: 1894 witnessed the deaths of three people who, each in a different way, had been important to her. Some time that year her father died. Nothing survives that records her response to his death, but it is reasonable to suppose that she met it with some feelings of ambivalence. She had been distant from her family, geographically and emotionally, ever since she left home twenty years previously.[81] Her northern

[76] MacColl, 'Jane Harrison'.

[77] R. A. M. Stevenson, 'Greek Vase Painting', *The Art Journal*, NS 57 (1894), 208–9.

[78] Anonymous review, 'Fine Arts', *Athenaeum*, 20 Oct. 1894, 533–5.

[79] Anonymous review, *Nation* (NY), 24 May 1894, 394–5.

[80] Anonymous review, *Illustrated London News*, 28 July 1894, 118.

[81] Sandra Peacock (in *Mask and Self*) claims *passim* that Harrison's relationship with her father was always close. Similarly, Thomas Africa ('Aunt Glegg among the Dons, or Taking Jane Harrison at her Word' in Calder (ed.), *The Cambridge Ritualists Reconsidered*, 24) refers to Harrison as the 'darling daughter of a doting widower'. However, I can find no evidence for

upbringing would have trained her to 'thole' the pain.[82] Sir Charles Newton, who had been her mentor and in that sense a sort of spiritual father to her, died on 28 November. But the most devastating loss was the death of Henry Butcher's sister, Eleanor. Of Eleanor's friends Jane was the closest, the two women having shared with each other similar emotional burdens. Eleanor had been recovering in a nursing home from what had appeared to be a successful operation which Harrison had urged her to go ahead with. Her death came suddenly, after an afternoon of receiving visitors.[83]

At this time she was particularly attracted by a book on Greek beliefs about the afterlife, by the German Erwin Rohde, which she reviewed for the *Classical Review*.[84] Rohde argued that Homer, who is usually taken as a starting point for Greek religion, represents a 'break' in the mythological tradition. Nowhere is this break more clearly seen than in his beliefs about life after death. The fundamental belief, held by primitive people in many parts of the world, is that the ghost of the deceased haunts his tomb, and must be appeased by 'an elaborate cultus of the dead, hero-worship, and the whole apparatus of a faith that recognises the power of the departed soul'. Homer, on the other hand, speaks of 'a psyche, a shade, which on leaving the body goes away to a place apart, and which once gone, has no power over the living'. However, even in Homer Rohde thought he could detect 'survivals' of the earlier, prevalent practices. Rohde's observations became the keystone of Harrison's research methods. 'So long as the mythologist insists on beginning with the poetic and ultimately orthodox Olympian system,' she wrote, 'so long will he work with the cart before the horse and any intelligible sequence be impossible.'

Rohde's investigations into the possible origins of belief in the immortality of the soul touched Harrison at another level. Rohde found in the

---

such a relationship after Charles Harrison's remarriage when Jane was 5 years old. Peacock and Africa rest their case on Freudian theory alone.

[82] See, for example, her transparently autobiographical remark about children and a parent's remarriage: 'If the father is a man who cares for truth, . . . he will perhaps say, "Everything *is* different. In the old days, when life left *me* cold and desolate, *you* were the focus, the fire at which I warmed my frozen hands. On my hearth a new fire is lit now, by the side of which your flame is pale and cold. By it you cannot stand. Face facts. You are young. Go out into the cold and rain, make for yourself no false shelter; for my sake and for yours, flinch as little as may be." And the girl, if she is wise and brave, accepts the inevitable. She will stretch out no appealing hand; she will silence the reproach upon her lips' ('Homo Sum', in *Alpha and Omega*, 96–7).

[83] Mirrlees's draft biography.

[84] Erwin Rohde, *Psyche: Seelenculte und Unsterblichkeitsglaube der Griechen*, 2 vols. (Freiburg: Mohr, vol. i, 1890; vol. ii, 1894). The reviews of the two parts of Rohde's book appear in *Classical Review*, 4 (1890), 376–7; and 8 (1894), 165–6.

worship of Dionysos, or Bacchus, 'the touchstone of any religion worth the name, the keystone of spirituality' so lacking in the worship of the other Olympians. The goal of the worshippers of Bacchus was no less than that of union with the god. The worshippers,

in furious exaltation and divine inspiration, strive after the god; they seek communion with him. They burst the physical barriers of their soul. A magic power takes hold of them; they feel themselves raised high above the level of their everyday existence; they seem to *become* those spiritual beings who wildly dance in the train of the god. Nay, more, they have a share in the life of the god himself.[85]

The key elements of the religion of Bacchus are *ecstasy* and its correlative, *askesis*. Ecstasy means, literally, 'standing outside oneself' with the religious sense of the soul being 'liberated from the cramping prison of the body'; *askesis* 'training', the preparation of the soul. 'To dance till we are dizzy, to toss our heads in ecstasy,' as did the Bacchae, 'may not seem the best means of promoting spirituality, but to any one who has watched either the dancing or the howling dervishes at work the whole faith becomes historically intelligible', she claimed. That the worshipper has actually become divine is attested to by the fact that at the close of the dance he has miraculous powers. These ideas of Rohde became seminal for Harrison's *Themis*, published eighteen years later.[86] The importance to her of Rohde, however, went beyond the intellectual stimulus. As always, she read with emotional commitment. 'What we think about Greek religion affects what we think about everything else', she was later to write. 'The mind is not made in water-tight compartments.'[87] Rohde's conception of spirituality became a model for her own, and parallel to her writing on the religion of the Greeks can be discerned the development of a personal spiritual quest, which for the rest of her life she sought to bring into line with the latest in sociological and psychological research. At this particular juncture, Rohde's exposition of asceticism resonated with the emotional void of her experience.

About the same time she began to see clearly the direction that her research would need to take her. In 1892, her friend and former student Katherine Raleigh published a translation of A. H. Petiscus's *The Gods of Olympos: or, Mythology of the Greeks and Romans*[88] and Harrison obliged with a

---

[85] Erwin Rohde, *Psyche: the Cult of Souls and Belief in Immortality Among the Greeks* (London: Routledge & Keegan Paul, 1950), trans. W. B. Hillis from the 8th edn. (London: Routledge & Kegan Paul, 1950), 258–60.   [86] See *Themis*, esp. 47–8.

[87] *Themis: a Study of the Social Origins of Greek Religion* (Cambridge: Cambridge University Press, 1912), p. xxii.

[88] A. H. Petiscus, *The Gods of Olympos*, trans. Katherine A. Raleigh (London: T. Fisher Unwin, 1892).

preface. Petiscus's book, written in 1863 and intended for elementary students, presented traditional material as established fact, distasteful to Harrison who was always more interested in the newest discoveries and theories. Whereas it was sufficient for the elementary student to be familiar with established facts, the teacher, she believed, should be aware of the current state of scholarship and know that 'the gods as they appeared in Homer are not the primary imaginations of the gifted Greek, have not sprung, like Athene, full armed from the creative brain, but are the late and literary stage of a long evolution. Poseidon, it is whispered, was not originally the god of the sea; Artemis and Apollo had originally nothing to do with each other; the marriage of Zeus and Hera was a latter-day thing.'[89] In her preface Harrison gives a critique of the state of mythological research in the 1890s and states her own position. Max Müller's theory that myth is a 'disease of language', with myths evolving from a misunderstanding of names, and the 'cosmical' method whereby a god is reduced to a single natural phenomenon, fail to account for all the evidence; the 'folklore' or anthropological method, espoused by Andrew Lang and J. G. Frazer[90] was likewise inadequate, although she saw a substantial soundness in the comparative approach. It 'leaves us with the beginning of things, with certain primitive elementary conceptions, and takes no heed of the complex structure reared on the simple base. The seductive simplicity of the "Corn-mother" and the "Tree-spirit", and worst of all, the ever-impending "Totem" is almost as perilous as the old Sun and Moon snare.' In the place of these failed methodologies Harrison proposes another 'so complex, so difficult, that [the mythologist] may well shrink'. He must discover the links in the chain from primitive demons and spirits to the gods of Olympos.

It is not enough for him to hint airily that Dionysos may have been a bull or a tree, that Apollo may take his choice between a dog, a wolf, and a mouse . . . what he must do, or fail, is to trace each Saga to its local home, to carry out the work that the great H. D. Müller [*sic*: Karl Otfried Müller is meant][91] began before his time, to disentangle the 'confederacy of local cults' from which the ultimate Olympian assembly was evolved.[92]

[89] Jane Ellen Harrison, Preface to *The Gods of Olympos*, p. vii.

[90] Presumably by the time she wrote this she had read Frazer's *The Golden Bough* (1890). However, Robert Ackerman observes 'Jane Ellen Harrison: the Early Work', *Greek, Roman, and Byzantine Studies*, 13 (1972), 209–31, 'what she must have gained from Frazer was not the crucial connection between myth and ritual, for she had that already in 1890 in *Mythology and Monuments*, but the comparison between Greek religion and "savage" folklore. . . . [B]y the early nineties Miss Harrison had been persuaded of the basic worth of the anthropological approach; what she had now to do was to become enough of an anthropologist to employ it' (p. 228).

[91] The correction is made by Ackerman, 'Harrison: The Early Work', 229.

[92] Preface to *The Gods of Olympos*, p. vi.

In stating the problem in these terms she thus combined what to her mind was sound in the 'folklore' method with the dawning realization, articulated by Rohde, that the origins of Greek religion are not to be found in Homer. If Petiscus's approach was 'safe', integrity demanded that her own research be dangerous, and reflection on the contrast spurred her to chart her own course. To what she here calls the 'tribal' method she was to devote the next ten years of her life. However, as she became increasingly absorbed in the task she grew more and more committed to one particular outcome of her researches and never again was she to write with such detachment about the comparative merits of different approaches to the interpretation of myth.

In 1891 Henry Butcher had published a volume entitled *Some Aspects of the Greek Genius*[93] containing an essay on 'The Melancholy of the Greeks', which not only echoes some of the tenets which Harrison espoused during this period, but also perhaps puts into words some of her own experience of these dark years. From the beginning she had always read her own experience into Greek literature, and the passages from Homer, Pindar, Mimnermus, and Euripides that Butcher singles out must have captured her feelings with peculiar poignancy.[94] Against the popular view of the Greeks as radiant men and women secure in the serenity of their rational thought, he underlines those other moods and sentiments in which 'we may catch many plaintive tones and some accents even of despair'. And how should we who live respond? Butcher concludes by quoting Pindar: 'Forasmuch as men must die, wherefore should one sit vainly in the dark through a dull and nameless age, and without lot in noble deeds?'[95]

The publication of further articles and reviews in the next couple of years helped to dispel the spectre of a 'dull and nameless age'. In 1895 she returned to Athens to examine the progress of the excavations, and to Delphi where excavations were now under way. The Director of the French excavations, Théophile Homolle, conducted her all over the site, and to her delight she found archaeological evidence to support a nascent thesis she was beginning to formulate about the early development of Greek cults. This visit had important consequences for her career a few years later, when she published

---

[93] S. H. Butcher, *Some Aspects of the Greek Genius* (London: Macmillan, 1891).

[94] To Harrison, now in her forties, Mimnermus would have spoken most eloquently when he linked the generations of leaves to the passing of youth. To Pindar, man is 'the dream of a shadow'. Euripides, always Harrison's favourite poet, is 'saturated with a profound feeling for human suffering, human ignorance, human infirmity. In him, if anywhere in Greek tragedy, *Sunt lacrimae rerum*' (literally, 'There are tears for things'; the poignancy of the Latin is untranslatable).

[95] Pind. xvii. 446–7, quoted Butcher, *Some Aspects of the Greek Genius*, 176.

her conclusions in an article in the *Journal of Hellenic Studies*[96] and gave a lecture in Cambridge. No diary of this journey to Greece survives, and of her travels only one incident has been chronicled. In Athens she met Samuel Butler. It was their second encounter.

In 1892 Butler had given a lecture at the Working Men's College, Great Ormond Street, and Harrison and the three Butcher sisters had been in the audience. She was shocked by his irreverence. The topic was 'The Humour of Homer', and Butler's thesis was that the interest of the *Odyssey* lies 'mainly in the fact of a bald elderly gentleman, whose little remaining hair is red, being eaten out of house and home during his absence by a number of young men who are courting his supposed widow—a widow who, if she be fair and fat, can hardly be less than forty.' The lecture met with vicious reviews, one of which, published anonymously, caught the eye by its caption: 'How to Vulgarize Homer'. Butler immediately suspected Harrison, whose glowering face had not escaped his notice during the lecture. 'I think most people will see that it is by an angry woman', he countered.[97]

Seeing that 'odious woman' in his hotel in Athens, Butler went up to her and reintroduced himself. He recalled,

She was still sore about the lecture and I apologised, reminding her that I had had to keep a room full of working-men in good humour.

'Besides,' I added, 'you chastised me quite severely enough at the time.'

'Was I rude?'

'Yes', said I, laughing, 'very rude'.

So we made it up and smoked a couple of cigarettes. We dined together during the rest of my stay in Athens, and I tried to ingratiate myself with her, but it was rather up-hill work, and I shall never be genuinely forgiven.[98]

She spent the summers of 1895 and 1896 in France with MacColl, his sister Lizzie, and Roger Fry, enjoying the new sport of bicycling. Roger Fry found Harrison with her masculine mind 'quite apostolic'.[99] Meanwhile, in the summer of 1895 MacColl's attention was riveted by a young woman named Andrée Zabé whom he met on a beach in Normandy where she was on holiday with her family, and he resolved to make her his wife.

Of the second summer MacColl remembered, 'J.E.H. made herself

[96] 'Delphika', *Journal of Hellenic Studies*, 19 (1899), 205–51.

[97] See Peter Raby, *Samuel Butler: a Biography* (London: Hogarth Press, 1991), 241–2.

[98] Ibid. 258.

[99] Letter from Roger Fry to R. C. Trevelyan, 15 Aug. 1895, published in *The Letters of Roger Fry*, ed. Denys Sutton (London: Chatto & Windus, 1972). The 'Apostles' were a select club of the social and intellectual elite among Cambridge undergraduates.

conspicuous by wearing silk breeches and a Bishop's apron (the garb was the latest fashion and she was proud of her legs) . . . I had to ward off a small riot of French bystanders at the Gare St Lazare.'[100] On this occasion Fry and Harrison returned to Dieppe, while MacColl and his sister travelled to Paris to visit Andrée Zabé's parents. The imminent loss of her closest friend moved one step closer to reality.

By now her work was receiving scholarly recognition. She had been made a corresponding member of the Berlin Archaeological Institute and served on the council of the Hellenic Society. Then, on 30 March 1895, on the strength of her lectures and publications on Greek mythology and art she received the distinction of an honorary LLD from the University of Aberdeen. It was noted by the press that the occasion marked an epoch in the annals of the university, the first occasion in the four centuries of the university's history that the degree had been conferred on a woman. Not only was it an honour for Harrison herself; it was also 'a compliment to the young lady undergraduates who have now obtained a footing at King's College on a level with their sterner fellow-students. The authorities could not have more fittingly indicated their sympathy with the new movement for opening up the University to women than by offering the degree of LL.D. to Miss Harrison.'[101] (Two years later the University of Durham was to confer on her an honorary D.Litt. in recognition of 'one who as a student of classical Archaeology and interpreter of Greek Art has made for herself a reputation which will last as long as any interest in Hellenic monuments and legends or any memory of the past glories of Athens lives in the minds of men'.)[102] When in 1896 the Yates Chair again fell vacant on the death of Reginald Stuart Poole, with high hopes she applied.

Of the six applicants, only she and one other, Ernest A. Gardner, met the criteria for the position, which now included an expertise in classical studies as a first requirement. On this occasion, the issue of gender was brought to the fore before any decision was made between the two shortlisted candidates. It was unanimously agreed that the committee should decide on merit alone. Several members were in fact in favour of appointing a woman. When the two candidates were interviewed, Harrison's comparative weak-

<hr />

[100]   DSM to Jessie Stewart, 1 Nov. 1943. MacColl's memory was inaccurate as to the date: he attributed this occasion to 1905.

[101]   *Press and Journal* (Aberdeen), 1 Apr. 1895.

[102]   This quotation is taken from a cutting in the Jane Harrison Archives, Newnham College: *Newcastle Daily*—(the paper is torn), 27 Sept. 1897. The ceremony was held at Newcastle. It is noteworthy that this account gives a list of all the distinguished men in attendance, followed by the observation that 'There was a large gathering of fashionably dressed ladies'.

ness in Roman archaeology and Latin authors became apparent, and Ernest
Gardner won the nomination on account of the breadth of his knowledge of
the ancient world.[103] One of his strongest claims lay in his teaching record as
Director of the British School at Athens.

Harrison now felt that all chances of a university appointment were lost.
That it should have been Ernest Gardner who defeated her added to her bitterness. He was what she contemptuously referred to as a 'sound scholar',
conservative in his views, preferring a position that had stood the test of time
to the latest hypothesis.

MacColl's marriage to Andrée Zabé in 1897 brought on a depression that
again took her close to breaking-point (a pattern that was to repeat itself
in her life some ten years later). He remained her friend to the end of her
life, but after his marriage she could never feel that things were the same.
She began to hate marriage, seeing it as what she called 'le grand égotisme
à deux'. She could not allow herself to face the unalterable truth that her
single life of scholarship had been bought at a high price: an aching void of
loneliness. From this point on, broken only by a couple of years when the
writing of *Themis* brought her satisfaction, her experience was played over
this haunting ground bass.

In 1898 she turned down an invitation from Miss Beale to lecture at
Cheltenham, pleading the difficulty she found in fitting teaching into her
research, as she found the two states of mind antagonistic. She had already
committed herself to a series of lectures on Delphi at the Passmore Edwards
Institute in Bloomsbury, in which she propounded a universal evolution
from a primitive matriarchal order, in which the mother was the head of the
family and the earth goddess the centre of worship, to the later patriarchal
order.[104]

An article in the *Edinburgh Review* gathers all the emotion of these years as
Harrison reviews a number of recent publications by Mannhardt, Ridgeway
and others that in different ways testified to Greek beliefs about death. It was
from reading Mannhardt that she lost the last flicker of any personal faith;
confronted with the loss of nearly everything that made life meaningful
to her, she now faced the implications. Her article, 'The Sculptured Tombs
of Hellas', seeks to relate funeral monuments to the art and thought that

---

[103] See Calder, 'Harrison's Failed Candidacies', 58.

[104] See *Englishwoman's Review*, 15 Apr. 1898. A synopsis of the lectures was also carried in *The
Times*, Feb.–Mar. 1898. For a contemporary reading of the same evidence from Delphi in more
recent years, written from a structuralist viewpoint, see Christiane Sourvinou-Inwood, 'Myth
as History: the Previous Owners of the Delphic Oracle' in Jan Bremmer (ed.), *Interpretations of
Greek Mythology* (London: Routledge, 1987), 215–41.

preceded them, but it passes beyond this stated aim to become a personal confession, an *apologia pro vita sua*.[105]

In 1861 the construction of a road between Athens and the Piraeus had lighted on a number of ancient 'stelae', or gravestones. Further discoveries followed and similar monuments from other parts of Greece had been collected, examined, and catalogued. Of the grave monuments she writes,

> They are as a class admirable examples of just those qualities we expect from the Greeks, dignity, restraint, good taste; as such they strike us by their contrast with the vulgarities of our own sepulchral monuments . . . We realise from the Attic stelae, with something of a shock of surprised pleasure, that [the Greek] . . . was more human than we thought him, he loved and even honoured wife and child. Moreover he contrives to touch us without any such squalid emotionalism as seems inseparable from the pathos of the modern stonemason. He achieves just what we would and cannot.

Harrison had seen enough of the work of the 'modern stonemason' of late, and characteristically, in her grief, found solace in the voice of the ancients, speaking across the years. Following William Ridgeway's ethnographical conclusions, argued in an article 'What People Produced the Objects Called Mycenaean?',[106] she found further evidence in sculpture for the 'two distinct currents of thought' that Rohde had claimed for Greek religion, for she discerned in the portrayals of sepulchral banquets a *contaminatio*, or conflation, of 'a banquet in Hades with offerings at the tomb made in the upper actual world', or of a Homeric picture of the afterlife with un-Homeric ancestor worship. Such a *contaminatio*, she states with the characteristic over-confidence that Ernest Gardner repudiated, is the *real* explanation of the scenes on the reliefs.

The article foreshadows what was to become a major part of *Prolegomena to the Study of Greek Religion*. She drew attention to the pictures of little black, winged ghosts, *eidola*, or *keres* on Athenian lekythoi, 'their gestures sometimes of entreaty and lament'. These are 'simply the reminiscence of the Homeric ghosts . . . the woeful piteous sprite of Patroklos and many another hero. At the grave we are none of us over-logical, and no Greek with his Homer in his head would query too strictly a *contaminatio* in art that found its answer in his own tangled convictions.' A discussion of the Lesche at Delphi, as described by Pausanias, but not yet—and still not yet—unearthed by archaeologists, leads to a recapitulation of her theories about

---

[105] Jane Harrison, 'The Sculptured Tombs of Hellas ', *Edinburgh Review*, 185 (1897), 441–64.
[106] William Ridgeway, 'What People Produced the Objects Called Mycenaean?', *Journal of Hellenic Studies* 16 (1896), 77–119.

Orpheus. There follows what can only be read, *mutatis mutandis*, as a commentary on her own spiritual journey. Turning from Ridgeway's 'Pelasgians' (the hypothesized autochthonous inhabitants of Athens) to the later Athenians she asks:

What echo is there of all that pictured certainty of the after-life, that fear of retribution, that hope, that certainty of divine communion, that Orpheus brought? . . . Bring the Athenians face to face with all these hopes and fears and faiths, add to them the great heritage of Pelasgian ancestor-worship, and we can only say that in their sepulchral monuments they 'renounced them all'. Nor is this a mere fancy based on the study of a small class of monuments. The final, the fullest commentary on these grave reliefs is the funeral oration of Perikles, and he speaks with no uncertain sound. He does not say with Plutarch 'to die is to be initiated into the greater mysteries;' he never even hints at a personal existence after death; the dead live only in the memory of their deeds. . . . Man, whatever Orpheus may say, is expressly forbidden to aspire after mystical communion and union with the gods—he may not seek to transcend the limits of his human personality.

She draws to a close by quoting from Butcher's volume of 1891:

In his beautiful chapter on 'The Melancholy of the Greeks', Professor Butcher dwells on the constitutional sadness of the Greek temperament. We find it already in Homer, and the source, to our minds, is the same as in the Attic stelae, the brave rationalism that looks on death simply as the end of life. 'Achilles knows his doom and accepts it; his one wish is that, seeing his span of life is slender, it might not be without honour.' The line sums up the spirit of the man, and, we may add, of the whole Hellenic race:—
'In death I shall die low, but now I would win goodly fame.'

But the final paragraph is all her own. Her prose reaches its heights as the grief of personal experience touches her scholarly criticism:

In Homer we have the pure Hellenic strain, with its instinct for rationalism; but the wonder is greater, the pathos more intimate, in the Attic stelae, fashioned in Pelasgian Athens, where Orphism was rife, and Plato the mystic taught; for it is the pathos of ancestral faith renounced, a heritage forgone.

The cadence of these words brings to a close another chapter of Harrison's life. At the age of 48, with academic hopes crushed, friends lost through death and through marriage, no consolation to be found in family or in faith, she stared bleakly at the future. At this point she received an invitation to return, under special conditions, to Newnham College.

5. Woman and Knowledge: Newnham 1898–1901

S HUT your eyes and what do you see of Newnham? I see the grounds with the double-blossom cherry trees all white, the red buildings with the undergraduate's libellous quip 'Queen Anne in front and Mary Anne at the back', the long corridors within, especially the ground-floor one in Clough because my first room was at the end and looked out on the garden. There was the Library with Jane Harrison's Charioteer at the entrance;[1] also Jane herself was on hand and you had to go down to dinner early for the privilege of sitting at her table, but it was worth it.[2]

Here [in Clough Hall], B. A. Clough's deep voice and endearing chuckle could be heard; the Swedish Miss Paues, as large in heart as in body, brought warmth into donnish contacts; and Jane Harrison with her originality and her penetration into the world of Ancient Greece brought glamour into scholarship. (There was a society for damming the Jordan, in my day. Miss Jordan, an earnest student, was monopolizing the seat next to Jane at dinner; Jane's admirers set out to thwart her and share out the honour. They had to get there early.)[3]

I first saw Jane Harrison when I went up to Newnham in '98. I had heard a great deal about her and she was one of the very few who come up to one's expectations. I was very shy and I found her brilliancy of appearance and the bantering vein of her talk a little overwhelming. She was so exhilarating and so much more alive than other people. One needed physical fitness and all one's wits to respond . . .

But I like best to remember her in the big arm-chair of her room on a Sunday morning. On fleeting visits to Cambridge when college days were past, she invited one for long, delightful talks. I can see her lighting a cigarette, crossing her knees, fumbling with rather helpless fingers in a heap of quotations and inscriptions, and prints of Greek vases pasted on loose sheets of paper—and the deep repose of the figure when once she settled down and gave one her mind.[4]

---

[1] The beautiful Yates Thompson Library, designed by Basil Champneys, had been built in 1897. A cast of the recently discovered Charioteer of Delphi stood outside.

[2] F. M. Brown (Sturton), quoted in Ann Phillips, *A Newnham Anthology* (Cambridge: Cambridge University Press, 1979), 47.

[3] F. M. Wilson, quoted ibid. 67–8.

[4] V[ictoria] de B[unsen], *Newnham College Letter*, Jan. 1929, 66.

Returning to Cambridge after the bitter events of the 1890s, Harrison determined to start life afresh. Rationalizing that MacColl's marriage was not after all such a great personal tragedy to her, since she had forsworn marriage and family life for herself, she vowed that from now on she would 'keep clear of passion' and throw all her energies into close friendships based on work.[5] She already had a circle of good friends to return to, and her work brought her into contact with other scholars who became vitally important to her, both academically and as friends. The intellectual environment was richly stimulating. She returned to an academic setting which included Henry Sidgwick,[6] the Jebbs,[7] the Verralls,[8] the Marshalls,[9] and the Darwin family.[10] (J. G. Frazer, author of The Golden Bough, was a Fellow of Trinity, but after his marriage to Lilly Grove he withdrew from all social life.)[11] It was, in Jessie Stewart's words, a 'brilliantly intellectual company, interested in scientific and especially psychical research, like-minded in loyalty to Newnham and in zeal to break down barriers in the University, not only with regard to the higher education of women.'[12]

Harrison returned to Newnham under conditions that suited her ideally.

---

[5] The evidence for this is to be found in a cryptic and garbled entry in Hope Mirrlees's notebook, under the heading 'The Cornford Letters'.

[6] Sidgwick died of cancer in 1901, shortly after Harrison's return to Newnham. There is nothing in her extant papers that mentions his death.

[7] Sir Richard Claverhouse Jebb, Regius Professor of Greek 1889–1905 and MP for Cambridge University.

[8] Arthur Woollgar Verrall, Fellow of Trinity, went on to hold the first Chair in English literature.

[9] Alfred Marshall, after four years as Principal of University College, Bristol (1877–81) and two as Fellow of Balliol College, Oxford, and lecturer in political economy, returned to Cambridge as Professor of Political Economy. The Newnham College Register recognizes the contribution of Mary Paley Marshall as an unofficial collaborator in much of his work.

[10] Francis Darwin, a university lecturer in botany from 1884, became Fellow of Christ's College in 1886, and a reader in botany from 1888–1904. For a delightful portrayal of the social life of Cambridge during this period, seen through the eyes of a child, see Gwen Raverat, Period Piece: a Cambridge Childhood (London: Faber and Faber, 1952). Gwen Raverat was a daughter of George Darwin, granddaughter of Charles Darwin, and related through her mother to Sir Richard Jebb.

[11] Frazer shared Harrison's preoccupation with anthropology and folklore. She attributes the rise of interest in anthropology and classics to The Golden Bough (Reminiscences, 83), and in the preface to her Prolegomena asserts that his writings had become part and parcel of her mental furniture. He assisted her when she consulted him on individual points. But he lived a life of relentless routine which left no time for social contact, (and little for his wife).

[12] Stewart, Harrison, 12. See 'Annexe: The Intellectual Aristocracy' in Noel Annan, The Dons: Mentors, Eccentrics and Geniuses (London: HarperCollins, 1999), 304–41, for the kaleidoscopic familial relationships among Cambridge intellectuals of this period.

She loved the quiet of Cambridge, and the community life enshrined in its colleges. During the twenty years since she had been a student the college had grown and matured: Clough, Sidgwick, and Pfeiffer Halls had been built, providing accommodation for a hundred and fifty students. The magnificent Yates Thomson Library had been recently built and now held a collection of 10,000 books. Enclosing a large garden, the college no longer stood isolated in a field. Academically, a position on the staff of Newnham was surely preferable even to the Yates Chair at London. In addition she was fortunate enough to be able to negotiate her own terms of employment. A normal appointment to the Newnham staff carried with it a heavy teaching load, exacerbated by the need for remedial teaching; Harrison's gifts and her interests were focused on research and writing, two activities which she declared in her case to be incompatible with teaching. Newnham was willing to offer her a research position, feeling that having her on staff would enhance their academic reputation ('as an ornament' was her own way of putting it). Henry Sidgwick proposed that the college offer her a fellowship with minimal teaching responsibilities. She was asked to 'reside during the coming Michaelmas and Lent terms, with free board and lodging', and to give 'one lecture a week during these terms'. Unlike the rest of the Newnham staff she was not required to give undergraduate tutorials.[13] She appears later to have taken certain students under her wing, but she did so voluntarily.

The initial appointment was for two terms only; she was either 'on probation' or the irregular appointment was seen to be viable for a short period only. But for a while, at least, she was offered the ideal conditions under which to develop her work on the primitive origins of Greek religion. The following year the Council of Newnham College elected her to their first Associates' Research Fellowship 'so that she might have a period of academic calm' to write up the material she had collected during the last thirteen years. The three-year appointment was renewed successively, with the same favourable terms, in 1903, 1906, and 1910. In addition to the dispensation from undergraduate teaching she also received occasional release from lecturing duties, leaving her free to travel (as in 1901) or for 'literary work' (1908).[14]

[13] I am grateful to Mary Beard for drawing to my attention the very favourable terms granted to Harrison.

[14] I wish to thank Claire Breay for directing me to the entries in Newnham Council's Minutes, vol. 2: 1897–1912, from which these details are taken. See also Claire Breay, 'A Gentleman's Education? Women and the Classical Tripos 1869–1910' (Part II diss., Classical Tripos 1991).

Her initial course of lectures was on Delphi and was given at the Archae-ological Museum, beginning on 11 November 1898. Her purpose was to trace 'the origin and development of the successive cults of Delphi, from the first beginnings of the oracle to the final supremacy of the Olympian Apollo'.[15] The archaeological excavations at Delphi which had been begun in 1892 furnished further evidence for her belief that one could distinguish in Greek religion 'layers of cult'. Although Apollo presided over the oracle in Classical times, he was, according to the literary myths, a usurper, a late-comer, and the oracle was originally an oracle of the earth.[16] It had fallen first to Themis, an early earth-goddess whose function came to embody the pre-serving of social custom, before being taken over by the Olympian god. Now archaeology, too, bore witness to the earlier cult, with the discovery of the *omphalos*, a strange stone covered with a network of bands to resemble woollen fillets, a cult object of an earlier worship of the earth. Encouraged by such confirmation, Harrison extended the reading of the texts so as to find similar 'clues' in literature to the original character of the Furies, or Erinyes.

Fusing literary sources with Rohde's theories about ghosts, Harrison saw in the Erinyes another version of local ancestral ghosts, locally influential after death, with powers for either good or evil. Dwelling as they did below the earth, they were especially potent in matters concerning fertility. She argued that in the early period of anthropomorphism, in which the earth was characterized as the mother, such genii as the Erinyes were naturally conceived of as her daughters—particularly since in primitive communities agriculture is the concern of women. The sex of the Erinyes, in other words, makes sense if we understand them as creative genii of fertility, not if we think of them as avengers of blood. Their original form was that of snakes, and they bear witness to an early snake-cultus (also to be found in the worship of Athene and Demeter), at Delphi particularly connected with the legend of the Python. The snake-Erinyes haunted a grave, surmounted by a fetish stone, whose worship evolved into the later worship of Gaia and Kronos. Already by Homer's time these beliefs had been overlaid by the patriarchal Olympians, and the 'real' meaning of the Erinyes was eclipsed. The *Choephori* of Aeschylus, dealing as it does with the ritual of the grave, reverts to the earlier religious conceptions, and the *Eumenides*, the third play of the trilogy, resolves the conflict between old and new by transforming the Erinyes into the very benign beings from whom the literary form had itself sprung.

[15] Prospectus, JHA.   [16] See Aesch., *Eumenides*, 1–20; Soph., *Iphigenia in Tauris*, 1249 ff.

Her lectures on Delphi presented these conclusions, dramatically corroborated by photographs lent to her by Homolle. For the first time an English audience could see for themselves the *omphalos*, or 'navel stone', archaeological evidence for what might otherwise have been no more than speculation. The lectures were published the following year in a long article in the *Journal of Hellenic Studies*.[17]

In the published article she takes her conclusions one stage further, and here we see for the first time some of the hostility towards the Olympians that so characterizes Harrison's later work. 'All is fair in theology and war', she writes, while accusing Aeschylus of theological animus. His misrepresentation of the Erinyes is 'wilful and deliberate' when he portrays them as hideous and makes them unrecognizable to everyone except Clytemnestra. With reasoning somewhat circular she seeks to clinch her argument (that Aeschylus knew perfectly well who the Erinyes were), by citing as 'conclusive proof' the fact that he turned them in the end into benign spirits and restored all their ancient functions.[18] In fact, her 'proof' is rather a clue to her methodology. She loved to invert the myths on the assumption that some patriarchal usurper had turned them upside down in the first place in order to serve his own ends.

In arriving at these conclusions Harrison has indeed read the myth backwards: the resolution of the Erinyes into Semnae is the clue to their real origin as friendly spirits. Her imaginative insight into what she believed to be a genuine religious practice, something real as opposed to literary convention, was no doubt stimulated by her own travels in Greece. Twelve years later John Lawson was to write his powerful book, *Modern Greek Folklore and Ancient Greek Religion*,[19] in which he observes the parallels between peasant beliefs among Greeks of the twentieth century and primitive religious conceptions. Harrison anticipated, without systematically chronicling the practices of Greek peasants, some of Lawson's conclusions. Both Harrison and Lawson imaginatively understood primitive rituals as something living and powerful.

In the audience was a young man of 24, a fourth-year student at Trinity College, who, in order to gain her acquaintance, sent her a letter about some point that had struck him. She invited him to meet her to discuss it, and so began a 'series of innumerable conversations over the black brew of Indian tea which we both found needful to revive the powers of thought after the

---

[17] 'Delphika', 205–51, especially 205–6.   [18] Ibid. 250.

[19] John Cuthbert Lawson, *Modern Greek Folklore and Ancient Greek Religion: a Study in Survivals* (Cambridge: Cambridge University Press, 1910).

idleness of the early afternoon'.[20] The student was Francis Macdonald Cornford. Born the son of a clergyman in 1874, he had won a scholarship to Trinity College, Cambridge, in 1894, where he had become a pupil of Henry Jackson, praelector in ancient philosophy, and Walter Headlam of King's College. After winning a first in both parts of the classical Tripos, he continued to live in Cambridge as editor of the *Cambridge Review*, having failed in his bid for the Professorship of Greek at the University College of South Wales in 1897. In 1899 he won a Fellowship at Trinity. Unorthodox by temperament, he would have been attracted by Harrison. She in turn would have been drawn by his loneliness at the time, and by his courteous, somewhat aloof, manner.[21]

Her lectures made a vivid impression on him:

I have a vision of her figure on the darkened stage of the lecture room at the Archaeological Museum, which she made deserve to the full its name of theatre—a tall figure in black drapery, with the touches of her favourite green, and a string of blue Egyptian beads, like a priest's rosary. The rather low voice vibrated with the excitement that had been working in her for many hours of preparation. The hushed audience would catch the nervous tension of her bearing, even before the simple conversational tones began to convey the anticipation of some mystery to be disclosed. . . . At one of her Newnham lectures on Orphism she enlisted two friends to swing bull-roarers[22] at the back of the room that the audience might learn from the 'awe-inspiring and truly religious sound' what Aeschylus' Edonians meant: 'Bull-voices roar thereto from somewhere out of the unseen, fearful semblances, and from a drum an image as it were of thunder underground is borne on the air heavy with dread'.[23]

Her association with Cornford marks the beginning of the most fruitful period of Harrison's work. She may have been twice his age, but interaction with young people always stimulated her. Her approach to research was young. She always believed that there was more at stake in her research than just the accumulation of scholarly data; she approached her work as if she were seeking for the key to the universe itself. She was forever searching for

[20] F. M. Cornford, 'Jane Ellen Harrison', *Newnham College Letter*, 1929, 72.

[21] See Douglas Kellogg Wood, 'F. M. Cornford' in Briggs and Calder, *Classical Scholarship*; Shelley Arlen, *The Cambridge Ritualists: an Annotated Bibliography* (Metuchen, NJ and London: Scarecrow Press, 1990) 299–301; and Gilbert Murray, obituary of Francis Cornford, *Proceedings of the British Academy*, vol. 29 (1943), 421–32.

[22] See Jane Harrison, *Themis*, 61–6: 'The "bull-roarer" was a bit of wood to which a string is tied, and it is whirled round and round at initiation-rites to make a whirring sound.' The bull-roarer was a 'singularly illuminating instance of sanctity, and of a sanctity actually observable in Greece'.

[23] Cornford, 'Jane Ellen Harrison', 74.

some deeply hidden truth under the surface of what the Greeks thought, seeking to draw closer to some thrilling reality. For the next ten years the 'innumerable conversations over the black brew of tea' became an integral part of her creative process. Many years later she analysed the nature of the help she received from her male colleagues:

Now, emphatically, I never looked to man to supply me with new ideas; he might, accidentally, or as oftener happened, we might flash them out together; but that was not what I wanted. Your thoughts are—for what they are worth—self-begotten by some process of parthenogenesis. But there comes often to me, almost always, a moment when alone I cannot bring them to the birth, when, if companionship is denied, they die unborn. The moment, so far as I can formulate the need, is when you want to disentangle them from yourself and your emotions, when they are sending out such a welter of feelers in all directions, setting up connections so profusely and recklessly that you hold your sanity with both your hands, and yet it seems going. Then you want the mind of a man with its great power of insulation. That is why a man's mind is so resting. To talk a thing over with a competent man friend is to me like coming out of a seething caldron of suggestion into a spacious, well-ordered room.[24]

Francis Cornford was certainly an ideal colleague. If Cornford offered Harrison the intellectual insulation she needed, she reciprocated with a sympathy and attention that sharpened his own focus.

Her association with Robert Alexander Neil, senior tutor at Pembroke College was significant in a different way. Unlike Cornford, Neil was a contemporary, just two years her junior, a Scot whose 'sympathetic . . . silences made the dreariest gatherings burn and glow'.[25] She must have first met him as early as 1892 when they served together on the Council of the Society for the Promotion of Hellenic Studies. Neil had begun his academic career in medicine before changing to classics, and after taking his degree was elected a Fellow of Pembroke College. He became interested in Sanskrit, and for the remainder of his life he spent one or two afternoons a week reading the Rig Veda and other Sanskrit literature with Professor Edward Byles Cowell, Fellow of Corpus Christi College and the University Professor of Sanskrit.[26] The antithesis of J. G. Frazer, who secluded himself like a hermit in order to

---

[24] 'Woman and Knowledge', *Newnham College Letter*, 1913, 22–5; repr. 'Scientiae Sacra Fames', 130–1.   [25] *Reminiscences*, 55.

[26] With Cowell he published an edition of the 'Divyavadana' in 1886. At the time of Harrison's return to Cambridge he was working on a translation of the 'Jataka', or Birth Stories, from Pali into English, as well as an edition of Aristophanes' *Knights*. He was an accomplished scholar in the comparative philology of the classical languages, Sanskrit and Celtic (also an interest of Cowell's).

devote his entire energy to writing, Neil published little, being always ready with his time to place his extensive knowledge at the service of others and to solve difficulties for his friends—inspiring, suggesting, emending. His Sunday luncheons Harrison described as 'the best intellectual thing in Cambridge'.[27] She found in him just the colleague she most needed to help her with the details of her work, an expert in the very areas of classical studies in which she felt the most deficient. ('I *think* I can arrange that for you', she quotes him as saying, when she was in need of philological underpinning for an argument.)

Their friendship seems to have gone deeper than mere academic collaboration. Neil was physically attractive and strongly built. Her allusion to his 'silences', reminiscent of her descriptions of her father and contrasting with those of her garrulous stepmother, is an indication of the attraction he held for her. The breadth of his learning and interests, which extended beyond the fields of his academic expertise to include the whole range of literature, would have generated further sympathy between them.

Through the Verralls she made another important friendship, an association that was to have the most profound influence on her life and work. Gilbert Murray (Fig. 10) was born in Australia in 1866 and educated in England. He had become Professor of Greek at Glasgow at the age of 23, and in 1898 had married Lady Mary Howard, daughter of Lady Carlisle of Castle Howard.[28] The Verralls had known Murray since 1894, when they had met him on holiday in Switzerland. Verrall and Murray shared a deep interest in Euripides: both men were engaged in recovering for their contemporaries an appreciation of his genius which had been considerably undermined during the Victorian era. Verrall had published *Euripides the Rationalist* in 1895;[29] Murray was engaged in preparing an edition of the works of Euripides for the Oxford Classical Texts Series. At the time of their holiday in Switzerland they were collaborating over a projected Lexicon of Euripides. At the same time Murray was working on a project for a wider audience, making verse translations of the plays. He had begun these for students with the purpose of communicating not only the sense but the aesthetic power of

[27] JEH to Jessie Stewart, n.d., JHA.

[28] See Jean Smith and Arnold Toynbee, *Gilbert Murray: an Unfinished Autobiography* (London: Allen and Unwin, 1960); Francis West, *Gilbert Murray: A Life* (Beckenham: Croom Helm, 1984); Duncan Wilson, *Gilbert Murray, OM, 1866–1957* (Oxford: Clarendon Press, 1987); and Robert Fowler, 'Gilbert Murray' in Briggs and Calder, *Classical Scholarship*, 321–34.

[29] Arthur Woollgar Verrall, *Euripides the Rationalist* (Cambridge: Cambridge University Press, 1895).

10. Gilbert Murray, 1934

the original Greek. Now in 1900, Murray and the Verralls were holidaying together again in Switzerland, and this time were joined by Jane Harrison. Murray wrote to his wife: 'I like her very much indeed . . . she strikes me as having a generous mind, which is rare among scholars—she is overflowing with interest in all sorts of subjects.'[30] Later the same year Murray came to Cambridge for a reading of selections from his latest translation of Euripides and met Harrison for a second time, at the Verralls' home.[31] Lady Mary Murray described the occasion: 'G read the Hippolytus quite admirably,

---

[30]   GM to MM, 9 July 1900, MS Gilbert Murray 455, fo. 86. Quoted in Wilson, *Gilbert Murray*, 119. In the account of what follows, Wilson has conflated the two occasions of Murray's visits to Cambridge to read *Hippolytus*.

[31]   The exact chronology of these events is confusing. From the evidence of letters (JEH to GM and Bertrand Russell to GM), Murray visited Cambridge on two separate occasions to give public performances: a play-reading of the *Hippolytus* in Feb. 1901 (postponed from Jan. because of the death of Queen Victoria), and a lecture in Mar. 1902, which was arranged by Harrison herself.

audience most appreciative, Miss Harrison audibly weeping. B. Russell said he thought he had never been so much moved.'[32]

In August 1900 there begins what became at times an almost daily correspondence between Jane Harrison and Gilbert Murray. She claimed that she preferred getting and even writing letters to seeing people—'letters do not abash and confound one by their personalities—but I rarely find this morbid taste is shared'.[33] Lady Mary Murray carefully collected the letters, which are now housed in the archives of Newnham College. Sadly, Murray's side of the correspondence is missing, as Hope Mirrlees prevailed upon Harrison to burn all of her papers when she finally left Cambridge in 1921. However, the correspondence is so frequent that it is often not difficult to reconstruct what Murray must have written to her. The letters are remarkable for a number of reasons. First, they exemplify a thesis that she herself articulated: that letters should be about the recipient, not about the writer. Whether she was pouring her heart out or requesting help with a problem in her work, her focus was nearly always on the person she was writing to, and her relationship with that person. As a result she rarely mentions anyone else, except, occasionally, mutual friends. During the period when she was writing almost daily to Gilbert Murray she was working in close co-operation with Francis Cornford and the Verralls, yet their names hardly appear in the correspondence at all, despite the fact that she was sharing with them the same scholarly issues that she was writing to Murray about. Secondly, she wrote with a flair that is uniquely her own—the letters to Murray sparkle with humour, allusions, teasing, and at times a perilous baring of her own emotions. When she was angry or disappointed she made no attempt to hide her feelings, but clothing them in humour and hyperbole she communicated without ever giving offence. At other times she would write pure nonsense, and the letters that have survived from this period of her life give us a clue as to what Alice (Lloyd) Dew-Smith had meant when she described her conversation of student days as 'a continual stream of delightful nonsense'. Her command of language is superb, even when she is tossing off a quick note to catch the post. Her writing is alive with metaphor, much of it from the Bible she had memorized as a child, and which still lived in her imagination long after she had rejected its teaching. One of the first letters asks for Murray's views on a line of Euripides:

---

[32] Lady Mary Murray's diary, MSS Gilbert Murray 559, Bodleian Library, Oxford.
[33] JEH to MM 14, n.d. [June 1901?].

Mr Verrall is the bad serpent who tempts me . . . he said you had views. It was most indiscreet, for he knows the fell curiosity of this particular Eve. Could you bear to tell me on a postcard what it means? I and the hungry young sheep who look up and are not fed would burn incense to you for ever, but if this prayer is μέγ' ἀναιδές [greatly presumptuous] as indeed it is, do not write . . .[34]

The first few letters from Harrison are remarkable for the speed with which the formality of her initial overtures develops into a language of closeness. By December, her manner with Murray had become much more personal. All formality is gone, and she begins to write in a mock-obsequious style which becomes a feature of much of the later correspondence. In the next few years, as Harrison's relationship with Murray became progressively more intimate, she was to agonize over what she once again so passionately desired: not sexual fulfilment, emphatically not (or at least not consciously), but an uninterrupted personal intimacy, based on their work. Since, for her, work was primary, this relationship must also be primary. That Murray was married was inconvenient but irrelevant; Lady Mary Murray belonged to a part of Murray's life that Harrison found difficult to understand and allow for. As if aware, perhaps subconsciously, that her growing companionship with Murray was excluding his wife, she made strenuous attempts at friendship with Lady Mary. But a lack of sincerity in her letters to Lady Mary betrays her attempt to build a relationship on a false foundation. The fact of the matter was that she and Lady Mary had very little in common.

The problem was compounded by stresses within the Murrays' marriage, of which Harrison may or may not have been aware.[35] At the very time that Harrison's close friendship with him began, Murray had just severed his connection with a former student, Janie Brailsford. Janie was married to another former pupil, Noel Brailsford, and there is no reason to believe that her relationship with Murray was anything other than a lively friendship in which their common interest in Greece played the central role. Lady Mary, feeling that she had failed her husband if she could not be all in all to him, had grown increasingly jealous. He, in return, increasingly resented his wife's attempts to restrict his friendships with other women. 'I want to act consciously on my own judgement and responsibility and not to feel you are "forbidding things" ', he wrote to her in May 1900. At root they understood the marriage

---

[34] JEH to GM, Dec. 1900, JHA, GM letters, 2. The letters to Gilbert Murray, many of them undated, have been numbered with two different sets of numbers, presumably by Hope Mirrlees and Jessie Stewart. I am using the reference numbers in square brackets. Of the letters from Jane Harrison to Lady Mary Murray, some are included with the Gilbert Murray letters, and numbered accordingly, others are not and remain unnumbered.

[35] The quotations in this paragraph are taken from West, *Gilbert Murray*, 34.

relationship differently. She had entered into it as 'perfect unity, utter love', in which husband and wife would be totally absorbed in each other. 'I tell you that my love will wrestle with yours to be the greater . . . till we can lay [our souls] without fear at the feet of the One Unknown God and let them die together in the service of humanity', she had written. He, no less high-minded, found such 'perfect unity, utter love' not to be incompatible with a variety of other close friendships, especially friendships based on his work. The very fact that his work, around which his life revolved, was closed to her, intensified Lady Mary's jealousy. She seems, besides, to have been afflicted with all sorts of self-doubt about her ability to be a good wife, and was con-tinuously in a state of nerves. She could not have been easy to live with. Bertrand Russell wrote (cattily) of her:

She sees, poor woman, so much more of what is right than she can accomplish. Her faults are (1) jealousy, (2) too much care for her rights and for those people she cares for, (3) too much anxiety over trivial things, such as details of housekeeping, (4) bad temper, (5) general restlessness and rebellion, (6) lack of self control. Her virtues are (1) public spirit, (2) a great love of virtue and desire to do right, (3) a very strong impulse to all sorts of kind actions, (4) a real care for good work, even Gilbert's. Both lists might no doubt be lengthened. Her attitude to Gilbert is curious. Anxious about his welfare, but jealous if he is praised.[36]

When Murray renounced his friendship with Janie Brailsford for his wife's sake they felt they had reached a *modus vivendi*, although the fundamental issue was never resolved. Such was the situation when Harrison began writing to him, and, shortly afterwards, pleading for him to come and visit her in Cambridge.[37]

She had written to him earlier about a difficult passage in Euripides' *Hip-polytus*, in which Phaedra, tormented by the illicit love she feels for her stepson, deliberates over the two senses of the word αἰδώς ('shame'). What Euripides means is not clear. Murray's reply has not survived, but his note in his translation of the *Hippolytus* (1902) are suggestive. He writes of Phaedra:

The 'delights' that have tempted and undone her are, first, the pleasure of long talks—with Hippolytus, or about him; next, the pleasure of losing herself in dreams; and thirdly, in some sense not precisely explained, but surely not difficult to

---

[36]   Bertrand Russell diary, 19 Feb. 1903, BRA.

[37]   Francis West writes that 'When he went to Italy in February 1903 to consult Euripides' manuscripts for his edition of the Greek text, Lady Mary was jealous *even* of the companionship of Jane Ellen Harrison, . . . who, he had to reassure Mary, was not in love with him' (*Gilbert Murray*, italics mine). West has greatly underestimated the tensions in the relationship between Lady Mary Murray and Jane Harrison, as events of 1903 testify.

understand, a feeling of shame or cowardice. She feels that if only she had had more courage all might have been well! Why this 'shame,' this yielding to fear, strikes her at this moment as a 'delight,' is not explained; but it does not seem to me unnatural.[38]

It is doubtful that Murray read anything personal into her letter about Phaedra (or, for that matter, that Harrison herself had any conscious intention of self-revelation), but Murray's rather curious description of Phaedra's 'not unnatural' delight captures the state of Harrison's emotions. The relationship between them was precarious. Murray was good-looking, gracious, and unfailingly courteous, and had repeatedly in the past attracted devotion from women students. Harrison would have been drawn to him from the start by his encyclopaedic knowledge of Greek literature, a fund from which she could draw for her own work.[39] Moreover, he shared her anthropological approach to classics. What probably fuelled their relationship more than anything else was Murray's remarkable intellectual tolerance. He was 'open-minded to a fault', and 'prepared to see the good in anyone's point of view, perhaps especially if it was a radical one.'[40] She could count on Murray for a sympathetic listening to anything she wanted to try out. Lastly, he was not only a classicist, but also a poet, who could resonate to her own emotions about poetry. 'When you first say those lovely verse things to me I feel dazed & a little frightened', she wrote to him in November 1901. His translations of Euripides set her 'a whole new standard of trying to understand. . . . [I]t is only a poet in one's own language that can help to the understanding of a poet in another.'[41] Later she wrote:

I found peace in the train & the Bacchae—it was good of you to bring it for me—for they simply fill me with content & happiness—You will laugh I know & well you may but I think the reason why yr verses give me such intense & almost immeasurable

[38]   Euripides, *Hippolytus*, trans. Gilbert Murray (London: G. Allen & Sons, 1902). Murray's interpretation is surely very strange. Surely Phaedra's delight in 'long talks' (λέσχαι, l.384) refers to gossip, not talks *with Hippolytus*. Murray's odd interpretation is itself an indication that he is writing more out of his own experience than from what is in the text.

[39]   He had written in *A History of Ancient Greek Literature* (London: Heinemann, 1897) how our conception of the Greeks varies from one generation to another. The 'serene and classical' Greek had yielded to the 'aesthetic and fleshly'; both were now phantoms of the past. 'There is more flesh and blood in the Greek of the anthropologist, the foster-brother of Kaffirs and Hairy Ainos', claimed Murray. 'He is at least human and simple and emotional, and free from irrelevant trappings.'

[40]   Robert L. Fowler, 'Gilbert Murray: Four (Five) Stages of Greek Religion', in Calder (ed.), *The Cambridge Ritualists Reconsidered*, 93–4.

[41]   JEH to GM [18], n.d.

delight is that they are just what I wld have given my soul to do myself. As a quite young girl I had a dream of being first a poet & next a scholar & tho both dreams faded swiftly & completely they have always left a sort of empty ache of something never found.[42]

By January 1901 she was writing to Murray quite openly—though in a bantering style—about the intensity of her intellectual friendship. When she found out that the London production of his *Andromache* had been postponed she scolded him, 'You are too hateful and abominable for words. . . . Do you realize that I (in the biggest capitals) shall have gone Crete-wards—I don't believe anyone in all London wanted to see it as much as ME.'[43]

In February 1901 she left for an extended visit to Italy and Greece. She had several reasons for visiting Europe at this time. The International Historical Congress took place in Rome in February. In Greece there was much new archaeological material to see, and Dörpfeld was giving guided lecture tours around the sites. In Crete, in particular, Sir Arthur Evans's excavation of Knossos was uncovering new material with every passing day, much of which was directly pertinent to Harrison's study of religious origins. Not only did Harrison herself need to keep abreast of the mass of new material, but she also wanted one of her students who was just about to begin Part II of the Tripos examinations, Jessie Crum (later Stewart), to experience Greek archaeology at first hand.[44]

'She adopted me', Jessie Stewart remembered, 'after she had seen hanging in my room her favourite scene of initiation ritual from the Villa Farnesina ceiling which I had newly brought back from Rome. She termed herself my Director of Studies.' Jessie had still to complete Part I of the Tripos, so her relationship with Harrison at this stage was purely informal, cemented by the painting. But it was typical of Harrison to notice an unusually gifted student and offer encouragement. She invited Jessie to join her on a trip to Greece prescribing some preliminary reading, demanding for a second-year student.[45] But Harrison always thought her students knew more than they

---

[42] JEH to GM [49], 22 Apr. 1902.   [43] JEH to GM [9], n.d. [Jan. 1901?].

[44] See Christopher Stray, 'Digs and Degrees', *Classics Ireland*, 2 (1995), 121–31.

[45] As preparatory reading Harrison had prescribed W. Robertson Smith, *Lectures on the Religion of the Semites* (Edinburgh: Adam & Charles Black, 1889) and Henry Sumner Maine, *Ancient Law: Its Connection with the Early History of Society and its Relation to Modern Ideas* (London: John Murray, 1861). Jessie Stewart wrote: 'From Robertson Smith's splendid blaze of imagination came the explanation of sacrifice and the communal character of primitive religion. Oldenberg, the Buddhist Scholar, showed how myth arose out of cult; and Sir Henry Maine, after numerous editions and editions, is still the standard authority on ancient Law and the "Themistes" which preceded any conception of law' (Stewart, *Harrison*, 14).

did, and to the gifted among them her high estimation of their ability came as a compliment and a challenge.

Before she left the Murrays invited her to spend a weekend at their home at Barford, Surrey. To her embarrassment, she ended the weekend by fainting. Her friends were concerned about her health, especially as she was about to leave on an extended study period in Europe. However, as Margaret Verrall wrote to Lady Mary Murray on 14 February, Harrison was much better by the time she left. 'She swore by all the gods—and she has more than the rest of us!—that if she were the least ill on the way she would stop at Dover. The sea air always sets her up.'[46] Leonard Whibley of Pembroke College gave a farewell lunch for her on 8 February, and she left two days after. Jessie Crum and Margaret Tuke, lecturer in French at Newnham, were to join her later.

In Rome she attended the International Historical Congress, after which she wrote to Lady Mary, 'I have lapsed into bed for a day slain by the polyglot hospitality of five nations. Rome is an awful whirlpool & over-play is much worse than over-work.' J. G. Frazer and his wife were also there:

Mrs Frazer (your double!) has been sitting by my bed for two hours, telling me 'who not to know' i.e. who has not paid Mr. Frazer 'proper attention!' This is the price I pay for a few shy radiant moments under the Golden Bough—good conservative tho' I am I am ready for any reform in the Game Laws for the preserving of Eminent Husbands.[47]

Lilly Grove Frazer, described by Malinowski as Frazer's 'redoubtable companion'[48] was remembered by all who knew her as a 'dragon', and persisted in keeping people away from her husband on the grounds that they only wasted his time. However, Harrison hints at a subtext with the words 'your double': though Lady Mary Murray was nothing like Mrs Frazer in either her personality or her behaviour, perhaps Harrison's remarks about 'the Game Laws for the preserving of Eminent Husbands' contain something more than banter. A year later her relationship with Lady Mary was sufficiently strained that one wonders whether there is not more in her comments about Lilly Frazer than at first meets the eye.

---

[46] Margaret Verrall to MM, 14 Feb. 1901.   [47] JEH to MM, 24 Feb. 1901.
[48] Quoted by Robert Ackerman, *J. G. Frazer: His Life and Work* (Cambridge: Cambridge University Press, 1987), 126. Ackerman, after a charitable attempt at putting the kindest possible interpretation on the evidence, records some of the behaviour that her contemporaries found so objectionable: 'She was rude, overbearing, and peremptory with people who worked for her . . . she was devious and manipulative with those whom she could not order about.' She persistently believed that her husband did not receive 'proper attention'.

Jessie Crum joined them at Bari where they visited the Etruscan museum before crossing from Brindisi to Patras. At Athens they avoided the grand European hotels built for the tourists, choosing instead to stay at the 'genuinely Greek Hotel d'Athènes where we lived on Yogurt and resinated wine'.[49] (Perhaps Harrison also wanted to avoid the kind of awkward situation that had arisen when she met Samuel Butler on her last visit). They walked round the acropolis looking at the strongholds of all the Dörpfeld theories, Harrison 'wildly excited about him & all he does in abject admiration'.[50] Dörpfeld showed them over the new excavations at the agora and the Lenaion. He showed them Dionysus' wine vat at the corner of what he believed to be the original scene of Aristophanes' *Frogs*, the old theatre of Dionysus-in-the-marshes. They saw the Hero shrine of Sophocles, where he received Asklepios The Protector, in the form of a great snake. 'How I wish Euripides had had to receive that snake', was Harrison's comment.[51]

It was not only the excavations themselves but also the archaeologists that caught Jessie's attention. 'Did I tell you about the German party?' she wrote home:

It was such fun, all the greatest archaeologists in the world, none of them on speaking terms! Dr Dörpfeld brought Prof Furtwängler & made him say How do you do to Jane & he looked so furious, I thought there was going to be a scene & Jane rose with her most gracious smile & shook hands. They all flock round her & appreciate her far more than the English. Everybody is divided into two camps, Dörpfeld & anti-Dörpfeld & I go their lectures alternately. Jane is a tremendous admirer of Dörpfeld—Avtos—she calls him, so we spend hours over every stone that he has excavated. He seems to be a sort of Schliemann with a wonderful intuition & he began as an architect, so he studies all the topographical & architectural questions from a common sense point of view, & doesn't depend entirely on the interpretation of some obscure passage as most of them do.[52]

Robert Carr Bosanquet, Director of the British School at Athens also showed them around, taking them 'to all sorts of exciting caves in the side of the Acropolis, & then to the top of the Parthenon from which one gets a glorious view of everything. Miss Harrison gets all the great men to let us in everywhere! She is tremendously excited about one great German professor who is here,[53] & we are going to a party at his house tomorrow evening! I am so alarmed.'[54]

When a large horde of Cambridge people arrived with Ernest Gardner,

[49] Stewart, *Harrison*, 13.   [50] Jessie Crum to Mrs Crum, Mar. 1901.
[51] Stewart, *Harrison*, 15.   [52] Jessie Crum to Mrs Crum, 2 Apr. 1901.
[53] Presumably Adolf Furtwängler.   [54] Jessie Crum to Mr Crum, 27 Mar. 1901.

Harrison and her party were most thankful they were not in the same hotel. They went to hear Gardner lecture and 'we flocked round the Acropolis like sheep on a "personally conducted" Perowne tour'.[55] They also met the Swedish scholar Samuel Wide 'who says it is a great incentive to all the archaeologists here that the best book on Athens has been written by a Fraülein! Jane becomes more and more a prophet! She is a most delightful travelling companion.'[56]

The main purpose of Jessie Crum's visit to Greece was to experience the much more demanding 'Peloponnesian Reise' guided by Wilhelm Dörpfeld. The last day they regretted leaving Athens and their comfortable hotel, but, Jessie conceded, 'it will be very exciting. We do Corinth tomorrow, & Mycenae on Thursday, Epidaurus on Sat. which Jane says is the most beautiful place in Greece, then back here.'[57]

The 'master' took them, a polyglot company, on an intensive tour. The day began at six o'clock and they worked until eight o'clock in the evening without any siesta in the heat of the day. The itinerary took them through Eleusis, where he lectured on the Hall of the Mysteries, to Epidauros to see the fourth-century theatre, and to prehistoric Tiryns. They went to Mycenae where he explained the *tholos* (the Treasury of Atreus), the shaft graves, and the Lion Gate. Corinth was still unexcavated but 'we rode up Akrokorinthos on mules'.[58] After Jessie Crum left her to return to Cambridge, Harrison stayed on to visit Crete, where the excavations at Knossos begun the previous year had already brought to light written tablets, frescoes, and the whole labyrinthine Palace of Minos—an 'extraordinary phenomenon: nothing Greek—nothing Roman—perhaps one single fragment of late black varnished ware among tens of thousands. . . . Nay its great period goes at least well back to pre-Mycenaean period.'[59] The second season began in 1901, and by the time that Harrison reached Crete the digging was in full swing. She wrote to Murray,

I simply must write to you from Phaedra's home address[60]—whether you want to hear is quite irrelevant. But you *will* want to know the last great find, Mr Evans showed it me an hour ago—the Minotaur himself, *seated on a throne* (a seal impression) with a worshipper before him. Zeus is nowhere. I always knew he was a tire-

---

[55] A cruise conducted by Connop F. S. Perowne had just arrived in Athens with 192 school teachers.

[56] Jessie Crum to Mrs Crum, 20 Apr. 1901.   [57] Jessie Crum to Mrs Crum, Apr. 1901.

[58] Stewart, *Harrison*, 15.

[59] From Evans's notebook, 27 March 1900, quoted by Joan Evans, *Time and Chance* (London: Longmans, Green and Co., 1943), 330.

[60] Phaedra was the daughter of Minos, King of Crete.

some parvenu, and I have been doing my best to discredit him for years, he is so showy and omnipotent, and now at last I can chant a true Magnificat to the old bull-headed god. He has a beautiful curly tail in the seal, which would pervert the most orthodox. What a dear delight it is to 'put down the mighty from their seat!'[61]

Three days later Evans wrote of how he was able to reconstruct a religious scene from another seal: a goddess on a sacred peak with a lion on either side of it, her temple behind, and a worshipper in front.[62] Harrison had seen a picture of this seal in the *Annual of the British School at Athens*,[63] and at first thought it too good to be true, 'a veritable little manual of primitive Cretan faith and ritual',[64] a portrayal of the Mountain Mother, a standing monument of matriarchalism. At Knossos Evans now allowed her to examine the fragments from which he had constructed the scene. Satisfied that the reconstruction was correct, she paid tribute to Evans's highly trained eye, and the perception of the excavator who had first observed that these separate clay impressions had all been made by the same seal.

From the 'land of Phaedra' she also wrote to Murray her further reflections on the *Hippolytos*:

It is a conflict not merely of moral ideals but, which is much more important, of racial cults—it is just the Eumenides over again, but I can't put this in the space of a letter, besides, it will probably bore you. . . . Oh, why are you not here? Please tell Lady Mary that I have taken rooms for her next year in a beautiful little Turkish hareem, with a well and a loggia and a lemon tree, and a few rugs—not much else . . . I think of her with mixed emotion, every time I drink too much wonderful Cretan wine, which is daily. . . . Everything is beautiful here. I know now why Phaedra was homesick for her great sea palace; it makes Athens seem cramped and chilly and meagre. But you will come next year, won't you? I can't think how you *can* stay away.[65]

She returned to Athens to join Dörpfeld, who had 'angelically invited her' to join him on his *Inselreise*, which would include Crete again. 'I learn more from him in an hour than from anyone else in a year', she confessed. The cruise took in Delos, from where she wrote to Jessie Crum, 'How I wish you had come on this Reise. It is horrible for most things though the Perrys are a comfort[66] but there are always Avtos' Vorträge [lectures] which get more and

[61] JEH to GM, 21 Apr. 1901 (I have taken this from the typescript copy in the Newnham archives, not having seen the original).

[62] Evans, *Time and Chance*, 337.

[63] *Annual of the British School at Athens*, 7 (1900–1), 29, fig. 9.   [64] *Prolegomena*, 496–7.

[65] JEH to GM, 21 Apr. 1901 (from typescript).

[66] Edward Delavan Perry was director of the American School at Athens. She wrote later of him and his wife: 'they were extraordinarily kind to me out in Greece, he has written the worst Sanskrit "Method" it has ever been my sorrow to use, & he does inscriptions, but he is kindness

more geistreich and anregend [ingenious and stimulating]. We had roughish weather and are six in a cabin. I need not enlarge. But these islands are divine!' And from Santorini: 'Thera! Do you realize this amazing place? I do, for I have scuttled over it on a donkey with a wooden saddle and am black and blue. The Felsinschriften [rock inscriptions] are most beguiling and I could have spent all day over them. I long for you daily.'[67]

It had been her intention to visit Troy, but she was forced to change her plans when she found herself quarantined for chicken-pox. 'I parted from Avtos this morning,' she wrote to Jessie, 'I (inwardly) in floods of tears, he smiling radiantly at the prospect of starting without me to Troy . . . He has no sentiment',[68] and to Gilbert Murray, 'What a horrid diseased world it is! I am sure we want another Flood badly.'[69] Disease was not the only trouble of this world that oppressed her at this time. She had just received news that the two daughters of her friends the Turnbulls had died in a house fire.

By the end of May she was back at Newnham, intoxicated with new things and new ideas. She confessed that in Greece she had grown faint with longing for the sight of British rain and mud, 'after the horrible glare & those dreadful clear-cut outlines people rave about' and longed for the scent of an English east wind. The greenness of England enraptured her. 'I am still in the newly home stage when one gets hysterical at the sight of every lilac bush, but it will pass.'[70] She now began work on 'a long dull article on the "Mycenaean Question", which will keep me laid low for many days'.[71] She was grappling with a formidable problem, trying to sort out the complex questions of ethnology that had been raised by the recent discoveries in the Aegean. For her own purposes of tracing the separate cults of Greece back to their local origins, she needed a foundation of ethnology. However, there was no agreement among scholars over a number of important but perplexing questions of anthropology.

She began the article by surveying the field, and then devoted most of it to a review of William Ridgeway's recent book, *The Early Age of Greece*. During the previous twenty years an enormous amount of new archaeological material had come to light. Heinrich Schliemann, though not the first to make discoveries, had been the first to attract scholarly attention, and he had done so by making connections with Homer. Harrison perceptively

---

& goodness incarnate & both of them have a real sense of humour' (JEH to GM [308], 20 Apr. 1907).

[67] JEH to Jessie Crum, quoted in Stewart, *Harrison*, 15–16.
[68] JEH to Jessie Crum, 23 May 1901.   [69] JEH to GM [13], 30 May 1901.   [70] Ibid.
[71] Jane Ellen Harrison, 'The Dawn of Greece', *Quarterly Review*, 194 (1901), 218–43.

observed that 'to arrest the attention of classical scholars there was needed, not mere facts, but facts that could be related to orthodox tradition'. Initially, then, the question aroused by the archaeological finds was 'What light did they shed on Homer?' But under the pressure of accumulating facts the questions changed. In 1896 Ridgeway's article 'What People Produced the Objects Called Mycenaean?'[72] had provided Harrison with a useful base. The problems which now confronted classical scholars were large and diverse, and concerned questions of race, language, and chronology of the inhabitants of the early Aegean, the causes of the rise and fall of their civilizations, their relationship to the other peoples of the Mediterranean, and how all of the new data fitted with the literary tradition of ancient Greece which spoke of peoples such as Pelasgians, Achaians, and Hellenes, to name a few. By 1900 a bewildering variety of explanations were being put forward, but a consensus was beginning to form that an indigenous civilization had existed for millennia in the Mediterranean, and that this had been overlaid by an immigrant people. Herodotus had stated as much in the fifth century BC. Ridgeway now proposed that the indigenous, dark-haired stock were Herodotus' Pelasgians, and that these were the people who had built the walls and tombs at Mycenae. Homer's Achaeans, he argued, were fair-haired immigrants, and he identified them with the Celts. Harrison leaped at his conclusion: 'We are suddenly at home among the long-haired Achaeans because they are ourselves. These banquets of abundant roast flesh are Homeric, but also British, and contrast significantly with the dainty fish diet of the Pelasgian Athenians', she exclaimed.

But Ridgeway's 'solution' was fraught with as many problems as it solved, and caused a minor furore.[73] No-one before him had taken Herodotus' Pelasgians seriously, and now Ridgeway was not only proposing their historical existence but also giving them the Mycenaean artefacts which Schliemann had attributed to the Achaeans. He argued in support of his Pelasgians that there were a number of discrepancies between the archaeological data and Homer, the most significant of which was the manner of burial of the dead. This issue was particularly important for Harrison because it had implications for her theories of beliefs about an afterlife. She pointed out that the way Homer narrates the story of Odysseus' visit to the underworld attests

[72] William Ridgeway, *The Early Age of Greece* (Cambridge: Cambridge University Press, 1901).
[73] There is still no scholarly consensus on these issues, which have proved exceedingly complex. As Harry Payne has observed, part of Harrison's difficulty in writing anything that would have any lasting value to the study of the classics was the exceedingly difficult nature of the material she was working with—be it mythological, anthropological, or historical.

to two such different 'conceptions' of what happens to the soul after death, for having told us that Odysseus is about to go 'down', Homer takes him north instead, to the land of the shadowy Cimmerians. The blending of two incompatible ideas was to Harrison 'plainly apparent'.

She concludes by considering the significance of all this for scholarship at large, and it is in the bold sweep of her conclusions that we have Harrison at her best, displaying her gift for metaphorical thinking, enlivened by the way in which she characteristically gives mythological beings a life of their own:

In the course of the discussion it has, it may be hoped, become abundantly evident that the access of the material, and the adoption of scientific method necessitated by this material, have given to classical studies a momentous impulse. They have transfused new life into a plant which was beginning to perish from atrophy. We were all of us taught in our childhood that Athene sprang full-grown from her father's head. Athene herself now abjures this monstrous origin. With the humility born of contact with actual fact, she owns herself 'the daughter of the Earth, our mother'; and from every fresh contact with the earth, with reality, Antaeus-like,[74] her strength is renewed. To drop metaphor, we renounce perforce that academic phantom, the insulated and 'ideal' Greek, and find in his place the actual man, the outcome of a long past, the Greek of anthropology and archaeology. The 'great age' is still there, but, as prologue to it we thankfully accept the unrolling of the great panorama of history, the shiftings of populations, the action and reaction of North and South, the eternal πάντα ῥεῖ ['everything is in flux'].[75]

(The astute reader will have observed that Harrison is unable to drop metaphor even when she tries, so eidetic is her imagination.)

She was aware, however, of the resentment with which the application of the newer sciences, archaeology and anthropology, to classics was likely to be received. Her passions aroused, she concluded her article with an abundance of metaphor:

The citadel of scholarship, we are told, is undermined, the enemy is inside the camp, archaeology, which should be 'ancillary'—a word hateful to the free republic of science—threatens the master-function of literary scholarship. 'I had rather a young man knew a single book of Homer than he should dig up and date all the crockery in the Archipelago.' Why this antithesis? Is it impossible to examine scientifically the stones of the palace at Knossos and yet to know and love the deathless tragedy of the princess who dwelt there? In the infinite web of human knowledge, who is to say

[74] Antaeus was a mythological giant of Libya, son of Poseidon and the Earth (Ge). He was a renowned wrestler, and overcame all his adversaries by his power of renewing his strength from the earth, so that, if perchance he was thrown, he arose with fresh vigour. He was finally overcome by Heracles, who crushed his body while holding him in the air.

[75] 'The Dawn of Greece', 242.

which thread lends most to the weaving of the ultimate pattern? For the literary and linguistic scholar there will always remain the garden enclosed—let him see that it be not a *hortus siccus*—a garden full of rare and delicate flowers, which he may gather at his will. Is he any way the poorer because in the wider horizons around him the broad fields of archaeology are outspread, white to the harvest?[76]

Finally, to reassure the sceptical she closed the article by stressing how conservative is the new scholarship, for it serves to rehabilitate the old traditions. Archaeology, tradition, and language, as Ridgeway was at pains to point out, were all in harmony.

Ridgeway invited Harrison to attend his Part II lectures on archaeology, where students sat around the table and learned to 'strip off the layers' until they reached the ultimate authority for proof. 'Proof', Jessie (Crum) Stewart recollected, 'was largely found in the collection of coins and other objects in his own pockets.' Ridgeway's approach was in direct opposition to that of Harrison's other great mentor at Cambridge, J. G. Frazer, whose *Golden Bough* Ridgeway dismissed as 'theories built upon unproved assumptions and guesses and "supposes."' Stewart gives a succinct portrait of Ridgeway: a 'great figure with splendid unkempt Irish head—half blind and prodding his way along with a stick; stopping as he walked down King's Parade to show a new Roman coin or to reveal a new academic plot to a friend.'[77] Harrison, with one foot in Ridgeway's ethnological camp and the other in Frazer's anthropological methods, was always afraid that the great Irishman would 'slay her with his shillelagh'. 'God *is* good', she wrote to Gilbert Murray in 1904, 'who made Ridgeway & Ernest Gardner & you and gave me eyes to see his human comedy.'[78]

Two weeks after her return to Cambridge Harrison received the shattering news that R. A. Neil had died suddenly of appendicitis. Instantly her double hope of human companionship and scholarly co-operation was devastated. Hope Mirrlees believed, on the testimony of Elinor (Ritchie) Paul, that they were engaged to be married. It is quite plausible that Harrison, by now 50 years old and released from the fear not only of pregnancy but also of the family life she so abhorred, was ready at this point to reconsider marriage. Marriage to Neil could have offered her exactly what she wanted without all the drawbacks that would have attended marriage to MacColl ten years previously. But for Harrison, who once said that she was convinced that if she wanted anything really badly it was sure not to be, the dream of such a lifelong companionship was to be denied. 'Things are horribly sad just now', she wrote to Jessie Crum. 'He was almost the best and quite the oldest

---

[76] Ibid. 243.   [77] Stewart, *Harrison*, 17–18.   [78] JEH to GM [206], 5 May 1904.

of my friends here—I lunched with him after the Reed lecture & planned all sorts of work in the vacation—& the next time we meet he is lying there in the college chapel. . . . and the worst of it is that every scrap of my present work has been discussed with him & simply aches with remembrance.'[79]

It was impossible for her to work under the circumstances, and there was no solace to be found anywhere in Cambridge, for wherever she turned her surroundings 'ached with remembrance'. There may have been an added unpleasantness to the situation, in a rumour that it had been necessary for her to be absent from Cambridge for the previous period. A cryptic entry in Hope Mirrlees's notebook refers to a 'disaster' that fell on Harrison after her new appointment to Newnham in connection with her relationship with a man (unnamed). As a result of this disaster, Mirrlees adds, it was imperative for her to be separated from him. It is not at all clear who Mirrlees had in mind when she wrote this. Was it Neil? And if so, what was the scandal? Nothing else survives that helps in the elucidation of this passage, but if the reference is to Neil, and if she went to Europe to separate herself from him, not from choice but from necessity, his death on her return must have been unbearable.

The situation is reminiscent of her early years in London, when some kind of malicious gossip had sent her fleeing to the Continent. Now, in 1901, she was once again hounded by accusations. It was not, as Duncan Wilson alleges in his biography of Gilbert Murray, that she was 'something of a Bohemian'[80] if we take Bohemian to imply disregard for morals, especially in the matter of sex. In the stricter sense of Bohemian, defined in the *Westminster Review* in 1862 as 'simply an artist or littérateur who, consciously or unconsciously secedes from conventionality in life and art'[81] the term describes her quite accurately. There were two elements in her behaviour that would have stirred up gossip. First, she was openly scathing towards Victorian hypocrisy in ethics. Secondly, her research in ancient religion was uncovering pagan beliefs that undoubtedly held appeal for her, and which she spoke about with unabashed enthusiasm. The reviews of her early books reveal the reactions of many of her contemporaries to her theories. As early as 1882, when she had published *Myths of the Odyssey*, she had been sarcastically stigmatized as an 'advanced thinker' for comparing the results of listening to the Sirens to the consequences of eating the forbidden fruit 'in the Semitic saga', and worse, she had written that 'the boundary between

---

[79] JEH to JS, n.d.   [80] Wilson, *Gilbert Murray*, 119.
[81] *Westminster Review*, July and Oct. 1862, 32–3.

good and evil is a soft shadow-land to a people whose moral standard was in the main aesthetic'.[82] The *Athenaeum* had published a review of *Mythology and Monuments of Ancient Athens* that attacked her with similar venom:

The school which holds that a study of the mental condition of savages is the best foundation of a scientific mythology, and that the legends of the Greeks resolve ultimately into traditions from ancestors on a level with Eskimo and Bushmen, can boast of an accomplished adherent in Miss Harrison . . . [T]he aim and end of truly scientific study is to demonstrate how the spirit of Hellenism subdued to its purposes of truth and beauty the most refractory legends and unpromising types, rather than to be bend on resolving all that is most gracefully expressive into the vile conceptions that habitually circle round a wigwam.[83]

If she had been able to keep academic distance between herself and her research it might have been possible to shrug off such criticism, but her approach to her studies was just the opposite: she believed, and made it quite clear that she believed, that what we learn from ancient Greek religion has everything to do with the way we live our present day lives. Now, with *Prolegomena to the Study of Greek Religion* taking shape in her mind, she was pointing enthusiastically to a society where there was (or so she believed) no institution of marriage—connections had taken place at random and people lived in joyful freedom from societal constraint.[84]

It was but a short step from these doctrines to the rumour that Jane Harrison was preaching promiscuity at Newnham. To make matters worse she taught her students Sappho, and was prepared to explain to the innocent what was meant by 'Sapphism'. Dean Inge reputedly said that Newnham was a dangerous place because of her, and her old friend Henry Butcher now joined her accusers, warning parents not to send their daughters to Newnham where Jane Harrison preached free love.[85] One may perhaps conjecture that a spiteful tongue or too ready an imagination extended the rumour to suggest that Harrison was living in some sort of illicit sexual relationship, either homo- or heterosexual. That there was such a rumour is quite probable; that it had any foundation is inherently improbable. Gilbert Murray, who knew her better than anyone, described her on one occasion as being 'like Aunt Fanny trying to be naughty'.[86] In other words, she enjoyed shocking people with her ideas and delighted in being unorthodox; nevertheless she was 'guarded by a native sanity and the ineradicable habits left by

---

[82] *Athenaeum*, 21 Jan. 1882, 87.   [83] *Athenaeum*, 2 Aug. 1890, 167.
[84] *Prolegomena*, 262.   [85] 'V[ictoria] de Bunsen' in Mirrlees's notebook.
[86] GM to MM, MS Gilbert Murray 456/178.

an old-fashioned and somewhat severe education, with its good manners, its fastidious taste, its personal dignity and power of self-control. These things remained', wrote Murray, alluding to her ethical standards, 'like the original writing in a palimpsest, clear and indelible beneath the superficial and fast-fading script of the last new philosopher or psychologist.'[87]

[87]   Murray, 'Jane Ellen Harrison: Address', 21.

6. *Ker* and *Cheiron*: Jane Harrison and Gilbert Murray 1901–1903

HARRISON spent the remainder of 1901 and 1902 working out her theories of Greek religion, incorporating the new material brought to light by archaeology. In the autumn of 1901 and spring of 1902 she gave a lecture series in the Cambridge Archaeological Museum on 'Primitive Greek Ritual and Mythology'. The first part dealt with primitive ritual and service, demonology, and 'theology' including sections on 'the making of a god' and 'the making of a goddess'. The second part addressed the mystery religions and bore the subtitle 'Many bear the wand, but the Bacchants are few'. As she worked through the material she constantly appealed to Murray for confirmation of her interpretation: 'I had worried over the Bacchae till it had become an excited tangle & a positive nightmare when I could not sleep, but you smoothed it all out so beautifully—I wish I had yr mind which thinks things right thro' instead of my own troublesome one which stops short just to be a curse to myself & my too kind friend.'[1] She had some misgivings about bothering Murray, who had been tired and ill, and added a fear that she played the part of a 'fatigue bacillus', a role she was to adopt frequently. But she needed Murray, and her questions could not wait.

She stayed with the Murrays again during the Christmas vacation. Lady Mary was by this time pregnant again—a state of affairs that threw Harrison into a turmoil of emotion:

I always feel when it happens to any one one knows that it must put everything & all the world out of focus or rather into a new focus. I should feel like God when he made the world—but alas, from being much with many sisters who suffer untold miseries I know too well there is another side—it is part of the horrible tangle of things that it should be so & always makes me want to curse. I daresay you have found a way of not cursing.[2]

---

[1] JEH to GM [17], 2 Sept. 1901.   [2] JEH to MM [21], 10 Dec. 1901.

She had at first protested that Lady Mary had much too much on her mind, quite apart from her state of health, to think of having guests, but Lady Mary must have persuaded her to accept. Staying in their home Harrison became aware of the Murrays' high-principled lifestyle. She was afraid that she had come to know them 'on false pretences', and the next couple of letters reveal her distress:

I can't tell you how upsetting & bewildering it is to me to find all these things that I have labelled 'fads' held steadily as principles by you two—who—much against my will I am forced to feel are far away above & before me. I have never known any one before you held these views—I mean any one I took seriously—people like my dear Alys Russell[3] . . . I can't take quite seriously. I don't know the least whether you are right or wrong, but if you are wrong yr wrong is something that makes me more ashamed than any right. . . . But the worst is that I know with a horrid certainty that you have let me get to know you on false pretences. I never shall be like that—it isn't in me—all I can say is that some things will be different ever after, I mean I shall never again sneer or laugh at the things that are sacred to you.

Well it is no use repenting on paper—& I am glad I did get to know you even on false pretences! I never felt so happy & at home in any one's house before.[4]

Quite seriously you are both bad for me—Lady Mary I think worst because she is best but you are both so hypermoralized & super-spiritualized that you force me to think of 'righteousness, Temperance, & judgment-to-come' &, in the words of my own Baptismal Service, I have by a healthy instinct of self-preservation 'renounced them all'. Everything is a danger to me that cannot be instantly translated into hard thinking. Mr Verrall always says & he is right that I am by nature rotten with superstition & emotional mysticism. As I said to Lady Mary I say to you that you have done me good in one way. I will never set my influence as I have done in the past, against good things because I see in you two how beautiful it all is—but I will not think about these things or try to practice them because for me that way madness lies & in my family we are already liberally supplied with lunatics![5]

She was sensitive enough to have been affected by the Murrays' idealism. Their lifestyle was austere and high-minded, ruled by a sense of duty that expressed itself partly in selfless hospitality. It is possible that the Murrays' self-imposed discipline in matters of diet had made a special impression on her. They had become vegetarians in the 1890s partly for health reasons, but also out of a conviction that eating meat involved cruelty to animals, though meat was always provided for guests. Harrison had a peculiar tenderness towards animals (a typical example was her comment on the death of a friend's dog: she described him as 'the only real Christian I have ever met')

---

[3] Alys Russell (née Whitall Smith), wife of Bertrand Russell, was a Quaker.
[4] JEH to GM [26], n.d.   [5] JEH to GM [25], n.d.

and must have been brought up short by this aspect of animal rights. The Murrays' plain living and teetotalism contrasted with Harrison's habits. She was known, said Bertrand Russell, for her capacity for whisky and cigarettes, of which she smoked thirty a day.

Ever since she had heard Murray reading his new translation of Euripides' *Hippolytus* she had been working to persuade him to come and give a lecture on Hippolytus at Cambridge. At this time Gilbert Murray, having resigned the Chair at Glasgow because of ill health, was living at home in Surrey (a state of affairs made possible by the generosity of Lady Mary's wealthy family). Reading Harrison's letters one does sense a certain measure of hypochondria. Toothache, sore throats, colds are all given as reasons for cancellation of engagements. By 13 February, after the date of the lecture had been changed several times, she wrote, 'Yes the 28th & let us have no more nonsense about our vile bodies or I shall begin to put D.V. after my dates.'[6]

On 14 March the lecture finally took place. She had by this time worked herself into a state of high nervousness, wanting everything to be quite perfect. Her feelings afterwards were ambivalent. 'Of course it goes without saying that it was a brilliant & beautiful success', she crooned to Lady Mary, who did not attend after all (and perhaps had never seriously intended to). But the first half had been 'solid politics—exquisitely done, but still politics'.[7]

Murray's translation of the *Hippolytus*, published in 1902, paved the way for Harrison's *Prolegomena* by daring to criticize the Olympian gods. The plot of Euripides' play deals with the destruction of the hero Hippolytus by Aphrodite, whom he had slighted by his devotion to Artemis. 'It is noteworthy how Euripides' moral hatred of the orthodox Olympians breaks out', Murray writes in the notes.

The human beings are full of love and mutual forgiveness. The goddess, radiantly lovely as she is and pure with the purity of dawn, still thinks of revenge, and—as appears at her departure—is, in some profoundly tragic sense, unloving: a being to be adored, not to love back. The last consolation of Hippolytus is the thought of his perfect devotion to one who in the nature of things can care for him only a little: 'I have obeyed Her all my days.'[8]

She spent the summer of 1902 with the Verralls in Switzerland, where she joined them for the 'air.' However, it was no holiday from work. 'I am working so hard', she wrote to Murray,[9] '. . . recasting the argument of Dionysos & in part re-writing Orpheus—that is chiefly why I wish you were

[6] JEH to GM [39], 13 Feb. 1902.   [7] JEH to MM 44, 15 Mar. 1902.
[8] Eur. *Hippolytus*, trans. Murray, 85–6.   [9] JEH to GM [74], 26 June 1902.

here. I can scarcely read my own script & realize to the full how good you were to labour thro' it.'[10]

Her letters reveal the extent to which her work and life were one. The Murrays' fourth child, Basil, had been born in June, just before Harrison had left for Switzerland, and she had dashed off a letter: 'Oh I am more glad than I can possibly say—& *so* relieved to get the news before I start. . . . I am so glad it is Basil not Ruth tho' it's sad for Ruth not to come into this good world,' and advised her 'if he cries too loud get a 'liknon' & set him in a ploughed field—that will still his crying. . . . Well I hope he will grow up to be just like his father (only not *quite* so pragmatical) & to write beautiful things tho' I shall be gone to the home of Hades & never read them.'[11] To Gilbert she wrote separately, candidly—and revealingly—, 'The dogma of the Fatherhood of you I have always found difficult to grasp—even when I saw all those absurd children asking you riddles at breakfast. This world is a splendid place but I am always *furious* when any one comes into it & so would you be if you were a reasonable Woman [sic].'[12]

Another person who played a significant role in Harrison's life during the years she was writing *Prolegomena* was Bertrand Russell, a cousin of Lady Mary Murray. Russell had married the American Alys Pearsall Smith in 1894, and now, seven years later, realized he was no longer in love with her. For a period in 1901 the Russells shared a house with the philosopher Alfred North Whitehead and his wife Evelyn, and Russell had fallen in love with Evelyn, drawn to her by her experience of acute heart pain. Russell had been present with his wife Alys that evening in 1901 when Murray had read his *Hippolytus* at the Verralls' house. Later that evening, returning home to find Evelyn in extreme pain, Russell had undergone a strange mystic experience, leaving him with a vivid awareness of 'the unendurable loneliness of every human soul'.

It follows that . . . in human relations one should penetrate to the core of loneliness in each person and speak to that. . . . I felt that I knew the inmost thoughts of everybody that I met in the street, and though this was, no doubt, a delusion, I did in actual fact find myself in far closer touch than previously with all my friends.[13]

---

[10] Her handwriting was atrocious, the bane of publishers and biographers alike.

[11] JEH to GM [71], 16 June 1902. The *liknon* was 'the shovel-shaped basket used for the carrying of fruits, served in primitive days another purpose, that of cradle for a child' (*Prolegomena*, 523). For the festival of the Liknophoria, see ibid. 517 ff. 'The child rises out of a cornucopia, symbol of fertility . . . It is all the same beautiful symbolism tht refuses coldly to discriminate between the human and the natural, that sees in marriage the plough, in man the sower, in earth the mother, and in the fruits of the earth the new-born child' (ibid. 525–6).

[12] JEH to GM [72], n.d.

[13] *The Autobiography of Bertrand Russell*, 2 vols. (London: Unwin Brothers, 1967), i. 145–6.

His new awareness of the pain of existential loneliness must have touched his relationship with Harrison, so accurately did this perception apply to her own condition. At Whitsun 1902 Harrison was among a group at the Russell's home at Friday's Hill, Surrey, not far from the Murrays' home at Churt. The party included Sidney and Beatrice Webb, and Gilbert Murray was there for part of the time. Alys had left for a 'rest cure' in Switzerland. On the Monday Russell and Harrison had gone for a walk alone, and she confided to him all her troubles.

Russell's own emotional life at the time was in chaos. Nine years later he confessed to Ottoline Morrell that in 1902 there had been a woman in his life whose identity he guarded closely:

> Again I loved, piercing the prison of flame
> Where one stern soul in lonely anguish burned
> Forgetting the earth once more with love I came
> Into that hell whence no light hopes returned[14]

Russell's biographers, Ronald Clark and Ray Monk, have tentatively taken this woman to be Evelyn Whitehead. However, Russell recorded in his journal an aspect of the Whitsun weekend that he did not divulge to Alys. He wrote on 18 May 1903 how that day the previous year stood out as a happy one:

At that time I was inspired; my energy was ten times what it usually is, I had a swift insight & sympathy, the sense of a new and wonderful wisdom intoxicated me. But I was writing cold letters to Alys in the deliberate hope of destroying her affection . . . Also I was reckless in giving sympathy where it would have been better to withhold it . . . I had not learnt to forgo the affection of people I was fond of.[15]

Ronald Clark quotes this diary entry in connection with his friendship with Evelyn Whitehead. But on this occasion it was Jane Harrison, not Evelyn Whitehead, who inspired Russell. Interestingly, the language of the journal entry echoes that of his mystical experience after the Hippolytos lecture, when he had first become aware of the 'unendurable loneliness' of every human soul. It is pointless to try and sort out the details of their emotional entanglements, but clearly, for this weekend at least, Russell and Harrison found solace in each other. If there was anything more to their relationship, both of them kept their silence.

He had been present at the *Hippolytus* lecture that year and attended Harrison's lectures with interest—and not a little humour and raillery. By this time she was grappling with Dionysos, whose worship embodied 'a new

[14] Bertrand Russell to Lady Ottoline Morrell, quoted in Ronald Clark, *The Life of Bertrand Russell* (London: Jonathan Cape, 1975), 88, 151.   [15] Diary, 18 May 1903, BRA.

religious impulse, an impulse really religious', a 'return to nature', a 'breaking of bonds and limitations and crystallizations, and a desire for the life rather of the emotions than of the reason, a recrudescence it may be of animal passions'.[16] The mysticism attracted her, but not the 'animal passions'. There were two major difficulties for her in his cult: the eating of raw flesh—live flesh—and the drunkenness which accompanied his ecstasy. 'To become a "Bacchos" it was necessary to do a good deal more than dance enthusiastically upon the mountains', she concluded. The tearing of live flesh was an integral part. 'I wish you could persuade her', Murray wrote to Russell, 'that she cannot—no, nor all Newnham together—tear a live bull to pieces with her bare hands . . . she believes that some Cretan women actually did it'.[17] Russell replied that he would provide the bull if she would undertake to tear it limb from limb at her next lecture in the Archaeological Museum. 'That absurd B[ertrand] R[ussell] came in the other day' she protested to Murray, 'with his eyes shining & a sporting offer to "stand" a Wild Bull if I wld rend it limb from limb.'[18]

By July she was 'in sore straits' about a number of technical details regarding the meaning of specific words in the Orphic fragments, crucial for her understanding of the religion of Dionysus. She was 'desolate' without the Verralls while Arthur was away at a spa in search of cures for his arthritis ('Poor Mr Verrall has had to go off to Harrogate to be boiled and baked'),[19] but even more desolate when Murray took issue with her over points of scholarship:

I behave like the thing I most despise in the world, a half educated scholiast piling up odds & ends of information & not taking the time or the trouble to see what they are really worth & how things really were (& herein lies the sting!) I see you have been laughing at me, & thinking me, of course in yr polite way, a pretentious fool—& so I am.

Why can't I behave with dignity, recognize my limitations of mind & training & keep my second rateness to myself? Something that I have struggled against all my life compells [sic] me to write books but at least I needn't inflict my proofs on you. I know the rest will be full of this sort of badness—it is partly hurry & partly, oh well, just me. I shld like to begin everything all over from the beginning & pray to the Lord for a new mind. My heart is all right, its my head damn it, & that's the only thing that really matters.

Yrs. JEH

[16] *Prolegomena*, 363–4, 444.   [17] GM to Bertrand Russell, 26 Apr. 1902, BRA.

[18] JEH to GM [141], n.d. Jessie Stewart has added the date 15 May 1902 (perhaps from the envelope), and has then wrongly assigned the letter a place in the correspondence of May 1903.

[19] JEH to GM [81], 3 Aug. 1902.

I shall finish the horrid book somehow because I am caught in the Wheel of Things, but I won't bother you any more—do yr own beautiful work in peace, & sometimes if you are kind send me a little verse to cheer me & make me feel that nothing else matters.[20]

Two days later,

Thank you—this is a kind & most comforting letter—it came on my birthday! to help me to make Good Resolutions.

Perhaps I was rather morbid. I had spent a sleepless night. . . . & things looked black. Also, as always happens, everything came together. Mr Verrall had just done looking over the Erinyes & tho he was as always, angelically kind, I cld see that he thought it was all much ado about scarcely anything, & was puzzled as to why a sane or fairly sane person shld write such stuff.[21]

In October Murray shared with her the new preface he had written for *A History of Ancient Greek Literature*, in which he wrote of his methodology. 'I have tried', he wrote, '. . . to realise, as well as I could, what sort of men the various Greek authors were, what they liked and disliked, how they earned their living and spent their time.' He acknowledged how the conceptions of the Greeks change with the passing generations, declaring his debt to the anthropologists:

The 'serene and classical Greek' of Winckelmann and Goethe did good service to the world in his day, though we now feel him to be mainly a phantom. He has been succeeded, especially in the works of painters and poets, by an aesthetic and fleshly Greek in fine raiment, an abstract Pagan who lives to be contrasted with an equally abstract early Christian or Puritan, and to be glorified or mishandled according to the sentiments of his critic . . . There is more flesh and blood in the Greek of the anthropologist, the foster-brother of Kaffirs and Hairy Ainos.[22]

Murray had expressed his aim to maintain a proportion between 'the scientific and the aesthetic' aspects of his subject, acknowledged his dependence on 'philological and antiquarian' arguments, and explained his decision to keep his exposition clear of technicalities and references to other scholars. Harrison told him she was 'quite sad I am not in it',[23] and went on to reflect on what she learned from him:

I don't think I ever understood till I knew you what taking the right sort of fruitful pains meant—one sees so much barren classical effort that I had let myself grow to despise minute work & take a sort of stupid pride in splashing round inaccurately or

---

[20] JEH to GM [89], 7 Sept. 1902.   [21] JEH to GM [90], 9 Sept. 1902.
[22] *A History of Ancient Greek Literature* (repr. New York: Appleton, 1932), p. ix.
[23] JEH to GM [104], 28 Oct. 1902.

superficially, & now you show me the beauty of all that burrowing, a peculiar beauty something like yr 'atmosphere of creativeness steeped in critical meditation'.[24]

She may have gushed over Murray's preface and admired his methods, but was never able to make them her own. They disagreed fundamentally about the need for footnotes and documentation. She differed from Murray in her need to share with her readers the long—and often tedious—path that led to her conclusions. In a moment of self-knowledge she confessed to Murray the central weakness in her own work: 'Very tardily I admit that one of yr criticisms was just. I see I have not stated fairly the views of my opponents, I didn't bother to consider what they really *did* think. It's very troublesome bothering with other people's minds but I will try to do it—as you bother with mine.[25]

Forms of address were a problem for Harrison's generation, a problem poignantly illustrated in a postscript she wrote to Lady Mary Murray in January 1903: 'Cld you ever bear to use my plain name [Jane]? You have never had to bear the ugliness of being called Miss. I don't believe yre properly thankful for yr mercies but they ought to make you thoughtful for others.'[26]

All of her early letters to Murray begin *in medias res*, avoiding the problem by omitting the customary 'Dear . . .', and she signs herself JEH. After a while she must have begun to feel that this was too stark. Nicknames among friends were, at that period, a way around the difficulty. In January 1903 she subconsciously defined their relationship with a name that playfully alluded to her dependence on him and her fear that she plagued him with her requests for help. She began signing her letters 'Ker' or 'Potnia Keron'— 'Lady of the Spirits' (a pun on the title 'Potnia Theron', or 'Lady of the Wild Things')[27] The word 'ker' is hard to translate. In *Prolegomena* she likens 'keres' to 'a sort of personified bacilli', which could cause disease, blindness or madness, 'little inherent physical pests'.[28] There is a menacing aspect to the name of which she seems to have been dimly aware. As her dependence on

[24] JEH to GM [105], 29 Oct. 1902.   [25] JEH to GM [108], 7 Nov. 1902.

[26] JEH to MM, 2 Jan. 1903.

[27] See Homer, *Iliad* 21. 470, where the epithet is applied to Artemis the huntress. Harrison discusses the iconography of the Lady of the Wild Things in *Prolegomena*, 264, 497.

[28] Ibid. 166, 171. Chapter 5 of *Prolegomena* is devoted to an analysis of 'The Demonology of Ghosts and Sprites and Bogeys', vengeful spirits and ministers of death. Renate Schlesier, in a personal conversation, suggested to me that the name carries a sinister sense of bringing death, and indicates that all her life Harrison saw herself as the one who had caused the death of her mother. Given Harrison's expressed fears that she was to Murray a 'fatigue bacillus', I do not think it is necessary to read such an interpretation into her adopted nickname.

Murray grew, so did her jealousy. She resented his involvement in politics and anything else that took him away from his work on Greek literature, and so from her—she joked about it but the jealousy was real—expostulating in June 1902 that his activities confirmed her 'hatred of History Newspapers Politics & Politicians, but how you *can* see all this & go on as you do wasting yr time & strength on such things'.[29] Unlike Murray, Harrison was, to use her own phrase, 'blinded by over-focus', and her single-mindedness put a continual strain on her relationships. For Murray, as her mentor, she coined the nickname 'Cheiron' after the wise centaur who was entrusted with the rearing of heroes, and most commonly refers to him simply as 'Ther' ('beast').

The 'wild bull' was not the only topic of ritual research that attracted interest from other Cambridge dons. 'My book it wld seem is being written by everyone except me!',[30] she cried as she wrestled with 'edible cereals and grasses', elucidating the origin of intoxicants, a topic which Francis Darwin as a botanist insisted was important.[31] On another occasion he found her busy writing an article on the 'Mystica Vannus Iacchi'. The mention of 'Iacchus' mystical fan' is found in Vergil's *Georgics* without elucidation, in a list of the husbandman's equipment.[32] The article attempted to answer two questions: In what sense is a winnowing-fan 'mystical'? and What is its connection with Iacchus? She argued that the winnowing process was 'mystic' in that the Greeks believed that the fan which physically purified grain had a mystical power to purge humanity, and that purification and fertility were closely linked in the primitive mind. The *vannus*, she claimed, had always been associated with Dionysos / Iacchos, the god of the Northerners' beer before he encountered Mediterranean wine.

She records in her *Reminiscences* how Francis Darwin interrogated her:

'What is a *vannus*?' he asked. 'Oh, a "fan",' I said; 'it was a mystical object used in ceremonies of initiation.' 'Yes, but Virgil says it is an agricultural implement. Have you ever seen one?' 'No,' I confessed. '*And you are writing about a thing you have never seen*,' groaned my friend. 'Oh, you classical people!' It did not end there. He interviewed farmers—no result; he wrote to agricultural institutes abroad, and, finally, in remote provincial France, unearthed a mystic 'fan' still in use, and had it despatched to Cambridge. Luckily he also found that his old gardener was perhaps the last man in England who could use the obsolete implement. On his lawn were to be seen a gathering of learned scholars trying, and failing, to winnow with the *vannus*. Its odd shape explained all its uses, mystic and otherwise.[33]

---

[29] JEH to GM [74], 26 June 1902.   [30] JEH to GM [101], 11 Oct. 1902.
[31] See *Prolegomena*, ch. 8.   [32] Vergil, *Georgics* I. 165.   [33] *Reminiscences*, 57–8.

Even that was not the end of the matter. Francis Darwin's son, Bernard, crowned the occasion with a poem, gently poking fun at his father's insistence on scientific detail and exactitude:

> Oh! where shall be found
> The real scholarship sound
>   The prop and the pride of the Briton,
> When ladies of note
> Spurn what Aeschylus wrote
>   And that which he ought to have written.
>
> Oh! to think that she might
> Shed a flood of new light
>   On the rise and the fall of the Gracchi
> But prefers to explore
> That insoluble bore
>   Called the Mystica Vannus Iacchi.
>
> Just this and no more—
> E'er his corn he could store
>   In his ante-pelasgian hovel
> Did primitive man
> Use a winnowing fan
>   Or only a winnowing shovel?
>
> Oh! had I the pen
> Of a Phillimore, then
>   I could say what I thought, but alack! I
> Am powerless quite
> To throw even that light
>   On the Mystica Vannus Iacchi.
>
> Now somebody may
> Be a Triton some day
>   Mid anthropological minnows
> By tracing the plans
> That were primitive man's
>   From the way that a Finlander winnows.

11. A 'winnowing fan' by Bernard Darwin

> But persons of sense
> And of true eminence
>   Should turn and come sorrowing back, I
> Shall venture to hold
> Into scholarship's fold
>   From that dreary old Vannus Iacchi.[34]

That was November. The allusion to the Finlander refers to a letter, complete with photographs of winnowing-fans Darwin received from a Finnish writer who had recently written a book on primitive agriculture in Finland. By the time she had assimilated all the material she received from different parts of Europe on winnowing, she had material for two long articles. On 16 February 1903, Harrison gave a lecture on the 'Mystica Vannus Iacchi'. On a side table lay some object covered with a cloth. At the moment of revelation she flourished a genuine 'winnowing-basket', identical to the Greek reliefs that she had illustrated with her slides. The *Cambridge Review* reported the lecture as an 'intellectual treat'.[35]

Her final version of the *vannus* lecture was published in the *Journal of Hellenic Studies*.[36] She devoted a great deal of attention to an examination of winnowing practices, drawing on evidence from literature, art, and present-day peasant practices, and stressing the difference between a *ptuon*, or shovel, which was used to throw the grain into the air to be sifted by the wind, and a *liknon*, in which the grain was shaken in a flat basket in such a way as to eject the chaff and keep the grain. The article was complete with a photograph showing winnowing-fans in use:

Happily baskets of precisely the same shape . . . are still in use for winnowing, and the process, though almost obsolete owing to the introduction of winnowing machines, can still be seen. I should like to say at the outset that what is new in my discussion so far as it relates to the shape and use of the 'fan' is entirely due to the kindness of Mr. Francis Darwin, to whom this paper owes its inception.[37]

'It was a lifelong lesson to me,' she admitted.

It was not quite all my fault. I had been reared in a school that thought it was far more important to parse a word than to understand it. I had myself, as a student, eagerly asked why the *vannus* was mystic, and the answer had been, 'You have construed the

---

[34] The poem (in Bernard Darwin's hand) is included with the letters from GM to JEH [93].

[35] *Cambridge Review*, 19 Feb. 1903, 194.

[36] *Journal* of *Hellenic Studies* 23 (1903), 292–324, with supplementary notes in 24 (1904), 251–4.

[37] Ibid. 23 (1903), 299–30 and 292, n. 2.

passage correctly; that will do for the present.' And as my 'coach'[38] closed his Virgil, he remarked sadly, 'Bad sport in subjunctives today.' Such training was perhaps the best possible for my always flighty mind.[39]

Her study of the religion of Dionysos led naturally into an examination of Orphism—a path up which she was led with the enthusiasm of the initiate herself. 'The full significance, the higher spiritual developments of the religion of Dionysos are only understood through the doctrine of Orpheus, and the doctrine of Orpheus apart from the religion of Dionysos is a dead letter', she wrote in *Prolegomena*.[40] Research into Orphism was stimulated at this time by the discovery of eight inscribed tablets on gold leaf. Six of these were found in tombs in Southern Italy, one in Rome, and one in Crete. 'Buried with the dead they contain instructions for his conduct in the world below, exhortations to the soul, formularies to be repeated, confessions of faith and of ritual performed, and the like.'[41] They are an important source for Orphic ritual, and despite the fact that they had already been much discussed, Harrison felt that their full importance for the history of Greek religion had not yet been appreciated. It was imperative for her to see them at first hand. One of them, the so-called Peteleia tablet, had been acquired by the British Museum, where she had studied it. It was difficult to decipher, the text is fragmentary, and the end of it makes no consecutive sense. Murray came to her rescue. 'I am glad you like the tablets,' she wrote to him on 1 May 1902, 'they seem to me the only really inside evidence we have.'[42] It was obvious that she needed to travel to Italy to see the rest of them, and needed Murray to be at her side.

Her plans coincided with those of Murray. There were manuscripts of Euripides to be studied in the Laurentian Library, and Murray had repeatedly received invitations from Bernard and Mary Berenson to visit them in Italy where Berenson, a connoisseur and collector of art, housed his collection in the famous villa at I Tatti, near Florence. Mary Berenson was a sister of Alys Russell, and so distantly related to the Murrays. Murray, nervous about his health, was attracted by a visit to a warm climate, and finally decided to accept the Berensons' invitation in March of 1903. Meanwhile Harrison travelled to Sicily with other friends, the Dakynses,[43] before accepting the Berensons' invitation to join the party at I Tatti.

[38] Presumably Henry Butcher, who might also have argued that it was not quite all his fault, either.   [39] *Reminiscences*, 57–8.

[40] *Prolegomena*, 572.   [41] Ibid.   [42] JEH to GM [55], 1 May 1902.

[43] Henry Graham Dakyns, senior (1838–1911), was a Xenophon scholar and had been tutor to the children of the poet Tennyson. He had a son of the same name who was a friend of Bertrand Russell and G. E. Moore.

The mixture of personalities at I Tatti led to a variety of tensions, recorded in a number of different letters. Harrison got on well with BB (as Bernard Berenson was known), who talked anthropology and ethnology with ease. Mary Berenson found her very silly, and believed she was in love with Murray. She wrote to her mother, Hannah Whitall Smith, of the 'amusement' they were deriving from the comedy playing under their roof. Harrison's whole 'feu intérieur', she wrote, was taken up with 'amourous [sic] adventures', as she raved about MacColl's beautiful eyes, while the rest of them winked behind her back.

And now, sad to say, poor Gilbert is to be torn from his house of repose for an 'amourous adventure' of which he is, and will remain, perfectly unconscious. She is going to take him off to that hell of church bells, Perugia, for a week, then to Rome, then to Naples . . . He said he would 1000 times rather stay here . . . but nothing will induce her to listen to so much as a day's delay. He even thought of feigning illness (I suggested it!) but in the end his Puritan conscience would not allow him to adopt that ruse. He says she would be fearfully offended and say that he was throwing over his old friends for new ones. And, it appears, she has taken the journey to 'take care of him'. She is not a woman of character sufficient for anyone to suggest her altering her plans for *his* benefit, for she is very selfish and jealous, and obviously 'soft' on him (he doesn't know it). Indeed, I, taking it for granted she was like Alys and me, *did* tell her that it would be better for him (as it clearly would) to remain in the quiet here instead of being chivied about in noisy hotels, and she took such a hatred for me that not all my most 'winning ways' can overcome it.

I daresay she is very nice when she is not bent for flirtation, but I can only say that now she is quite disagreeable. Logan and Emily say they think it isn't really Miss Harrison but a pseudo-Jane who has come in her place. She is so dull and heavy, will talk hardly at all, except about MacColl's divine eyes, & in tête-à-tête about 'dear Gilbert' and the nervousness and stupidity of Lady Mary (she admits she is 'awfully good'), and so we are fairly 'stuffed' as the Italians say. She 'loathes whist' and our evenings seem *nearly interminable*!! Gilbert proposed a game last night, & she was distinctly huffy! She is determined to carry him off on Tuesday, and I should really rather not have him if his presence entailed hers, although for his sake—he dreads the journey so!—I did invite them to stay on another week. But she won't, thank goodness. She is such an awful warning to Emily and me not to pursue flirtations beyond the limits set by nature. She is 53!!![44]

Two events ruffled emotions still further. Murray 'threw a bomb' into the midst of the company by expressing a liking for Tennyson, and shocked the company by reciting *Maud*. Mary Berenson concludes this letter with an

[44] Mary Berenson to Hannah Whitall Smith, 15 Mar. 1903. Formerly in the private collection of Barbara Strachey Halpern.

insightful observation: 'The truth is, I think, that Murray has never distinguished clearly among his different sets of interests, his aesthetic, technical, dramatic & benevolent interests. He is very aristocratic & exclusive by nature in his tastes, but forces 'catholicity' on himself by principle. At least, this is how we read his strange lapses from *our* standards!!' The second incident occurred over the game of the 'Golden Urn': a game in which they judged the merit of famous passages from English poetry, making emendations and occasionally bracketing a line or word. Harrison said little, but retired early. Murray came upstairs to find her pacing the floor. 'The fops, the insolent fops!' she wept.[45] 'I was rather disconcerted,' Murray wrote to Lady Mary. 'Of course I agree with her; perhaps if I had been alone, I should have felt the same rage, instead of taking it good-humouredly and chaffing them.'[46]

Harrison had no desire to stay long at I Tatti, feeling hopelessly out of place, and was making attempts to tear Murray away to Naples to look at an Orphic tablet. 'You may trust me absolutely that he shall not help me in any way that can hurt him', she wrote to Lady Mary. 'I think he has had enough of this house and is ready to go. They are just kindness itself but personally I don't think I *cld* stay long.'[47]

The whole episode is interesting for the light it sheds on how differently different personalities can perceive the same situation. Murray's biographer, Duncan Wilson, aptly comments on the Berensons' perception of Murray: 'Mrs Berenson was left with the impression of an utterly charming, high-minded, unworldly academic, unable to cope with any intrigue or practical demand. She did not realize . . . what strength of conviction and purpose was concealed by those delightful manners, and what nervous strain was involved in the concealment.[48] Murray wrote to his wife that he scarcely realized till he got away what a strain I Tatti had been.[49] Harrison could not wait to get Murray to herself; Murray on the other hand confided to Bertrand Russell that 'Miss Harrison and I go to Perugia tonight. I do so want to go home!'[50]

Nevertheless, Murray could write to his wife from Perugia, 'I like Perugia & this hotel very much, & on the whole find Miss H a good companion. She is sensible, amusing, quick in the up-take & very interesting. On the other hand some things set her on edge—as the Berensons did!'[51]

[45] Wilson, *Gilbert Murray*, 101. See also Stewart, *Harrison*, 28.
[46] GM to MM, 15 Mar. 1903, MS Gilbert Murray 456/139.
[47] JEH to MM [137], n.d.   [48] Wilson, *Gilbert Murray*, 102.
[49] GM to MM, 21 Mar. 1903, MS Gilbert Murray 456/144–5.
[50] GM to BR, 17 Mar. 1903, BRA.
[51] GM to MM, 19 Mar. 1903, MS Gilbert Murray 456/141.

Harrison could be extremely demanding. On this occasion Murray could scarcely conceal his irritation with the imposition she placed on him. He found her nevertheless 'an admirable companion—friendly & easy & extraordinarily interesting. And she goes her own way & works by herself in a manner that lightens the slight burden of companionship.' He helped her with the proofs of *Prolegomena*, ('she is indeed a most able writer, though her views seem to me often foolish—like Aunt Fanny trying to be naughty') and then left her to finish them while he went to look at paintings.[52]

He was beginning to think she was older than he had thought. Not only did she speak of him and the Berensons as belonging to another generation, but also was 'quite unfit to walk in the sun or uphill', though this difficulty may have been due not so much to her age as to her chronic respiratory problems. He had not forgotten the fainting episode at Barford, and was perpetually afraid of a recurrence.

In Rome they worked on the tablets together, Murray finding he could read them much better than Harrison, from his knowledge of manuscripts and palaeography, not to mention better eyesight. There was an unpleasant sequel. Harrison, stupefied by the tablets, reached a state of mental bewilderment. Unable to read or to make up her mind what to do, she started wandering about, straying into the path of trains. Murray was understandably anxious.

All her life Harrison made strenuous demands of her friends, and could be blind to their own rights, needs, or plans. Murray now discovered that she was really nervous of travelling alone, especially by night. She was even more fearful of being left alone. 'And of course she could not *bear* to join herself to an ordinary English party!'[53]

Lady Mary was suspicious. Her husband tried to reassure her that he told her everything, while Harrison wrote enthusiastically about how the warm weather was good for his health:

I think what he wants is a long, quiet stay in a *warm* climate. . . . It is quite pathetic to see how he thaws & brightens when his feet are in a spot of sun! . . .

Well I need not tell you that I have had a beautiful time—getting his help over the Orphic tablets has made me too happy for words. I[t] was just what I wanted most in the world. If you had been here it wld have been just perfect. My inhuman heart is very full of Orphic tablets & the like, but I feel by sympathy other people's aches & emptinesses & have some human longing of my own after you—& yesterday when we went to the Aquarium I even longed for the children, the fishes were so preposterous & sailed up in the glass wall apparently with express intent to make

---

[52] GM to MM, 21 Mar. 1903, MS Gilbert Murray 456/144.
[53] GM to MM, 9 Apr. 1903, MS Gilbert Murray 456/180.

faces at us. Do not write, you have enough letters as it is. I shall send another report soon.[54]

The note of insincerity rings again in these letters—her professed devotion to Murray and the good of his health, the expression of regret that Lady Murray was not there to make it 'just perfect'. All she really wanted was to be alone with Murray (and the Orphic tablets)—a hankering she could in no way share with Lady Mary.

[54] JEH to MM [138], 28 Mar. 1903.

7. *Prolegomena to the Study of Greek Religion*: Newnham 1903–1906

THE summer of 1903 was spent on the manuscript of *Prolegomena*, 'writing too much and too fast'. 'My head has completely & abruptly stopped work . . . (My vile body is quite well)', she wrote to Murray on 15 May.[1] She prevailed upon Murray to provide an appendix on the Orphic tablets, but warned him that if it struck her as pedantic she would rewrite it ('I won't have any nice human book stuffed with saw-dust').[2] By July it was done and met with her approval. 'What a beautiful learned appendix & how "ther"-ish it is in places. I do like the plan of putting curses in the middle of hexameters, it was what I always wanted to do when I had to write them. Seriously I think it is all very interesting & will make a dear little book by itself. . . . Thank you very much. What a lot of work it must have meant.'[3]

On 28 August she received the news that Ellen (Crofts) Darwin had died. Ellen Darwin had suffered from heart disease for so many years that, as Bertrand Russell said, 'everyone had given up thinking of her as likely to die'. The end came as a great shock to all her friends, but Harrison was particularly affected. The death of any close friend brings intimations of one's own mortality, but Harrison's identification with Ellen Darwin was intensified: she too suffered from a chronic heart condition. 'Yes, Ellen Darwin was my oldest & in some ways my closest friend', Harrison wrote to Lady Mary Murray.

I fell in love with her the first night we came up together as students & it has been so ever since—she was to me one of the best things in my life, perhaps *the* best. There was a sort of moral sureness that made her a real refuge; she was not popular here, very few knew her & fewer still cared for her & she was very intolerant of any ordinary human worldliness—her utter lack of *spiritual* conventions made many people here uncomfortable with her—it often made me ashamed & rebuked & it *was* a sort of limitation but such a beautiful one.[4]

[1] JEH to GM [141], 15 May 1903.   [2] JEH to GM [152], 24 Sept. 1903.
[3] JEH to GM [148], 20 Jul. 1903.   [4] JEH to MM [149], 10 Sept. 1903.

Ellen had been chronically unhappy for years, and Harrison tried to comfort herself by the thought that her suffering was finally at an end.

To make matters worse for Harrison, after Ellen's death Francis Darwin found Cambridge intolerable:

> I don't think he can face it, so I shall almost lose him & Frances the child. I wish people who talk about Xian faith cld see the wonderful brave patience of these two who are utter agnostics. It is a thing I can never forget tho' I can scarcely bear to see it. You will understand. . . .
>
> Yes, it has been a great comfort to have Orphic tablets & Mr Murray just now. It was my birthday yesterday—so you wrote me a birthday letter unbeknown—& I had a tea-party of him only we talked about nothing sad but I felt befriended.[5]

The Russells, despite the severe stresses in their own marriage, also stood by her in her loss, inviting her to join them on a bicycling holiday in the Lake District in September. 'Miss Harrison has a curious antipathy to moral senti-ments', he wrote to Gilbert Murray on this occasion, 'which causes always a more or less latent unhappiness between her & me, & makes my liking for her less than my respect & admiration. She says she likes or dislikes people chiefly according to their behaviour to her, which is very feminine & rather a pity; but I am sure it not wholly true.'[6] Russell had just completed *The Principles of Mathematics*,[7] which Harrison had attempted to read. 'I tried to murmur his tenth axiom in BR's ear at the [Newnham College] Council, but broke down in the middle from emotion at its luminosity—but if *you* can understand his book of course *I* can. There's a real axiom for you', she wrote to Gilbert Murray.[8] Comparing the averred sanity and wholesomeness of her own writing to Russell's 'relations of P,R,Q', she wondered why it was that she found his company infinitely refreshing, even though she could never understand one word of his dark sayings. 'Is it that Personality is sovereign or Reason the merest subject? He wouldn't like that solution', she mused.[9]

It had been a hard summer. She can hardly have failed to notice the strained relationship between Bertrand and Alys Russell. Lady Mary Murray, hypochondriac as ever, complained of ill health, and Gilbert also was 'moderately ill'. Verrall's health was steadily deteriorating. Harrison had worries of her own, too, since her fellowship had been granted her by Newnham College to write *Prolegomena* and was due now to expire, though Newnham had invited her to stay on as a lecturer for three more years.

---

[5] JEH to MM [149], 10 Sept. 1903.　　[6] Bertrand Russell to GM, 26 Sept. 1903, BRA.

[7] Russell, *The Principles of Mathematics* (Cambridge: Cambridge University Press, 1903).

[8] JEH to GM [143], 16 Jun. 1903.　　[9] JEH to GM [144], 18 Jun. 1903.

Murray must have looked for opportunities for her. 'How kind of you to think about fellowships', she wrote to him.

It touches me deeply, but tho the Fellowship lapses & leaves me less income by a third I still stay here—the arrangement is that I live here for nothing, giving in return the blessing of my presence (no small thing) & lecturing for part II & on other things, like Kers, when I have anything to say.[10] It suits me perfectly & if I were decently economical (which I am not) I shld still be quite rich. I loathe money—it is so ugly & abstract & unmeaning & really ought not to exist in a decent state.[11]

A more immediate anxiety was accommodation for the short period before the beginning of term when the college was closed. She found a place at High Wycombe,

a *real* workman's cottage, all cleaned & painted & furnished but still a real one & in strict confidence I *hate* it—I can't even think, the walls are so close—why is it that every attempt to lead the simpler life is either farcical or hideously uncomfortable. Give me a good old rotten civilization with marble halls & pampered menials—also the air is bad. I can't stand it . . .[12]

With the feeling of being pushed from pillar to post she spent the few remaining days of her exile staying with her friend Bella Napier in London, trying to work on the proofs of *Prolegomena*, and feeling helpless without 'Mr Verrall & Liddell & Scott'.[13] The publishers, she complained, were so hideously learned. They were now querying 'turndun' and 'Nova Zembla', wanting to spell it 'Zemlya'. 'I refused with an oath', she inveighed.

Worst of all, her own health was troubling her and her doctor suspected that her thyroid gland was the root cause of her shortness of breath, fainting, and nervousness ('but for it a great strong cow like me wld have no nerves at all, for my heart is as the heart of a wild bull'). The doctor also told her she was on no account to be worried. ('Remember this and accept all my theories & emendations unquestioned henceforth.')[14] Her one solace was Murray's friendship and their shared work. For her birthday he had sent her a copy of August Nauck's *Fragments of Euripides*. ' "Nauck" was sitting in my room looking so stout & comfortable & comforting—for I am a deeply dejected Ker—but after all what does it matter if they do cut my throat as long as there are all these dear little lonely fragments to be translated & put together?'[15]

---

[10] She had in fact been appointed to lecture for two terms each year. See Newnham Council Minutes, 16 May 1903, published in vol. 3: 1897–1912.

[11] JEH to GM [154], 27 Sept. 1903.   [12] JEH to GM [156], n.d.

[13] JEH to GM [159], n.d. The reference is to Liddell and Scott's *Greek Lexicon*.

[14] JEH to GM [160], 11 Oct. 1903.   [15] Ibid.

Her doctor advised her to give up smoking and prescribed the drugs akapnia and strophanthus to ease the withdrawal. 'He says there is no disease in the heart at present,' she wrote to Lady Mary, 'but the thyroid mischief wld easily set it up if not checked & at present my poor old heart is doing all its work twice over. I am so relieved that he doesn't want to operate. I am a horrid coward & I have seen so much of the resulting shock from operations.'[16] After a fortnight's treatment he described the improvement in her heart's action as little short of incredible, but her relief at this news was counteracted by the misery of withdrawal.

I ought to be glad & relieved, She wrote to Gilbert Murray, for I am a contemptible coward about physical pain, but yet I feel I cld screw myself up to any operation rather than face this dreariness—it is a daily hourly misery that one cannot even dignify by the name of pain—just to be told to get over a bad habit—ugh. If giving up drink is like the wrench from a lover—who all the time you half-despise—giving up smoke is like parting from the best friend who always comforts & never torments.

Also I hate asceticism & am compelled to practice it. All my life I have meant to behave handsomely to my body & it has done the like to me & now it goes & plays me a low trick & I have to paint my throat a bright orange & take vile drugs.[17]

Prolegomena to the Study of Greek Religion was finally published at the beginning of November. She wrote it to counter the tendency of prevailing books on Greek religion to treat the subject as mainly a matter of mythology, and mythology derived from literature at that, with Homer taken as the starting point. Her aim was to examine the substratum of religious conceptions earlier than Homer, which surface in later poets and which can be detected in ritual.

She begins by establishing that the Greeks themselves recognized two forms of ritual, Olympian and chthonic, which she characterizes by two distinct formulae: the Olympian, 'Do ut des' ('I give that you may give'), and the chthonic, 'Do ut abeas' ('I give that you may go away'). 'Do ut des' represents a transaction which has nothing religious to its name. By contrast, 'do ut abeas' derives from a real fear of the power of evil, something 'truly religious'. She examines the Athenian festivals of the Anthesteria, Thargelia, and Thesmophoria for their elements of the rites of the lower stratum. Recognizing that Zeus, for example, was worshipped as Zeus Meilichios in the form of a snake, she concludes that the anthropomorphic Zeus has 'slipped himself quietly into the place of the old snake-god. It is not that Zeus the Olympian has 'an underworld aspect'; it is the cruder fact that he of the upper air, of the thunder and lightning, extrudes an ancient serpent-demon

----

[16] JEH to MM [161], 15 Oct. 1903.   [17] JEH to GM [164], 8 Nov. 1903.

of the lower world, Meilichios'. Greek religion for all its superficial serenity had within it and beneath it elements of a darker and deeper significance, with the 'strange fierce loveliness that lurks in rites of ignorance and fear, rites stark and desperate and non-moral'.

A chapter on 'The Demonology of Ghosts and Sprites and Bogeys' begins with an observation that is fundamental to all her work, that to understand Greek religion we must think ourselves back to a time before human beings engaged in clear, analytical thought, when 'all things were in flux', when individual gods and spirits had not been distinguished. Furthermore, we must understand that we are dealing with a mentality alien to our own. It was art, which makes images, and literature, which crystallizes things, that fixed this 'shifting kaleidoscope'. There were at first no gods at all, only conceptions of the human mind. The 'ker', which she proceeds to examine in art and literature, was a vague spirit, capable of manifestations in many forms: evil sprite, bacillus of disease, old age and death, Harpy, Fate, Gorgon, Siren, Sphinx, Fury. Turning from Homeric Olympus to local cults she discovered survivals of a civilization far from patriarchal: primitive goddesses who traced their descent through the mother. Identifying three stages of a woman's life as maiden, bride, and mother she saw these stages crystallize into separate goddesses. Demeter and Kore are but two facets of the same goddess. 'The relation of these early, matriarchal, husbandless goddesses, whether Mother or Maid, to the male figures that accompany them is one altogether noble and womanly, though perhaps not what the modern mind holds to be feminine. It seems to halt somewhere half-way between Mother and Lover, with a touch of the patron saint.'[18] With the coming of patriarchal conditions the women goddesses are 'sequestered to a servile domesticity, they become abject and amorous'. In this connection she understands Pandora as in origin simply the Earth-Mother, the 'All-Giver', but an irresponsible patriarchal mythology changed her into a lovely temptress; in Hesiod 'there gleams the ugly malice of theological animus' so he unmakes and remakes Pandora, she who made all things, into the plaything of the gods. 'To Zeus, the archpatriarchal *bourgeois*, the birth of the first woman is but a huge Olympian jest.'[19]

On the topic of matriarchy Harrison is elusive. She certainly believed, largely on the evidence of the Cretan seal of the 'mistress of the animals' perched on the mountain-top, that in its early stages Greek religion was 'matriarchal'. By this she meant that cult was mainly in the hands of women, that the object of worship reflected the worshipper, and that the line of

---

[18] *Prolegomena*, 273.   [19] Ibid. 285.

descent was traced through the mother since the paternity of the father could never be established.[20] Though a nostalgia for such conditions permeates *Prolegomena*, she nevertheless writes that the shift from matriarchy to patriarchy is 'a necessary stage in a real advance. Matriarchy gave to women a false because a magical prestige.'[21]

Athene is the Parthenos, the maiden, whom the Athenians turned into a sexless thing; she is 'laden with attributes, charged with intended significance, but to the end she remains manufactured, unreal, and never convinces us'. As for the story of her birth, fully grown from the head of Zeus, it 'remains a desperate theological expedient to rid an earth-born Kore of her matriarchal conditions . . . it is all an unreal theatrical show . . . we cannot love a goddess who on principle forgets the Earth from which she sprang'.[22]

Aphrodite is clearly the bride, but a bride of the old order, she is never a wife. Vase paintings of Aphrodite rising from water depict her as year by year she renews her virginity by matriarchal baths.[23] Hera is clearly the wife, forcibly married to the invading patriarchal Zeus after ruling supreme in Thessaly and Argos. Male gods are derived from heroes who in turn have their origin in ghosts. The new Olympian religion was superimposed on the old, powerless to alter its rituals, changing only the form and the name. It is to Dionysos we have to look for religion in any deep and mystical sense.

The Dionysos of *Prolegomena* comes from Thrace (that is 'certain beyond question'), though two years later she reversed her position and had him coming from Egypt. In Euripides, she acknowledges, he comes from the east to his birthplace in Thebes ('He came unto his own and his own received him not');[24] the apparent contradiction is easily resolved by a piece of legerdemain and the casual comment that Euripides as a poet can afford to contradict himself (a dig at Murray?). Dionysos, alone of the Olympians, comes with a revel rout of satyrs and maenads. His story is riddled with seeming contradictions. He comes as a young man, but Plutarch has him worshipped as a baby in the cradle. He is the god of the grape, but Thracians drink beer,

---

[20]   *Prolegomena*, 261, 561, 246.   [21]   Ibid. 285.   [22]   Ibid. 302–3.

[23]   Not surprisingly, Harrison was pilloried for the 'matriarchal baths', which added to the rumours of how dangerous it was to send your daughter to Newnham.

[24]   John 1: 11; one of many biblical allusions she harnesses for her own purposes. The dissonance is probably intentional, and serves her purpose by implying that Christianity is but one manifestation of 'survivals' from primitive religion. The anonymous reviewer of *Prolegomena* in the *Athenaeum* comments: 'Where the underlying religious idea is essentially the same, such a use of familiar words is suggestive; but where the resemblances of circumstances is only superficial, the association of ideas is actually misleading, and further many readers, whose feelings deserve to be respected, may find it offensive' (*Athenaeum*, 3983 (27 Feb. 1904), 278).

not wine. These difficulties are tackled in a long and convoluted philological argument.

Finally she is ready to state the characteristic essence of the worship of Dionysos. 'The fact however repugnant must be faced. The essence was intoxication'.[25] But he was also a tree god and bull god, a primitive nature god informed by a spirit of intoxication. As for his epithet 'dithyrambos', she rejects the traditional interpretation 'he of the double door' and tentatively suggests in its place a connection with the Greek word θρίαμβος, the name for a song to Dionysos. The Greeks of the sixth century, she suggests, may have grown weary of their Olympians and looking for a return to nature they found in Dionysos that 'desire for the life rather of the emotions than of the reason, a recrudescence it may be of animal passions'.[26] The savage, taking alcohol for the first time, experiences a new awakening within himself. He is, he declares, possessed by a god. If Degas, in his painting *L'Absinthe*, had chosen to celebrate the beauty of a woman besotted with absinthe, the 'peeping moralist that lurks in most of us intrudes to utter truth beside the mark and say that she is wicked. To the Greek artist there was no such extreme issue between art and morality.'[27]

She had come to terms with the drunkenness of Dionysos worship after reading William James's recent lectures at Edinburgh on 'The Varieties of Religious Experience'. In 1902 she had written to Murray how the mysticism and drunkenness parts had delighted her, and how his description of experiences of anaesthetic paralleled her own; 'morphine cured me far more of materialism—& laughing gas convinced me of the existence of god. I am quite serious.'[28] James articulated her own experience precisely when he wrote of the 'deepened sense of significance' that can be aroused by certain sights, sounds, and odours, and that intoxicants intensify further.[29]

When Orpheus, whom she insisted was a historical person, came on the scene, he so refashioned the religion of Dionysos that it is hard to think of one without the other. Orpheus, more of a priest than a musician, modified the Dionysiac rites by spiritualizing the ecstasy. Whereas Dionysos is

---

[25] *Prolegomena*, 424–5.   [26] Ibid. 444.   [27] Ibid. 449.

[28] JEH to GM [85], 14 Aug. 1902.

[29] James wrote: 'The sway of alcohol over mankind is unquestionably due to its power to stimulate the mystical faculties of human nature, usually crushed to earth by the cold facts and dry criticisms of the sober hour. Sobriety diminishes, discriminates, and says no; drunkenness expands, unites, and says yes. It is in fact the great exciter of the *Yes* function in man. It brings its votary from the chill periphery of things to the radiant core. It makes him for the moment one with truth' William James, *The Varieties of Religious Experience* (London: Longmans, Green and Co., 1908), 387.

drunken, Orpheus is sober. 'But this new spirit of gentle decorum is but the manifestation, the outward shining of a lambent flame within, the expression of a new spiritual faith which brought to man, at the moment he most needed it, the longing for purity and peace in this life, the hope of final fruition in the next.' There is nothing in the Bacchae to suggest that a human being may ever become a god; the cardinal doctrine of Orpheus is the possibility of attaining divine life and immortality. The means was asceticism.

Orphic mysteries consisted first of 'omophagia', and despite Russell's ridicule she continued to maintain that the women of Crete actually tore a live bull limb from limb, though she was forced to concede that the practice must have fallen into abeyance in Periclean Athens.[30] The point was crucial to her, for the goal of her argument (to which she was driven more by emotion than reason) was that the Orphic followers of Dionysos believed that by partaking of an animal that was a divine vehicle, it was possible to be made one with the god. Her exposition continues by showing from vase paintings Dionysos in ecstasy; he is drunk, but with music, not with wine.

She concludes with a paean:

There are some to whom by natural temperament the religion of Bromios, son of Semele, is and must always be a dead letter, if not a stumbling-block. Food is to such a troublesome necessity, wine a danger or a disgust. They dread all stimulus that comes from without, they would fain break the ties that link them with animals and plants. They do not feel in themselves and are at a loss to imagine for others the sacramental mystery of life and nutrition that is accomplished in us day by day, how in the faintness of fasting the whole nature of man, spirit as well as body, dies down, he cannot think, he cannot work, he cannot love; how in the breaking of bread, and still more in the drinking of wine, life spiritual as well as physical is renewed, thought is re-born, his equanimity, his magnanimity are restored, reason and morality rule again. . . .

Those to whom wine brings no inspiration, no moments of sudden illumination, of wider and deeper insight, of larger human charity and understanding, find it hard to realize what to others of other temperament is so natural, so elemental, so beautiful—the constant shift from physical to spiritual that is of the essence of the religion of Dionysos. But there are those also, and they are saintly souls, who know it all to the full, know the exhilaration of wine, know what it is to be drunken with the physical beauty of a flower or a sunset, with the sensuous imagery of words, with the strong wine of a new idea, with the magic of another's personality, yet having known, turn away with steadfast eyes, disallowing the madness not only of Bromios but of the Muses and of Aphrodite. Such have their inward ecstasy of the ascetic, but they revel with another Lord, and he is Orpheus.[31]

---

[30] *Prolegomena*, 487.   [31] Ibid. 452–3.

The sacramental nature of life at its simplest and most precious is older than any historical referents—certainly older than Christianity—and universally human. It is in passages such as these that the reader begins to feel the full force of her emotions about Greek religion.

The publication of *Prolegomena* did little to cheer her, but rather added to her depression, for she now complained of having no work to interest her. 'The Fat One', as she nicknamed her book, 'at last sits on my table & grins at me & I don't care enough for him even to turn over his horrid pages.'[32] Characteristically, as her student Jessie (Crum) Stewart pointed out later, it was the process of research that she loved, not its conclusions. As soon as one project was complete she put it behind her, restless for a fresh challenge. Moreover, she worried about the reception of *Prolegomena*.

Reviewers found much to admire in the book: its enormous scope, its originality, the boldness and occasional brilliance of its theories, and the daring imagination of its author. 'Even if it should be thought that at times the writer's fancy outruns the warranty of facts, yet Greek religion, as handled by Miss Harrison, has this supreme merit, that it lives.'[33] They also pointed out that these qualities were also its weakness. Time and time again the evidence is not sufficient to support her conclusions, her use of sources was uncritical and selective, and the whole characterized by enthusiasm and dogmatism rather than careful scholarship.[34] Farnell, after summarizing her argument and acknowledging the importance of her subject, concludes that she has failed in her collection and evaluation of the evidence. She lacked the ability to discriminate between her sources, and was deficient in her knowledge of comparative philology. She had been quite frank in her admission that she was no philologist, but this did not excuse the 'hopelessly unprovable—and therefore gratuitous' etymologies, for some of which Verrall was responsible. Farnell accused her of being deeply attached to a theory of matriarchy, which inspired in her the kind of passion one finds vented at meetings on women's rights.

No anthropologist living or dead is responsible for the amazing vision of a matriarchal earth which reveals itself in these pages: of the time when no child necessarily knew his own father; when Zeus was not yet come 'with his virtuous thunderbolt' . . . to destroy free love; when there was mere σύμμιξις but no γάμος [intercourse but no marriage], nor 'the squalor of domestic happiness'; when women, being in power, evolved goddesses after their own image, the mother and the maid, or

---

[32] JEH to GM [164], 8 Nov. 1903.   [33] Anonymous, *Cambridge Review*, 10 Mar. 1904, 245.
[34] For a list of reviews, see Arlen, *The Cambridge Ritualists*, 28–9.

Amazonian deities like Athena, who took 'matriarchal' baths to restore their virginity . . . or, if the women tolerated a male divinity, they always endeavoured to keep him an infant.[35]

This is a distortion. Her vision was not of a 'matriarchal earth', but of a time when lineage was traced through the mother, and women held power in the family. Cult, she had stated, was in early times in the hands of women, who fashioned their gods after their own image. Yet in other ways Farnell's review was judicious. He found her account of the ritual of the dead 'mainly good and sound', praised her account of Orpheus, and concluded, 'The whole book is attractive because of its vitality and happy flashes of imagination; at the same time it is provocative and disappointing because of its animus and uncritical temper.'[36]

Gilbert Murray, writing for the *Speaker*, while acknowledging his own contribution to the book, realized that it possessed 'peculiarities of style and treatment which may exasperate one reader as much as they charm another' and that it was 'full of new ideas and disputable, though never indolent or uncritical, statements'. Murray particularly liked her section on Orpheus, which shed light on 'that most marvellous of subjects, the natural religion of man' in which a rite that originated with drunken Thracians passed into a higher ascetic mysticism, and became filled with longing for spiritual purity, its drunkenness sublimated into a 'brotherhood with the wild beasts of the forest'. Her vivid imagination, he continued, enabled her to write about the *keres* 'as if she could not sleep for fear of them; about the Earth-Maidens as if she had attended their chapels from childhood and regarded the adherents of Zeus and Apollo as little better than Papists!' He did not spare her from criticism for her 'arrant partisanship', for loving goddesses and hating gods, for affection for 'Pelasgians' and coldness towards 'Achaeans'. He feared she had underrated the living influence of the Olympian religion.[37]

In the end she was vindicated by her own university. The examination papers for the classical Tripos in May 1904 testified to the importance of her work. 'I blush for the Examiners,' she wrote with elation, '5 questions straight out of the F[at] & C[omely] One.'[38]

However, when *Prolegomena* first appeared she had no such confidence. Suffering from a kind of post-partum depression in addition to bereavement, exacerbated by nicotine withdrawal, she felt 'dull & empty & miserable' and planned to take herself out of the country and go with Kate Raleigh to Sicily 'because I don't feel fit for human society & the Sicilians

---

[35]   Lewis R. Farnell, *Hibbert Journal*, 2 (1903–4), 825.   [36]   Ibid. 827.

[37]   Murray, *Spectator*, 27 Feb. 1904, 519.   [38]   JEH to GM, [215], 8 June 1904.

won't know'. These plans fell through and instead she found herself accompanying the Verralls to Algeria, where Arthur Verrall had been ordered in a continuing search for a cure to his gout. May Verrall was not well either, suffering from rheumatism and 'neuralgia'. 'I thought it was no time for finesse', she explained to Lady Mary, '& blurted out that I was free & they both jumped at me with open arms! One never believes enough in one's friends [sic] friendship, that is my constant experience & if I can be the least good to them it will be an immense joy for they are ceaselessly good to me.[39]

Her relationship with the Verralls, going back to her student days, was a curious one. She described her friendship with May as 'the only cloudless friendship I have ever known,'[40] yet they had very little in common. May Verrall, after her collaboration with Harrison in *Mythology and Monuments of Ancient Athens*, abandoned her interest in classics for psychical research, determined to find out whether there was any scientific basis for parapsychology. Arthur Verrall, a textual critic best known for his work on Euripides, whose scepticism and irrationality appealed to him, and for his far-fetched emendations (which earned him the nickname 'splendid emendax'), had no interest whatever in the anthropological and sociological 'stuffage' (his word for the historical evidence supplied by archaeology) that was of consuming interest to Harrison. He could not endure controversy, and although he was of continual help to Harrison whenever she needed advice on philological matters, he stayed out of all her academic skirmishes. He was 'angelically kind' and tolerant, but could never see why a sane person could write as she did. (On one occasion she had expostulated over some scholar with whom she differed: 'It's intolerable that people should be allowed to go on talking and teaching such nonsense', to which he replied: 'All right, let's have back the Inquisition'.)[41] Over the famous issue of the wild bull he had eventually taken up arms. Harrison wrote to Murray, 'You know don't you that AWV has discovered that the earthquake & fire in the Bacchae are all hallucinations. I did not realize how he hated the Bacchos whom I love so & he declares he sympathizes with Pentheus—we got quite stormy over it.'[42] On another occasion he declared in a lecture that 'any gentleman wld be justly annoyed if he found a Wild Bull in his stables', causing Harrison to fear that his audience would giggle over the Bacchae for the rest of their lives.

[39] JEH to MM, 167, 14 Nov. 1903.
[40] Obituary of Margaret de Gaudrion Verrall, *Newnham College Letter*, 1916.
[41] Jane Harrison, 'Dr Verrall: a Remembrance', *The Common Cause*, 27 June 1912, 188.
[42] JEH to GM [309], 14 May 1907.

'The sheer comedian gets hold of him almost to a dangerous point when he is lecturing specially to his undergraduates who demand that he shld play the brilliant fool', she ruefully reflected.[43] It was probably a combination of their genuine kindness towards her and their incessant love of wit and humour that made the Verralls two of Harrison's dearest friends.

They left for Hamman, Algeria, in January 1904, where she shared the Verralls' pleasure in the thermal baths. She wrote to Murray:

They are half underground & the light that comes in on the pale green water is quiet & beautiful & Bethesda like, & sometimes at sunset, a ray comes slanting in on the water & it seems as if in a moment there must be a Holy Dove & from shere [*sic*] exhaustion & excess of sulphate of magnesia one feels so good & meek & limp & new-born. But Madame la Baigneuse does not approve of me, because, if I go into the hot bath I have battements de coeur & if I stay in the tepid one I 'transpire' less than the smallest political scandal. She speaks of making a 'bonne transpiration' as yr Mother Church speaks of making a good death.[44]

Arthur Verrall became his old self again, 'bright and cheery and preposterous, . . . with all the querulousness and gloom that you saw and realized, completely gone'. The 'cure' was less successful with May, who remained depressed and missed her psychical research.[45] Letters to the Murrays were more replete even than usual with Biblical imagery, but, she explained, 'if you were here and cldn't put yr nose out of doors without seeing Abraham & Isaac & Jacob all rolled up in bundles you wld write like that'.

She left the Verralls in Algiers to continue their cures, returning through France. From Nimes she sent Murray a postcard of the Roman arena: 'On great Festivals of yr Church this is still full of Wild Bulls. How more than ever I detest the Romans & all their work',[46] and from Avignon:

I expect you know this place off by heart. I expect also that Rosalind has been decently educated on Allgemeine Weltgeschichte [general world history] & knows why the Popes came waltzing over to Avignon & built this amazing palace & then waltzed back again—for anything that I know they might as well have gone to Hamman R'Hira. Before I was born I think Popes & Avignon ran in my head together but I never knew why & it is now too late to ask.

As usual tho one finds bits that need no history—there is the broken bridge & the empty chapel of S. Benizet on it—utterly empty with a stone altar-table & the sunlight streaming in. 'Desolation is a delicate thing.' It made me think of a possible worship when all religions have been swept clean away, like that lovely faith Bertie preaches . . .

[43] JEH to GM [334], n.d. [1908].   [44] JEH to GM [186], 1 Feb. 1904.
[45] JEH to MM, 181, 17 Jan. 1904.   [46] JEH to GM [188], 12 Feb. 1904.

At Arles I found a delightful Xian sarcophagos with a Nativity & the Holy Child in a liknon. Some nice cows were nosing at him wch shows clearly that the type of Hermes in liknon with cows has been taken over![47]

Meanwhile Murray was making preparations for a stage performance of his translation of Euripides' *Hippolytus* in London, at the urging of his friend, William Archer. Archer had noted similarities between Euripides and Ibsen, and saw the possibilities of presenting the ancient play as though it were a contemporary psychological drama. This goal accorded well with Murray's objectives in translation. Granville Barker, as director, had a similar interest in making ancient drama come as naturally to the theatre as possible.[48] The *Hippolytus* is framed by speeches of Aphrodite and Artemis, pitted against each other as Hippolytus spurns the one to worship the other. Their role in the action of the drama illustrates exactly the concept of a 'goddess' that Harrison had presented in *Prolegomena*. The part that each plays is not so much that of the modern conception of a divinity as that of a 'Force of Nature, or a Spirit working in the world' explained Murray.[49] Aphrodite is a personification of sexual attraction: to deny her existence would be a denial of obvious facts. 'For the purposes of drama,' Murray went on, 'this "thing" must be made into a person, and even represented in human form according to the current conceptions of mythology.' It was Murray's idea to have on stage statues of the two goddesses, and ('as archaic goddesses are not found ready made')[50] Harrison had been commissioned with the design of the statues. She insisted that they be archaic. While passing through Paris on her way back to Cambridge she took the opportunity of studying possible models in the Louvre, and revelling in the thought that there would be two archaic statues of goddesses on the stage, 'enough to make a success of any translation, however bad'. Knowing that Murray would have preferred classical to archaic she teased him, 'Well, you just *won't*! Artemis shall have a bow & Aphrodite shall be divinely stiff with a dove & a flower & a smile. Oh such a smile! I long to be at them.'[51] 'All my heart just now is in the making of graven images', she added in a letter to Lady Mary.[52] The actual execution of the goddesses was delegated to Jessie Crum (Stewart), who, with the help of her sister Edith, made masks on the model of Athenian *korai*. *Korai*, literally 'young girls' were marble statues of the Archaic period, characterized

[47] JEH to GM [191], 14 Feb. 1904.
[48] See Dennis Kennedy, *Granville Barker and the Dream of Theatre* (Cambridge: Cambridge University Press, 1985), 42.
[49] Eur. *Hippolytus*, trans. Murray, 77.   [50] Stewart, *Harrison*, 63.
[51] JEH to GM [no number], n.d.   [52] JEH to MM, 200, 23 Mar. 1904.

12. Drawings for the statues of Aphrodite and Artemis for the Lyric Theatre production of Euripides' *Hippolytus*, 1904

by a 'Mona Lisa' smile. The bodies of the goddesses were made by draping linen in stiff folds around wicker mannequins.

By April the goddesses were ready and Harrison was pleading with Murray to come to Cambridge to give his approval. When he pleaded lack of time she chided him: 'Why are you not staying the night? The Verralls have heaps of room in their home & their hearts . . . The goddesses don't like being hurried when they have got their smiles on. . . . Mr Barker *must* look at the Goddesses to see if they are right from the stage point of view. If you are very tired I will take him alone—in the afternoon—but they (the Goddesses) wld be hurt.'[53]

The goddesses had to be transported and provided some amusement to those who saw her wheeling them down the street in a 'very old-fashioned pram.' One of the goddesses lying on its back in the pram had an out-stretched left arm 'held up to high heaven, and the effect was most extraordinary. Miss Harrison had wheeled this through the streets of Cambridge completely unperturbed.'[54] She was in her element with the whole business. Her knowledge of vase painting was also put to use in the hair-dressing of Theseus and Hippolytos, and she confessed her enjoyment at 'working these things up'. 'While I was looking up people's hairs I simply longed to do the *Bacchae*, one cld make a separate loveliness of each figure.'[55]

The rehearsals of the *Hippolytus* were not without problems. The chorus presented the main obstacle to an appearance of modernity, a difficulty which was compounded by the inaudibility of the 'cantilation' led by Florence Farr. Farr's musical accompaniment on the psaltery was not to everyone's taste, though the poet W. B. Yeats was delighted,[56] and Harrison admired her.[57] Some of the actors left much to be desired, all of them except Granville Barker making Harrison feel 'sick with nervousness'[58] The Nurse and Aphrodite were pronounced by Harrison to be 'absolute horrors', though they did improve with rehearsal. 'Could that beautiful Artemis be got to part her hair straight?' pleaded Harrison, 'the parting to the side & crooked is all too human & just mars the divine on her. Hippolytus was wonderfully brushed up & really seemed to have some hair & 29 years gone from his stupid face—but Lord—how long, how long?'[59] On the other hand Edyth Olive as Phaedra and Granville Barker as the messenger carried the day. 'Very few seem to realize that there were two actors acting beautifully & the rest so much pernicious lumber, but all that is secondary.'[60] The performances, held on the afternoon of Thursday 26 May and three afternoons the following week, surprised Murray with their popularity. The audience grew from about fifty on the first day to a full house on the third. On the fourth, when he found a crowd stretching down Shaftesbury Avenue, he thought he must have come to the wrong theatre.[61]

In their foremost aim the performances succeeded. Desmond MacCarthy

[53] JEH to GM [203], 25 Mar. 1904.

[54] E. G. Brown, 'In Newnham Walk' in Phillips (ed.), *A Newnham Anthology*, 50.

[55] JEH to GM [207], 7 May 1904.   [56] Murray, *An Unfinished Autobiography*, 109.

[57] JEH to MM, 212, n.d.   [58] JEH to GM [213], 1 Jun. 1904.   [59] Ibid.

[60] Ibid.   [61] Gilbert Murray, 'Unfinished Battle', *Listener*, 5 Jan. 1956, 13.

declared that Murray's translation turned Euripides into an English poet-dramatist, and that Granville Barker's production naturalized him on the English stage.[62] In the end Harrison declared she could 'let the beauty of it flow over me & at the end of the first act it just dissolves one's very spirit. I don't know which is to be thanked & blessed, Euripides or you, for the life of me I don't—perhaps you both had to be. I read it all thro again in the train. I was filled to the full with happiness.'[63] The following day, reading the reviews, she was ecstatic. 'The papers cry aloud, all of them, in yr praise—you have done to the full what you worked to do—made a great mass of people—who never cld have understood it any other way realize the greatness of Euripides'.[64] *The Times* admired Edyth Olive for transforming Phaedra from lines of text to be studied for examinations into a 'living, palpitating, wailing woman', and praised the costumes, the grouping, and posing, though admitting tactfully that sometimes the 'plastic disposition of the scene' interfered with the audibility of the actors.[65]

Murray generously wrote to Bertrand Russell to thank him for the reception that he had given to his reading of his translation at Newnham in 1901. The 'ecstatic letters' he was now receiving, together with 'ecstatic newspaper articles' led him to believe that there was 'a kind of "boom" in Euripides. It all makes me grateful to you and Miss Harrison and the one or two people who told me about it long ago.'[66] The success of the performances and the good reviews in the press were to Harrison a magnificent vindication of her twin cult of Euripides and Murray. The public had now made the discovery 'much to their manifest astonishment that Euripides is a great dramatist & has been translated by a poet. . . . I think you must be very proud & happy. I am *so* glad', Harrison concluded.[67]

The goddesses also had an influence of another kind, as they inspired Francis Cornford with the material for his first book, *Thucydides Mythistoricus*. Applying Murray's and Harrison's theories to historiography, Cornford now read Thucydides with fresh insight. Thucydides, he argued, thought in mythological language no less than the dramatists, and understood the

---

[62] Desmond MacCarthy, *The Court Theatre* (London: A. H. Bullen, 1907), 18.

[63] JEH to GM [210], n.d.   [64] JEH to GM [209], 27 May 1904.

[65] *The Times*, 27 May 1904, 4.

[66] GM to Bertrand Russell, June 2 1904, BRA. The *Hippolytus* at the Lyric was followed by *The Trojan Women* (1905); *Electra* (Jan. 1906); *Electra* and *Hippolytus* (Mar. 1906); and *Medea* (1907). The scanty receipts from these productions indicate that he may have overestimated the 'boom' in Euripides. See also Wilson, *Gilbert Murray*, 422, n. 27.

[67] JEH to MM, 212, n.d. For an assessment of the impact of Murray's popularization of Euripides, see Patricia E. Easterling, 'Gilbert Murray's Reading of Euripides', *Colby Quarterly*, 33/2 (June 1997), 113–27.

historical events of the Peloponnesian War to have been determined by 'Forces of Nature, or Spirits working in the world'; Luck, Persuasion, Hope, Eros, and Nemesis are all characters, as it were, in the drama. The anthropomorphic mode of thought, he argued, was engrained in the Greek mind. Even the rationalist Euripides could not shake himself free of it.

when we read the *Hippolytus*, and still more when we see it played, the feeling grows upon us that reason falls back like a broken wave. A brooding power, relentless, inscrutable, waits and watches and smites. There she stands, all through the action, the white, implacable Aphrodite. Is she no more than a marble image, the work of men's hands? Is there no significance in that secret smile, no force behind the beautiful mask, no will looking out of the fixed, watching eyes? And yet, how can there be? Is she not one of the outcast, dethroned Olympians, a figment of bygone superstition, despised and rejected of an enlightened age? No, she is more than this, and much more.[68]

The book, published in 1907, is dedicated to Jane Harrison, 'a dream in exchange for many fine dreams', in an echo of Socrates' words in Plato's *Theaetetus*.[69] Can one detect in this dedication a trace of some of those conversations over the brew of black tea? Socrates' 'dream for a dream' tells of elemental things which we can know but can never explain. Complex things can be traced back to their roots, and knowledge for Plato is a matter of being able to 'give account', but the roots themselves remain solely as objects of perception and admit of no explanation. Such are the roots of religion, 'things which are', as Harrison later phrased it, and among them, with her archaic smile, stands the 'white, implacable Aphrodite'.

After the sustained effort of writing *Prolegomena* Harrison turned her attention to two requests for shorter publications. The publisher Constable had asked her to write a simple handbook of mythology. She was not at all suited to such a task, being by nature inclined to pursue all the complexities of a subject, and averse to popular and conventional handbooks. Conventionality was exactly what the publishers probably wanted. She was plagued with self-doubt. Murray restored her confidence by telling her that it was 'valuable'. When the proofs came she was relieved that they were not 'wholly condemned', but nevertheless the primer was pronounced 'queer'. 'A great deal will have to be done to it', she groaned.[70]

The reason the book was thought 'queer' was due no doubt to the originality of her approach to the subject. The study of mythology, she had

[68] Francis Cornford, *Thucydides Mythistoricus* (London: Arnold, 1907), 243.
[69] Plato, *Theaetetus*, 201D–E.   [70] JEH to MM, 224, 28 Aug. 1904.

claimed more than ten years previously, in her preface to Petiscus's *The Gods of Olympos*, was a subject in a state of flux. Its very methodology was hotly debated, as Andrew Lang discredited the search for origins by means of linguistic comparisons (the 'Indo-European' or 'nomina-numina' method), and a new method of comparative anthropology was finding favour, particularly after the publication of Frazer's *Golden Bough*. For Greek mythology there were huge gaps in the data. The mythologist, she had written in *The Gods of Olympos*, has the demons and spirits of primitive man at one pole, and the 'gods of Olympos' at the other; while a link in this chain is wanting, he knows no rest.[71] While in writing the preface for Petiscus's book she had settled for the traditional view of the Olympians as being the easiest starting-point for the student, in the primer she tackled the difficulties.

The introduction opens by drawing the reader's attention to three problems within the study of Greek religion. First, although religion, she wrote, comprised two elements, theology, or mythology (what people *think* in relation to their gods), and ritual (what people *do*), the study of Greek religion had hitherto concerned itself solely with mythology. Secondly, mythology had not been studied as an independent whole, but only as an ancillary to literature, an investigation of 'allusions'. And thirdly, until very recently the subject had always been studied through the medium of the Romans or the Alexandrians, with the result that the Greek gods were known by the names of their Roman counterparts. It was a small step from there to invest the Greek gods with the nature of the Roman, and to read Roman religious attitudes back into the very different Greek religious conceptions.

Taking for granted the assumption that all cultures evolve through similar stages, she proceeds to consider what Greek religion holds in common with all religion in the early stages of development. Her list comprises ghosts, spirits and nature-gods, ancestor worship, family religion, tribal religion, anthropomorphism, the formation of a pantheon, individual religion, magical rites, purifications, prayers, and sacrifices.[72] She then attempts to give an account of religion before Homer, when the gods were undifferentiated, when they were worshipped as fetish-stones and pillars, overlaid with oriental and Egyptian influences. Following Ridgeway's ethnology in *The Early Age of Greece* she believed that material finds corroborated literary accounts of early Greek religion (e.g. in Herodotus, Pausanias, Plato, Xenophon). This 'Pelasgian' period was followed by the arrival of 'Hellenes' from the north. At this point Homer transfigured the gods with his poetic

---

[71] Petiscus, *The Gods of Olympos*, pp. vi–vii.
[72] *The Religion of Ancient Greece* (London: Constable, 1905), 12–13.

imagination. Most of his Olympians, lacking religious feeling, are northern gods, big and boisterous; occasionally his theology reflects racial fusion, notably in the unending conflict between 'Northern' Zeus and 'Pelasgian' Hera, who once ruled alone at Samos, Argos, and Olympia. Greek ritual likewise reflects racial differences. The Olympians are worshipped with sacrifice, as befits northern gods, but heroes are remembered with different rites which belonged to a 'Pelasgian' stratum. To these two strata of theology and ritual ('Pelasgian' and 'Olympian') must be added a third, the mysteries of Demeter and Dionysos. Dionysos was a fusion of the Thracian beer-god, Sabazios, and the Cretan mystery-god, Zagreus, akin to the Egyptian Osiris. Unlike the Olympian gods, the mystery-god was mortal (died and came to life again), offered union with the divine, and was worshipped in asceticism. In contrast to Homer's Olympians of epic, the religion of the mystery-gods was characterized by a sense of evil, the need for purification, and the hope of immortality.

Poetry and philosophy, she concludes, civilized the raw material of religion. Whereas Homer created the anthropomorphic Olympians, the philosophers—Thales, Empedocles, Plato—fashioned a beatific vision from the material of the mystery-gods.

It is the peculiar merit of Greek religion that from the outset, as we know it, these elements of licence and monstrosity, the outcome of ignorance and fear, were caught, controlled, transformed by two things—by a poetry whose characteristic it was to be civilized as well as simple, and by a philosophy that was always more than half poetry. For the Greeks, the darkness and dread of the Unseen was lighted, purified, quieted by two lamps—Reason and Beauty.[73]

The second request came from Dörpfeld, and was no doubt the result of their meeting at the International Congress of Archaeology in Athens in April 1905, which Harrison attended with Cornford. The occasion was redolent with that sense of destiny, of classical studies 'coming of age', that was so characteristic of the early years of the twentieth century. It was attended by about six-hundred delegates and two-hundred associate members from all the countries (with the exception of Spain) that 'derive through Greece their civilization from the Mediterranean area'.[74] It was inaugurated with much pomp and ceremony, enhanced by its coinciding with the festivities for Greek Independence Day. The delegates and associate members of the congress met in the Parthenon for the beginning of the official proceedings, presided over by Prince Constantine. His address in Greek

---

[73] Ibid. 64.   [74] Louis Dyer, *Nation*, 80/2079 (4 May 1905), 351.

was followed by speeches in French and German, with Wilhelm Dörpfeld paying tribute to Ludwig Ross and K. O. Müller, while declaring Ernst Curtius as 'the latter-day winner of an Olympic crown of immortality'.[75] The co-operative international spirit that characterized archaeology in Greece was glowingly commented on, while other speakers the following day drew significance from the date of the congress, the rector of the university proclaiming that the liberation of Greece made it possible to 'usher in a festival truly Panathenaic, because all civilized nations had responded to the summons and were joining in it as the spiritual sons and common defenders of ancient Athens—chips of [sic] the old Hellenic block'.[76] In response Percy Gardner declared that Athens was the

> inevitable meeting-place for the first archaeological congress, since the beauteous fragments of ancient Greece first taught archaeologists to use their eyes, and mankind first learned from Greece to think methodically. What Olympian and Delphian assemblages did for ancient Greece, our modern congresses did . . . for Europe, whose peoples were bound together by common Christianity, and also by their common growth from seeds derived at the time of its splendor from ancient Hellenism.[77]

The first day ended with illuminations, torchlight processions, and fireworks which lit up the whole Acropolis. The effect of this was noted to be curious rather than impressive. The Parthenon, then as now, defies all human attempts to add to its splendour, and will always look best in natural light, whether of the sun or the moon.

The sessions began on the evening of 8 April. They were divided into seven sections: classical archaeology; prehistoric and oriental archaeology; excavations and museums, and preservation of monuments; epigraphy and numismatics; geography and topography; Byzantine archaeology; teaching of archaeology. Of over one-hundred papers, only two were given by women, Jane Harrison and Harriet Boyd, the excavator of Gournia in Crete. Harrison had apparently stood her ground on a matter of principle and would not agree to participate unless admitted on the same terms as the men, as a delegate rather than as an associate member.

Harrison's paper, entitled 'The E at Delphi', was scheduled for the evening of 11 April. In it she proposed a mythological interpretation of a symbol, resembling the letter 'E' lying on its back, that appears in front of the temple of Apollo on coins of the second century AD. Rejecting earlier interpretations (that the E was the letter epsilon indicating the number 5; or

---

[75] Louis Dyer, *Nation*, 80/2079 (4 May 1905), 351.
[76] Ibid. 80/2080 (11 May 1905), 370.   [77] Ibid.

that it stood for 'ei', and meant either 'if' or 'you are'; or that it represented a trident) she argued that it was a representation of the Charites, or Graces. These had been deposed at Delphi when the god Apollo took over the oracle, but, she claimed, were piously remembered by this symbolism. For their representation in the form of an 'E' she cited parallels to support her theory that the symbol was that of three sacred baetyl stones, or meteors, set, like columns, on a basis.[78]

The rest of the papers in the classical archaeology section dealt with various points of interpretation of artefacts. Most of them, she confessed, she found boring. Doubtless she could find in their conclusions nothing that would throw light on religion or mythology. Narrowly focused as she was, she had little patience for scholarship in other areas.

The congress was enlivened by a plethora of social events: receptions, garden parties, and a ball ('all . . . scurry & formalities & polyglot conversations. Mr. Cornford is a great comfort, as much as anyone merely human cld be').[79] Harrison would have found more congenial two special side attractions: a 'pious pilgrimage' to Eleusis on the Saturday afternoon and a performance of Sophocles' *Antigone* by the Society for the Performance of Attic Dramas on the Monday. All in all, she described it as a 'loathesome Congress', but 'now and again we managed to put in beautiful days'.[80]

For those who wished to tour the sites of excavations two special excursions had been arranged to follow the congress, one to the mainland sites of Greece, the other to the islands and to Asia Minor. The second had tempted Harrison, who had written to Murray of her dilemma ('it is dreadful to be whisked over Crete at that pace but I have never seen Phaestos & want to badly').[81] Fortunately, however, an 'English boat' was hastily got together and she went to Crete after all. Only a brief postcard to Murray from Crete survives as a witness to this part of her visit. She had hoped to see the great German scholar Ulrich von Wilamowitz-Moellendorff at the congress, but Murray's letter of introduction had not reached her and she was disappointed.[82]

Harrison had been approached by Macmillan back in 1901 for a new edition of her *Mythology and Monuments of Ancient Athens* in the light of recent excavations. Now in 1905 Wilhelm Dörpfeld pressed her to write a

[78] Harrison, 'The E at Delphi', summary in *Proceedings of the Cambridge Philological Society*, 70 (1905), 1–3. Also, summary in *Comptes Rendus de Congres Internationale d'Archéologie* (Athens: Hestia, 1905). Noted in the *Cambridge Review*, 9 Feb. 1905, 179, and 5 Mar., 227.

[79] JEH to GM [243], 1 Apr. 1905.   [80] JEH to DSM, n.d., MS MacColl, H176.

[81] JEH to GM [241], 29 Feb. [*sic*] 1905.

[82] JEH to GM [244], n.d. (postcard with picture of Mount Ida, postmarked Heraklion).

new book on the interpretation of these excavations. As secretary of the German Institute at Athens, Dörpfeld had devoted himself to a study of Athenian topography, but had reached conclusions that were at odds with the positions of J. G. Frazer and of Ernest Gardner in his *Ancient Athens*.[83] Frazer, in his commentary on Pausanias, published in 1898, had already taken up cudgels against Dörpfeld, writing, for instance, with gratuitous animosity,

Here, too, I desire to correct a mistake of my own. I have spoken of Athens as if it were an unwalled town at the time of the battle of Marathon. I did this, not in reliance on the opinion of Professor von Wilamowitz-Moellendorff . . . and Dr Doerpfeld (in Miss Harrison's *Ancient Athens*, p. 21)[84] that it was so, but merely because I overlooked the testimony of Herodotus (ix.13) and Thucydides (i.89) that it was not. On the question of the state of Athens in the fifth century BC. I decidedly prefer the evidence of Herodotus and Thucydides to that of Dr Doerpfeld and Professor von Wilamowitz-Moellendorff.[85]

Dörpfeld found in Harrison a ready disciple. From the first time she attended his lecture tours in 1901 she had followed him with a devotion so abject as to be almost unseemly. His wide imagination excited her 'like poetry', and she would go to any lengths to defend him from a '10th rate idiot like E[rnest] G[ardner]'.[86] As a result she was prepared to write for him a book on topography, a subject which really did not interest her very much, except inasmuch as it cast light on ancient religion. Nevertheless, she readily acceded—though not without revealing where her own real interests lay. The manuscript is punctuated with long discursions on matters of ancient art, mythology, and ritual, all written in the personal style that was by now her hallmark. No one but Harrison could have so identified with the visitor to the Acropolis Museum:

As he passes in eager excitement through the ante-rooms he will glance, as he goes, at the great blue lion and the bull, at the tangle of rampant many-coloured snakes, at the long-winged birds with their prey still in beak and talon; he will pause to smile back at the three kindly 'Bluebeards,' he will be glad when he sees that the familiar Calf-Carrier has found his feet and his name, he will note the long rows of solemn votive terra-cottas, and, at last, he will stand in the presence of those Maiden-images, who, amid all that coloured architectural splendour, were consecrate to the worship of the Maiden. The Persian harried them, Perikles left them to lie beneath his feet,

[83] Ernest Gardner, *Ancient Athens* (London: Macmillan, 1902).

[84] Frazer is referring to her *Mythology and Monuments of Ancient Athens*.

[85] Frazer, *Pausanias' Description of Greece*, 6 vols. (London: Macmillan, 1898), Paus. 2. 528–9, quoted in Ackerman, *J. G. Frazer*, 137.   [86] JEH to GM [273], n.d.

yet their antique loveliness is untouched and still sovran. They are alive, waiting still, in hushed, intent expectancy—but not for us. We go out from their presence as from a sanctuary, and henceforth every stone of the Pelasgian fortress where they dwelt is, for us, sacred.[87]

Of the Mycenaean art on the acropolis she wrote, 'Man in art, as in life, is still at home with his brothers the fish, the bird, and the flower. After this ancient fulness and warmth of life a pediment by Pheidias strikes a chill. Its sheer humanity is cold and lonely.'[88]

'Truly, a little archaeology is a dangerous thing', she wrote as she discussed other views which conflicted with those of Dörpfeld.[89] In 1905 there were so many competing claims for the location of the agora that she could write, 'The agora, conducted by successive theorists, has made the complete tour of the Acropolis'.[90] Dörpfeld situated the agora in the hollow between the Acropolis, Areopagus, Pnyx, and Hill of the Muses, buttressing his position with arguments that to Harrison were 'simple and convincing'. Now that the agora has been found to occupy the site to the north of the acropolis and has been largely excavated, the whole of Harrison's book is out of date, the arguments irrelevant and tedious. Some of the hotly debated issues, such as the exact location of the Enneakrounos, or Nine Springs, while still not settled, have lost interest—at least until evidence more compelling than was available to Dörpfeld should come to light. Perhaps because visitors to Athens in the twenty-first century are no longer steeped in classical literature they no longer come, Pausanias in hand, with the thought of identifying all the literary landmarks. Topography is no longer a matter of consuming importance for the traveller.[91]

---

[87] Harrison, *Primitive Athens as Described by Thucydides* (Cambridge: Cambridge University Press, 1906), 2–3.

[88] Ibid. 29.   [89] Ibid. 141.   [90] Ibid. 87.

[91] See Beard, 'Pausanias in Petticoats', for further discussion of the transient interest of this debate.

8. The Pillar and the Maiden: Newnham 1906–1907

> IF one man depends on you for his supply of butter and you on him for your supply of tea, you are drawn into a real relation; but if the interchange be of thought and sympathy induced by that material commerce, the links are closer, more vital.[1]

The completion of the hated primer left Harrison with a clear idea of the direction that lay ahead for the study of Greek ritual. The history of Greek religion was yet to be written: Homeric religion needed to be rewritten in the light of archaeological discoveries; the individual Olympian gods needed to be variously related to 'Pelasgian', oriental, Hellenic, and northern influences; the origins of the mystery religions needed to be linked to the 'Pelasgians', and to the people of Crete, Phoenicia, and Asia Minor. 'How, in its early stages,' she asked, 'did religion act on philosophy? philosophy re-act on religion? Finally, a difficult and delicate task, what is the attitude of each literary author, his personal outlook and bias, how did each modify the material ready to his hand?'[2]

Such an agenda was clearly designed with Cornford and Murray in mind, and Harrison's fervour inspired much of Murray's *The Rise of the Greek Epic* (1907) and *Four Stages of Greek Religion* (1912), together with Cornford's *From Religion to Philosophy* (1912). Her own volume *Themis* was also published in 1912. Harrison saw their researches as charting a new course for Western thought (much as Bertrand Russell felt he was doing during the same period in his work on mathematics and religion) and to some extent the other two genuinely shared her vision, if Murray's memory served him correctly. He wrote to Jessie Stewart in 1953, 'We were as you say a remarkable group. We somehow had the same general aim and outlook, or something, and the work of each contributed to the work of the others. We were out to see what things really meant, looking for a new light our elders had not seen', glossed

---

[1] Jane Harrison, *Heresy and Humanity* in *Alpha and Omega*, 36.

[2] *The Religion of Ancient Greek*, 62–3.

by Jessie Stewart as 'Cornford in the *Presocratics*, Murray in the *Bacchae* and *Euripides*, and Jane everywhere.'[3] Both men could be pressed into service to write chapters for *Themis*, and the prefaces of all their books of this period ring with acknowledgements to one another's work. They shared a progressive outlook and an interest in widening the traditional discipline of classics by the application of new work in the social sciences. However, although they were united in their search, they found their answers in different places. The interests and instincts of her two male colleagues were not as closely allied to Harrison's as she believed. Whereas she insisted that *only* primitive religion was of value, for both Cornford and Murray it was no more than a starting point. They differed fundamentally in their understanding of what was meant by 'religion'. Murray's elucidation of it as 'man's attitude towards the Uncharted', no man experiencing quite the same as his neighbour,[4] is a long way from Harrison's 'what we feel together, what we care for together, what we imagine together'.[5] She intuited that what was emotionally satisfying to her was the 'truth', rarely stopping to think that other people might see things differently, and failed to see, during this period, the cracks that were already beginning to open up in her relationship with the two men. It had always been her fatal flaw not to consider points of view other than her own ('it's very troublesome bothering with other people's minds', she had confessed to Murray in 1902[6] when he had counselled her to pay attention to other people's opinions). Least of all did she suspect that Murray and Cornford, drawn into that 'real relation' with such close and vital links, might soon come to feel that their more important work lay elsewhere. However, for a time they acceded to her agenda.[7]

Cornford was a willing collaborator, and many of her ideas were thrashed out in endless discussion in his rooms. Two or three times a week they went riding together on their pennyfarthing bicycles, as Frances Darwin remembered: 'Francis very upright, with his usual rather Spanish dignity, she with her sibyl-head (which yet always had an indefinable look of a sailor about it) thrown back and a long sea-green or silvery scarf blown about her, that somehow managed never actually to be caught in the mudguard.'[8]

---

[3] Stewart, *Harrison*, 83.   [4] Murray, *Five Stages of Greek Religion*, 183, 198.

[5] Harrison, *Themis*, 487.   [6] JEH to GM [108], 7 Nov. 1902.

[7] For a detailed discussion of the divergence between Harrison's views and Murray's, with its implication that the label 'Cambridge ritualists' reifies a non-existent 'group', see Annabel Robinson, 'A New Light our Elders had not Seen', 471–87, and Beard, *Invention*, 109–28, esp. 116–17 and n. 18, p. 202–3.

[8] Quoted in Stewart, *Harrison*, 104, a covert reference to the tragic death of the dancer Isadora Duncan.

13. Jane Harrison, Hugh Stewart, Gilbert Murray, and Francis Cornford in the Malting House garden, Cambridge

Sometimes they spent holidays in the same place, 'working separately or together, but always in close touch'.[9]

She said of this period of her life that she drifted into the most beautiful happiness she had ever known. 'I never consciously fell in love,' she confided to Hope Mirrlees, 'but bit by bit I came to depend entirely on him', thinking somehow that he would never marry and that their sort of 'unmarried–married' life would be for always.[10]

Research was interrupted, greatly to her annoyance, in the spring of 1906 when she was required to move houses within Newnham. 'What a fearsome thing a move is', she wrote to Murray. 'Well it is partly over tho my books lie in heaps on the floor & "Bill" (all British Workmen are called Bill—never Tom) is dropping paint on them. When you next come to see me you will find me in a superior sort of cave with two mouths like Pan's. Well to-morrow I start for Marazion'[11] and, after spending Easter in Cornwall, 'You will find me in an entirely new cave. I feel old for the first time because I take no interest in the excitement of a move & I hate carpets & curtains—the state ought to provide them.'[12]

It would be more than twenty years before Virginia Woolf gave her seminal paper at Newnham in which she insisted that if a woman was to write she must have money and a room of her own,[13] but the idea had first been articulated by Harrison,[14] who called her room her 'cave' after her claim that the guardians in Plato's *Republic* were Orphic initiates in their cave.[15] She had written to Lady Mary Murray on an earlier occasion that if she had Lady Mary's domestic responsibilities she would go and live in a cave. The word carried for her the double connotation of a place of deep insight with primitive simplicity. When Newnham closed for a period every summer to allow the servants a holiday she felt uprooted in every way: physically, intellectually, and emotionally.

In May her three-year appointment at Newnham came to an end. She

[9] Francis Cornford, *Newnham College Letter*, 1929, 72.

[10] 'The Cornford Letters', Mirrlees's notebook. This cryptic section of the notebook contains her version of what Harrison had apparently admitted to her in connection with letters she had received from Francis Cornford. The allusions are not at all clear, though Mirrlees's later attempt to scratch out all personal names was not entirely successful.

[11] JEH to GM [290], n.d.   [12] JEH to GM [293], n.d.

[13] The lecture was subsequently published as *A Room of One's Own*. See p. 6.

[14] Harrison wrote, 'One of the most ominous signs of the times is that woman is beginning to demand a study' ('Scientiae Sacra Fames' in *Alpha and Omega*, 128). See Robinson, 'Something Odd at Work' in McNees (ed.), *Virginia Woolf: Critical Assessments*, 215–20.

[15] Plato, *Republic* 514A. JEH to GM [102], 14 Oct. 1902. She adds that the 'cave' is also the cave of Trophonios.

seems to have had no anxiety over the matter, and, indeed, the Newnham College Council renewed it for a further period of three years, with the requirement that she lecture for two terms out of three each year. As with her previous appointment, Harrison succeeded in securing for herself terms of employment that must have been the envy of all her Newnham colleagues. Teaching in Part I of the Tripos was regarded as sheer drudgery, and once again Harrison got out of it, teaching only in Part II, in which students chose among five specialist options (language, which was compulsory, history, philosophy, art, and archaeology). Harrison thus secured a double advantage: she lectured in the two fields of her research interest, art and archaeology, and her teaching duties were extremely light compared with her women colleagues. She negotiated her terms of employment the way that the men did at their colleges, with the result that she had time for research.[16] Even with these terms she appears to have had no qualms about travelling overseas during term time.

Some of her students must have felt that all this was a loss, that Harrison's foremost gift was that of teaching, and that when she died, her greatest contribution to the world had died with her. She taught not to any curriculum, (which is perhaps why she was spared the duties of Part I), but taught on the edge of her own research. Many students testified to her freshness, originality and infectious enthusiasm. On occasion she gave tutorials in Greek to non-Tripos students who knew none, and experimented with a method all her own. Disdaining the heavy memorization of paradigms that was the hallmark of all traditional methods, she plunged her students straight into real Greek literature. She herself described her method to Murray in 1905:

I am trying an experiment with yr Hippolytus on a girl who has learnt Greek for one fortnight . . . I read a short chunk of it aloud to her—Greek & yr translation—then I just show her roughly how it fits in grammatically & she learns the Greek off by heart. After she knows it thoroughly we discuss the details but never before. She picked up the first chorus metres without any effort apparently—she is musical—she does not at present know a single technical name, it is all by ear. To such base use do you come.[17]

She presented her method at a meeting of the Curriculum Committee of the Classical Association where it met with a predictably mixed reception. From a student's point of view:

---

[16] See Breay, 'Women and the Classical Tripos' in Stray (ed.), *Classics in 19th and 20th Century Cambridge*, 49–70, esp. 60–1.   [17] JEH to GM [261], n.d.

'Was she a good teacher?' I am hardly the one to give an answer for she used to single me out as her failure *par excellence*. She certainly failed signally to teach me Greek. But then she only set out to teach it by the way. She tried the experiment of starting me straight away on the *Choephori*, expecting that the language would come with a rush from the sheer driving force of the subject matter. It did not. The seduction of corn-babies and *pharmakoi* and the like proved far too strong for proficiency in verbs and declensions. It was putting the cart before the horse all the time—it was no use for examinations. But of course one got something from Jane that one got from no other teacher of her time. One caught the strong breath of intellectual passion. There was about her very presence the glow of a heightened imagination; and it shed a radiancy over many things in life besides the matter to hand. It was almost a new revelation to some of us.[18]

Hope Mirrlees unwittingly testifies to the weakness of the method: she refers in her notes on Harrison to Aeschylus' 'Co-ephorai' [*sic*],[19] revealing that she had missed the point of the title of the play itself. Nevertheless, for all its eccentricity, such an early example of the use of the 'direct method' in teaching languages is most interesting. By the last quarter of the twentieth century, the same principle of using 'real' Greek in teaching beginners was becoming the norm, even if its merits were still hotly debated. Few perhaps would start students out on Aeschylus, or even Euripides, but what is clear is that Harrison understood the supreme importance of sharing with students from the start the experience of reading great literature. The method is very successful with students who are gifted linguistically, and often a dismal failure (if measured by examination success) with those who are not. It was Harrison's genius to recognize that what a student carries away at the end, if not grammatical mastery, may be something she will ultimately value more highly.[20]

---

[18] Victoria de Bunsen, 'Jane Ellen Harrison', *Newnham College Letter*, 1929, 69.

[19] The *Choephori* are the bearers of the *choes*, or 'pots', that Harrison so frequently refers to in her *Prolegomena*. The play is perhaps better known with its title translated into English: *The Libation Bearers*. The plays of Aeschylus are notoriously difficult in their language, and it is nothing short of amazing that Harrison would consider using them for teaching Greek to the beginner. Mirrlees, who failed to make the connection between the 'pots' of the *Prolegomena* and the 'pots' of the *Libation Bearers*, shows that Victoria (Byxton) de Bunsen was not Harrison's 'failure par excellence'.

[20] I have experimented myself with a method not dissimilar to that of Harrison, when I took a small class of highly motivated students who wanted to read Homer. By traditional standards they were not 'ready for it', so I began by teaching them the metre, then I had them memorize a passage, and then we read in the traditional way, but learning the grammar as it came up. Their achievement far exceeded all my expectations.

One of the greatest gifts Harrison brought to all her teaching was her own lively mind, and one cannot separate her method of teaching Greek from the fact that all this while she was working at different languages herself. In the course of a decade she tackled hieroglyphics, cuneiform, Syriac, and Russian. She, together with Cornford and Sir James Frazer, comprised a Hebrew class taught by Professor Kennett. To her, the acquisition of a language was the discovery of a fresh personality, a new way of seeing the world. 'All her teaching', wrote Cornford, 'glowed with the excitement of discovery; the gleam of an untravelled world had never faded from the second aorist of the most eccentric verb.'[21] Teaching and learning were for Harrison a joint discovery, and if she often overestimated what her students were actually learning, they remembered with affection that she never adopted a patronizing attitude: on the contrary, she treated them as equals. There was no sense of teacher and pupil. Jessie (Crum) Stewart recollected how Harrison always treated her as an intellectual equal, and her teaching was as one scholar sharing something new and vital with another. She had no interest in simply imparting knowledge, and refused to teach the orthodox views. Rather, she would invite the student to join her in an adventure of learning, laying out the evidence: poets, scholars, early Fathers, all rather daunting to an undergraduate, but intensely stimulating to the gifted student.

She could also be kind to her students, and took an interest in some of their struggles, never forgetting what it was like to be in their shoes. Writing to one young woman who was concerned about conformity, she shared, 'I have been through so much distress of mind on the question of conformity myself that I do not think there is any form of human problem that I have so much sympathy with. . . . [I]f you have time perhaps we could talk it out a little some evening. . . . My view of conformity has modified a good deal. I used "to bow in the house of Rimmon" much too much, I fear.'[22] Later she wondered if she had said the wrong thing, but was reassured, and wrote again:

It confirms me in a sort of instinct that I have—based I suppose on the old *tout comprendre, c'est tout pardonner*—that the more one takes those near and dear to one into confidence, the more one can show of oneself to them, the less danger there is of misunderstanding and being misunderstood. I often feel that most of one's

---

[21]   Cornford, 'Jane Ellen Harrison', 72–3.

[22]   JEH to Miss Potter, n.d. An allusion to the Old Testament character of Naaman, commander of the Syrian army (2 Kings 5: 18), who begged the prophet Elisha for indulgence when he was obliged to 'bow in the house of Rimmon' with his master, the King of Syria.

difficulties in life come from not getting deep down enough into what people really feel & mean, but just contending on the outside, & it is just these outside moulds that are different for each generation and cause the confusion.[23]

One sees here not only Harrison's concern for a troubled student and readiness to give of her time, but also her affinity with those of a younger generation. She understood the 'outside moulds' for what they were, and could live comfortably within those of her younger friends. It is interesting to see how, now that she was a Fellow of Newnham, she looked back on her own student days, when her own hatred of conformity had got her into trouble.

The summer of 1906 Harrison travelled with Francis Cornford to the Loire Valley in France. There she visited the Benedictine Abbey at Fontevrault which, like so many religious establishments, had been seized during the French Revolution and turned into a prison. The incongruity came as a shock: one moment she was moved by the peace and loveliness of an exquisite oratory, the next the guide was demonstrating various subterranean dungeons with their instruments of torture. Despite her attachment to primitive religion, all of her work had (paradoxically) been underpinned by a faith in human progress, and proof positive of the moral advance over the centuries was (or so she had thought) the decline in cruelty.

The holiday was marked by an experience which imprinted itself powerfully on Harrison's mind and became the icon of her thought for the next couple of years. They visited Chartres with its magnificent cathedral, at the north entrance of which Harrison experienced a moment of epiphany. Standing before the north façade of the cathedral her eye was caught by a 'pillar-shrine'. Her mind flew back three-thousand years to Crete and a feature of Minoan art: a central pillar with a figure or figures in poses which suggest worship.

In 1901 Sir Arthur Evans, the excavator of Knossos, had given a lecture to the Hellenic Society in which he had drawn attention to the omnipresence of trees and pillars in Mycenaean (including Minoan) art, and by careful comparison with what is known from literary as well as archaeological sources from the Eastern Mediterranean had argued that trees and pillars were worshipped 'aniconically', that is, without anthropomorphic representation of any god.[24] Evans concluded with a personal experience he had had in Macedonia, participating in a Muslim ritual that involved

---

[23] JEH to Miss Potter, 17 Nov. 1907.

[24] A. J. Evans, 'Mycenaean Tree and Pillar Cult and its Mediterranean Relations', *Journal of Hellenic Studies* 21 (1901), 99–204.

worshipping a sacred pillar in a shrine. Harrison was doubtless present at the lecture, which may have been the reason for her visit to his excavations later that year. Now she could testify that she too had witnessed a modern-day survival that added validity to Evans's conclusions. This was exactly the kind of experience that thrilled her. She loved the sheer persistence of certain practices down through time. She loved the irrationality of these rituals; the fact that the people who perform them, though they have no idea why they do what they do, are in fact maintaining a living contact with their ancestors. The persistence of Authur Evans's 'pillar cult' was all that was needed for her to accept his theory. It was not in her temperament to sift and weigh the evidence.

Her experience at Chartres was so profound and suggestive that when Harrison learned that the *Vierge du Pilier* had her own week-long festival, more ancient than the saint it purported to celebrate, she returned to Chartres in September to witness it all. She sent Murray a postcard with a picture of the Virgin, and described to him the hundreds of tapers burning in honour of her birthday, with throngs of the faithful kissing her pillar. She was only slightly unnerved by the opening prayer for the increasing number of those who had lost their faith. She began to ruminate on the episode as material for three separate papers on pillar cults.

The previous year Murray had been offered a fellowship at New College, Oxford, from October 1905 for three years, lecturing three times a week for two terms on subjects of his own choosing. He had spent much of the past few years working on Euripides, editing and translating texts as well as overseeing stage productions, and although he continued on his textual work he began to consider a change of direction in his scholarly activities. Early in 1905 he had corresponded with Evans about the possibility of assisting him in the excavations in Crete. When nothing came of that proposal, Harrison reminded him of her intentions for him, the 'difficult and delicate task' of elucidating how each Greek author worked with the material ready to his hand, modifying it according to his own personal outlook. He considered Sophocles, but Harrison was insistent: 'Homer, of course. If you dare to choose the Antigone! I know in yr deceitful & desperately wicked heart you are longing to entirely re-write the whole of Sophocles & to prove thereby that he was the long lost uncle of Euripides.'[25] She implored him to tackle the problems of Homeric religion. Now that she had finished with *The Religion of Ancient Greece* and *Primitive Athens as Described by Thucydides*, she

[25] JEH to GM [282], n.d.

complained that she felt like a bear robbed of her cubs, and ready to tackle the 'Homeric question' again. Dörpfeld had unsettled her mind with a paper that did not take Ridgeway's ethnography into account, and she needed someone with whom she could talk it all over.

About the same time Murray received an invitation from Harvard to come and give six public lectures on some aspect of Greek literature. Although he was not free to take up the offer until 1907, he began to think about what he would choose as his topic. He decided to study the development of Greek poetry from a particular angle: the gradual evolution of what he called 'a force making for the progress of the human race' and which he further defined as 'some gradual ennobling and enriching of the content of life'.[26] The Greeks rose above their barbaric ancestors by valuing the virtue of *sôphrosynê* (self-restraint), tempering their violent emotions by gentler thought.

When Murray finally left for America in April 1907, he left Harrison lonely and desolate without her *sôphrôn* Cheiron in his 'cave'. So dependent had she become on his letters that she could not bear the six-day delay it took them to reach him: 'the Lord knows what may have happened and what yr mind has turned to.'[27] Just how much the usual regular interchange of letters controlled Harrison's natural impetuosity became clear from the fracas she became involved in during his absence.

She had been asked to review volumes III and IV of Lewis Farnell's *The Cults of the Greek States* newly published by the Clarendon Press.[28] 'I simply pine to be spiteful', she confessed to Murray. 'Those two huge volumes are just *nil* and now I shall have to try and be kind and Xian just because Woe is me, I have the fear of you before my eyes.'[29] But with the Atlantic separating them, Murray's *sôphrosynê* failed to temper Harrison's emotions. The review she sent to the *Cambridge Review* was filled with venom.

Books, she claimed, are of two kinds. Some are written because the

[26] Murray, *The Rise of the Greek Epic*, (Oxford: Clarendon Press, 1907), 1. Murray's 'pagan man' was characterized by 'a certain primitive effortless level of human life, much the same all the world over, below which society would cease to be; a kind of world-wide swamp. . . . *La nostalgie de la boue*—"home-sickness for the mud"—is a strong emotion in the human race. . . . Now, as Greek civilization rose from the swampy level of the neighbouring peoples . . . it could not shake itself clean all at once. Remnants of savagery lingered on' (p. 10). What Murray seeks to do is to change the dividing line of the prevailing antithesis between the pagan Greek and the civilized Christian by setting the Greeks firmly within the category of 'civilized man' and to show that Hellenism is a collective name for the very forces which strove for the regeneration of the pagan.   [27] JEH to GM [308], 20 Apr. 1907.

[28] Farnell, *The Cults of the Greek States*, 5 vols. (Oxford: Clarendon Press, 1896–1909).

[29] JEH to GM [308], n.d.

author has something original to say; others are written to meet a need. (After all, she had just herself completed two books of the second sort, and she knew it.) Since Farnell, she claimed, had nothing new to say, *The Cult of the Greek States* fell into the second class. The reader, she claimed, would be looking for a book that would take all the new material of ethnography, archaeology, and anthropology, and apply it to the study of Greek religion using the new scientific and historical methods. He needed a book that would clarify what their gods meant to the Greeks, the significance of their cult, ritual, and mythology, and how it came to be. Anything less 'is only so much new debris in an already crowded lumber-room'. Warming to her topic, she continued to attack Farnell for starting with the Olympians and for thinking of them as personalities. Four volumes and there is no word of Hermes, 'the ancient Herm-god, the pillar-cult incarnate'.[30] She berated Farnell for his slight treatment of Hermes and Dionysos and failure to discuss hero-worship. But it was the last paragraph of the review that stirred up the most trouble. She had written,

Frankly, the time for writing a history of Greek religion is not yet come, and the separation of its two factors, ritual and mythology, which mutually explain each other is . . . a barren and lamentable schism. When the time is ripe, when a vast amount of pioneering work has been done, when Cretan and Mycenaean cults have been properly explored, and a solid foundation has been laid, then no doubt there will appear a Master Builder. He will do for Greek Religion what another Oxford scholar, Mr Gilbert Murray, is doing—alas, in America—for Greek Literature. He will not only know all the facts, but he will divine their real significance, what religion really meant to a Greek, and how he came to fashion his gods. . . . Meantime Mr Farnell leaves us in the valley full of bones and 'Lo, they are very dry,' and the voice is still heard crying, 'Son of man, can these bones live?'[31]

Farnell was on leave at the time, and so Percy Gardner, Professor of classical archaeology at Oxford, felt it incumbent on himself to come to Farnell's defence. He called the article 'neither a review nor criticism, but a call to repentance' and accused Harrison of assuming an unwarranted tone of superiority. If she preferred ghosts to deities and Dionysiac revels to the Panathenaic procession, that was her affair, but if Farnell on the other hand preferred 'the religion of Homer, Pindar and Sophocles, of Pheidias and Polygnotus, to that of the Athenian rabble', it was surely excusable. As for

[30] Hermes was worshipped right through classical times as a square pillar with a phallus and a human head. In *The Religion of Ancient Greece* (18–19) she had begun with Hermes in order to come to grips with the stark contrast between the Olympians of art and ritual and their counterparts in Homer.

[31] *Cambridge Review*, 30 May 1907, 440–1.

the 'Master Builder', Gardner acknowledged that he was yet to come, but not in the guise envisaged by Harrison. He would, rather, 'lay a broad basis, and try to account for every discoverable fact in a reverent spirit'. Dryness, of which Harrison had accused Farnell, was no fatal fault in a serious book. A scientific work is not a poem nor a dream of a new social system. The 'Master Builder' certainly will not 'start with some wild theory and twist all his facts to adapt them to it'.[32]

The *Cambridge Review*, which was not due to appear again till October, forwarded Gardner's letter to Harrison in advance, and permitted her to reply in the same issue. It must have distressed her that it was Gardner who undertook to defend Farnell, since he had always commanded her respect. However, she did object to his saying her article was not a review. The substance of the article had been to point out two 'defects of method' in Farnell's work: the classification of Greek cults under the headings of the Olympian gods, and the separation of mythology from ritual. In the face of such defects Farnell's book could not be said to provide the 'broad basis' upon which 'a reverent spirit' could account for 'every discoverable fact'. That the review was in fact a 'call to repentance' she acknowledged, adding that 'such a call is not unneeded by contemporary writers on Greek religion'.[33]

Word of all this must have reached Murray. His letter to Harrison has not survived, but one can imagine something of his reaction by her letter to him:

Now just look here—why *do* you go to America? If you had been this side of the pond I should have sent you proof of my intemperate review (or rather I shld never have dared to put you into it) & you wld have *re*-written it in words of one syllable & terms of the Xian religion & now here I am embroiled with 'old Percy' whom I adore & he says my review is no review . . . & his dear foolish old head is stuffed with cotton-wool, but I do crawl in the dust before *you* for dragging yr Holy Name in the mire, but I seemed to see how good the world wld be if only you were a mythologist.

To make matters worse I have a long screed just gone to press in the Athenaeum[34], not signed but an unborn babe (Mr Cornford says) wld know it was by me—well that's a 'review' anyhow with chapter & verse. And you have got hay-fever. Oh dear what a black world. Don't ever go away again or I shall go straight to perdition.[35]

She jokes about it, but Harrison's relationship with Murray, with its curious combination of dominance and dependence, was becoming

---

[32] Gardner, Correspondence, *Cambridge Review*, 13 June 1907, 482.   [33] Ibid. 483.

[34] Presumably this refers to her review of *The Rise of the Greek Epic*, which was published anonymously in the *Athenaeum* (1908), 596-7.

[35] JEH to GM [311], n.d.

problematic for her, both emotionally and intellectually. She was setting herself up for grief. He was bound eventually to pull back from her control, while her reliance on him was depriving her of independent judgement. The following April she described for him how she would like her life to be. She would like it to consist of her reading and writing 'stuffage' (Verrall's name for archaeological source material) and for him to walk in every morning for about half an hour and say it was all wrong! In fact, Murray dealt faithfully with her in his criticism, and did not hesitate to correct her on matters of fact or interpretation. It would appear that she always deferred to what she felt was his better judgement. Moreover, as the row over her review of Farnell serves to illustrate, Murray, whose own *sôphrosynê* was proverbial, constantly toned down Harrison's polemical stance.

What Harrison failed to perceive at this stage was the beginning of a more serious rift between them. It was her tendency to see everything through a prism of her own perspective, and she seems to have read Murray's American lectures as though they were part of her grand scheme for the understanding of origins. But while he in no way undervalued Harrison's work in religion, Murray's own leanings were tending in the direction of the Classical period of Greek literature. The attraction of origins was only that they could show just how far, by contrast, the Greek of the fifth century had come.[36]

Reeling from the criticism of Percy Gardner and reprimand from Murray, she spent the summer searching out her spirit and reconsidering her views on the Olympian gods. Gardner had accused her of taking undue interest in 'ghosts, bogies, fetiches, pillar-cults'. In matters of ritual, he contended, her heart 'was not in the right place', preferring as it did 'savage disorders, Dionysiac orgies, the tearing of wild bulls to the ordered and stately ceremonial of Panathenaic processions'.[37] It is unlikely that she had any misgivings about where her sympathies lay, but she certainly felt the need to defend herself, or, in her own words, 'to submit an *apologia pro haeresi mea* ('In defence of my heresy')'.[38]

She had been invited to address the Classical Association in October 1907. 'Shall you mind writing my paper for the Class. Ass. for me?' she asked Murray. 'It is called "The Pillar and the Maiden" but you cld say anything you like in it.'[39] The paper she eventually read began with a pose of humility, as if

---

[36]   Harrison periodically claimed this as her own perspective, but everything that she published belies this attitude. It would appear to be an instance of her acquiescence to Murray's views without her perceiving how contradictory her own position then became.

[37]   Harrison, 'The Pillar and the Maiden', *Proceedings of the Classical Association*, 5 (1907), 65. The Latin is a pun on *Apologia pro Vita Sua*, the title of John Henry Newnhan's autobiography.

[38]   Ibid.   [39]   JEH to GM [349], n.d.

she had come to the conclusion that it was she, not her critics, who needed to repent. Then, moving to her subject of the persistence of ancient ritual, she described her experiences of primitive ritual at Chartres when mothers and babies had flocked to the cathedral steps from miles around, tapers had been lit, and after 'much trafficking in holy cakes and pictures and images' the celebrations had closed with evensong in the cathedral and the 'real business': the procession and worship of the 'Vierge du Pilier'. She went on to describe the throng of young girls, all in blue, carrying tapers, who went first into the crypt then up again to take their station beside the Maiden of the Pillar. 'It was all so frail, and young, and virginal . . . It was the old pagan thing back again, the maidens worshipping the Maid—*their* Maid. My matriarchal soul was glad within me.'[40] It was, she claimed, the same worship as Roman children paid to Diana, and Greek children to Artemis. The ceremony closed when the maidens had sung their last hymn to the Maid, and the congregation crowded round to kiss the Pillar.

The pillar, she believed, was the original object of worship. Hermes was a pillar long before he was a bearded man. Atlas, who holds up the heavens, was a pillar before he was an anthropomorphic god. Even Prometheus is associated in Hesiod with a pillar; even—'dare we think it?'—Odysseus, bound to a mast while he sailed past the Sirens. The pillar came first. Later, an anthropomorphic tendency began to form a human likeness of the object of worship, and place it on top of the pillar. At this point Harrison parted company with Sir Authur Evans. The Pillar and the Maiden, the aniconic and the iconic, did not represent two chronological stages of the evolution of religion, which Sir Arthur Evans had labelled 'lower' and 'higher,' but two 'deep-down tendencies of the human mind', and the preference for one over the other is temperamental. On this score she identified herself unconditionally as an 'aniconist':

I had often wondered why the Olympians—Apollo, Athena, even Zeus, always vaguely irritated me, and why the mystery gods, their shapes and ritual, Demeter, Dionysus, the cosmic Eros, drew and drew me. I see it now. It is just that these mystery gods represent the supreme golden moment achieved by the Greek. . . . The mystery gods *are* eikonic [*sic*], caught in lovely human shapes; but they are life-spirits barely held; they shift and change. Aeschylus, arch-mystic, changes his Erinyes into Eumenides, and is charged with impiety. Dionysus is a human youth, lovely with curled hair, but in a moment he is a Wild Bull, and a Burning Flame. The beauty and the thrill of it![41]

Proclaiming herself a mystic and an aniconist by temperament, she told her audience that she threw herself on their mercy, hoping that there was

---

[40] Harrison, 'The Pillar and the Maiden', 68.   [41] Ibid. 77.

room in the world for all temperaments. (It is not hard to imagine their reaction to such a theatrical gesture.) Perhaps, she concluded, iconism and aniconism represent the workings of the conscious and the subconscious. 'The subconscious makes for fusion, union, emotion, ecstasy; the conscious for segregation, discrimination, analysis, clarity of vision. On the action and interaction of these two our whole spiritual vitality would seem to depend. It is a far-reaching thought.' It needed now only two men, a philosopher and a sociologist, to provide her with some useful labels for her ideas and she had the material for her next large volume, *Themis*.

9. Crabbed Age and Youth: Cambridge 1908–1909

To complicate her life during Murray's absence in America, she had been 'beset by evil Keres' at this time:[1] symptoms of pain and depression which were diagnosed, probably correctly, as connected with heart disease. All her life she had had problems with shortness of breath, nervousness, and fainting, which had previously been attributed to a thyroid disorder. She had been persuaded to give up smoking and was advised to cut down on alcohol.[2] In 1908 she began to see Murray's homeopathic doctor, Christopher Wheeler (whose wife Penelope had acted in some of Murray's Euripides productions in London). Wheeler diagnosed an 'area of leakage' in a valve. 'To put it simply', she wrote to Murray, 'I am a worn out pair of bellows.'[3] There was talk of sending her to Bad Nanheim in Germany (a place famous at the time for the treatment of heart disease) for a cure ('perhaps he will commute the penalty to a voyage round the world, which wld be worse').[4] For a while she improved under digitalis and 'a new drug called "Actaea"' and wrote to Murray, 'I may live till 1910.'[5] The 'evil Keres' also took the form of recurring spells of blindness which on one occasion lasted as long as an hour. Possibly these, as well as the heart disease, were connected with rheumatic fever from her childhood, and may have been psychosomatic as well. Wheeler forbade her to strain her eyes with the scripts of Hebrew, hieroglyphics, and Sanskrit, and also to read by artificial light; he also prescribed exercise, something she had never enjoyed. By this time she was prepared to try anything that would bring relief. Cornford graciously agreed to accompany her on bicycle rides two or three times a week, and friends remember her struggling laboriously on her old pennyfarthing, or clattering over the cobbles. But heart problems continued to plague her, she was often out of breath, and the nervousness to which she had always been prone intensified to 'nameless terrors' as well as a fear of train journeys: 'I have what I and the books call

---

[1] JEH to GM [309], 14 May 1907. [2] JEH to GM [346], June 1908?
[3] JEH to GM [352], May 1908. [4] JEH to GM [348], Mar. 1908.
[5] JEH to GM [347], Mar. 1908.

"siderodromophobia"—[fear of railways] & many other interesting symptoms denoting senile decay.'[6] At these times she could not bear Cornford to leave her side.

On top of this, Francis Cornford had been suddenly taken ill in May 1907 with appendicitis. The news must have struck panic into Harrison, who lived with a constant fear that anything or anyone good would be snatched away from her. She had already seen first her sister Jessie, and more recently R. A. Neil, die from the disease. 'Men are so melodramatic in their ilness [*sic*]', she wrote to Murray. 'They go a long bicycle ride with you one day & the next you find them in bed with doctors & a trained nurse.' Cornford was soon out of danger, but not without leaving Harrison in a state of strained nerves. She accompanied him to Southwold in Suffolk, where he went to convalesce in the belief, prevalent at the time, that the bracing air of the east coast was especially restorative. As she cared for Cornford and, for her own part, recovered from the shock of it all, she became aware that her feelings for him were more than ordinary friendship. 'I seemed to have found myself married in spirit before I woke up to love', she later confessed. 'I had so learned all my life to live in the things of the mind and to find my great joy and peace there. I always seemed to fall in love with my mind.'[7] There began the onset of an emotional nightmare from which she was never to recover.

These events are known to us only in the barest outline. On the other hand, much of what happened subsequently can be reconstructed from letters and an unpublished memoir of Frances Darwin, the daughter of Frank and Ellen Darwin. Ellen's early death in 1903 had devastated both her husband and her daughter, aged 17 at the time, and they had left Cambridge, unable to live in the house which was full of her memories. Frances's mental health had deteriorated further, and she had been sent to the Continent for a cure. In Switzerland she had met Gilbert Murray's daughter Rosalind, who was likewise seeking a cure from some undiagnosed complaint, and the two had become friends. Very suddenly, in 1908, Frances recovered her spirits, and returned to Cambridge in a buoyant mood. (Writing of these events thirty years later, she said that she had since learned that she was 'cyclothymic', suffering from a mild bipolar disorder.) She had decided to study art, and began to take drawing lessons with the painter William Rothenstein.

Frances's return to Cambridge happened to coincide with the Tercentenary celebrations of the birth of John Milton. To mark the occasion Professor Shipley of Christ's College conceived the idea of a stage production of

---

[6] JEH to GM [333], n.d.   [7] 'The Cornford Letters' in Mirrlees's notebook.

John Milton's *Comus*, and broached the idea to the newly-formed Marlowe Dramatic Society, which had been founded the previous year in protest against the entrenched conservatism of the University Dramatic Society. Justin Brooke, a gifted actor, and Rupert Brooke (no relation) were invited to participate. Francis Cornford had been asked to lend his influence as a senior member of the university by acting as treasurer. It was decided to hold the performance during the summer vacation to enable female students to take part, and Harrison was charged with recruiting—and chaperoning—the women, a role she described as 'maiden-aunting'. Frances Darwin and her cousin Gwen (later Raverat) were put in charge of costume and scenery, and persuaded the painter Albert Rothenstein to design the set. The casting gave some trouble when the student who had been chosen for the part of Comus proved unequal to the part, and Frances and Gwen Darwin were convinced that the part should be reassigned to Francis Cornford. After some discussion in Rupert Brooke's rooms in King's, the views of the Darwin cousins carried the day, despite the fact that Francis Cornford was a senior member, and he was '*so* old, over thirty' (he was, in fact, 33). Following strict protocol the two Brookes auditioned Cornford and offered him the part. It must have suited him in more ways than one: with his swarthy skin and dark, curly hair he must have looked the part of the pagan god as well as investing it with his affinity for primitive religion.

The scenery represented a night sky in a wood. Frances Darwin described the fun of 'slodging' huge brushes into the paint, which resembled blue butter, and then 'scrubbling'and 'schlooping' it onto a sheet, lowered for them every ten minutes by Rupert Brooke hanging on to a pulley. Combined with all the fun was a sense of intense seriousness about the poetry, which they felt they understood in their bones. When one of them pierced the deep blue of the night sky with 'one tinsel star', Rupert Brooke brooded a whole afternoon about the vulgarity of their minds, and 'how he had been deceived in thinking that anybody understood Milton but himself'.

Watching them fuss over their costumes Frances was struck by the observation that men are vainer than women, though of course 'women dress up more or less every morning of their lives, so it's nothing new to them',

but to see the Attendant Spirit (Rupert Brooke) doing his hair—solemnly holding his golden head upside-down—as we had taught him—and shaking it from side to side, or later rumpling his fingers through the front and gazing in the glass with melancholy flower-like eyes. 'I can't get it right. Is it right now? Will my hair do now?' Or Comus with a stern intellectual expression spending at least half-an-hour every time getting his gold sandal-ties exactly right round what Aunt Jane calls his 'absolutely hopeless legs' (I suppose because they were too long and slender for the purpose).[8]

The performance, which took place in the New Theatre on 10 July 1908, with Thomas Hardy in the audience, was less than an unqualified success largely because the actors, especially Comus, lacked the professional skill to project their voices, and much was inaudible. But to Frances, Comus was a born actor, giving himself up to the poetry with a sure instinct. Dressed in a panther-skin and glistening robes, he moved with mystery, 'a dark sorcerer with a strange and somehow disembodied grace'.[9] But what stood out in Frances's memory in later years was the beauty of Rupert as the Attendant Spirit, speaking the final benediction,

> Mortals, that would follow me
> Love Virtue; she alone is free.
> She can teach ye how to climb
> Higher than the sphery chime;
> Or, if Virtue feeble were,
> Heaven itself would stoop to her.[10]

The whole event was watched by Harrison with searing emotions. To begin with, her attitude to theatre in general was one of ambivalence, more pronounced as she grew older. 'I am weighed down by Comus', she wrote to Murray. 'I wrestle with my loathing of things theatrical & I see the Beast-Rout in a vision which will never be accomplished—what beautiful preposterous stuff it is.'[11] Murray at this time was working in London with a production of the *Medea* of Euripides, which drew from Harrison the affected observation:

I am always aware that there is a passion in you quite left out in me—that dramatic one—& it is very strong in you for it makes you bear so much incidental squalor. I also believe that one reason why you can bear it is that you either are or have trained yrself to be less easily irritated & upset by merely sensuous tawdriness—both in sights & sounds—you live so much by the inward eye. . . . I know what I feel is—here are these lovely words, altogether lovely which I read by myself in great & pure joy & they are going to be presented in a medium both muddy & violent.[12]

She professed to share with Frances Darwin the worship of great poetry, but in fact there was something else that prevented her from enjoying *Comus*. Rupert Brooke had remarked carelessly in her presence that 'no one over thirty is worth talking to'. These words struck her at a sore point. She had

---

[8] Frances Darwin, memoir.   [9] Ibid.   [10] Milton, *Comus* 1018–23.
[11] JEH to GM [356], n.d.   [12] JEH to GM [357], n.d.

always prided herself on her ability to relate to young people. Francis Cornford was, after all, twenty-four years younger, but this had no bearing on the way she related to him. All of a sudden she found herself an outsider, a spectator to a production in which the actors, *including Cornford*, were a generation younger than herself.

In fact, the production of *Comus* was a watershed in her life as she began to sense that her young friend was in love with Francis Cornford. With this insight both her mental and her emotional worlds were thrown into complete confusion. Frances, the daughter of her dead friend, she had known from her childhood and still thought of as a child (as indeed Frances seems to have regarded herself at the time, writing to her aunt about 'the grown-ups' at dinner). Frances, for her part, felt herself to be Harrison's 'newest human discovery and plaything'. Frances further recollected a tea party that Harrison held in her rooms to introduce her to Francis Cornford, not indeed in any propulsion towards marriage, but thinking that her 'plaything' would entertain him. She felt afterwards that Harrison had thrust them together. Soon afterwards Frank Darwin had begun to invite Cornford to join Harrison on the frequent occasions when she dined at the Darwin home. In all of this Harrison's individual relationships with Francis Cornford and with Frances Darwin were so vastly different that it never occurred to her for a moment that the two were in any sense of the same generation. There were eleven years between them. Initially, that also seemed a great gulf to Frances ('he was *so* old, over thirty').

One night after a rehearsal Harrison walked up and down the 'Backs' by the river, alone, all through the night, while the emotional impact of this development sank in. Her first instinct, if we are to believe her own word, was to broach the subject with Cornford, fearing that Frances, in her present mental state, might go mad if emotionally overwrought. It is hard to know what Harrison was thinking at this point. She 'decided to play providence', telling herself that Cornford would be able to help Frances. She certainly had no inkling of what was to follow.

Reconstructing these events one can't help marvelling at the naïveté of both Harrison and Cornford. Harrison herself apparently believed that her relationship with Cornford was so close that nothing, *not even his marriage*, could affect it. She (astonishingly) felt that he was 'years older and maturer' than herself. Cornford, when Frances asked him later if he was unaware that Jane Harrison was in love with him, claimed that it never crossed his mind. He perceived her not as an equal, but as a mentor a generation older than himself (which she was), and called her privately to Frances by the name by which Frances had always known her, 'Aunt Jane'. He wrote to Frances:

About Aunt Jane we shall have to be thoughtful. You see she and I were both rather lonely people, we foregathered and made friends and we have been a good deal together. Now she is feeling that someone else will be more than all friends to me henceforth—and that someone she loves very dearly. Of course I shall care for her more than ever. It was she who brought us together and I shan't forget that. But she can't help feeling a little lonely and it is distressing her that such a feeling should interfere with her gladness at your happiness and mine.[13]

Later in life Frances put on paper with considerable insight what her own attitude had been:

I still thought of those figures who had always been in my life, as Jane had, just as grown-up people. I credited them with a selfless affection which found complete fulfilment in contributing to the well-being of the younger generation—that they might still be able to change and grow, like us, never entered my head, still less that they could feel inward conflict or any such thing as an agonising ambivalent emotion; even Francis—so much more adult than I—never fully reflected at this time, I think, that it was because Jane had been like a key for him which unlocked the closed door of his personality, that I was now able to turn the handle and walk straight in. And there I stood surrounded by treasures in the very centre of the secret room: not a scholar, without her genius, or her passion, and partly through the simple accident of being more than thirty years younger than she was. I sometimes supposed myself in those days to have the gift of imagination, and yet there I was contentedly blind to this great cruelty of Fate.[14]

Jealousy turned to hatred of Frances, whom she treated spitefully for several years before she finally got her emotions under control. In 1914 she used the experience in a paper read to the Trinity Essay Society. Her anguish at being displaced in Cornford's affection must have been cruelly fuelled by Comus's lines:

> Meanwhile, welcome Joy and Feast,
> Midnight shout and revelry
> Tipsy dance and Jollity.
> Braid your Locks with rosy Twine,
> Dropping odours, dropping Wine.
> Rigour now is gone to bed;
> And Advice with scrupulous head,
> Strict Age, and sour Severity,
> With their grave saws in slumber lie.
> We that are of purer fire
> Imitate the Starry Quire,

[13] Quoted in Stewart, *Harrison*, 109.   [14] Ibid. 110.

Who in their nightly watchful Spheres
Lead in swift round the Months and Years.[15]

Were these lines in her mind when, six years later, she penned the essay entitled 'Crabbed Age and Youth'?[16] Its theme is the difficulty experienced by 'fairly mature youth and quite early middle age' in living together. She begins by quoting the comment 'No one over thirty is worth speaking to' (without mentioning the name of Rupert Brooke), and explores the typical pursuits of the young and the middle-aged. Firstly, in her view, the young love to masquerade, and to be part of a great, egocentric chorus. Then, in parallel sequence to the evolution of Greek tragic drama from choral dance, Youth eventually specializes 'through the compulsion of life', by accepting a post, by marriage or some other life-changing event, whereupon he mellows, and becomes easier to live with. Companionship between Youth and Crabbed Age is possible so long as they both are bent on some common inquiry. 'Who, save as a matter of curiosity, asks whether a fellow man of science is twenty or forty?' she inquires. She goes on to analyse some of the mistakes they make in trying to live together. Here Age 'sins worse than Youth. Age dominates, possesses Youth, uses Youth for its own selfish purposes, demands its sympathy and adulation, and then expects Youth to be grateful.'

The word 'grateful' touches off a painful memory, which she proceeds to narrate. The identity of the characters is too thinly disguised:

I once knew a tutor who, rash man, thought he had made a friend of a pupil. The pupil wrote, as it happened, to announce his marriage, and used the occasion to say how 'grateful' he was and for what. 'I owe to you eternal gratitude: *you have helped me to find . . . myself*—that self which I am now about to dedicate to another.' The tutor's face was old and grey as he laid down the letter. But the young man was quite sincere: his tutor had been to him, not a friend, but a door by which he might enter, a ladder by which he might spiritually climb. The friendship between Crabbed Age and Youth is always beset on both hands by the fiend of megalomania; the younger enhances himself through the skill and knowledge of the elder, the elder feeds his vanity on the open-eyed admiration of the younger. Only very delicate souls can live unhurt in such an atmosphere.[17]

After *Comus*, evicted from her rooms at Newnham for the summer, Harrison took lodgings at Southwold, and Cornford kept up his habit of accompanying her, presumably to combine something of a holiday with the

---

[15] Milton, *Comus*, 102–14.
[16] 'Crabbed Age and Youth', read to the Trinity Essay Society in 1914, and published in *Alpha and Omega*, 1–26.   [17] Ibid. 21.

opportunity to work together. Three weeks later Frances Darwin and her father joined them. Harrison kept up the appearance of welcoming them, but inwardly, as she later confessed to Frances, her heart sank with the realization that things would never be the same again. Later that summer Cornford asked Frances to marry him.

The perception that marriage and sex is 'le grand égotisme à deux' was to dominate her thinking and writing for several years. Her feelings again spilled over into an article, published the following year under the title 'Homo Sum'.[18] Harrison declares that the words 'Homo sum should be blazoned on the banners of every suffrage society.' Ostensibly 'a Letter to an Anti-Suffragist from an Anthropologist', the first part of the paper is an articulate explanation of why she had changed her mind over the past ten years over the question of the vote for women. The different ways that the words 'womanly' and 'manly' are applied to morals, she argues, reveal that the behaviours they supposedly connote are not in fact related to gender at all. If by 'womanly' we mean 'gentle', 'modest', 'tactful', we are using the word to refer to the virtues of the weak, physically or socially. These are the attributes of the governess and the companion, but also of the private secretary and the tutor; 'they are virtues not specially characteristic of the average duchess'. She then considers the egotism of sex, and contrasts it with the 'herd instinct'.[19] 'The instinct of sex is anti-social, exclusive, not only owing to its pugnacity; it is, we have now to note, anti-social, exclusive, owing also to the intensity of its egotism.' As the argument continues it becomes patently autobiographical, and it is hard to see how parts of this essay have anything to do with the argument about votes for women. Her examples of such egotistical delusion could hardly be more telling, and all the more so for their conjunction: the letters of the newly engaged ('We shall try not to be more selfish than we can help'), and the counsel of a widower to his daughter on his remarrying ('The love I feel for my new wife has nothing to do with my affection for you'). 'There is no such devastating, desolating experience as to have been at the centre, warm and sheltered,' she wrote, 'and suddenly

[18] 'Homo Sum', Being a Letter to an Anti-Suffragist from an Anthropologist (Oxford: Blackwell [1909?]) repr. in Alpha and Omega, 80–115. The reference is to a declaration of the Roman playwright Terence: homo sum, nihil humani alienum a me puto ('I am a human being; nothing that's human do I account alien'). Latin has the advantage over English of two distinct words for 'man': homo (man as human being), and vir (man as male, as opposed to mulier, woman).

[19] She makes reference to W. Trotter, 'Herd Instinct and its Bearing on the Psychology of the Civilised Man', Sociological Review, 1 (1908), 227–48 and 'Sociological Application of the Psychology of Herd Instinct', ibid. 2 (1909), 36–54. These articles are reprinted in W. Trotter, Instincts of the Herd in Peace and War (3rd edn. London: OUP, 1953; 1st edn. 1915), chs. 1 and 2.

to be at the outmost circumference, and be asked to revolve as spectator and sympathizer round a newly-formed centre.' The rise of Greek drama parallels human experience, for it arose out of the chorus, which then 'differentiated into chorus and spectators, and ultimately into actors and spectators. *This is what happens . . . in life.*'[20]

Lady Mary Murray read 'Homo Sum' before it was published, and wrote warning Harrison that she had lapsed into autobiography and advising her to delete the references to the father's second marriage. Harrison replied, thanking her for her criticism, and adding, 'Yr instinct was sound—that *was* autobiographical & one should not put one's father's sins in a tract, you have saved me from a piece of bad taste. I felt (when I read it after yr letter) that it was splenetic & personal. . . . I always felt that it was not the second marriage but the early Victorian *lies* that poisoned my life—nothing is poisonous except lies.' Nevertheless, in the version that went to print the passage remained. Also left in against Lady Mary's advice was a purple passage about falling in love—included lest 'the paper might, without something of that sort, leave the impression that it was a tirade against sex & that would have been so dreadfully untrue for I think it *the* wonder & beauty of the world— only apt to go all wrong and ugly'.[21]

It is all too clear what had happened. As Harry Payne has observed, the Cornford marriage opened up wounds more than half a century old with the spite of a child and without an adult's understanding. Her reaction to her father's remarriage is understandable, but that she never got over it 'marks the central emotional dynamic of her later life'.[22]

Physical problems continued to compound her misery. She had written to Murray in April, 'I go to London Friday to see Mr Wheeler in the morning & yr foot man at two in the afternoon. I now have a doctor for every limb.'[23] In May her foot doctor (Robert Jones) prescribed surgery for her toes, 'cusped' as the result of rheumatoid arthritis. It would involve not walking for six weeks, but the alternative was worse: iron bars fitted on all her boots and shoes, and no guarantee even so that she would not deteriorate. 'I am "flabby" with a flabby heart—it is disgusting', she groaned, 'sodden and depressed'.[24]

Surgery on her toes was arranged for 31 July 1908. Margaret Verrall, whose interests by this time were entirely taken up by psychical research, had a macabre curiosity about the effects of the anaesthetic, and planned to be

---

[20] 'Crabbed Age and Youth', 12–13 (italics mine).   [21] JEH to MM, 28 Aug. 1909.
[22] Payne, 'Lady of the Wild Things', unpub. typescript.
[23] JEH to GM [351], n.d.   [24] JEH to GM [355], n.d.

present when Harrison came round. 'She is going to suggest things to me when I am subconscious & see what occurs.'[25] What occurred is not recorded, but she could write to Murray that the ether was 'quite a nice treat'. To Lady Mary she wrote of the ambulance:

it was most comfortable & ingenious & the three men who carried me were so kind & cheery & clever, but they simply reeked of spirits & tobacco—I was almost moved to give my first temperance address, but after the almost morbid purity of a model antiseptic sick room it was such a whiff of the dear disgusting old world I was coming back to that I refrained my lips & forgave them.[26]

Cornford escorted her to Devon to convalesce under the care of the Murrays, and from there she went to stay with her sister Lucy in Yorkshire, where in the company of her family she felt more lonely than ever, feeling that she belonged to no-one, least of all to her own kin.[27] She was not well enough to attend the Third International Congress for the History of Religions which was held in Oxford the following September, though she submitted a paper on 'Bird and Pillar Worship'. Cornford read it for her.

She returned to Newnham in the autumn to begin work on an article on the study of religion which had been commissioned for the centenary of Charles Darwin's birth. But writing did not come easily. 'I have piles of things to say & no power to say it, & it is dull, dull.'[28] She was not only physically but also emotionally drained, and blamed Cornford for her lack of inspiration. When the article finally went to proof she wrote to Murray that she had 'put in all yr Great Thoughts & modified the greatness of some of my own . . . but any really offensive words I can still take out'.[29]

She was right about lack of inspiration. The Darwin article is the dullest thing she ever published. Nevertheless it is significant for an understanding of the state of her thinking about religion at this point.[30] The first part is an account, perhaps an unintentional parody, of what she considered to be the accepted attitude to religion in England in the first half of the nineteenth century; the second, much longer part attempts to evaluate the influence of Darwin and contains, along with a resumé of recent books and articles,[31]

[25] JEH to GM [367], n.d.   [26] JEH to MM, [369], 6 Aug. 1908.
[27] JEH to GM [371], 30 Sept. 1908.   [28] JEH to GM [374], 4 Nov. 1908.
[29] JEH to GM [383], 29 Dec. 1908.
[30] Harrison, 'The Influence of Darwinism on the Study of Religions' in *Alpha and Omega*, 143–78. Martha C. Carpentier calls this article 'seminal'. See *Ritual, Myth, and the Modernist Text* (Amsterdam: Gordon and Breach, 1998), 10.
[31] She lists as books that have influenced her own views (p. 498, n. 1): W. Wundt, *Völkerpsychologie* (Leipzig, 1900); P. Beck, *Die Nachahmung* (Leipzig, 1904), and 'Ernkenntnisstheorie des

some thinking of her own. Before Darwin, she argues, religion was regarded as a body of doctrine, revealed once and for all by an anthropomorphic God. Only at the end of the century was the importance of ritual recognized. By this time anthropologists and missionaries were studying 'savages', and at the time of the Darwin centenary in 1909 (also the fiftieth anniversary of the publication of *The Origin of Species*) thought they had some understanding of 'the primitive mind'. Harrison accepts uncritically the assumption that bedevilled ritual studies at this period, that what the anthropologists learned about savages was indicative of the early development of human beings everywhere at all times. The primitive man had not yet begun to distinguish objective and subjective; his dreams, aspirations, and memories and a host of abstract ideas are all equally the furniture of a real, if secondary, world. Naming things could call them into being. The traditional view of the origins of religion would argue from this point that out of this inchoate cluster of ideas developed, first, polytheistic gods, then monotheism. But Harrison takes a different tack, emphasizing that 'man has ritual as well as mythology; that is, he feels and acts as well as thinks; nay, more, he probably feels and acts long before he definitely thinks. . . . and out of his feeling and action, projected into his confused thinking, he develops a god'.[32] Ritual, far from being the dead practice we so often associate with the word, was for primitive man a real, live thing, as by a practice of imitation he worked to bring about the state of affairs in the world that he so desired. The notions of *mana*, *orenda*, and the like, as used by savages, have brought home to us what primitive man is doing as he performs his rituals. So far Harrison is summarizing the writings of others, but now she inserts what she describes as 'my own most serious contribution to the subject' as she addresses herself to the question, 'Why do the world of thinking and the world of doing combine?' Her answer runs as follows.

The world of *mana* and magic on the one hand, and that of dreams and ghosts on the other, combine when we try to give reality to our egocentric desires. The supernatural world is malleable as the natural world is not, 'space and time offer no obstacles; with magic all things are possible'. She concludes this section with an extraordinarily revealing example. It had already been assumed by Edward B. Tylor that the mind of the primitive

primitiven Denkens' in *Zeitschrift f. Philos. und Philos. Kritik* (1903), 172, and (1904), 9; Henri Bergson, *L'Évolution Créatrice* and *Matière et Mémoire* (1908); Dr. Preuss, 'Ursprung der Religion und Kunst', *Globus*, 86 and 87, and in the *Archiv f. Religionswissenschaft*; and for the subject of magic, MM. Hubert et Mauss, 'Théorie Générale de la Magie' in *L'Année Sociologique*, 7.

[32] 'The Influence of Darwinism', 161.

resembled that of a child; Harrison's illustration catches her in the act of actually entering into the mind of the child:

The child helps us to understand our own primitive selves. To children animals are always people. You promise to take a child for a drive. The child comes up beaming with a furry bear in her arms. You say the bear cannot go. The child bursts into tears. You think it is because the child cannot endure to be separated from a toy. It is no such thing. It is the intolerable hurt done to the bear's human heart—a hurt not to be healed by any proffer of buns. He wanted to go, but he was a shy, proud bear, and he would not say so.[33]

Religion grows, then, not out of primitive *thinking* but out of primitive *feeling* and *acting*. Is it then purely a delusion? No, because religion may be the only way of apprehending things that cannot be put into language without distortion, things that have to be felt and lived. These things may be enormously important. Moreover, it is only when we think of religion as continuously evolving, rather than an unchanging revelation, that we can attain to a spirit of real tolerance. We may have renounced the practice of magic, yet there is still in the mystery and ambiguity of religious ritual an opening for our insistent emotions.

Much of this material would find its way into the full-length book that was forming itself in her mind, eventually published as *Themis*, where she worked out a more satisfactory, if highly idiosyncratic, conclusion about the value of religion.

Her heart still gave her problems. A second opinion from a Dr Rogers brought the same diagnosis, but the opposite treatment: Rogers urged complete rest. Frank and Frances Darwin kindly took her in and nursed her in their home on Madingley Road until she was pronounced well enough to travel. She was sure that her 'grey sea-mother' would help, and in the middle of December 1908 took refuge with Alys Russell at Aldeburgh, Suffolk, where she stayed for about a month taking with her to read 'the Word of God in Hebrew, James's Psychology, Lehmann's Aberglaube [superstition, myth] in . . . a vast book I cannot even hold'.[34] She had always looked to the sea for its restorative powers; now she had also come to realize that Cambridge was the worst place in the world for her to be until after the Cornford wedding.[35]

That Christmas Frances Darwin drew a Christmas card for her fiancé, depicting them both, together with her father and Jane Harrison, forming a procession, each carrying a piglet (Fig. 14). The drawing, done in the style of

---

[33] 'The Influence of Darwinism', 173.
[34] JEH to GM [381], 22 Dec. 1908.   [35] JEH to GM [387], 8 Jan. 1909.

14. Christmas card by Frances Darwin, 1908, showing herself, Francis Cornford, Frank Darwin, and Jane Harrison

a vase painting, is a spoof on an illustration in *Prolegomena*.[36] It bears the inscription 'ΥΣ ΚΑΛΟΣ' ('pig is beautiful'), a parody of the inscription often found on Greek vases that bear the name of a (homosexual) lover. Underneath are the words 'ΑΛΑΔΕ ΜΥΣΤΑΙ' ('to the sea, ye mystics'), the words that accompanied the act of purification at the Eleusinian Mysteries, and a reference to Harrison's discussion of the formula in *Prolegomena*.[37] The celebrants on that occasion carried pigs, which they drove to the sea before bathing with them. The fact that the animal involved was a pig is, according to Harrison, without any significance. The meaning of the whole ritual is elusive, but in Harrison's account it is at heart a ceremony of purification coupled with one of initiation. The Christmas card is no less elusive, no doubt referring to a private joke between the engaged couple. They may indeed all have been going to the sea; they believed in its power to heal. There are suggestions here of Frances's recent recovery from depression,

---

[36] Harrison, *Prolegomena*, 126.   [37] Ibid. 152 ff.

her forthcoming marriage, and perhaps an intimation that the relationships between the four of them would be 'purified', anticipating Harrison's 'conversion' a few years later.[38]

At some time during her stay in Aldeburgh (Harrison had an aversion to dating her letters) she wrote to Frances a most personal and revealing letter. In an era when strict etiquette about forms of address was beginning to break down, the name by which a young person should call an older friend was problematic. Nicknames were one solution. They were also intimate, which could be awkward. The letter is worth quoting in full.

My dear F,

About names—how strange & wonderful they are. I think one will always—in the New Jerusalem[39]—have official names for public use & one's secret names for those who are near to one, known only to a very few ('σιγῶντα ὀνόματα' ['silent names'])—a secret name should mean only just one's own personal relation that no one else could have & the public name is just a label which you have in common with a jampot. 'Francis' will do quite well as a label for Francis—'Comus' cannot go on and 'Frank' I always flatly declined to call him. I don't like the name *in itself* and all its associations for me are round yr father—tho it expresses him as little as it expresses 'Francis'—in time I daresay I shall get used to saying the label name & he had better label me in the family 'Jane' tho he has never called me that in his life. Long ago as I daresay he has told you he announced by letter (he always announces everything by letter) that he meant always to call me Shvah, wch is Hebrew for the Queen of Sheba. It was because . . . but you know yr Bible. So then I fell into calling him Shlomoh (accent on the last syllable) which is Hebrew for Solomon. So if you want to understand our signatures you will have to learn one Hebrew letter ש—he *is* very wise. Long before that when we were in Greece together he got called the Bear—I will show you some day the photograph that will explain why he was called that—& then Shlomoh became the name of the Ur-Bear because it is soft & padding & fumbles & shuffles—but these names & great truths are known only to me & him & you.

I think you & I have felt about for names for each other & never found them. Frances doesn't somehow mean much to me—I think that is why I shorten it to F. but it means a remembrance as it was a great deal to yr mother. I shall perhaps some day find the right beast for you, but it certainly isn't a bear—you haven't a scrap of one in you, wch is odd because yr father *has*.

[38] In her interpretation of this drawing (*Mask and Self*, 160), Sandra Peacock is almost certainly wrong. She ignores the parallel between the drawing and the vase painting in *Prolegomena*, together with Harrison's commentary on the pig procession, while adducing an anachronistic Freudian reading that goes against the grain of the sensibilities of all the players involved.

[39] An allusion to Revelation 3: 12 (compare 2: 17). This is but one of the countless allusions in Harrison's writings to the Bible she had memorized so thoroughly in her childhood.

Jane is a dignified label for me, but I want you to drop 'Aunt.' Aunt & Uncle have to me always a touch of comedy & even farce about them—perhaps you won't agree. You know not what being a real Aunt is. I don't think it is much of a relationship anyhow, I mean, I find that with my real nieces I have to make separate friends with them individually or not if I am to have a real relation. Anyhow I am not yr *real* Aunt, & you not my real niece—you are first & foremost the child of my friend whom I chose for myself & who is gone & *that* is more than any *un*chosen relationship & you are next my friend for yr own sake—so let our label be Jane. One cannot always find a *real* name—it either comes or doesn't come & it is useless to hunt. I think very often just as the Greeks had Augenblicksgötter who developed into permanent gods so the real names are flashes of sudden intimacy & contact caught in a moment & then kept for always.

It is horrible cold blooded work labelling one's jampots. I think that is why to me marriage has in it so much that is noisome—it brings about all sorts of official states & relations. Francis becomes suddenly 'Aunt Maud's' nephew & has to be rechristened & so on. . . .

About work. Yes, the world *is* a ruthless place & sex the most ruthless thing in it. Thank you for seeing that. I am just now faced by the blank unalterable fact that for more than 5 months Francis has not cared & could not care at all for the work that has been for years our joint life & friendship—but I have faith to believe it may not always be so. While it *is* so it is better that he & I should *not* be together. I also absolutely believe that you reverence work, tho you could & ought not to understand, nor can he, how—late in life—work & friendship come to be the whole of life. I trust you always.

　　Jane

I think yr secret name for Francis ['Tiger'] is really yr *own* name. You always seem to be crouching mentally waiting to give a splendid spring straight to the mark—that is why my dear one when I am weak tho you often delight me you never rest me. Someday I shall be stronger.[40]

In another letter she wrote to Cornford,

Of course you understand—you and she are by nature birds of prey, you pounce straight down on what you want and eat it up and the devil take the other birds'—isn't it so? I knew it was—well if we are two birds of prey, the Old Eagle and the Young One shall we try at least not to prey on each other? The Old Eagle would like to try—for she loves her Young One.[41]

Francis Cornford and Frances Darwin were married in June 1909. Harrison wrote from Aldeburgh that she would not be there 'in my vile body—it is too vile just now, but my spirit will shake hands with you at the garden parties,

[40]　Quoted by Ackerman, 'Some Letters of the Cambridge Ritualists', 121–4.
[41]　This letter is taken from a transcription in Mirrlees's notebook.

and that the choice of the Registry Office was 'hideous but right, and one has to do right—still I wish you could have been married under a tree by the old snake'.[42]

The year of 1909 was also one of change for Murray as he took up his new responsibilities as Regius Professor of Greek at Oxford. He had accepted the position with some hesitation, conscious of the differences between himself and his predecessor, Ingram Bywater. His inaugural lecture, delivered on 10 February 1909, reads as a manifesto. Cambridge had led the way in expanding the scope of classical studies to include archaeology, literary criticism, and anthropology, and Murray proposed incorporating such developments into the 'Greats' curriculum at Oxford. Murray felt, moreover, that the study of classics at Oxford, with the first five terms devoted to language and literature ('Honour Moderations'), history and philosophy ('Greats') being studied by students in their senior years, had fostered an attitude of condescension towards Greek literature as a subject to be outgrown, and he sought for ways to reintegrate the two parts of the degree. The inclusion of cognate subjects would further this end. Moreover, he would carry into his work as Regius Professor the mission, already expressed in his London performances of Euripides, of making accessible to non-specialists what the scholar has felt in the beauty and power of great literature. For Murray the calling of the scholar was to be a mediator 'through whom the power of great men over their kind may still live after death'.[43] Murray had learned from Harrison that in order to understand Greek literature, we must also feel. With her he shared the conviction that 'feeling', far from being an indolent substitute for the exacting task of scholarship, entailed more, not less, hard work. For many people, the sheer task of intellectual analysis dulled the edge of imagination, but for a scholar, that is exactly what it must not do.

All of these sentiments, expressed publicly on so significant an occasion, must have been most gratifying to Harrison. However, there was another aspect to his new position that was less welcome. Prior to his appointment he had agreed to give the Gifford Lectures on some aspect of religion in the winter of 1908–9. Harrison's heart had leapt at the opportunity:

Splendid, splendid—just what I have longed for that you shld do the religion of the gods. Do it? There is no one in the whole world that I know who can do it but you—& under the head of religion you can say just everything you want, all leading up to Euripides. Oh it is too beautiful & delightful & I begin to believe that 'God's in his

[42]   JEH to Frances Cornford, n.d. box 8.
[43]   Gilbert Murray, Inaugural Lecture, University of Oxford.

heaven'. And I will grub up all the primitive preliminary 'stuffage' in fact I *shall* be doing it anyhow for the *Epi-* or *Meso*-legomena. . . . Oh you will have a dreadful time—but I am so happy thinking of it.[44]

Harrison, always ready to dictate to Murray and Cornford what she thought should be their joint agenda, saw in the Gifford Lectures a project that would absorb herself together with Murray. Now, with the assumption of new duties as Regius Professor he had felt it necessary to cancel the arrangement. She was devastated.

What *can* I say? I hoped that the Professorship would give you more leisure for other work not less. It is such a crushing disappointment that you should give up the Gifford lectures that I can not look at it with clear eyes, but that is just rank selfishness [,] just the wish that for a time you should be looking at things more from my angle so as to help *me*!

That and also the feeling that what you were going to do for the Gifford was really, I mean all the primitive religion part, *necessary* even for yr final Euripides pronouncements, but I may be wrong to attach too much importance to these things, & if you feel the thing is too much for yr physical strength the Gifford must be given up. I hoped now you are free to lecture as you please the one could work into the other. Must the decision be made absolutely at once? The gist of the disappointment is to me—that I feel you will drift away from mythology & religion & *origines*. You see there are only two people who are scholars & with literary minds who understand that these things are at the back of everything—FMC here for Cambridge & I hoped you for Oxford—the specialists don't count—they grub up the facts but don't see the relations, & it wld have been so splendid that you as Professor should give these lectures.

But again I say I can't see clearly. Perhaps there are tears in my eyes. Follow yr own conviction of what is best for work—& I will not uselessly lament.[45]

She could see the world only through the lens of her own interests. It was all but impossible for her to grasp the fact that Murray, unlike her, did not see the study of origins as essential to his work, and that in fact his approach to Greek literature was guided more by where it was leading *to* than where it came *from*. For Murray, origins were of interest only inasmuch as they indicated how far humans have progressed, a perspective tellingly revealed in the title of his book published the previous year: not 'The Origins of the Greek Epic' but 'The Rise of the Greek Epic.' Similarly, when Murray was invited to give a course of lectures at Columbia University in 1912 on the origins of Greek religion, he wrote to the President, 'I can't resist coming to Columbia, and the subject you propose is just the one that I happen to be full of at the

<hr/>

[44] JEH to GM [353], n.d.   [45] JEH to GM, [378], n.d.

present moment. I would sooner make it "Greek Religion" than "The Origins of Greek Religion." '[46] At this point Harrison intuited that the scholarly collaboration they had enjoyed together with Francis Cornford was beginning to unravel. In an undated letter (perhaps 1911) she reproached Murray again for abandoning her: if he had done the Gifford Lectures she felt that he would have cleared up the quagmires, instead of which he went on to other things, '& now all my stuff is so outside yr real work that tho you are infinitely patient & good, I always feel it is an effort to you to refocus yr attention on it'.[47]

All these events—Cornford's marriage, Murray's Regius Professorship, and the implications for the future of their scholarly collaboration with Harrison, together with her deepening depression—led to further complications for Murray in his friendship with her. His relationship with Lady Mary, which had never been easy, was undergoing severe strain at this time. She had given birth to their fifth child, Stephen, in February 1908, and neither she nor the baby was in good health. Lady Mary took Stephen to Sidmouth to convalesce. Meanwhile Gilbert took the children to Rottingdean, where he shared a house with the homeopathic doctor Christopher Wheeler and his wife Penelope. The sheer number of letters between them in 1908–9 testifies to how frequently they were apart. This would put a strain on any marriage, but a strange cavalier spirit in Murray made the situation intolerable for his wife. When the hay-fever season drove him to the sea, he took the children with him and stayed with the Wheelers in Cornwall. Penelope Wheeler, who was studying for the part of Phaedra in one of his Euripides productions, was an attractive woman, and when Murray wrote to his wife of the fun they had had playing with kites on the beach, she was understandably distressed. His reply would have done nothing to put her mind at rest, as he confessed that he did indeed 'become charmed by a certain kind of beauty' and that although he professedly loved her more than ever before in his life, these 'rather emotional friendships' did nevertheless come drifting across his heart. He certainly saw nothing wrong or treasonous in them.[48] 'Not for him *le courage du mensonge* or even *le courage de se taire*', as Wilson so aptly comments.[49]

Harrison's depression, her constant longing for his company, no less concealed, combined with his genuine friendship for her, placed him in a difficult position *vis-a-vis* Lady Mary. In the summer of 1909 the whole family

---

[46]   GM to Nicholas Murray Butler, 9 Oct. 1911. Quoted in Wilson, *Gilbert Murray*, 157.

[47]   JEH to GM [503], n.d.   [48]   GM to MM, 25 June 1908, MS Gilbert Murray 459/105.

[49]   Wilson, *Gilbert Murray*, 146.

went to Aldeburgh to be near her, but Gilbert stayed on after his wife returned to Oxford. He tried to explain to her that it was only out of duty that he stayed on, feeling 'unamiable and grumpy and depressed',[50] finding Harrison's depression contagious.

Meanwhile, in Cambridge, Frances's cousin Ruth, daughter of Horace Darwin, had begun canvassing friends of Harrison with a view to raising subscriptions for a portrait. Harrison realized that the proposal for a portrait offered an opportunity to a young artist, and suggested that Ruth write to D. S. MacColl, now Keeper of the Tate Gallery, for advice, pointing out that he 'knew her well' and that she had absolute confidence in his judgement. Harrison had been in touch with MacColl a few years previously, apparently in reply to an invitation to join him once again on a holiday. Her reply included a suggestion that he 'come and paint the portraits of our Eminences here—they are gnarled and twisted enough to give you full scope in lights and shadows'.[51] MacColl recommended as his first choice Augustus John, though expressed fears that the name might terrify the committee. Other names that were considered were Francis Dodd and Wilson Steer. Steer, MacColl ventured, had reached an extraordinary sensitivity in his drawing of faces, but 'his tastes lie in the direction of young girls'.[52] On hearing of MacColl's suggestions from Ruth Darwin, she wrote to him directly, in a letter that was a little more self-revealing than her previous one, 'Of course I shld like John if he would do it. He has seen the vision of the Beauty of Ugliness &, which is still harder, of Plain-ness.'[53] Steer, she thought, would not be able to make anything of her. Weighing the choice between John and Steer, Harrison reflected that John was by now 'too big a name to terrify', and that his portraits captured the 'character that comes into all faces, however plain, that belong to people who have lived hard'. However, she was not averse to Steer taking a look at her, and felt that a Steer would certainly be a great acquisition for the college. She had some personal acquaintance with Steer, having bought, under MacColl's advice, one of his paintings at a time when he was unknown. If she could once again help a struggling young artist (this time John), she would be very pleased, for 'artists appeal to me just as bears do—they are so dumb & helpless in matters of this world's goods'.[54]

It was agreed that John should be approached, and in July 1909 Harrison returned from Aldeburgh to Cambridge to sit for the portrait. Murray had

[50] GM to MM, 12 July 1909, MS Gilbert Murray 460/52.
[51] JEH to DSM, n.d. [1905 by internal evidence], MS MacColl H17.
[52] DSM to Jessie Stewart, 27 May 1909, Harrison paper, box 10.
[53] JEH to DSM, 30 May 1909, MS MacColl H177.   [54] JEH to Ruth Darwin, n.d., box 9.

realized the emotional strain entailed in returning to Cambridge. He coun-selled her to try to fill her days with work rather than dwell on the long lonely years that lay ahead, and graciously helped to make that a reality by coming to visit her for the duration of the portrait. In a curious way the painting itself helped her as she reflected on how an artist's eye sees charac-ter in the lines of a suffering face. Meanwhile she wrote to Murray that 'The immortal & immoral John is painting me day by day & so swiftly that I think it will be done before you come—if he is here & you see him I believe you will say his face is beautiful. I entirely refuse to believe that he is evil—a good god may have denied him all moral sense . . . but he is better without it.'[55]

Murray arrived later that week, and engaged her in scholarly conversation while John painted. The artist broke with convention and instead of insisting on a formal pose he simply let her recline in her *chaise-longue*, as she had been doing for months, smoking almost incessantly. (She had apparently lapsed back into the habit she had so painfully given up.) For a background Harri-son suggested her Steer painting *Yachts*, an idea which John seized upon. She was delighted as he spent two days working on it in oblivion of herself and commented to MacColl that she felt as if she were an episode in the career of a painting that had given her much joy over the years: 'He was delightful. I felt spiritually at home with him from the first moment he came into the room, he was so quiet & real, and sympathetic too. He came to Cambridge in two vans with 6 horses, 7 sons & I never was quite clear how many wives. I asked the chief one to come & see me but she couldn't or wouldn't.'[56] She thought it best not to enquire further about his domestic arrangements 'lest his habits should be patriarchal & scriptural'.[57] Jessie Stewart recalled how a party of Gilbert Murray, his daughter Rosalind, Helen Verrall, and Gwen Darwin had walked out to Grantchester to visit him, finding his children unkempt and untended, sleeping under an awning on straw.[58]

In the event the choice of Augustus John was felicitous. The portrait is colourful and original, just like its subject, and, like its subject, provoked strong and conflicting reactions. Harrison liked it, though she wrote that she looked like 'a fine distinguished prize-fighter who has had a vision & collapsed under it'.[59] D. Piper, speaking on the BBC Third Programme described it somewhat cryptically as 'the only existing humane portrait of a Lady Don',[60] whereas Arthur Benson wrote that 'the portrait of Jane Harri-son, with its clay-coloured face, claw-like hands, coloured cushions and rugs

---

[55] JEH to GM [409], 19 July 1909.   [56] JEH to DSM, 15 Aug. 1909, MS MacColl H178.
[57] JEH to GM [409], 19 July 1909.   [58] Stewart, *Harrison*, 129.
[59] JEH to DSM, 15 Aug. 1909, MS MacColl H178.
[60] Quoted in Stewart, *Harrison*, 130. No date is given for the broadcast.

is perfectly *horrible*.[61] (The same writer records sitting next to Harrison at a dinner at Newnham College when she discoursed on her love of beauty. 'Poor woman', he sighed. 'How she must hate mirrors.')[62]

The painting now hangs in the Senior Combination Room at Newnham. The face that looks out from it stares into the distance, tired, tight-lipped and stoical. There is little hint of the playful humour that still shone out from her letters. The expression suggests rather that she could not find the resources within herself to heed Murray's advice and not think of the endless lonely years that now lay ahead. The positive side of his admonition was easier to heed, and she began to concentrate her energies on her next major book.

[61] Arthur Christopher Benson, Diary, Magdalene College Cambridge Archives, F/ACB/110, 3–4.

[62] Ibid. F/ACB/87, 11–12. On another occasion he described her as 'a ruinous sight, with a face torn to bits by nerves, & strange sheaves of variously tinted false hair bound on her head by a ribbon—but she is a pleasant woman, & can sustain a conversation' (Ibid. F/ACB/121, 45–6).

10. Heresy and Humanity: 'Other Worlds' 1907–1915

THE plan for the book that was to become *Themis* (she at first thought of it as her *Epilegomena*) had been in her mind since 1907, when her work on revisions to *Prolegomena* for a second edition had made her realize that its theories seemed to her already outdated. There had been archaeological discoveries and fresh perspectives from sociology, providing her with much more new material than *Prolegomena* could accommodate. More seriously, her own life experiences had changed her focus, and, as much in a search for personal meaning as for scholarly insight, she had read widely in the intervening years.[1] All these factors combined to lead her to change her mind on too many matters to be content with *Prolegomena* any longer.

In June 1907 she could write to Murray that 'the first chapter of my next book is curdling up in my brain. It's going to be on mysticism in relation to sympathetic magic.'[2] By the following April she had enough preliminary ideas to share with him and had a perfect opportunity to discuss them, since at this time he was sitting for a sketch by Frances Darwin, who did not like to talk while she was drawing. Harrison had just read Henri Bergson's *L'Évolution Créatrice*, and warned Murray that she 'might be a nuisance about it' when she came.[3] Bergson had given her a key to understanding both her own world and ancient religion in his theory of durée, 'true time', 'that life which is one, indivisible, and yet unceasingly changing'. We are, each of us, he argued, like a snowball, consisting of all that has gone before, organically

---

[1] Her letters to Gilbert Murray between 1908 and 1911 refer to the following authors and, where she gives them, titles: Otto Seeck, *Untergang der Antiken Welt*; [Leopold von Schroeder] *Mysterium und Mimus* (a book on the Vedic hymns); the Hebrew Bible; William James's '[The Principles of] Psychology'; Alfred Georg L. Lehmann *Aberglaube und Zaunberei*; F. von Hügel, '2 volumes on Mysticism and Religion'; Rivière; Gruppe; Glotz; Durkheim; Reinach; Stewart, *Doctrine of Ideas*; Leuba; W. M. McDougall; Nietzsche (rereading); R. R. Marett 'From Spell to Prayer', *Folklore*, 15 (1905), 132–65; van Gennep, *Rites de Passage*; Foucart; *L'Année Sociologique*.

[2] JEH to GM [314], n.d. The finished book bears little relation to this proposed outline.

[3] JEH to GM [359], n.d.

connected to our collective past.[4] Here was something that spoke directly to her own condition, struggling with ageing and loneliness, and disconnected from the present. As she explored this idea she began to see why Dionysos had always held appeal for her, where the Olympian gods held none.

She explained her thesis to Murray as mysticism as an antithesis to Olympianism. Unfortunately, Murray did not think she had either side clear, and his criticisms were so unsympathetic he was worried that he had made her ill. 'I thought she was going to have a palpitation at dinner',[5] he wrote to Lady Mary, fearing that he had been insensitive to her heart condition and the potentially serious effects of emotional distress. He backed off, and 'things got better afterwards'. Harrison returned to Cambridge, from where she wrote to him that she intended to leave mysticism quite alone for a bit while she worked on the Sun and the Moon, after which she would go back and 'purge it from all indiscretions'.[6]

The book that was stirring in her mind would preach her new gospel of *durée*. By applying Bergson and Durkheim to the data of Greek religion she could reach back into the past and find connection and meaning, if not with her contemporaries, with a great sequence of those who had experienced the same emotions from the earliest times. But to do this meant renouncing many of the ideas she had put forward in *Prolegomena*.

One of the fundamental changes that had taken place in her thinking since *Prolegomena* was a deepening of the conviction that the essence of Greek religion would never be found in the Olympian gods. The Olympians were not only non-primitive, but 'positively in a sense non-religious'.[7] They were neither starting points for Greek religion, nor satisfactory goals. The mystery-gods, Dionysos and Orpheus, by contrast, seemed genuinely religious. (Murray had made this point, interestingly, in *A History of Ancient Greek Religion* as far back as 1897, where he had written, 'A "real" religion is a people's religion. The great complex conception of Dionysus-Bacchus was a common folk's god.')[8]

With such reflections she could not side-step the massive and intractable question: what did she understand by the term 'religion'? The topic was under intense scrutiny at the time, as anthropologists and psychologists were pointing out the shortcomings of Frazer's assumptions about the linear evolution of religious thought, the same in every society, and his understanding of religion as a purely intellectual matter. Frazer had made a

---

[4] Henri Bergson, *Creative Evolution*, trans. Arthur Mitchell (London: Macmillan, 1960), 1–6.

[5] GM to MM, 21 Apr. 1908, MS Gilbert Murray 459/35.

[6] JEH to GM [350], 23 Apr. [1908].   [7] Harrison, *Themis*, p. xi.

[8] Murray, *Ancient Greek Literature*, 64.

clear differentiation between religion (intellectual) and magic (practical); this was challenged by R. Marett in a paper entitled 'From Spell to Prayer'.[9] Marett also drew attention to the importance of emotion in religion, and to the importance of emotion felt in a group, what he dubbed its 'mobbish' aspect. (Others, notably William McDougall, Lucien Lévy-Bruhl, Arnold van Gennep, and Émile Durkheim were all engaged, with Marett, in formulating a social psychology of religion).[10] 'Frazer I am almost sure is all wrong', Harrison wrote to Murray.[11] She was convinced by Marett's case for a stage of 'pre-animism' and that 'magic is just what marks the border land between man & beast & ultimately gives rise to religion, art & many other civilized things. Then half way it is met at fairly late stage by animism . . . as an advance on magical pantomimic daemons.'[12]

But it is not to Marett but to Bergson and Durkheim that Harrison attributed the flash of insight that enabled her to formulate her own concept of religion. From Bergson's *durée*, she saw that Dionysos was really religious, whereas the Olympians were 'a late and conscious representation, a work of analysis, of reflection and intelligence'. Primitive religion, was not, as she had drifted into thinking, 'a tissue of errors leading to mistaken conduct; it was rather a web of practices emphasizing particular parts of life, issuing necessarily in representations and ultimately dying out into abstract conceptions'.[13] Frazer's 'religion' was something too purely intellectual. Marett's came closer to what she needed.

The issues that had been raised by the performance of *Comus* were related to all this in a complex way. She had partially worked them out in 'Crabbed Age and Youth', which must now be read as a commentary on *Themis*. Her exclusion from 'le grand égotisme à deux' of the Cornfords had raised other existential anxieties, mostly to do with ageing. It was not just that she was a generation older than the couple. She had also been an outsider to the whole production, a chaperone, not an actor, and the displacement from the stage was almost unbearable. A 'rite of passage' had taken place. When in her reading of anthropology she came across accounts of tribal initiation ceremonies she found herself personally and emotionally involved in the life of the savage. She notes the 'inherent and inevitable friction' between the young and the old, and attributes this to a contrast between the rationalism of youth and the tradition, and consequent

[9] R. R. Marett, 'From Spell to Prayer', 132–65, repr. in R. R. Marett, *The Threshold of Religion* (2nd edn. London: Methuen, 1914; 1st pub. 1909).

[10] See Ackerman, *J. G. Frazer* 224–9 for the exchange between Frazer and Marett over the relation of religion and magic.

[11] JEH to GM [317], n.d.   [12] Ibid.   [13] *Themis*, p. xii.

altruism, of 'Crabbed Age'.[14] This conclusion, she states, was shaped by the three things she was working on at the time: savage initiation ceremonies, the rise of the Greek drama, and the philosophy of Henri Bergson. In initiation ceremonies we see life as consisting of stages, with prolonged, anxious, and painful transitions. At and through his initiation the initiate is brought 'into close communion with his tribal ancestors: he becomes socialized, part of the body politic. Henceforth he belongs to something bigger, more potent, more lasting, than his own individual existence: he is part of the stream of totemic life, one with the generations before and yet to come.'[15]

As she thought about the 'plot' of her new book, Durkheim's 'collective representations' provided an answer to why Dionysos (like Milton's 'Comus') is always accompanied by his band of revellers, his *thiasos*, 'a matter cardinal for the understanding of his nature'.[16] She now looked for the origin of the god in the emotion of the group, not in any individual consciousness. The Olympians are

the last product of rationalism, of individualistic thinking; the *thiasos* has 'projected' them utterly. Cut off from the very source of their life and being, the emotion of the *thiasos*, they desiccate and die. Dionysos with his *thiasos* is still—*Comus*, still trails behind him the glory of the old group ecstasy.[17]

But she still had an enormous collection of intractable material that she wanted to include, and recognized the problems of organization that it posed. What she needed was an organizing principle, and, with the sense of good luck that characterized and bedevilled so many of her serendipitous finds, lit upon one near at hand. 'By the most fortunate of chances, at Palaikastro, on the eastern coast of Crete, just the very material needed for this study has come to light, a ritual Hymn commemorating the birth of the infant Zeus', she explained in the first chapter of *Themis*.[18] Unfortunately she was in such emotional distress that she read the hymn, or rather Murray's emendation of it, through the lens of her own need. 'I am getting so fond of that dear little hymn', she wrote to him. 'You have made it so neat & complete & what a mess it wld have been left in if you hadn't tidied it up.'[19]

What the hymn seemed to her to celebrate was an initiation ceremony

---

[14] 'Crabbed Age and Youth' in *Alpha and Omega*, 5.

[15] 'The Kouretes and Zeus Kouros', *Annual of the British School at Athens*, 15 (1908–9), 308–38, at 325; quoted in *Themis*, 19.

[16] *Themis*, p. xiii.   [17] Ibid. 48.

[18] Ibid. 1. She had already written an article on the hymn in 1908, 'The Kouretes and Zeus Kouros'. The material and the argument in this paper are essentially the same as the first chapter of *Themis*.   [19] JEH to GM [467], n.d.

of a youth into the life of the tribe (interpretation taken from Durkheim), with the remarkable feature that not only is the youth a god, but the god Zeus. More remarkably, the band of youths who traditionally surrounded the baby Zeus, clashing their cymbals to protect him—the Kouretes—here appear as a *thiasos*, or band of revellers dancing attendance on the god. The *thiasos* is usually found in connection with Dionysos; that it should appear here with Zeus gave Harrison just the key she was looking for. She could now apply Durkheim's theory that the origin of the Greek gods is to be found not in an intellectual process that grew out of the worship of heroes (as she had argued in *Prolegomena*), but in the emotion of the group. The group is primary, the god secondary. Once there was no god, only the group of Kouretes, but the emotion of the group, intensely felt, was perceived to exist outside of it: from this it was a short step to perceive the chief Kouros as divine, a *daimon* or demi-god, and ultimately as a 'full-blown' god—whether Zeus or Dionysos is irrelevant. The fundamental value to Harrison in reasoning like this was that she now had 'evidence' for Greek religion without a god. She was well aware that this situation obtained in Buddhism, and confessed that 'I always wanted to be a Buddhist and now I know I *am* one.'[20] From the 'hymn of the Kouretes' she also understood that the god was being invoked to 'leap for the Year . . . for full jars . . . fleecy flocks . . . fields of fruit . . . and for hives to bring increase, and to leap for godly Themis'. She now saw Themis (social custom), together with Dike (justice), lying at the origin of religion. (In the original Greek, written all in capitals, there is no way of distinguishing proper names, and no hard and fast distinction between animate and inanimate, abstract and concrete.) Harrison chose to understand Themis and Dike as goddesses, and hit on a perfect title for her book, no longer *Epilegomena*, but *Themis: A Study of the Social Origins of Greek Religion*. She wrote to Murray, 'I begin to see—please don't say No—that Themis Dike etc. who always seems so late yet appear in Hesiod as seasons are all part of the socializing of things.'[21]

Her letters to Murray during the years taken up with this research are full of discussion of work in progress, enlivened by a world of private paronomasia—though perhaps not so private as she thought. She wrote to him in July 1910,

. . . Oh dear, I do want to hear what you are doing with the Durkheim chorus . . . The Epic [*The Rise of the Greek Epic*] must be got thro—it is such a dear old Epic. Do you put all the new stuff in the preface? I do wish it was the drama but it will be next year, & then I shall have cleared off the curates [Kouretes] & the Dithyramb. I do hope my

---

[20] JEH to GM [333], n.d.   [21] JEH to GM [487], n.d.

letters to you will all be published in yr 'Remains'. Think of the notes required 100 years hence—on the Durkheim chorus & the curates.[22]

They are nearly always witty:

I . . . met at the Vice-Chancellor's a gentleman called Marcus Aurelius. . . . His other name is Dr. Stein.[23] I loved him, he had lost several toes in a snow storm in central Asia & he was very sympathetic & interested about my great toe joints being extracted. It is so seldom one can pour out about one's toes at dinner. I am sure you wld like him. What things they found in Central Asia, only it seems that there as in Crete no one cares to keep anything but their weekly accounts & their title deeds—anyone can write another epic any time—but yr butcher's bill who can replace that?[24]

In anticipation of the sustained hard work of writing her new book, she went to Sweden to see if a month at a spa under a certain Dr Emil Zander would improve her health. The fun of another language and her eye for the absurd seem to have done more for her than the heart doctor:

The Baths have such adorable names that I mean to try them all. You have 'Köhlen-säurebäder [carbonic acid baths], Fangoeinpackungen mit Lanolinseife-oder-Cocosbutter [mud packs with lanolin soap and coconut oil]. Think of being eingepackt in Cocosbutter . . . & I am doing this just to get a new heart for the Epile-gomena, & the sea is 'vaguing' & on Saturday (30th) I sail to Gotenberg. I am learn-ing Swedish hard. When one's brain softens there are always new lingos to learn thank the Lord.[25]

Later during the trip she recorded,

I have just recovered from a severe *Mag- och Tarm-sjuk-dom* [stomach and intestinal sickness] brought on I fear by greed & a diet of cream & a surfeit of lampreys, & it has made me quite thankful that the Lord as a rule afflicts this his servant with a presentable *Hjärt-sjuk-dom* (A language that allows you to say frankly that you are heart-sick is nice & primitive & refreshing.) & you wld like this place. You have cream with yr soup & custard pudding with yr fish . . . I am far from sure if the air of this place suits *me* but I am almost certain it wld just do for you. It is mild & bland—the Saltsjö is just what I suppose it means—a salt lake. You see no outlet, it is covered with little white yachts & islands. This anstalt is perfectly peaceful. There is a vast Ligghalla wch faces both ways & is perfectly sheltered & nobody comes there.

---

[22] JEH to GM [468], 26 July 1910. The Durkheim chorus refers to the first chorus in Euripides' *Bacchae*, in which she thought she found elements of Durkheim's theories.

[23] Sir Mark Aurel Stein (1862–1943) was at this time working for the Indian education service. A man of wide interests and expertise, he published translations from Sanskrit, made valuable archaeological discoveries in India, and explored Baluchistan and Persia studying their ancient history.

[24] JEH to GM [442], 30 Jan. 1910.   [25] JEH to GM [468], 26 July 1910.

Zander is a nice kind slow man with an acute face. He took nearly a week to recover from the shock of finding that I bathed in the 'Oppen See'. His only fault is that he *will* speak English, not a word of which he understands. I am getting to love Swedish. It is so crude & Viking like. One really knows nearly all the words but they are unrecognizable.[26]

She wrote to Murray about the massage treatments, complaining how painful they were. The doctors put it down to 'intercostal neuralgia', '& their pleasing plan is to grip hold of the spot that hurts worst & just wrestle with it. Their eyes shine with joy when you flinch.'[27] Murray was working on a translation of *Oedipus the King* at this time, and sent her a draft. After a fruitless journey into Stockholm to get hold of a text she vowed she would never again travel without a text of Sophocles: 'no gentleman ever does'.[28] But she told Murray candidly that although she liked certain phrases the translation as a whole failed to thrill her in the way that the Greek did. 'Well, I am sure it is the fault of Sophocles if you can't translate him save with a sense of labour.'[29] Her final comment on Murray's *Oedipus* concerned the title. 'Please don't let it be "Oedipus King of Thebes". "Thebes" has no point & it spoils the king & the medicine man.'[30]

She returned to England on 5 September, a failure in the eyes of her Swedish doctor, having lost weight ('his ideal is a stoutness to which I cannot aspire'),[31] arriving back at Newnham to find herself in the chaos of changing rooms at Newnham. The worst part was the disarray caused to her books and waiting for new bookcases to be built, with fifty offprints of her article on 'Zeus Kouros' waiting to be sent to German 'Gelehrtes' [scholars] and needing copies of Murray's translation of the Palaikastro hymn to accompany them. A. B. Cook came to visit her and was 'greatly excited and delighted by the curates'. He had suggestions for minor emendations to Murray's text, but she was much encouraged when he told her he considered her main issue proved beyond doubt '& save you he is the only man who sees that it will develope [*sic*] out into all sorts of directions'.[32]

'Develope out into all sorts of directions' it certainly did, as she fleshed it out with a mass of detail taken from recent discoveries in anthropology— especially accounts of initiation rites, totemism, and sanctities such as 'mana', 'wakonda', and 'orenda' as manipulated by tribespeople in remote

[26] JEH to GM [471], Aug. 1910.   [27] JEH to GM [472], 10 Aug. 1910.
[28] JEH to GM [473], 25 Aug. 1910.   [29] JEH to GM [472], 10 Aug. 1910.
[30] JEH to GM [483], n.d., written from the 'native moors' referred to in the next paragraph, probably 22 Oct. 1910.
[31] JEH to GM [473], 25 Aug. 1910.   [32] JEH to GM [476], 12 Sept. 1910.

areas of the world, whose religion was for the first time being studied—and an enormous quantity of discrete material taken from ancient Greek literature.

Maintaining the importance of what people *do* in connection with their religion, as against what they *say*, she turned to the seasonal rites, in particular to those of the spring, when the inducement of the food supply was uppermost in the minds of worshippers. Parting company with Frazer, she emphasized not fertility, but the renewal of the year, of fresh life, and observed that in Greece these rites were associated with contests, the *agones* or athletic contests and the other contest significantly bearing the same name, the *agon* of the drama. Different though they may seem, and different as in fact they became, they arose from the same root, the spring *dromenon* (ritual) conceived of as a conflict, a dramatic setting forth of the natural happening of the spring. She prevailed upon both Murray and Cornford to contribute chapters. Murray's 'excursus' on the origins of drama had originally been given as a lecture in Oxford in 1910. In it he argued for a common pattern to be found in the life-cycle of all tragic heroes, commemorated in the annual dramatic festival.[33] Cornford offered a summary of a lecture course which he had given on Pindar and the Olympic games. His argument, which he had doubtless thrashed out with Harrison, was that their origin lay in a foot race of the Kouretes. The Olympic victor was not an individual hero, but a 'functionary', commemorated as the *daimon* of the group and the 'luck' of the year.[34] Thus the spirit common to all life was not the 'vegetation spirit' of Frazer and Mannhardt, nor even the spirit of ecstasy suggested by Murray in *Ancient Greek Literature* to lie at the root of the worship of Dionysus–Bacchus, but a 'year spirit', or, to use her pseudo-Greek term, the *eniautos-daimon*—'eniautos' denoting not so much the calendar year as periodicity, and meeting her need for a power that embodied the 'whole world-process of decay, death, renewal'. The term proved disastrous, calling forth scorn from scholars for its faulty construction (although in English we can happily speak of a 'year spirit', Greek cannot use the word *eniautos* as an adjective). She would have done well to leave it in English, but she wanted the Greek *eniautos* for its connotation. It is tempting to surmise that the renunciation of the vegetation-spirit for a spirit of recurrence—the very core of *Themis*—was triggered by Comus' lines:

---

[33] The pattern consisted of the sequence of *Agon* (contest), *Pathos* (suffering), *Messenger*, *Threnos* (lament), and *Theophany*, 'or, we might say, *Anagnorisis* (recognition) and *Theophany*'. If it be objected that tragedies do not normally end with a joyful theophany, Murray replied that they once did, in the Satyr plays which have been lost.   [34] *Themis*, p. xvi.

> We that are of purer fire
> Imitate the Starry Quire
> Who in their nightly watchful Spheres
> Lead in swift round the Months and Years.[35]

The *eniautos-daimon* thus grew, she argued, out of the collective representation of the group, whether as the winner of the Olympic games, the leader of the *thiasos*, or a primitive king, the hero of tragic legend. The anthropomorphic Olympian gods were a late and decadent development, the product of intellectual reflection, *objets d'art*, known, not felt and lived, desiccated and dead, chill and remote. In contrast, the *daimon* was not so much a personality as a potency, directly connected to life on earth.

Here the book might well have ended, and might have maintained greater unity if it had. However, it remained to return to the hymn and elaborate why the Kouros is bid to 'leap for goodly Themis', and, for Harrison, to find in her introspective account of religion a place for social progress and a personal way forward. She understands the goddess Themis not in the usual sense of Justice personified, but as the incarnation of social order impregnated with religion, who ruled at the dawn of Greece.[36] Here she finds 'the social fact . . . trembling on the very verge of godhead. She is the force that brings and binds men together, she is the "herd instinct", the collective conscience, the social sanction. . . . She is not religion, but she is the stuff out of which religion is made.'[37] Primitive people, under the sway of Themis, projected their sense of unity with their group upon their totem animal. Gradually, she argued, the power of the group was weakened, and the sphere of religion narrowed, until ultimately its 'representation' became 'that all but impossible conception', the god as an individual. The final stage of decadence occurs when the god becomes an *objet d'art*.

At this point, 487 pages into her argument, she reaches her own description of religion. While accepting Durkheim's definition ('Les phénomènes dits religieux consistent en croyances obligatoires connexes de pratiques définies qui se rapportent à des objets donnés dans les croyances [Phenom-

---

[35] John Milton, *Comus*, 111–14.

[36] See Reinach, A. 'Thémis: Un nouveau livre sur les origines sociales de la réligion grèque', *Revue de l'Histoire des Religions*, 69 (1914), 323–71, at p. 324. In her understanding of the goddess 'Themis' Harrison appears to have been influenced by a work she recommended to students of archaeology, Henry Sumner Maine, *Ancient Law: its Connection with the Early History of Society and its Relation to Modern Ideas* (London: John Murray, 1861), in which the author posited that 'Themis', who appears in the later Greek pantheon as the Goddess of Justice, originated in the primitive assumption that 'sustained or *periodically recurring* action', whether in the physical or moral world, was attributable to a personal agent (p. 3, italics mine).   [37] *Themis*, 485.

ena held to be religious consist in obligatory beliefs, connected with clearly defined practices which are related to given objects of those beliefs]'),[38] she felt that this, like all definitions 'desiccated' its object and 'chilled its life-blood'. Religious faith and practice, she wrote, is intensely obligatory, but

it is also eagerly, vividly, chosen, it is a great collective *hairesis*.[39] Religion sums up and embodies what we feel together, what we care for together, what we imagine together, and the price of that feeling together, that imagining together, the conces-sions, the mutual compromises, are at first gladly paid.

It is when religion ceases to be a matter of feeling together, when it becomes indi-vidualized and intellectualized, that clouds gather on the horizon. It is because reli-gion has been regarded as a tissue of false hypotheses that it has commanded, will always command, the animosity of the rational thinker. When the religious man, instead of becoming in ecstasy and sacramental communion one with Bacchos, descends to the chill levels of intellectualism and asserts that there is an objective reality external to himself called Bacchos, then comes a parting of the ways. Still wider is the breach if he asserts that this objective reality is one with the mystery of life, and also with man's last projection, his ideal of the good.[40]

Without making the parallel explicit, Harrison models her lady 'Themis' on Milton's 'Temperance'. The book concludes with a purple passage expounding the sympathetic resonance with which, according to the Greeks, the natural world responds to human morality. *'Themis was the mother of Dike*; the social conscience, the social structure, gave birth, not of course to the order of nature, but to man's conception, his representation, of that order.'[41] Comus-Dionysos, the emotion of the group, the loneliness of the spectator, the warmth of participation, the chasm that confronts Crabbed Age: all this is the subtext of *Themis*.

There remained the thorny question of the dedication. She badly wanted to dedicate it to Murray, who had 'talked it out' with her in the initial stages and who had read her drafts with critical attention. She wrote to him on 8 December 1911,

My dear Ther
I must just out with it—that Bad Book of Bulls & Bears—may it be dedicated to you? I wanted to ask you when you were here but a great aidôs [shame, embarrassment] fell on me & also I was feeling you were feeling how bad it was. Don't say yes in a hurry of compassion & Xian charity but just think it over & if either you or Mary feel

---

[38] Translation by Jacqueline Redding and W. S. F. Pickering, in W. S. F. Pickering (ed.), *Durkheim on Religion* (London: Routledge and Kegan Paul, 1975), 93.

[39] The Greek word means 'choosing'; it is the etymon of the English word 'heresy'.

[40] *Themis*, 487.   [41] Ibid. 533, italics Harrison's.

it is not the sort of book for a Regius Professor to be mixed up with say No. I shall feel for a bit like a rope & a bottle of poison & the nearest pond but 'tout passe'.[42]

When he agreed there was the problem of wording:

It now remains for you to give yr whole undivided mind to the question of verbage. I can't put, as I naturally should, Χειρώνι χαρίν [thanks to Cheirôn] because you are so Regius. I abhor 'Regius Professors'. I also loathe the name that 'yr godfathers & godmother gave you in yr Baptism'. Initials are undignified & ostentatiously obscure. I can't say 'to Him in Whom' etc. because of ABC. What is a poor Ker to do?[43]

She left it eloquently simple, 'a thank offering':

TO GILBERT MURRAY

χαριστήριον[44]

If *Themis* was hammered out of Harrison's life experiences, its argument is no less valid on that account. It is, however, hard to follow, and Harrison was aware of this from the start. She had written as she always wrote, 'in a white heat',[45] committing to paper ideas that had been in her head for as long as four years, at the pace of about a chapter a week, with the argument following a train of thought that is not necessarily clear to the reader. Cornford, who was astonished at the rate at which the finished chapters appeared once she had begun to write, provided invaluable help at the end by helping with a detailed table of contents which acts as a thread through the labyrinth, and perhaps encouraged the inclusion of the short resumés which are strategically placed throughout the book. Murray, who considered the book an important advance on *Prolegomena*, felt that it contained too many ideas for it to be easily assimilated.

She herself was aware of a central weakness in the book. 'I am intensely conscious', she wrote to A. B. Cook, 'that my theories (and the book will be a tissue of theories) need a broader basis of psychology and probably ethnography. It is probably rash to publish as it stands, and I stand to lose such reputation as I have.'[46] This defect did not escape reviewers. The *Saturday Review* (Andrew Lang?) attacked her: 'Miss Harrison confesses she is no philosopher and no sociologist, and has no ethnological capacity either. An excursion into the last two provinces might have given her ballast.' Accusing

---

[42] JEH to GM [532], n.d.

[43] Cook was an evangelical Christian, and would have been offended at her use of religious language in praise of Gilbert Murray.   [44] JEH to GM [533], n.d.

[45] The phrase is Lewis Farnell's, from his review in the *Hibbert Journal*, 11 (1912–13), 453–8, at 454.

[46] JEH to A. B. Cook, 8 Sept. 1911, quoted in *Newnham College Letter*, 1929, 59.

her of constructing God in her own image, the reviewer listed her defects as a scholar: 'excess of sympathy, over-eagerness to catch at coincidences, want of discrimination of evidence, and inability to conduct sustained thinking'.[47] Farnell, predictably, was contemptuous. He drew attention to her dogmatism of tone, and accused her of being 'the victim of the idea that happens to dominate her phase of thinking at any particular time', and criticized her tendency to bend the evidence to fit her theory.[48] The anonymous reviewer in the *Oxford Magazine* damned with faint praise: 'The book on the whole will appeal rather to the easy-going amateur than to the trained expert in anthropology and comparative religion. . . . Miss Harrison's work has always a freshness that is at first attractive; but the freshness is often found to be as that of the dew on cobwebs'.[49] W. M. L. Hutchinson in the *Classical Review* called her 'the Scholar Gipsy of Hellenic Studies'. 'The road to Truth is paved with good heresies', he continued, 'and if indeed *Themis* embodies one, it is of the very best kind—at once brilliantly suggestive and a direct incitement to controversy', going on to point out that Bergson's *durée* was no new doctrine: the theory that the instinctive idea of primitive man was the persistence of life through change had already been articulated by Sir Alfred Lyall.[50] The *Athenaeum* was more positive, and while expressing reservations about her bias towards matriarchy and totemism, alone intuited her metanarrative: 'She is a handmaid of the loom of the Time-Spirit. So it comes about that she is subjectively disposed to catch the note in early Greek religion which corresponds to the cult of the *Eniautos-Daimon*—the endeavour by sacramental means to help things to grow, and yourself to grow with them.'[51]

'This work will never be adequately reviewed', complained Farnell in the *Hibbert Journal*, quoting Andrew Lang, 'for no magazine can afford sufficient space.'[52] No English magazine, perhaps, but the *Revue de l'Histoire des Religions* found space for a 48-page review by the French sociologist Adolphe Reinach.[53] The article summarizes for French readers the content of *Themis*, chapter by chapter, interlaced with critical comments. The book reads, he says, like a scintillating conversation, which is its charm, but the author is guilty of looseness in her exposition (a fault of English writers, he notes), and complains that her insights get drowned in all the detail. One would have liked a consideration of other people's opinions, he complains, especially in

[47] *Saturday Review*, 113 (4 May 1912), 558–9.   [48] Farnell, *Hibbert Journal*, 454.
[49] *Oxford Magazine*, 28 Nov. 1912, 116–17.
[50] W. M. L. Hutchinson, *Classical Review*, 27 (1913), 132–4.
[51] *Athenaeum*, 4403 (16 Mar. 1912), 317–18.   [52] Farnell, *Hibbert Journal*, 453.
[53] Reinach, 'Thémis'.

the discussion of the controversial dithyramb, and one would have liked her to persuade the reason as easily as she does the imagination. The hymn will not bear the weight of interpretation she lays on it, for there are alternative interpretations, and many do not see it as a 'Hymn of the Kouretes'. Harrison has forgotten too easily that although it may contain primitive elements, it is for all that a Cretan text of the fourth century AD, where the preoccupation with Justice was historically justified. Crete, after all, was the land of 'Eunomia'. But for all these criticisms, the length and detail of the review testifies to the significance of the book, and when a second edition was called for in 1927, Harrison referred her readers to Reinach's article.

The book suffers from two main flaws. One is the amount of special pleading with which Harrison makes use of her sources. When the source fits with her conclusion, which she often seems to have arrived at independently by some previous intuition, 'the truth comes out'; when it does not, 'Homer, and sometimes Aeschylus forgot' the real meaning of the ritual.[54] This, and the failure to consider other points of view, leads to a book in which the author seeks evidence to support a position that she reached by other means. The second flaw is less reprehensible, and one of which Harrison was partially aware. By hitching her arguments to the latest in anthropological and sociological theory, she ran the risk of having her whole thesis undermined if the underlying theories were later disproved. In the event, this is exactly what has happened. The concepts of *mana, wakonda, orenda* have been more carefully studied, and cannot mean what Harrison has attributed to them. The theory of totemism can no longer be sustained. Few people read Bergson today. (It was unfortunate for Harrison that she lived too early to absorb Jung and his theories of archetypes and the collective unconscious, which would have served her better than Durkheim's 'collective representations'.) More seriously, what we now know about the ethnography of the early Mediterranean has undermined her account of the origin of the Greek gods. The Minoan civilization of Crete is now seen to be discontinuous with that of the Mycenaean and later Greek mainland. The origin and nature of the dithyramb is still a matter for disagreement. Her foundation is thus doubly insecure, for both her underlying social theory and the interpretation of Greek texts and artefacts have been supplanted, discredited, or abandoned because of insufficient data.

Harrison's attempt to formulate religious phenomena in non-Christian language was part of an intellectual current at Cambridge which can be

---

[54] *Themis*, 323, 417. One could cite a number of similar instances: see especially pp. 375, 502, 519, 520.

detected as early as Sidgwick's qualms at being required to assent to the Apostles' Creed. At the time that Harrison was working on *Themis* there were a considerable number of academics at Cambridge who, like her, felt that the institutional ties of the university to the Church of England were an intellectual straightjacket. Compulsory chapel attendance was a particularly sore point. Anthropology was beginning to be studied as an academic discipline, and yet there was no forum for the exploration of religious issues from a non-confessional standpoint. In 1909 a paper by Dr W. Chawner, Master of Emmanuel College, entitled 'Prove All Things' lent a focus to the general discontent, and twelve students wrote to Chawner asking for copies. They formed themselves into a society for the 'discussion on problems of religion, philosophy and art'.[55] Unlike the Apostles, whose membership was limited to twelve at any one time, the new society was open to all, and women were encouraged to participate. Meetings were of two kinds: those held in lecture halls four or five times a term to hear papers by well-known members of the university, and more informal gatherings every Sunday night, initially in the rooms of a first-year undergraduate, C. K. Ogden, in Magdalene College.[56] Ogden was at first secretary, then two years later the president of the society, a role he held until 1924.

Although she had hoped for a more intimate coterie and a more radical agenda, the society offered Harrison what she most keenly needed: a home for outcasts and misfits, a club at which women were warmly included, a gathering of young undergraduates at which she was welcomed. With its rational approach to religion she was fully at home. When it came to choosing a name, Harrison's 'The Heretics' won the day. It was a happy choice, with its connotations of anti-establishment free thought, with more than a hint of mischief, which would have appealed to Ogden's irrepressible sense of fun. Indeed, a sense of fun prevailed at the meetings, keeping them from becoming too earnest, and contributing to the success of the society. At the same time a high level of reasoning and informed opinion maintained the stimulating atmosphere. On 7 December 1909 Harrison read a paper at the inaugural meeting, appropriately entitled 'Heresy and Humanity'.[57]

She began with a magnificent flourish: 'The word "heretic" has still about it an emotional thrill—a glow reflected, it may be, from the fires at

---

[55] See P. Sargant Florence, 'The Cambridge Heretics 1909–1932', in A. J. Ayer (ed.), in *The Humanist Outlook* (London: Pemberton, with Barrie and Rockliff, 1968), 223–39, esp. 228.

[56] C. K. Ogden became well-known on the publication of his book, co-authored with I. Richards, *The Meaning of Meaning* (London: Kegan Paul, 1936). He acquired the reputation of an eccentric, fostered by his bizarre views on 'Basic English'.

[57] *Heresy and Humanity* (London: Watts, 1911), repr. *Alpha and Omega*, 27–41.

Smithfield, the ardours of those who were burnt at the stake for love of an idea.' After explaining its derivation from the Greek word for 'choosing', she asks why, when free personal choice sounds so splendid and inspiring, were heretics hated and hunted? 'To be a heretic in the days of Latimer and Cranmer was to burn. To be a heretic in the days of our grandfathers was to be something of a social outcast. To be a heretic to-day is almost a human obligation.'

She gave an explanation. Primitive society was held together by sympathy, similarity, and uniformity. Like his modern-day counterpart, the 'good soldier', the member of the primitive herd may not, for the safety of the herd, make a personal choice. Traditional views, including religious views, are tenaciously held because they are induced not by personal experience, but by 'herd suggestion'. This used to be called faith, and it is what holds a society together. However, two factors have changed the situation: science, and 'another movement towards what I will call Humanity'. Science, she argued, classifies and draws distinctions, breaking the spell of herd-suggestion which is 'always in a haze'. But

our keenest emotional life is through the herd, and hence it was that, at the close of the last century, the flame of scientific hope, the glory of scientific individualism that had blazed so brightly, somehow died down and left a strange chill. Man rose up from the banquet of reason and law unfed. He hungered half-unconsciously for the herd. It seemed an *impasse*: on the one side orthodoxy, tradition, authority, practical slavery; on the other science, individual freedom, reason, and an aching loneliness.[58]

Socially, she argued, with a nod to Durkheim, the impasse has been bridged by the division of labour, which has at once differentiated and organically united us in mutual interdependence. Out of this organic individuality emerges a true humanity: 'sympathy with infinite differences, with utter individualism, with complete differentiation, and it is only possible through the mystery of organic spiritual union.' Then, with the wound of Cornford's marriage only too visible, she concludes:

The old herd-problem remains of how to live *together*; and as the union grows closer and more intricate the chances of mutual hurt are greater, and the sensitiveness must grow keener. Others are safe from and with us only when their pain is our pain, their joy ours; and that is not yet. Meantime, whenever the old tiger-cat egotism snarls within us, we should resign our membership of the Society of Heretics, and go back for a season to the 'godly discipline' of the herd.[59]

---

[58] *Heresy and Humanity* (London: Watts, 1911), repr. *Alpha and Omega*, 35.   [59] Ibid. 41.

If this is not autobiographical it is nonsense. (Is the imagery of the tiger-cat a Freudian slip, seeing that 'Tiger' was Frances's pet name for Francis Cornford?) Worse still, the last sentence is mere cant. On no occasion did she ever give up her relish for heresy.

Membership grew rapidly, and by 1913, four years after its inception, had exceeded two hundred. Harrison had misgivings at this turn of events. The success of the society was in part due to the wide inclusiveness of its interpretation of 'religion'. In a university in which religion had come to be equated with an arid theology and dissociated from emotion and experience, Ogden's new society significantly took 'religion' to include art. It now recognized 'honorary members', which included not only Sir Francis Darwin, Francis Cornford, and Bertrand Russell, but other big names such as the Master of Emmanuel, J. T. Sheppard (subsequently Provost of King's), A. C. Seward (subsequently Master of Downing), J. B. Bury (Regius Professor of History), G. E. Moore, W. McDougall, G. Lowes Dickinson, George Bernard Shaw, G. M. Trevelyan, and J. M. Keynes. What had started as an iconoclastic and (dangerously) free thought society had caught on and become respectable.

The arrival of a new student, Hope Mirrlees, at Newnham in 1910 marked a turning-point for Harrison. The daughter of William Julius Mirrlees, whose career spanned that of engineer, military officer, and business man, living in England and South Africa, and a Scottish mother, Hope had first cherished ambitions as an actress. Virginia Woolf described her family as 'a typical English family, devoted, entirely uncultured, owning motor cars'.[60] After abandoning her theatrical dreams she came to Newnham, but left without taking the Tripos exams, and appears to have had a somewhat dilettante attitude towards her studies.[61] But she was clever, and gifted in modern languages.

The record has not been kind to her. 'Not my favourite lady' was the instant verdict of one woman who had known Mirrlees.[62] Virginia Woolf counted her with some ambivalence among her circle of friends in 1919.[63] In

---

[60] Virginia Woolf to Lady Cecil, 1 Sept. 1925, quoted in *The Letters of Virginia Woolf*, iii. *A Change of Perspective*, ed. Nigel Nicolson (London: Hogarth Press, 1977), 200.

[61] By this time the normal expectation was that a student coming to Newnham would take the Tripos.

[62] Jean Pace, in a personal telephone conversation.

[63] In the entry for 22 Jan. 1919 Virginia Woolf counts her friends: towards the end of the annotated list she writes, somewhat ambiguously: 'I have not placed Ottoline or Roger, & again there are Katherine & Murry & the latest of all, Hope Mirrlees' (*Diary*, i. 235).

her letters and diaries, Woolf describes Mirrlees variously as pretty, beautifully dressed, over-dressed, over elaborate, scented, extravagant, yet a little unrefined, clever, capricious, exacting, exquisite, very learned, powdered, cultivated, self-conscious, prickly, perverse. Others were not short of criticisms and described her as silly, affected, pretentious, ostentatious, spoiled, mannered, over-refined. On one occasion, a visit to Leonard and Virginia Woolf elicited the catty description: 'Her stockings matched a wreath in her hair; every night they were differently coloured; powder fell about in flakes, and the scent was such we had to sit in the garden.'[64] A year later, after Mirrlees had been to stay for the weekend Virginia Woolf wrote, after describing her with some of the adjectives above: 'It is easily explicable—the rich uncultivated father, brother a trim officer; wealth; health . . . & the greed, like a greed for almond paste, for fame.'[65]

One should perhaps temper these descriptions with the consideration that the Bloomsbury Group delighted in being caustic, and that Harrison was sufficiently attracted to Hope Mirrlees to accept her as her companion as her health declined, and more than that, to become close personal friends. A fellow student had memories of Hope darting into the room like a humming-bird, 'her sapphire eyes flashing, her pendant earrings swinging; a soft torrent of musical sounds issuing from her lips . . . a cross between a pixy and a genius'.[66]

The intimacy that developed between the two women reveals some fresh aspects of Harrison's personality. Mirrlees took Greek lessons from Harrison, without any great success, as has already been noted in connection with Harrison's unconventional teaching methods. No sooner had she become a student, however, than the two women began to form a friendship that was to develop in intensity until they had created for themselves an entire private world. Harrison had always been friendly towards her students—indeed one of her traits that was most appreciated by those she taught was that she never paid attention to their respective roles as teacher and student. Jessie (Crum) Stewart stands out among her former students as one who became a lifelong friend, as indeed did Victoria (Buxton) de Bunsen and Agnes Conway. But with Hope Mirrlees there were other factors involved. She arrived on the scene when Harrison was demoralized to the point that she could not see her way ahead, when her health was beginning to give her serious problems, and when she was desperately lonely. Years

[64] *Diary*, ii. 384, entry for 17 Aug. 1919.   [65] Ibid. ii. 75, 23 Nov. 1920.
[66] Stewart, *Harrison*, 174.

15. Hope Mirrlees and Jane Harrison

later Jessie Stewart wrote to Mirrlees 'wasn't it a miracle that you stepped into the breach and gave her new life?'[67]

The two women were, however, so different that one wonders what drew them together. It is not hard to see why the younger woman was attracted to the charismatic and famous older one. Why Harrison was prepared to let Mirrlees dominate her is not so obvious. At the simplest level, the answer can be found in the fact that she met her practical and emotional needs. The paraphernalia of daily life was becoming too much for Harrison, and Mirrlees was prepared to manage her. She was lonely, and Mirrlees offered friendship. Mirrlees's love of languages must have delighted Harrison. Mirrlees had other reasons also for attaching herself to the older woman. When she first came to Newnham her parents followed and bought a house nearby. She must have found this intolerable, especially since she and her mother had little in common. When in 1915 Harrison needed to go to Paris to see her heart doctor, Moutier, Mirrlees saw this as her only chance to break away from her over-protective parents, who would never have

---

[67] Jessie Stewart to Hope Mirrlees, 16 Aug. 1959. Letter in possession of Margaret Alexiou.

permitted her to travel alone, and the two women began their shared life. Harrison may well have recalled her own necessary break with her family when she similarly first travelled on the Continent.

Perhaps their shared sense of humour and playfulness also played a significant part in bonding them. There had always been a silly side to Harrison, which was beginning to grow more pronounced as she grew older, perhaps her way of disguising some of the physical and emotional pain she was suffering. It showed itself frequently in a conscious regression to nursery behaviour, nourished by a collection of props in the form of stuffed toys which perceptive students had given her. Although she had a strong antipathy towards children in general (because their entry into the world and their dependence on their parents interfered with the adult bonds between Harrison and her friends), she took individual children seriously as people in their own right and could enter very naturally into the imaginative world of a child. Helen Verrall (Salter) remembered vividly her faculty for make-believe. While on holiday with the Verralls in Normandy she and Helen invented a game of fantasy involving a bright green stuffed frog. In some way the frog represented Harrison herself and her emotions, and Helen remembered how, unlike most adults playing with children, Harrison took her imaginative world seriously. Helen never felt that Harrison had to make an effort to play with her, but that the frog's world was as real to the adult as it was to the child.[68]

In an important sense Harrison's whole *œuvre* was a game of this sort, more serious than real life, and her academic writing took her out of the stress of the world of Cambridge into an atavistic world created out of a fusion of archaeological fact and her own over-active imagination.[69] She could (and did) enter her primitive world to solve her own emotional problems and return whole again.

Perhaps in appreciation of the frog game, Helen Verrall presented Harrison with a stuffed bear when the teddy-bear first became popular in 1906. Harrison had always professed an affection for bears, which to her epitomized a combination of the characteristics she most valued in people: non-threatening masculine gruffness (was that why she so vividly remembered Heinrich Brunn's self-introduction: 'Brunn bin ich' with its suggestion of 'Bruin'?),[70] animals dumb and helpless (she likened artists to bears for these

[68] Helen de Gaudrion (Verrall) Salter in Jessie Stewart, *et al.*, 'Jane Ellen Harrison', obituary, *Newnham College Letter*, Jan. 1929, 71.

[69] Harry Payne first suggested this understanding of Harrison's life and work in his unpublished essay on Jane Harrison.

[70] I am grateful to Christopher Stray for this insight.

qualities), with ill-fitting coats and shuffling gait ('for heaven's sake let us all be shabby and comfortable'),[71] and of course Russia, with childhood associations, a land, language, and people she had always loved. She wrote in her *Reminiscences* that 'my friends tell me that at any mention of a bear I am apt to get maudlin'.[72] Earlier in the same book she had described the Athenian ritual in which young girls were dedicated to the worship of Artemis Brauronia, and how they must, to the end of their days, have thought reverently of the Great She-Bear, and how a similar reverence for bears exists among the Apaches today. 'Only ill-bred Americans or Europeans who have never had any "raising" would think of speaking of the Bear without his reverential prefix of "Ostin", meaning "Old One".'[73] She often called her stuffed bear "the Old One", or "O.O." as he appears on many postcards, and never allowed anyone to call him a teddy-bear: he was her 'authentic plaything'.[74]

At other times he was 'Herr Professor', perhaps with echoes of Brunn. He had spectacles and an umbrella, but no other clothing. Apparently he had only one good eye. Frances Cornford described how 'he lived in a sort of shrine on her mantelpiece', and how, shortly afterwards, she and Ruth Darwin happened on another endearing woolly bear when they were on holiday at Brides-les-Bains. 'We dressed it up as the Frau Professorin with a check blouse and gold buttons, and an alpen-stock, and sent her to Aunt Jane. She was received with apparent delight, but never really acquired any of the mana of the Herr Professor.'

The *mana* seemed to lie in the bear's embodiment of a number of incongruous qualities. Just as the fabrication of a Teddy-bear tames a dangerous animal into a huggable plaything, so Herr Professor cut the imposing real-life old-fashioned professor down to size. Harrison's love of animals was linked to her intense dislike of all strictly hierarchical and bureaucratic tendencies of humans. A visit to the Paris zoo to see a specially imported troupe of bears delighted her, for 'when the trainer man tried to make them do their stunts they just shambled past him & went nosing about their own business.'[75]

At this period of her life Harrison was beginning to abandon her 'atavistic world' of ancient Greek religion and grope towards a study of religion in general, and it is almost as though the bear functioned as a sort of transition

[71] *Reminiscences*, 20–1.   [72] Ibid. 49.

[73] Ibid. 70–1. This whole sentence is taken almost verbatim from A. B. Cook, 'Descriptive Animal Names in Greece', *Classical Review*, 8 (1894), 381–5, esp. 383–4.

[74] The phrase is recorded by Frances Cornford in her unpublished memoir of FMC.

[75] JEH to Prince Mirsky, 27 Feb. 1925.

object through this period of disorientation. Her personal recreation of primitive Greece, which had served as a fantasy world during the writing of *Prolegomena*, a private world shared with Cornford and Murray, now gave way to the world of the Bear, who like the Olympian gods of *Prolegomena*, gradually acquired his own life history. The world of the Bear was shared not with her male colleagues but with a new circle of younger women friends.

Much correspondence between Harrison and Mirrlees was carried on through the medium of the bear, who frequently professed minor ailments that (presumably) Harrison herself was suffering from, and lent expression to her emotions. A sample of the dozens of letters and postcards from Harrison to Mirrlees will serve to illustrate:

7 May 1912
. . . But 'bears first'. You *are* good to make a cave for the Old One & he thanks you from the bottom of his deep heart. Only he can't understand why you don't understand why he never travels. He can't leave the Polar Star! He is—as often announces with his strong left-arm uplifted

'true to the kindred points of Heaven and Home.'
. . . there is a special difficulty about his going abroad, he had so many quarterings & he wldn't like to be mistaken for a Travelling Bear. . . .[76]

22 Sep 1913
My dear Hope
I am glad you are coming back. This is just to say do look in on me. I am in Sidgwick Hall, first floor, end of the West wing. . . .

Thank you ever so much for looking after the old Bear & most of all for putting him back so beautifully into his cave. I flew across the garden the moment I got back but a 'pale green fear' got hold of me lest you might have forgotten and the cave be empty. It was faithless of me for you never do forget *really* important things like that.

But it's rather serious for he firmly tho quite politely refuses to move into Sidgwick Hall. He says you never lived there & it isn't a place for a Bear of his standing. . . . So there's nothing more to be said.

April 7, 1915
My dear Hope
I was very glad to get news of you & the Bear. I hope he did not frighten yr mother too much with his changeful glittering eye. He *is* frightening until perfect love casts out fear & I'm not sure it ever does.

[letter with no date]

---

[76] This and following items of correspondence re the bear: JEH to Hope Mirrlees mostly undated, box 9.

16. Hope Mirrlees and Jane Harrison in Paris with the bear, 1915, postcard sent to Gilbert Murray

. . . the Old Bear is much upset by yr not coming back. He says Ursula like all young people is fickle, so he has got a new love, a large & splendid Yorkshire Ram not wall-eyed at all. He has had a great compliment paid him: the Berne bears are having an Esperanto Congress & they sent a deputation to ask him to take the chair. He won't go because he is a really sound scholar but he thinks it a very proper attention.

[postcard with no date]

If you happen to be free tomorrow afternoon Wednesday about 6 do come & meet the Grey Mare. Something extraordinarily solemn is going on in the Cave.

More complicated is the relationship between Harrison and Mirrlees that is revealed (or rather, encrypted) in this correspondence. They affected to be the bear's two wives, the Elder wife and the Younger wife. Some read this as an indication of a sexual relationship between the two women, but given that there is no other evidence that Harrison, for her part, had any lesbian tendencies, it is more likely that the language points to a special relationship with Herr Professor that each of them claimed rather than to any sexual liaison between the two of them. It is difficult to know what to make of messages like the following post cards: 'I wish my morganatic wife to have my lawful wife's picture with the yaller spectacles (signed) [dots in the shape of the Great Bear]', and 'I desire that my young Wife do dine in Hall tomorrow with my elder Wife and go to the young ladies' Revue. I desire that my elder wife do not [illegible] my younger wife the whole evening. She is *not* a comic cut she is my young wife. Given in the cave—in the presence of Mrs Mutz and the Glass horse.'

Most probably it is all an elaborate game of language and make-believe. Carried on over years it created an increasing bond of intimacy as the code grew in complexity.[77]

There is extant a picture of the two women with the bear, taken in Paris during the First World War. Harrison was infuriated with the apparently meaningless red tape with which the French government bound up their lives while they were living in Paris. One regulation was the requirement to carry an identity card with a photograph. 'Perhaps the bear's photograph wld do—you are indistinguishable', Harrison wrote to Mirrlees. They decided to pose with the bear (Fig. 16).

[77] The problems of decoding language like this, and of understanding women's friendships of another era are discussed in Beard, *Invention*, 81–4 and 152–3.

11. Unanimism and Conversion: Cambridge and Europe 1910–1914

IN 1910 Gilbert Murray had been approached by the publishers Williams and Norgate to support a new venture. They felt there was a niche for short, inexpensive books to meet the needs of a growing number of people with secondary school education who were not in a position to consider university. The plan was to approach experts in various fields to come up with books of about 50,000 words on scholarly topics, written in an accessible style. Murray was an ideal choice: the education of the ordinary person had always been dear to his heart. He readily acquiesced. The Home University Library of Modern Knowledge was launched, with Herbert Fisher, J. Arthur Thomson, William T. Brewster of Columbia University, and Murray forming the Editorial Board. Murray set about looking for potential contributors and approached Harrison, who at this time was busy still trying to solve some esoteric philological problems in relation to *Themis*. She replied: 'How exciting about yr publishing scheme. Please let me know at once. If 50,000 words on the Dithyramb wouldn't interest 50,000 Gelehrtes [her mockingly deferential term for German scholars] what would? But seriously I do wonder what you are after.'[1] He must have explored a topic more seriously with her, for one month later she was overtaken by the speed of developments. At this time *Themis*, which she had just begun, filled her whole horizon. 'I am white with terror', she wrote him.

I only threw out the notion of Art & Ritual in a casual irresponsible way & here you are with yr Mr Perris & dates & agreements, like a cart-load of bricks!

Seriously I think *Ancient Art & Ritual* wld make the right sort of book. . . . It would be much better *ancient* than Greek. It wld leave me as you say a freer hand, but it wld all mean a lot of thinking as I shld not like to bring disgrace on yr cave . . . I think art & ritual are so like each other that they see-saw. The Romans had little art (*pace* Mrs Strong[2] & the Germans) & much ritual. A ritualist is never an artist: & an

---

[1] JEH to GM [475], 9 Sept. 1910.   [2] Eugénie (Sellars) Strong.

artist *pace* you is not strong in conduct. However what is the good of my saying anything because whatever I write you will rewrite upside down & in words of one syllable.[3]

At first the Home University Library was a success. Harrison began work on *Ancient Art and Ritual* as soon as *Themis* was out of her way, and Murray at the same time produced *Euripides and His Age*. The exchanges between Murray and Harrison illustrate a fundamental difference of opinion between them, which is continually surfacing in some form or another in their correspondence. Harrison dubbed it 'words-of-one-syllable-ness'. Murray had the gift of writing handbooks ('books to meet a need'), whereas Harrison found the task wearisome and distasteful. She had hated writing *The Religion of Ancient Greece* for the series 'Our Debt to Greece and Rome' in 1905. Without 'the real stuff behind' it seemed to her a book of 'imbecile stupidity'. She was adamant that a book must include full references if it was to be taken seriously. In 1907 she had argued with Murray about references for *The Rise of the Greek Epic*, trying uselessly to persuade him that they needed to be fuller throughout. She even offered to put them in herself, claiming that 'it would be a joy to do it'.[4] The root of the disagreement may have lain in the different readership that the two of them had in mind. Murray really meant to write for the bank clerk or shop assistant, whereas Harrison had in mind a readership that included her own students and doubtless the type of people who had flocked to her London lectures, the great majority of whom had been women from upper-class families, denied university education on account of their gender and more serious than the average bank clerk in their pursuit of learning.

Another facet of writing which she explored at this time was the place of imagination. Murray had claimed years previously that at the root of our emotions lie things 'utterly non-human and non-moral', which we cannot express, which we tend to worship, and which we consider the precious things in life. When we touch on them they can bring us ecstasy or tear our life to shreds 'without a break in their own serenity'.[5] They were Murray's 'God' and Harrison's 'gods' and 'life itself', things which we are afraid to face. On reading J. A. Stewart's *Plato's Doctrine of Ideas*, she felt she had discovered the underlying psychology of ecstasy in what Stewart called 'transcendental feeling': a feeling which appears in our consciousness as a visitant from that other world to which our common life belongs, and which holds

[3] JEH to GM [479], 8 Oct. 1910.   [4] JEH to GM [328], n.d.
[5] Murray, *Ancient Greek Literature*, 272, quoted by Harrison in *Prolegomena*, 657.

us spell-bound till we lose ourselves in gazing.[6] She wrote in excitement to Murray:

Just at this moment it seems to me to explain everything. It explains why thinking is no good at all unless one feels & is excited—it gives one the psychology of ecstasy & of beauty—same thing—& (tho' this may not so much appeal to you) it explains the difference between you & almost every other scholar & why everything you write excites me all over & everything yr pet lambs Percy & Mr Farnell write is so much dead lumber.[7]

An article by H. C. Goddard in the *Hibbert Journal* further stimulated her thinking on this issue by considering language as the expression of the whole person, not just the intellectual faculty. To illustrate the difference between 'intellectual' and 'vital' expression, Goddard compared the sentence 'That which was fragmentary in the temporal order is fulfilled in the Eternal Order' with 'And God shall wipe away all tears from their eyes; and there shall be no more death, neither sorrow, nor crying, neither shall there be any more pain: for the former things are passed away.'[8] Goddard maintained that reason and imagination are not enemies but allies, and that to express a profound thought simply is 'not an easy act of condescension, whereby the philosopher graciously brings down the truth from some high heaven to ignorant humanity, but an infinitely difficult act of creation whereby what was inert and impotent receives the breath of life'. She credited Murray with just such creative ability, whereas for her it was always a struggle. This explained, she wrote, why he expressed himself in words of one syllable when she used words of twelve.[9]

In all fairness, Harrison was dealing with an intractable topic, and for her the process of intellectual discovery was as important as its results—not what was needed for Murray's Home University Library. The writing drove her to near despair: 'I don't believe I ever can put the dithyramb into words of one syllable for the bank clerk.'[10] She pleaded for an extension of her contract.

Meanwhile Murray was preparing for a second visit to America in April 1912 to give a series of lectures at Columbia University, and Harrison could not see herself writing while he was 'away among the Apache Indians'. She

---

[6] See Stewart, *Plato's Doctrine of Ideas*, 139–40. In 1915 Murray published 'The Conception of Another Life', *Edinburgh Review*, 221 (1915), 122–39, developing this idea, distinguishing it from the immortality of the soul, and linking it with initiation ceremonies.

[7] H. C. Goddard, 'Language and the New Philosophy', *Hibbert Journal*, 9 (1910–11), 247–62.

[8] Rev. 21: 4.   [9] JEH to GM [497], 13 Jan. 1911.   [10] JEH to GM [505], n.d.

begged to be allowed to see his lectures in proof, perhaps even hoping for a way out of her contract altogether by sending him what she had written for inclusion in his book.

By the end of February she received a copy of Murray's first lecture, which was to become the first chapter of *Four Stages of Greek Religion*. In it he described the primitive 'Age of Ignorance', or, more colourfully, *Urdummheit* ('Primal Stupidity');[11] Harrison gleefully adopted this as a nickname for the whole book. The first chapter owes a great deal to Harrison's work, as Murray readily acknowledged in the preface when the book was published, with the warm testimony: 'I cannot adequately describe the advantage I have derived from many years of frequent discussion and comparison of results with a Hellenist whose learning and originality of mind are only equalled by her vivid generosity towards her fellow-workers.'[12] 'I must tell you how happy the Urdummheit is making me', she wrote to him. 'It *is* good & I am so proud that there are bits of Themis in it, tho they are all changed as tho their faces had been washed & they wore new holiday clothes.'[13]

Meanwhile *Themis* was published, and she reflected on the difference between their two books:

I am rather sad too reading thro the Urdummheit, because it is all so much clearer & cleaner & more convincing than the muddled furies of Themis. If I could have gone over things more with you & thought them out more fully in the light of you it wld have persuaded people. Now there will be the usual old row & people will be angrier than ever.

Well as soon as you get back you will publish the Urdummheit, & set it all straight.[14]

To clear her head before the fever of writing *Ancient Art and Ritual* (and perhaps also to be away from Cambridge while Murray was in America), she fled to the clearer air of Greece, taking a cruise on the RMS Dunottar Castle, visiting places inaccessible by road that she had not been to before. To travel with a party was a 'drastic remedy', but there were consolations. She enjoyed the monkey on board 'who is a comfort to watch in the rigging', and when the ship was held up by a formidable Mistral and the passengers lodged in a hotel she took the opportunity to visit the bears in the Marseilles Zoo. Best of all was her travelling companion, Logan Pearsall Smith, whose American 'careful, detailed politeness' pleased her. He too had written a

[11] The term had been coined by Preuss.
[12] Murray, *Five Stages of Greek Religion* (London: Watts and Co., 1935), p. xii. *Five Stages* is a revision of the original *Four Stages of Greek Religion*.
[13] JEH to GM [543], n.d.   [14] JEH to GM [555], n.d.

volume for the Home University Library, *The English Language*,[15] and delighted Harrison with his readiness to discuss etymologies and semantics and to teach her Old English.

The other passengers ('mainly Deans & Headmasters') provided some amusement: 'The deck of this absurd ship is simply strewn with copies of the Rise of the Greek Epic. . . . Next year I suppose the same deck will be strewn with "Urdummheit". . . . Today being Easter Day there is an *omophagia*[16] on the quarter deck & surplices are hurrying about looking important & carrying divers forms of hocus pocus. If I ever feared that my mother church was on her last legs I am undeceived.' On Easter Sunday she went to hear Edward Lyttelton preach on the Resurrection, curious to find out 'how they put it now-a-days'. 'Oh I do wish I understood the collective mind better', she sighed. 'I must try.'[17]

Rain brought disappointment as they travelled by train up the east coast of Greece, as she had been looking forward to seeing Mount Olympus ('I had a feeling that if I once saw Olympus I shld stop hating those old Olympians').[18] Pelion was similarly veiled in cloud ('I believe Cheiron was exceeding wrath with you for not visiting his holy mountain'). The narrow gorge known as the vale of Tempe, always spectacular, delighted her with its green beauty, as did the Plain of Larissa, with 'its immenseness and fertileness'. Pherae brought associations with the myth of Admetus and Alcestis, the 'hospitable' town of the myth. She was forced to admit that 'One certainly *does* get something from the places.' At Mount Athos it suddenly occurred to her that the monastery with its rigid exclusion of women and everything female was really a survival of the Mountain Mother, whose worship was taken over first by Zeus, then by Helios (the sun), and then by Elias (Elijah), with whose name Helios became confused; 'isn't it a splendid triumph of patriarchy that, tho the Panaghia[19] is still worshipped no woman may set her foot on the Holy Mountain? How things do last on.'[20] From there she began the return voyage via Crete and Syracuse. Unfortunately no letters survive to record any colourful details.

She spent the summer writing *Ancient Art and Ritual*, and had a draft ready

---

[15] Logan Pearsall Smith, *The English Language* (London: Williams and Norgate, 1912).

[16] Ritual of eating raw flesh. She is referring, of course, to the Anglican Communion Service.

[17] JEH to GM [560], Easter Day 1912. Edward Lyttelton was the headmaster of Eton at this time.

[18] The quotations in this paragraph are from JEH to GM [561], 16 Apr. 1912.

[19] Panaghia (lit. 'woman all-holy') in modern Greek refers to the Virgin Mary.

[20] JEH to GM [561], 16 Apr. 1912.

for submission by the end of July. Contributors to the Home University Library might reasonably have been expected to summarize scholarly thinking on their topic as well as offering their own views. But summarizing the views of others was something Harrison would never consent to do. Instead, *Ancient Art and Ritual* summarizes Harrison's own intellectual and spiritual journey to this point, all the way from *Introductory Studies in Greek Art* through *Themis* to her new-found interest in a group of French poets who called themselves 'Unanimists'. Her inveterate tendency to approach a scholarly topic from the angle of her own experience may help to explain the path that she intuits for the development of drama.

Art and ritual, she explains in the preface, might at first sight seem antithetical, but they come together in Greek drama, and art in this book means drama, though she inserts one short chapter on the visual arts and attempts to connect them to drama by a rather specious argument (drawn from the Elgin Marbles) that art is frozen ritual. She starts by considering ancient Egypt, where the representation of the death and resurrection of Osiris are set forth in both ritual and art, and extends this argument to Palestine and Babylon as she compares Adonis and Tammuz. It would seem from these examples that art and ritual start from the same impulse. But this impulse cannot be one of representation, for Osiris, Adonis, and Tammuz have no existence. To shed light on the origins she turns to 'savage peoples' of the twentieth century. From these we learn that art and ritual share a common emotional factor, the desire to 'give out a strongly felt emotion by representing, by making or doing or enriching the object or act desired.[21] She reminds us that art (i.e. drama) began with savages *doing* something to achieve their end by mimetic means, such as dancing for rain. We meet again the claim that in the beginning there was no god but only collective emotion, socially expressed. Ritual may seem dull to us, but that is only because the emotion has died down. In a section on pantomimic dancing, she draws on what she had learned from D. S. MacColl. But it is the psychology of it all that most interested her. Animals, she writes, act immediately on impulse, but

in man, where the nervous system is more complex, perception is not instantly transformed into action; there is an interval for choice between several possible actions. Perception is pent up and becomes, helped by emotion, conscious *representation*. Now it is, psychologists tell us, just in this interval, this space between perception and reaction, this momentary halt, that all our mental life, our images, our ideas, our consciousness, and assuredly our religion and our art, is built up. If the cycle of knowing,

---

[21]   *Art and Ritual*, 26.

feeling, acting, were instantly fulfilled, that is, if we were a mass of well-contrived instincts, we should hardly have *dromena* [ritual], and we should certainly never pass from *dromena* to *drama*. Art and religion, though perhaps not wholly ritual, spring from the incomplete cycle, from unsatisfied desire, from perception and emotion that have somehow not found immediate outlet in practical action,[22]

a point to which she will return. But first she turns to the dithyramb to establish a connection between magical ceremonies and seasonal rites. Here she overturns all her previous work on the origin and etymology of the dithyramb in a section that is, as she had feared, not at all clear to the reader. The dithyramb is now explained as a song sung at a spring festival, and the importance of the spring festival is that it magically promotes the food supply. Pindar wrote of the 'bull-driving dithyramb' and she devotes much space to an explication of this curious phrase in order to show, by means of anthropological parallels, how driving a bull helps the coming of spring. Having argued (by comparing the Greeks to the Ainos of Saghalien and their Bear customs) that, far from the god taking on the form of a bull, the real bull gives rise to a Bull-god, she concludes, 'The Ainos have their actual holy Bear, as the Greeks had their holy Bull; but with them out of the succession of holy Bears, *there arises, alas! no Bear-God'*.[23] The reader suspects that this section owes more to her self-confessed maudlin fascination with bears than to any real relation to the main argument.

Then quoting the Palaikastro hymn and describing initiation rites of Australasian aborigines, she shows how she believed the god arose from collective emotion, recapitulating the argument from *Themis*. The gods evolve in man's image, the old gods of group emotion yielding to the 'chilly', individualized, and anthropomorphic Olympians. And yet, taking its material from the Homeric *saga*, the drama maintained just the remoteness from immediate action that is needed, in Harrison's psychology, for the impulse to art.

Take a simple instance. A man—or perhaps still better a child—sees a plate of cherries. Through his senses comes the stimulus of the smell of the cherries, and their bright colour urging him, luring him to eat. He eats and is satisfied; the cycle of normal behaviour is complete; he is a man or a child of action, but he is no artist, and no art-lover. Another man looks at the same plate of cherries. His sight and his smell lure him and urge him to eat. He does *not* eat; the cycle is not completed, and, because he does not eat, the sight of those cherries, though perhaps not the smell, is altered, purified from desire, and in some way intensified, enlarged. If he is just a man of taste, he will take what we call an 'aesthetic' pleasure in those cherries. If he is an

[22] Ibid. 41.   [23] Ibid. 100 (italics mine).

actual artist, he will paint not the cherries, but his vision of them, his purified emotion towards them. He has, so to speak, come out from the chorus of actors, of cherry-eaters, and become a spectator.[24]

As a theory of painting, this makes no sense at all. In what sense does a painter have 'purified emotion' towards the cherries? Biographically, the paragraph is revealing. Resigned now to her role of spectator, Harrison still has to deal with her emotions. In embracing the poetry of the Unanimists she had begun the final stage of her emotional journey, accepting at last what she had repudiated earlier, a secular asceticism:

So again if we want to feel the splendour and vigour of a lion, or even to watch the cumbrous grace of a bear, we prefer that a cage should intervene. The cage cuts off the need for motor actions; it interposes the needful physical and moral distance, and we are free for contemplation. Released from our own terrors, we see more and better, and we feel differently. A man intent on action is like a horse in blinkers, he goes straight forward, seeing only the road ahead.

Our brain is, indeed, it would seem, in part, an elaborate arrangement for providing these blinkers. If we saw and realized the whole of everything, we should want to do too many things. The brain allows us not only to remember, but, which is quite as important, to forget and neglect; it is an organ of oblivion. By neglecting most of the things we see and hear, we can focus just on those which are important for action; we can cease to be potential artists and become efficient practical human beings; but it is only by limiting our view, by a great renunciation as to the things we see and feel. The artist does just the reverse.[25]

Apparently she believed that the reader would regard this as objective truth about art; did she not realize that it was also a confession? The point she thinks she has made is that ritual, a copy or imitation of life, has a practical end. Art, on the other hand, is cut loose from life. Ritual *makes, as it were, a bridge between real life and art*.[26] The italics are hers, and the metaphor of the ritual bridge was one she would frequently revert to.

She returns to ancient drama. At Athens, drama was originally a choral dance on the *orchestra*, or dancing floor, in which all participated; only later were actors differentiated from spectators and the theatre become a place where one watched rather than participated: this argument, based on the archaeology of the theatre of Dionysos at Athens, she had articulated in *Primitive Athens*. Originally the drama celebrated the 'year spirit' and brought in the spring, but the year rituals became monotonous, till happily Homer came to the rescue, and material for the drama was found in his epics and other heroic sagas, now lost. But with this development a great change

---

[24] *Art and Ritual*, 129.   [25] Ibid. 133–4.   [26] Ibid. 135.

took place, for in the old ritual dance the group was everything, whereas in Homer the individual is paramount.

The stages, it would seem, are: actual life with its motor reactions, the ritual copy of life with its faded reactions, the image of the god projected by the rite, and, last, the copy of that image, the work of art. . . . Track any god right home, and you will find him lurking in a ritual sheath, from which he slowly emerges, first as a daemon, or spirit, of the year, then as a full-blown divinity.[27]

'Track any god right home'; she had now in one sense completed the task she had set herself in 1892, when, with 'the demons and spirits of primitive man at one pole, and the "gods of Olympos" at the other' she had declared that while a link in the chain between them was wanting, the mythologist had no rest.[28] (The harder task, to trace each saga to its local home, awaited further ethnographic groundwork, and may in many cases be impossible.)

Having thus traced the origin of drama, she extends the argument to include the visual arts by quoting MacColl, who had recently described drawing as 'a kind of gesture, a method of dancing on paper'.[29] But if this sounds lively, sculpture is still frozen: 'by all manner of renunciations Greek sculpture is what it is . . . remote to the point of chill abstraction. The statue in the round renounces not only human life itself, but all the natural background and setting of life.'[30]

She then examines the relation of art to philosophy, science, and religion. Definitions were a problem, as she had discovered in correspondence with Murray, who had described the Olympians as ideal dreams, and made her realize that 'what you call Superstition I call Religion, & what you call Religion, I art'.[31] She now offers a new definition of religion: 'the worship of some form of god, as the practical counterpart of theology.'[32] Just as art has about it a sense of obligation: one feels one *ought* to value it, so religion lays obligation on its practitioners. There is also an emotional power common to both. Where they differ, according to Harrison, is that religion claims its object has objective existence. She is influenced by Tolstoy's dictum that all art is good *qua* art that succeeds in transmitting emotion, and then, by a drastically reductionist argument, arrives at her current espousal of Unanimism, claiming that 'It is the business of the modern artist to feel and transmit emotion towards this unity of man.' This categorical statement is followed by observations that show Harrison at her worst, seeing everything through the lens of her latest obsession, and making unjustified deductions from

[27] *Art and Ritual*, 191–2.   [28] Petiscus, *The Gods of Olympos*, pp. vi–vii.

[29] D. S. MacColl, 'A Year of Post-Impressionism', *Nineteenth Century* (1912), 29.

[30] *Art and Ritual*, 202.   [31] JEH to GM [570], n.d.   [32] *Art and Ritual*, 225.

personal experience. She cannot resist, in the midst of a larger argument, the temptation to refer back to the events that had most seared her own experience. The young, she declares, are temporary artists; they write lyric poems and love masquerading, and focus on life in a way that later on life itself makes impossible:

This pseudo-art, this self-aggrandizement usually dies a natural death before *the age of thirty*. [italics mine] . . . The real and natural remedy for the egotism of youth is Life, not necessarily the haunting of *cafés*, or even the watching of football matches, but strenuous activity in the simplest human relations of daily happenings.[33]

(Another year and much of that youth would enlist in the strenuous activity of a senseless war; two more years and Rupert Brooke would be dead at the age of 28.)

What the book still lacked, to Harrison's mind, was a 'moral', or some clear connection drawn from the ancients to the present day. A pivotal event in her life late in the summer of 1912 provided the key.

On 1 August she had left again for Europe with a 'contingent of Stracheys' to spend a couple of weeks at Beatenberg, staying at a pension that was 'einfach aber gemütlich' (simple but comfortable), and speaking French on account of Dorothy Strachey's French husband, the artist Simon Bussy ('good for me but rather wearing').[34] From there she went on to Geneva to see a doctor about her arthritis; the arthritis by now was much better, but her heart was not. She was joined by the sisters Alys Russell and Mary Berenson who took her for a run in their motor car—two hundred miles to Besançon and back—a thrill hardly calculated to slow down a racing heart. Mary she liked much better when not playing up to her husband. ('What a curse husbands are. They almost always demoralize their Fraus.')[35]

It was probably during this visit to Geneva that she experienced the second great psychological turning point of her life, analogous in some ways to the crisis she underwent in reaction to MacColl's criticism in 1887. On both occasions she used the word 'conversion' to describe her experience, and both led to a radical reorientation of her mindset and writing. With that the similarity ends. In 1887 her change of direction had been the direct result of pointed criticism from a friend, and resulted in a change of lecturing and writing style and a different focus to her work. What happened in 1912, if her own account is to be believed, was spontaneous. She described it in the language of religious mysticism and its effect on her emotions. The experience brought closure to the four years of emotional struggle that had started with

[33]   *Art and Ritual*, 242.   [34]   JEH to GM [575], 12 Aug. 1912.
[35]   JEH to GM [578], 2 Sept. 1912.

the production of *Comus* and had found outlet in hatred for Frances, expressing itself in cruel words and unkind actions, with associated guilt. In the aftermath, as she tried to understand what had happened and to live by the light of new revelation, she found new religious and literary interests. The 'atavistic world' of Greek religion began to lose its hold on her, and, like Bertrand Russell in 1902, she became more interested in 'the religion of today'. She explained it to Murray:

And now I must tell you a strange thing. I was wondering if I should tell you or not, when yr letter came & now I must tho' I am a little afraid, for you know so well the deceitfulness of the human heart & may dash my hopes.

Do you think a blasphemous Ker could be converted? Do you remember contending with me on the cliffs & maintaining that there was more in religion than the collective conscience. I think I know now at first hand that there is. Last night I was awake all night with misery & utter loneliness such as often comes upon me now that I have to go about alone, only it was worse than anything I had ever felt, like a black despair & I was full of hate against Frances, unjustly of course, as the cause of my loneliness. I fell asleep at last & woke about 6 bathed in a most amazing bliss & feeling that all the world was new & in perfect peace. I can't describe it—the New Birth is the best—it was what they all try to describe & it is what they mean by communion with God, only it seems senseless to me to give it a name & yet I do not wonder for it is so personal.

Something physical had happened for when I went to Röthlisberger the moment he put his instrument on my pulse he said 'Why, this is all better' & seemed astonished, but something not physical too for all the hate against Frances was gone clean. For the last year I have scarcely seen her. He found out, by my face he said, that every time I saw her it brought back the pain in my heart so he begged me not to see her & I didn't, but I felt mean & wretched. Of course I cannot be sure till I *do* see her, but I have no fear, it seems gone away clean.

I can't put it into psychology yet. What I feel most is that a wall of partition is broken down & a whole crust of egotism gone melted away & that I have got hold of something bigger than me that I am part of. But it was all done in my sleep, not by me at all.

What is it? I will never call it God—that name is defaced, but it is wonderful, and you were right as always.[36]

There is a striking resemblance between this and Bertrand Russell's experience of 'conversion' ten years earlier, when, after listening to Murray's reading of Euripides' *Hippolytus* at Newnham he had returned to the Whiteheads' home and witnessed the pain of Evelyn Whitehead. Overwhelmed with the sense of solitude of every human soul, he had felt the ground give

[36] JEH to GM [562], n.d.

way beneath him. Within five minutes he had become, by his own account, a completely different person. Russell never elaborated on the connection between his experience and the *Hippolytus*, but what they shared was a story of suppressed, illicit love. In the *Hippolytus*, Phaedra is destroyed by her secret passion for her stepson, Theseus, while Russell in 1902 was consumed by a secret love. In the heat of this experience Russell had written *The Free Man's Worship*, in which he advocated devoting one's life not to personal happiness but to the universal good. Harrison admired this beautiful religion, but cannot have failed to notice Russell's complete inability to live up to his ideals. Even at the time of writing he was nourishing hatred for Alys and love first for Evelyn Whitehead, then for Ottoline Morrell. Murray may have observed the similarity to Harrison's description of her 'New Birth' and urged caution, reminding her of the proof of the pudding, for she wrote to him on 2 September 1912, 'More psychology of the converted when we meet. It lasts.'[37] She would have liked to talk about what had happened with A. B. Cook, someone perhaps open-minded enough to help her understand it on her own terms, but she was inhibited by the thought of his wife knowing. It can be safely assumed that she did not discuss it with her close friend Alys Russell. Books were a great resource at this time: William James's *The Varieties of Religious Experience*, William McDougall's *Psychology* in the Home University Library,[38] a new essay by Bertrand Russell entitled 'The Essence of Religion',[39] and Julian Huxley's *The Individual in the Animal Kingdom*[40] all helped as she worked to understand her experience in terms of psychology. In a later letter to Frances she wrote

So we must face both of us, all three of us, the fact that my loneliness may be for life— it isn't I know that I am specially weak in moral courage, it just is that life is ebbing & with it the power to grow new spiritual tissues—one's life lives longest in one's brain & so my only life is really there now. . . . And also tho the loneliness is there & almost always aches, all the bitterness went in that miracle & has never come back—it has tried to once or twice, mechanically I have felt the old misery against you but it goes now directly—& that is due in part to the miracle but also in part to you, to the faith I have in you & your tenderness towards me.[41]

Perhaps it is true for every human life that a series of chance connections determines the course we take; for Harrison this seems to be especially true.

[37] JEH to GM [578], 2 Sept. 1912.

[38] William McDougall, *Psychology: The Study of Behaviour* (London: Williams and Norgate, 1912).

[39] *Hibbert Journal*, 11/1 (Oct. 1912), 46–62.

[40] Julian Huxley, *The Individual in the Animal Kingdom*, Cambridge Manuals of Science and Literature (Cambridge: Cambridge University Press, 1912).

[41] This letter is taken from a transcription in Mirrlees's notebook.

It shows up in her work, where she frequently refers to the 'happy coincidence' by which she discovered the key to a problem. Now, reading *The Poetry Review*[42] for August 1912 she was led, serendipitously, to a group of young French poets whose work exactly matched her psychological state, and it was they more than anyone who enabled her to articulate her newfound faith. After reading their poetry she was ready to speak of 'Unanimism and Conversion' to the Heretics Society on 25 November.[43]

The 'Unanimists' were a group of young French poets (including René Arcos, Charles Vildrac, and Jules Romains) who founded a community at l'Abbaye de Créteuil in which like-minded artists, artisans, and dreamers lived together with women and children, a monastery without an abbot. They were influenced by Walt Whitman and his dream of brotherhood. Their rejection of the traditional, of the academic world, of rationality, differentiated them as a group from others. As poets they stood for a reaction against the lyrical egotism of the end of the nineteenth century with its contempt for the *bourgeoisie*, and embraced instead a philosophy of inclusion. Their aim was 'so to write that each man should learn to love his own life, penetrate it, and see its beauty and value'.[44] They lived as a commune, setting up a printing press to provide a means of income as well as an opportunity for young authors to be published. In this way they also lived up to Tolstoy's ideal by learning a trade.

Significantly, and in this may well have lain a large part of their appeal, they were influenced by Harrison's two lodestars, Durkheim and Bergson. She wrote later of their common ideas:

Life is one—but you may think of that oneness in two ways. There is the stream of life in *time*, or, rather, in what Professor Bergson calls durée; that is one. Each of us is a snowball growing bigger every moment, and in which all *our* past, and also the past out of which we sprang, all the generations behind us, is rolled up, involved.[45]

But we may think of the oneness in another way, so to speak laterally or spatially, contemporaneously. All the life existing at one moment in the world, and at every successive moment, though individualized, is one. We are all of us members of one another. That is M. Romains' doctrine. So far as he has a philosophy, and he is very much a philosopher, M. Romains' is based on Professor Durkheim, M. Arcos' on Professor Bergson.[46]

She felt a 'burst of sympathetic Unanimism', and quoted H. G. Wells: 'This is as much as I see in time and space as I know it, *something struggling to*

---

[42] F. S. Flint, 'Contemporary French Poetry', *Poetry Review*, 1/8 (Aug. 1912), 381–92.

[43] 'Unanimism and Conversion' in *Alpha and Omega*, 42–79.   [44] Ibid. 47.

[45] Ibid. 48. This idea she had already seized on for *Themis*, and related to Dionysos.

[46] Ibid. 49.

exist. Above the heart in me is that: the desire to know better, to know beautifully, and to transmit my knowledge. That's all there is in life beyond food and shelter and tidying up.'[47] All of this fitted with her thesis in *Themis*, that religion is not the search of a soul for God but rather the projection of the emotion of a group.

Romains accepted these social forces, and organized them into a hierarchy. Durkheim had already written of the power of the group. Romains extended Durkheim's line of thought to smaller groups, as small as two people, who hold more power as a group than as individuals. He wrote in terms of a collective soul, which he termed 'the god of group two', 'the god of the family', of the village, of the town. There is also a diabolical 'god of the crowd'. Of these, the small is always the enemy of the larger group.

But it was Vildrac who most won Harrison's heart. 'He is more of a poet, less of a philosopher, than the other two,' she wrote, 'and his verse has a peculiar simplicity and poignancy that makes analysis almost impertinent.' His religious views were akin to those of the ancient Stoics: Vildrac's god was a 'vast elemental being', and his vocation was to awaken the 'archipelagos of solitude' scattered throughout the world to immersion in the great 'collective soul'. In *Livre d'Amour* (1910) he wrote not of the god of group two, but of the love of Everyman, in a style so personal and direct that she found it almost unbearable.

> I am weary of deeds done inside myself,
> I am weary of voyages inside myself,
> And of heroism wrought by strokes of the pen,
> And of a beauty made up of formulae.
>
> I am ashamed of lying to my work,
> Of my work lying to my life,
> And of being able to content myself
> (By burning sweet spices)
> With the mouldering smell that is master here.[48]

The poet leaves his work to meet 'this man and that', to show them the beauty of their lives, and to love each and every one.

But the printing press did not pay, and the community lasted for just fourteen months, until, broken by a terrible winter, they were scattered by hunger and poverty.[49] Even so, their spirit lived on, and in it Harrison found a home for her lonely heart.

---

[47] H. G. Wells, *Marriage* (London: Hogarth Press, 1986), 340; quoted in 'Unanimism and Conversion', 498.

[48] Quoted in 'Unanimism and Conversion', 57–8.   [49] Ibid. 43.

Harrison was now ready to expound her experience of 'conversion'. First and foremost, she claimed, there is no need of a god to explain it. We must drop theology if we would keep religion. As a psychological phenomenon she understood conversion to involve the following three factors: first, it arises out of an experience of desolation and despair; second, there follows a period of unutterable joy and peace, in which there is an 'almost intolerable significance in things' and individuality is broken down; third, the whole experience is involuntary. What has happened, in effect, is that the subject has been initiated into his social group; the individual spirit is socialized, or as Verrall translated the description of the ecstatic follower of Dionysos in the *Bacchae*: 'his soul is congregationalized'.[50]

In October she saw how to end *Ancient Art and Ritual*. Vildrac had said just what she wanted to say. Murray obliged with an English translation, drawing the following reply:

That translation is *just* what I want. It is so clean & plain. I tried to do it & got messy & tawdry. Thank you ever so much. . . . When I first said it I knew I had to write this sort of screed. It was sticking like a lump in my throat. And it must be Art & Ritual not as a superficial critic might say Ritual & Art, because the real object is art. It is first in importance tho not in history & tho my savage heart is more at home in ritual, that is the real difference between us (inter alia!)—that you have pushed right thro into art, I am still in the ritual stage.[51]

When in 1914 the artist Clive Bell published a small book on aesthetics, expounding his view of art as 'significant form',[52] Harrison let herself be lured, perhaps unwisely, into his long-standing controversy with Roger Fry. If Clive Bell was right in his assertion that representation is irrelevant in a work of art, the argument of *Art and Ritual* collapses. She responded with 'Art and Mr Clive Bell',[53] arguing from her own experience that a work of art that caused her aesthetic emotion had a trance-like quality, and that what sent shudders down her spine was not the form of a work of art, but *formal representation*.[54]

For her whole career Harrison had immersed herself in Greek art, but her interest was confined to its subject matter. She treated art, as she had always done, simply as a type of evidence, and her delight lay not in the form of the work in front of her but in unearthing some older, deeper meaning behind the representation. 'Aneikonism', she had written, 'finds . . . [its gods] in the life of nature outside man, or in the psychological experience, the hope, the

---

[50] Euripides: θιασεύεται ψυχάν, quoted in 'Unanimism', 65.

[51] JEH to GM [580], n.d.   [52] Clive Bell, *Art* (London: Chatto & Windus, 1914).

[53] 'Art and Mr Clive Bell', *Alpha and Omega*, 209–20.   [54] Ibid. 215–16 (*italics hers*).

fear, the hate, the love within him. It begins with fetishism, it ends in symbolism; its feet are in the deep sea-wells and in the primeval slime, its head is
swathed in mists and mysticsm.'[55] The representation of these primal emotions, not 'significant form', was what mattered.

[55] 'The Pillar and the Maiden', 11.

12. 'Tout passe, tout casse, tout lasse':[1] Cambridge and Paris 1914–1916

ALL her life Harrison had lived with a sense of foreboding evil; for most of her life her fears had proved to be well-grounded. When war with Germany broke out in August 1914, she was approaching the end of an academic career, failing in health both physical and emotional, keenly conscious of ageing, still finding it hard to come to terms with the loss of Cornford to his marriage. Now war, quite apart from its own intrinsic horrors, brought the desolation and the loss of nearly all that remained. 'War upsets every value', she wrote. 'Who cares to-day wholeheartedly for Hittites or Minoans? Who raises to-day the question of the Origins of Tragedy or Comedy?'[2] A bitter, added poignancy, perhaps accentuated by her gender, utterly confounded her: academic colleagues seemed actually to welcome the 'topsy-turvydom' that placed learning on the lowest rung and replaced it with a call to arms and the life of the barracks. A wedge was driven between her and Murray, who was increasingly drawn into politics in support of the government. Not only did this distance him from her by occupying his time (as his involvement in public affairs had always done), but for the first time she found herself unable to support his political stance. By her own confession she knew little about politics and cared less, and hitherto had always deferred to his opinion, but now, when Murray was convinced that war was a lesser evil than acquiescing to Germany, she was unable to reconcile his stance with her instinctive pacifism. She had only Hope Mirrlees to fall back on, and the two of them spent most of the war years together, dividing their time between England and Paris, where Harrison continued to go for treatment for her angina.

On 3 August 1914 Murray had sat in the Strangers' Gallery in the House of Commons and listened to the speech of the Foreign Secretary, Sir Edward

---

[1] 'Everthing passes, everything perishes, everything palls', French proverb.
[2] 'Epilogue on the War: Peace with Patriotism' in *Alpha and Omega*, 228.

Grey, and came away convinced that Britain had no choice but to go to war. He quickly became involved in the campaign to counteract German propaganda. He attended a meeting of eminent writers on 2 September, at which it was agreed to set up a 'Bureau of Information' (the 'Mendacity Bureau', he dubbed it), and immediately wrote a pamphlet, First Thoughts on the War,[3] ten thousand copies of which were sent to the Russian Foreign Minister for distribution. He admitted satisfaction at the news of German casualties, even writing that when he saw that 20,000 Germans had been killed on one day and only 2,000 the next, he was sorry, thereby shocking his close friend, Bertrand Russell. But, he argued, it was not the Germans but the system that must be crushed, and we must beware lest militarism corrupt our relations with one another. The danger he saw was that those who instinctively loathe war might be silent, leaving public opinion to the mercy of the militarists. In that event the war might deteriorate to just another of the sordid struggles of nation against nation.

The thrust of the paper was the importance of a sense of fraternity. To his wife he wrote:

I have hours in which I feel as you do, utterly abased and crushed by the misery of war, feeling that the death and maiming and starving of Germans and Austrians is just as horrible a thing as the same suffering in Englishmen. But mostly I feel strung up and exalted by a feeling of the tremendous issue and the absolute duty that lies upon us to save Europe and humanity. We did not know until the war revealed it what this German system meant. Once it is revealed I do feel that we must strike it down or die.[4]

Later, in another pamphlet How Can War Ever Be Right?, he added the observation that war is not all evil. It offers opportunities for heroism to the common man that he would never have in peace time. 'This is the inward triumph which lies at the heart of the great tragedy,'[5] a view surely formed from the kleos (renown) of the Homeric heroes, who would never have been heroes without the otherwise meaningless Trojan War, an irony of which even Homer seemed aware.

When Cornford signed up as a musketry instructor in October, Murray wondered if he should drill, and feeling he would 'rather like to', he joined the Oxford Volunteer Training Corps, then under the command of another classical scholar, A. D. Godley. He enjoyed the drill, and remained a faithful

---

[3] Murray, 'First Thoughts on the War' repr. in Faith, War and Policy, Lectures and Essays (Oxford: Oxford University Press, 1918), 3–19.

[4] GM to MM, 7 Sept. 1914, MS Gilbert Murray 462, fo. 74.

[5] Murray, 'How Can War Ever Be Right?' repr. in Faith, War and Policy, 20–45.

volunteer for two and a half years, being promoted to Corporal in 1916. The reactions of her other friends to the war also took Harrison aback, perhaps revealing how little she really knew them. She wrote to Murray in August,

Frances is very funny now-a-days, full of reactions, excited over the empire & the importance of people being simple & rather stupid & doing their duty at home & having a religion. Three years ago I was not allowed to utter the word 'duty'. I knew this Catholic reaction was on in France, but I didn't know that Jacques & Gwen [Raverat] & Rupert [Brooke] etc etc were all in it here! I hope Frances won't 'be received into' yr Holy Mother's bosom, it wld worry Frank, tho he wld stand aside & yawn heavily.[6]

Rupert Brooke, who had tried, but failed, to get a job as a war correspondent, was impressed with how the war transformed the 'intellectuals': 'Cornford is no longer the best Greek Scholar in Cambridge. He recalled that he was a very good shot in his youth and is a Sergeant-Instructor of Musketry. . . . Gilbert Murray and Walter Raleigh rise at six every day to line hedgerows in the dark and "advance in rushes" across the Oxford meadows. . . . I could extend the list. It's all a terrible thing. And yet, in its details, it's great fun.'[7]

Harrison struggled to understand how any of this could be 'fun'. She sought out the sea air in Norfolk, but found the lack of news eerie. Returning to Cambridge she lamely tried to do her duty, sensing all the while the meaninglessness of it, and went with Hope Mirrlees's mother Lena to pour out coffee in a camp at dawn: 'the beauty of the tents in the mist almost undid me—it was so Old Testament—like the hosts of Midian or the children of Israel or something. Why is a host of tents so horribly moving? Is is "tout passe", etc.?'[8] She visited the Cornfords, who now had a baby, Helena, born in October 1913, and came away feeling more empty than ever after a weekend of 'wallowing in an orchard & walking to & fro from the camp. They were trying new luminous bullets'.[9]

At Newnham she contributed to the efforts to raise funds for Belgian refugees, and gave a slide lecture on 'Hospital Life among the Ancient Greeks'. She wrote to Murray: 'The War is horribly exciting but I can't *live* on it. It is like being drunk all day & I want some hot milk, clean and feeding.'[10] She wrote out her own viewpoint to get it out of her system, with the same explanation she had put forward for her other writing, that it 'lies on my stomach' and 'makes me sick till I get rid of it'.

---

[6] JEH to GM [686], n.d.

[7] Rupert Brooke to Russell Loines, published in *The Letters of Rupert Brooke*, ed. Sir Geoffrey Keynes (London: Faber, 1968), 644.   [8] JEH to GM [687], 3 Sept. 1914.

[9] JEH to Hope Mirrlees, n.d.   [10] JEH to GM [688], 17 Sept. 1914.

She was unsettled by how the war had brought into focus the dark side of the 'herd instinct' which she had so enthusiastically embraced five years before. (Murray had perhaps provoked her with a comment in *First Thoughts on the War*, in which he had written wistfully of the working men who simply hail a stranger as 'mate', while dons and men of letters seem to have no mates and no gift for getting them.)[11] She wrote to him: 'I am beginning to feel as if the curse all over was the curse of a dominant *class*, a governing class, wch I used to think it so natural & fine to belong to,' and added abjectly, 'No one—except perhaps you—is to have power over anyone else. I mean power to compel.'[12]

Her article, *Peace With Patriotism*, was published by Deighton Bell as a pamphlet in 1915.[13] The glare of war had made her earlier work, she said, 'seem like faded photographs'.[14] But on further reflection, especially on the war itself, she came to the conclusion that the same realities underlie our academic thinking and our international conflict. Thinking and writing are solitary activities, she wrote, however much is undertaken collegially. 'Alone and safeguarded from emotion, all thinkers must be *while they think*; . . . that is the price they pay for their high calling.'[15] The don who enlisted discovered what he had probably never consciously known, a hunger for the common life, realized when the camp, with all its privations, seemed like a veritable paradise. Of the causes of the war she admitted she was not competent to speak, and she was prepared to accept on trust Murray's conclusion that under the circumstances Britain had no alternative but to fight. But she would admit no more than this, and against those who argued that war had a good side she inveighed, 'Are we to cause or allow or maintain war that our souls may be saved? Are cathedrals to be shelled and homes laid waste and children butchered that by terror and pity we may be made pure? My God! No! No! No!'[16]

War, she insisted, was a savagery, a set-back to civilization. In the 'depth of her fanatical heart' she dared to dream that on the day when every man, woman and child was prepared to march out, not to war but to martyrdom, no German soldier would be found who would cut down such a defenceless band. 'Hasn't the unarmed man who is ready to die for his faith some terrific power? even over Germans?' she asked Murray.[17] Possessed of a powerful instinct to protect the weak, she naïvely attributed such feelings to the rest of humankind. What then, could have driven Germany to war? Germany had

---

[11] Quoted in Wilson, *Gilbert Murray*, 221.   [12] JEH to GM [732], n.d.
[13] Repr. as 'Epilogue on the War: Peace with Patriotism'.   [14] *Alpha and Omega*, vi.
[15] 'Epilogue on the War', 231.   [16] Ibid. 233.   [17] JEH to GM [694], n.d.

become over-theoretical, over-intellectualized, 'seeking to understand and rule the world by abstractions'. In a deadly collectivism the whole nation became possessed of a single idea which it sought to impose. The Norman conquest had mercifully saved the British people and the English language from any delusions about racial purity.

There creeps into this article the thought that would not leave her, that at the root of all human conflict lies the ugly side of sex:

fighting must survive, because fighting and sex are inextricably bound up. Abolish these primal instincts, and the mainsprings of life are atrophied. Man is and must remain a fighting animal. True as to sex. No sane person seeks to free sex from jealousy, because sex is, in its essence, exclusive. All our most cherished institutions of marriage and the home centre round this quality of exclusion. Marriage *is* exclusion and jealousy, state-sanctioned. It is easy to see that here jealousy serves life, and has therefore its proper function. But need jealousy and exclusiveness spread from sex to the whole of life? So long as they do, so long we shall, I believe, have war. . . . We must cleanse our hearts not only from hate in war, but from those subtler poisons that fester unto war—from all rivalry, jealousy, and from all spirit of competition; . . . We must live and let live, tolerating—nay, fostering—in the life of individuals and of nations an infinite parti-coloured diversity, and so at last win *Peace with Patriotism*[18]

When she showed this to Murray he must have upbraided her, for she wrote to him in November, 'Well I never, I don't know what young Thers of forty are coming to, mocking at a respectable old Ker over 60 in a cap & spectacles. Am I really so absurd?' and accused him of corrupting her and muddling her mind by turning it from Pelasgians to current affairs.

That is I believe what is really wrong with me. My aunts on both sides were nearly all mad, & they have left me, stridently sane in body but with a mind only capable of one hot focus at a time & therefore of no practical use in a world of ten thousand focuses. . . . Why can you & almost only you be sane & yet not stuffy? . . . Well, it was good of you to read them thro & if I gave you one chuckle I haven't written in vain.[19]

Later she expressed relief that he had thought her tract only 'foolish', not 'vicious'. Her views on the 'herd instinct' interested him sufficiently to reply to them in a paper he gave at Bedford College in February 1915,[20] in which he used an argument from human evolution to assert that 'herd union' is an inherited trait in the human species, in itself neither good nor bad. 'It is nothing against a particular emotion that mankind shares it with the ape and tiger. Gorillas are famous for their family life, and tigresses are, up to their

---

[18] 'Epilogue on the War', 259.   [19] JEH to GM [698], 17 Nov. 1914.
[20] Murray, 'Herd Instinct and the War', *Atlantic Monthly*, 115 (1915), 830–9.

lights, exemplary mothers,' he wrote. Social class, professional groups, churches, parties in politics, cliques in art are all instances of the herd instinct. Strongest is the nation. As in all animals, once the herd is threatened, its response is 'to group, then fight or fly'. Harrison had noted with alarm how after a public meeting about the war the audience complained that the speaker did not tell them what they ought to think; Murray observed that ordinarily people feel small if they are given orders, but not so in wartime, when they are proud. Murray's chief concern was the potential effect of herd union on religion, for it discourages hard thinking. He predicted that once the war was over the aspiration after a better life and a world with more love in it would be drowned for a period in a flood of emotion, as disastrous as it was alluring.

On 16 December 1914 the Germans, targeting munitions factories, shelled the north-east coast of England, and in that instant the war ceased in her mind to be a matter of academic debate and became a present evil. Although Harrison's immediate family was safe, one of the family's former servants was killed in the blast with a grandchild on each knee. She remembered with affection this devoted maid who had left Yorkshire to look after her when she first went to London and was always a friend. 'One ought really to be glad that one's own country takes even such a small toll of the common suffering,' she wrote, 'but oh how it falls on the poor & defenceless.'[21] Murray wrote to console her, and she replied savagely how the thought of the Germans shelling the beautiful Whitby Abbey on the great cliff made her see red. Later, when she had collected herself she proclaimed herself a fool to mind so much. 'My cousin whose house at Whitby shook to its foundations writes as if the Germans had just been in to tea—that's the Yorkshire spirit.'[22]

By now she was suffering severely from angina, to the point where it incapacitated her for days on end and she had difficulty holding a pen. She complained of 'dying quietly for want of breath'. Only her French doctor, Moutier, was able to stop the pain, but had warned her that if she exposed herself to *les émotions* the *stigmates* would 'recrudesce'. It was difficult to avoid emotion at a time like this. However, as she pointed out, 'one can't well run over to Paris to see one's doctor now'. It was not just the danger that inhibited her, but also a fear of seeming egotistical to be worrying about her own pain at such a time. But in October 1914 when the pain grew worse she overcame her scruples. She sent Murray a postcard from Paris: 'It is wonderful to be here & somehow less unbearable for the nightmare becomes real. . . . Moutier received me with open arms in full uniform & "Vive l'Angleterre". It is very upsetting to be adored for one's group's sake.'[23] A few days later she could report that Moutier had pulled up her *chiffre* (blood pressure) but had warned her that it could keep going down till the war was over. 'He has also broken most of my knuckles with his ardent "poignées de main" ["hand shakes"] as an alliée', she added.[24]

On his advice she left Paris immediately after treatment. 'Antwerp had scared them, I think, but it is better now.' She realized on reflection that it is only an *imagined* thing that causes fear. The *real* thing has far less power.

When the pain returned in the spring, she went back, though not until after being detained by what she called a 'very *daimonion*' (eerie, miraculous) experience. 'I shld like to think it was my guardian angel but it may have been the Kaiser sending me his plans about Zeppelins & Paris. It is too long to write.'[25] (On another occasion in Greece she had been about to board a train, but saw her own figure sitting in the corner. Spooked by the experience, she changed her travel plans. She later heard the train had crashed.)

On this visit Harrison and Mirrlees made the discovery that just around the corner from the Hotel de l'Élysée was the École des Langues Orientales with courses in Russian. They now had a second reason for staying in Paris, and the hotel became for a while a second home to them. Their friends nicknamed it the 'Hotel du Lapin' after a rabbit which lived in a hutch at the bottom of the stairs. The rabbit would have appealed to Harrison's love of animals, but others of her friends found it *insupportable* and unhygienic, and when Jessie Crum (Stewart) visited them there her father, to Harrison's regret, insisted it be removed.

The discovery of the École Orientale was significant. Harrison and Mirrlees joined a second-year class, far ahead of their proficiency, but this, she wrote, was 'all to the good'. Three times a week it was taught by an irascible M. Boyer, 'but as most of his wrath falls on an adorable old M. l'Évêque, whose strong point is not grammar, I escape' she explained to Jessie.[26] He was in fact an admirable teacher. On the other three days a 'real Russian lady' gave them oral practice, using coloured pictures which she then described. Harrison was overjoyed to discover she could follow most of it. She wrote to Murray,

We are a queer class, M. l'Évêque, an Abbé, some (apparently) pawnbrokers, a French suffragette, etc. The fun is that the lady, a quite excellent teacher, simply takes M. l'Évêque's head off—he is muddle headed & rather idle, & so fat he can scarcely speak, but he has lived in Russia & thinks he knows Russian, & it all goes on in mixed

[23] JEH to GM [690], n.d.   [24] JEH to GM [691], 14 Oct. 1914.
[25] JEH to GM [718], n.d.   [26] JEH to JS 16 May 1915.

French & Russian. It is immensely instructive. I get in about 6 lessons a week (all at the expense of the State) & enjoy it hugely. I think I shall stay a month & give Moutier his long desired chance to surveiller me.

. . . It is too fascinating. I have always meant to devote my dotage to languages & now it is coming on.[27]

She was immediately captivated by the Russian language. 'Twice in my life, only twice', she wrote, 'it has happened to me to fall in love with a language. Once, long ago, with Greek, again, only yesterday as it seems to me, with Russian.'[28] Nothing, she claimed, had made her so happy since she first encountered particles in Greek! What enchanted her was the way the Russian language makes use of the aspects of the verb to distinguish between performing an action and seeing the action brought to fruition. 'Languages that use different roots [for these two aspects, e.g. English with the words 'seek' and 'find'] lose much of the inherent logic of life,' she concluded. Her premise was that a people's philosophy of life is expressed unconsciously in its language, and it was a small step for her to find in the imperfective aspect of the Russian language the *durée* of Bergson, the 'thing lived'. 'And our minds rush out to ask,' she continued, 'Is the perfective, then, the aspect of intellect, of the thing thought rather than the thing lived; of the mental net, in which, M. Bergson tells us, our mechanizing minds and brains have caught the living universe?'[29]

Living in France and learning Russian through the medium of the French language may have heightened her sensitivity on these issues. French, which she admired as the most highly civilized and rationalized of languages, has little facility for aspect. (Even the simple distinction in English between 'I go to Church' and 'I am going to Church' can be expressed in French only by a clumsy circumlocution.) Precise and rigid in its formulations, the French verb system is the antithesis of Russian (and Greek, for that matter). Harrison had expressed elsewhere her antipathy to dogma, to all theorizing and systematizing, be it in theology or politics or anything else, and had expressed it with unusual vehemence.[30] The French, just like the Olympians and the Germans, were 'over-intellectualized'. (Ironically, insisting on a rigid distinction between dogma and religion, abstraction and feeling, is itself a form of systematizing.)

At the same time as she was learning Russian she was brushing daily

---

[27] JEH to GM [721], n.d.

[28] Harrison, *Aspects, Aorists and the Classical Tripos* (Cambridge: Cambridge University Press, 1919), 5. This pamphlet is an expanded version of *Russia and the Russian Verb: a Contribution to the Psychology of the Russian People* (Cambridge: Heffer and Sons, 1915).

[29] *Russia and the Russian Verb*, 8.   [30] 'Sacra Scientiae Fames', 134–5.

against the red tape of life in France, its scrupulosity accentuated by wartime. She hated all officialdom, and now seemingly simple activities like posting a letter were surrounded with bureaucratic constraint. She described trying to send a telegram to Murray:

I all but languished in a felon's cell. They got a magnifying glass, detected the word 'Oxford' & immediately demanded my 'pièce de justification' . . . A 'pièce de justification' demands a 'permis de séjour' & a permis de séjour un permis d'arriver et de partir & a permis de partir involves a pièce de qualification from yr *patron* as well as the present of yr photograph to several commissionaires de police. It was like the house that Jack Built & didn't I learn a lot of French.

It was after this experience that she had the photograph taken with Hope Mirrlees and the Bear (Fig. 16), on a copy of which she wrote to Murray,

Here is the *pièce de justification*, taken hurriedly in the Tuilleries by a strolling bear. I never issue from the door without it & several flags. I utter piercing shrieks of Vive les Allies all day long. I'm worn out. . . . I was living peacefully not munie-ed with any pièces till I tried cabling to you. The official βάτραχος ['frog'] has a consuming passion for this photograph.[31]

She saw in the French the love of abstraction leading inexorably to 'moral, quasi-intellectual act[s] of judgment, the "clenched fist."' With the Russians it was otherwise. The Russian, or so she believed, longs for *durée*, as can be found in the writing of Dostoevsky, who does not judge the sinner, but sympathizes with him. 'It is not that he approves crime, but that he is not concerned either to approve or disapprove; he has not got there yet, he is living into it, understanding through feeling. . . . It is this living into things that a new generation demands, and it is this, because she is young among the nations, that Russia has to offer.' Using her favourite metaphor of warmth and cold she admits that the French language, though she greatly admired it, always struck her with a sense of chill. It pushed clarity 'to the verge of petrification'. Then, realizing the political danger of the opinion she had just expressed, she hastily adds that the great thing was to have both France and Russia as spiritual allies. As for the British, we recoil from abstractions, red tape, pièces d'identification, yet remain in our attitudes 'crudely perfective. We draw sharp lines, we circumscribe, we leave no open field for imagination and sympathy, and here we may well learn from the Russian'.

She presented these thoughts to the Heretics Society in the autumn of 1915.[32] In her *Reminiscences*, written ten years later, she writes with mawkish

---

[31] JEH to GM [724], postmarked 2 July 1915.
[32] The pamphlet *Russia and the Russian Verb* was originally given as a lecture.

sentimentality about Russia, and it is hard to know how literally to take her own claims. By the end of her life her memory was distorted by recent events, and her *Reminiscences* are demonstrably an attempt to rewrite her own life history. The very first sentence of the first chapter, entitled 'Yorkshire Days' begins, tellingly: 'In view of my present cult for Russia and things Russian, . . .' and proceeds to recall her father's business connections with Russia, bringing into her home caviare and cranberries and reindeers' tongues, which tasted 'not only of reindeer,—but of snow-fields and dreaming forests'. The Russians were, of course, 'Bears'. Was her sentimental attachment to bears traceable to an early passion for Russia, or was it the other way round? It is impossible to say. She loved them both for their slow ways, their love of silence and great spaces. Later in *Reminiscences* she gives an account of a dream:

One night soon after the Russian revolution I dreamt I was in a great, ancient forest—what in Russian would be called 'a dreaming wood'. In it was cleared a round space, and the space was crowded with huge bears softly dancing. I somehow knew that I had come to teach them to dance the Grand Chain in the Lancers, a square dance now obsolete. I was not the least afraid, only very glad and proud. I went up and began trying to make them join hands and form a circle. It was no good. I tried and tried, but they only shuffled away, courteously waving their paws, intent on their own mysterious doings. Suddenly I knew that these doings were more wonderful and beautiful than any Grand Chain (as, indeed, they might well be!). It was for me to learn, not to teach. I woke up crying, in an ecstasy of humility.[33]

This paragraph is enormously revealing. With Russia and bears are associated a number of words which have warm emotive force in Harrison's own idiolect: 'softly', 'shuffled', 'paws', 'courteously', 'mysterious', as well as the overtly favourable words, 'glad', 'proud', 'wonderful', 'beautiful', ending with the phrase that more than anything else she wrote captures Harrison's most characteristic, paradoxical pose, 'an ecstasy of humility'. There is something almost servile in her attitudes to those she most respected, especially Gilbert Murray. Was it her Yorkshire loathing of all domination, imperiousness, hybris, pompousness, and affectation that induced such an attitude in her? 'I like to think that we Yorkshire people have another trait in common with the Russians', she wrote. 'The vice we hate above all others is pretentiousness.'[34] She took the bear dream to be a symbol of what Russia meant to her.

And let there be no misunderstanding. It is not 'the Slav soul' that drew me. Not even, indeed, Russian literature. Of course, years before I had read and admired Turgenev

---

[33] *Reminiscences*, 77–8.   [34] Ibid. 13.

and Tolstoy and Dostoevsky, but at least by the two last I was more frightened than allured. I half resented their probing poignancy, and some passages, like the end of the *Idiot* and the scene between Dimitri Karamasov and Grushenka, seemed to me in their poignancy to pass the limit of the permissible in art. They hurt too badly and too inwardly. No, it was not these portentous things that laid a spell upon me. It was just the Russian language. If I could have my life over again, I would devote it not to art or literature, but to language. Life itself may hit one hard, but always, always one can take sanctuary in language. Language is as much art and as sure a refuge as painting or music or literature. It reflects and interprets and makes bearable life, only it is a wider, because more subconscious, life.[35]

   While she was in Paris she met the literary critic Prince Mirsky, a Russian aristocat and intellectual refugee, whom Leonard Woolf described as 'an unusually courteous and even gentle man, highly intelligent, cultivated, devoted to the arts', while noting that '[h]e had, at the same time, that air of profound pessimism which seemed to be characteristic of intellectual Russians, both within and without the pages of Dostoevsky.[36] He became a frequent visitor at her flat and an ardent admirer. In his memoir of Jane Harrison he tried to analyse the source and nature of Harrison's love for Russia. 'She loved it like a human being,' he wrote, 'in a way that could make, you, if you were a Russian, quite uncomfortable.' The reasons for this love were complicated. Partly, she believed that Russia, 'alone of all the nations of to-day, was earnestly and seriously intent on building a human society that would be worthy of man and of his reason'. As for the 'probing poignancy' of Russian literature, Mirsky saw her resentment as one of a piece with her loathing of a sick-room and her almost physical fear of all obsessions and insanity. Then there was her intense love of what she regarded as her totem, the Bear ('a shaggy, slothful, wild beast, in all respects like a man, and wishful to walk upright')[37] symbolizing to her the unity of all nature. She loved the Russian Orthodox Church and discerned in it the same elements of primitive religion she so loved. Unlike the Western Church, it respected the value of what Mirsky called the 'Vegetable Universe', and nurtured survivals of the oldest cults in its official theology rather than merely tolerating them.

   But the Russian language held more sway over her than any of this, because language, claimed Mirsky, is not only more subconscious than liter-

[35] Ibid. 78–9.

[36] Leonard Woolf, *Downhill all the Way: an Autobiography of the Years 1919–1939* (London: Hogarth Press, 1967), 24. Leonard Woolf kept up with Mirksy until he returned to Russia in 1931 to become 'entangled in the wheels of an idiotic, barbarous social and political system' and was probably liquidated. Leonard Woolf never saw him again and never heard anything of his fate.

[37] From the preface to *The Book of the Bear*, quoted in D. S. Mirsky, *Jane Ellen Harrison and Russia*, The Jane Harrison Memorial Lecture, No.2 (Cambridge: Heffer and Sons, 1930), 9.

ature, but also 'more unifying, more significative of the unity and reality of the human collective' and 'unlike most of her contemporaries, who hopelessly wallowed in an increasingly exclusive individualism, Jane Harrison was fundamentally social, a fundamental believer in the human group, in the People'.[38]

Mirsky points out that the Russia that drew Harrison was not the Russia of his day, but 'the civilisation of nineteenth-century Russia minus Tsarism', where she discerned a primitive folklore that expressed itself in the Russian language with its 'perfective' and 'imperfective' aspects, and he quotes the last paragraph of her *Aspects, Aorists and the Classical Tripos*:

> Immediately what we get from Russia, is the impulse to live in the living fact rather than outside it, to look to process, *durée*, rather than to achievement. Specially I think we need this in morals. We plume ourselves as moralists and have by more dispassionate critics been dubbed hypocrites. Morality is I think the vice of the perfective; it is the judging of an act by its results. A governing people will always emphasise results. Results can be tabulated, they are the basis of statistics, the stuff of which codes and strong government are made. . . . The Russian stands for the complexity and concreteness of life—felt whole, unanalysed, unjudged.[39]

It was the Russia of her dreams she loved, and as Mirsky discerned in 1930, 'the tabulation of results' was already becoming a Russian obsession. Nevertheless, these words 'open a window into the very heart of Jane Harrison's historic mission—the destruction of the morality on which the mentality of the "governing people" (people of course in the plural) of England was based'. Her turning away from her primitive Greek world to contemporary Russia was no new departure, it was rather her imaginative ability to see amongst the Russians around her those same attitudes she had always valued. Politically she was naïve, and her own comment that she was a 'little Englander with a dash of the Bolshevik' does not bear close examination.

Mirsky was struck, like all who knew her at this stage of her life, by the youthfulness of her intellect, which actually seemed to grow younger as she increased in age. It was as though her own year spirit infused her, rejuvenating her 'not ontogenetically, but phylogenetically' as she was reborn with each succeeding generation. 'For years', he wrote, 'she remained intellectually younger than the youngest of her pupils; younger not in personal experience, but in being reborn with a greater collective experience behind her.'

He saw her as an intellectual revolutionary who 'by the end of her lifework had emancipated herself—and others—from all the *idola* [sacrosanct

---

[38] From the preface to *The Book of the Bear*, 11–12.   [39] Ibid. 16.

ideas] that had presided over her coming into the world.' This she did in her own way as she trod the path from Greek vases through primitive religion to the Russian language. But paradoxically, and Mirsky thought this was at the root of her charm, she nurtured a revolutionary mind within the bounds of Victorian dignity and demeanour:

While her mind was busily destroying the rotting structure of Victorian ideas, while she was conjuring up out of the darkest past the Demons of Sex and Change, welcoming Freud and the Russians, lending a sympathetic ear to Joyce and refusing to say a word of condemnation against the Communist Revolution, her manners, her bearing, her talk, preserved the dignity and the delicacy of a more aristocratic and disciplined age. Her tastes remained Victorian, or even more disciplined and severe than anything that can be called by that name.[40]

In this respect she resembled the Russian revolutionaries born in aristocratic families who were never able to throw off their aristocratic habits.

All this while she had not totally given up her scholarly interest in classics, though the effort of putting her mind to it again 'stupefied' her, and made her homesick for the old days of learning 'when we talked of these really important things'.[41] She wrote the 'Greek Mythology and Religion' section of *The Year's Work in Classical Studies* in both 1915 and 1917, and an article on John the Baptist for the *Classical Review*.

The year of 1914 had seen the publication of the first volume of A. B. Cooks's *Zeus*. Harrison praised it in *The Year's Work in Classical Studies* (1915) on three counts: first, for its monumental learning; second, for its fearless, imaginative, and alert speculation; third for its 'epoch-making' inauguration of new directions in Greek religion. It was exactly twenty-five years since the publication of the first edition of the *Golden Bough*, a quarter century that had seen the adoption of the comparative method in the study of religion, the discovery of Minoan Crete, and the elucidation of Minoan religion. She suggests in her review that perhaps *ritual* had been over-emphasized, with its 'Mana, magic, double axes, horns of consecration, wild bulls [and] wood-peckers'; 'obscure sanctities' rather than 'anthropomorphic divinities and theology'. This is a major concession from one who had been totally absorbed in ritual, and had had no time for the Olympian gods. She goes further. Two dominant factors in religion had emerged: the King-god and initiation ceremonies, and an understanding of these had resulted in pro-foundly new thinking on Greek religion and literature, but A. B. Cook broke new ground by extending his attention northward from the primitive,

---

[40] Ibid. 6.   [41] JEH to GM [757], 22 Aug. 1917.

Mediterranean stratum of religion to the Indo-European, and upward from the sanctities of the earth to the gods of the sky. 'To one who . . . has long tarried perforce among the dead, among ghosts and *Keres* and field magic[42] and ancestor worship, Mr Cook's *Zeus*, with its sky and sunlight and dew and rain, is like the dawn of an Easter Day.'[43]

A. B. Cook, she observes, is a keen controversialist, but his monumental book on Zeus was written with such grace that it left her with the sense of Cambridge as a 'place where even scholars may dwell together in unity'.

This is a charming and generous tribute. Was it because Cook was a personal friend and was always kind to her? It was Cook she turned to for help with philology (though she had complained, 'he does not even care what a word means as long as he gets the silly form right').[44] Although his interest in Greek religion had much in common with that of Harrison and Murray, his Christian commitment left him at odds with both Harrison's and Murray's notion of what constituted 'real' religion. In spite of Harrison's statement that he was a controversialist, he had always sought to distance himself from the rancour that had characterized academic life in Cambridge during the previous decade, though he had been prepared to defend Harrison when her views had been attacked by Ridgeway. Her descriptions of him display the affectionate laughter she reserved for those she cared about. (He had, for example, helped her over her Victorian reluctance to discuss her views on the phallus: 'It is highly speculative besides being "obscene" but ABC stands by me. He hesitated as to whether it was publishable & then with a light in his eye said "Every work of the Lord of all life is good". I am not sure that I should go quite so far.')[45]

His evangelical convictions unnerved her. When she had been recuperating from surgery he and Cornford had come to see her to go over some proofs belonging to Cornford. She wrote to Murray on that occasion of how he had looked at her 'with a strange light in his eye as tho the Lord were chastening me & might even lead me to himself—I am rather thankful when he is safe out & nothing said about the Lord Jesus. Mrs ABC begins about the Lord Jesus *at once* while she is taking off her gloves. I respect her & despise ABC.'[46]

She didn't really 'despise' him at all. In many respects they were close colleagues and friends. Perhaps in 1915 her reflection on the similarities between

---

[42]   Walter Leaf coined this term for the religion of the conquered, the tillers of the soil.
[43]   'Greek Religion and Mythology', *The Year's Work in Classical Studies*, 10 (1915), 72.
[44]   JEH to GM [574], 12 Aug. 1912.   [45]   JEH to GM [524], 25 Oct. 1911.
[46]   JEH to GM [516 (2)], n.d.

academic strife and the things that lead to war had led her to a new appreciation of Cook's gentle temper.

Her infamous article entitled 'The Head of John Baptist' [sic][47] marks the culmination of her creative application of ritual theory to classics, and stands as an example of how ritual theory, tenaciously held and applied without respect for context, can lead to absurdity. She sees in the story of the death of John the Baptist[48] an instance of a widespread process, 'the legend of a historical personage cast in the mould of a primitive ritual'. The story is, she claims, *mutatis mutandis*, the same ritual dance as is found in the story of Agave and Pentheus, the dance of the New Year with the head of the Old Year, past and slain. Never mind that in the biblical story there is no ritual dance *with* the head, but rather, Salome's dancing evokes a rash promise from King Herod to give her whatever she desires; she appeals to an eleventh-century manuscript where the Devil is made to say to Christ that the head was given to Salome *for* the dance. Further comparisons with Adonis, Osiris, and Orpheus, together with their medieval analogues are brought in as evidence. A connection with the year-daemon is forged by the observation that John the Baptist's feast day falls in midsummer, six months from the nativity feast of the one whose way he prepared. His declaration, 'I must increase, but he must decrease'[49] may then be taken as a reference to the length of the solar day. Further parallels include the Russian marionnette play known as the *Vertep*, the English boar's head at Christmas, and even John Keats's poem *Isabella and the Pot of Basil*. She concludes that John the Baptist is a solstice-saint, the severed head becomes the vehicle of magic, and the reference to Herod's birthday reminds us, 'Le roi est mort, vive le roi!' Interpreted this way, 'the loathsome story of the Head and the dance is redeemed at once from its squalour of amorous license and dressed in a new ritual dignity'.

The article drew the criticism it deserved. The following issue of the *Classical Review* printed as its leading article a spirited rebuttal by the Provost of King's College in which he called her article 'amazing . . . confused and confusing', and in its use of texts 'grossly misleading'. Finally he accused her of careless thought, exaggeration of resemblances, ignoring of differences, and falsification of evidence, providing justification to those who denied comparative mythology the name of science. As a science only in the making, he believed that to teach it to students was to do them a gross disservice.

She was furious. She wrote to the *Classical Review* retracting some

---

[47] 'The Head of John Baptist', *Classical Review*, 30/8, (1916), 216–19.
[48] Matthew 14: 1–12; Mark 6: 17–29.   [49] John 3: 30.

inaccurate statements but remaining unmoved as far as her main contention was concerned. As for his remarks about the dangers of teaching comparative mythology, she responded, 'To me the keenest joys of science—as of sport—are always perilous, and I hope to die commending these perilous joys to a generation better equipped, and I trust more valorous, than my own'.[50] She immediately wrote to Murray, pleading with him to respond also on her behalf. Murray, however, sought not so much to support her as to mediate. In a letter to the *Classical Review*, while defending her interpretation of the Greek passages she had quoted, he concedes that in the article she had made mistakes. However, he suggests that the Provost had misunderstood the main thrust of her argument, taking it to suggest that John the Baptist was a year-daemon and not a historical person, and that, in the Provost's words, 'there were love-passages between Herodias' daughter and St John (on her side only) and that when she was repulsed . . . she demanded John's head out of spite'. Against this Murray maintains that it would never have occurred to him that any student of mythology would interpret Harrison's argument in this way, but that he understood her to mean that the historical story of John the Baptist became fused in legend with motifs frequently found in the myths of the year-daemon. Conciliatory to a fault, he expresses the view that should the evidence point to the conclusion that the Gospel story is in fact derived from the year-myth, no scholar should be debarred from saying so. But Harrison's point had simply been that 'John's death may have been put on Herod's birthday for a mythological reason, because in these stories the King is apt to die on the birthday of an enemy King'. Finally, he responds to the Provost's ending polemics about comparative mythologists with the ironic suggestion that they might have fallen into some shorthand language of their own which was liable to be misinterpreted by outsiders. If that was so, he acknowledged that they ought to be more careful.[51] It could not have been better put. And the caution was well-advised.

Harrison's review article 'Greek Religion and Mythology' in *The Year's Work in Classical Studies* for 1917[52] reads like a swansong. Whether or not she sensed that this would be her last article on a classical subject (she was still to write three more books on other topics), this review article elegantly, and without rancour, situates her own work within the current state of play in the discipline, and carefully restates her theory of the *eniautos-daimon* in a way designed to prevent the kind of misunderstanding that had occurred

[50] *Classical Review* 31/2 (1917), 63.   [51] Ibid. 63–4.

[52] 'Greek Religion and Mythology', *The Year's Work in Classical Studies*, 12 (1917), 79–101.

over *John Baptist*. She reviews favourably Rendel Harris's *The Ascent of Olympus*,[53] a title which she calls a misnomer, since Harris stays firmly on the bottom rung of the ladder as he links the Greek gods and spirits to the more primitive sanctities of animal and plant, especially plant. She admires the illustrations from old herbals, which 'give back to the mythologists the Herb-garden they had lost', linking the myths to the sacred orchard-garden of magic and medicine. Secondly, she reviews Walter Leaf's *Homer and History*, trembling 'lest he was about to play Herod to my own bantling, the Eniautos-Daimon, swaddled as he undeniably is in solar affinities'. She could relax again, for 'Dr Leaf is one of those rare combatants who take the trouble to understand the enemy's position before they proceed to demolish it' and he 'spared the divine babe, has seen that though anonymous he was not abstract, and has assigned him his due place as a factor in "the curiously composite faith of historic Hellas."' Leaf assigned the Olympian and chthonic forms of worship to the invading 'Achaeans' and conquered 'Pelasgians' respectively, understanding in both cases that the religion mirrors the experience of the worshipper.[54] She is less favourably disposed towards the work of her younger colleague and friend of her London years, Eugénie (Sellers) Strong, *Apotheosis and After-Life*,[55] which, though it deals mostly with Roman religion, touches on Greek in its section on Orpheus. Eugénie Strong linked (with approval) a resurgence in interest in Roman studies to British imperialism of the war years. 'It may be war prejudice—Mrs. Strong's enthusiasm is genuine and eloquent—but, somehow, just now, the figure of an Emperor "who will direct the human race to temporal felicity in accordance with the teaching of philosophy," even if Dante dreamt it, leaves us cold—nay, even inspires a certain misgiving. With all his faults, we prefer old father Zeus.'[56] (When this was published she confessed to being 'nasty and cattish' to Mrs Strong, but 'never did a book so stink in my nostrils'.)[57] As well as noting these three major publications, she takes note of lesser publications of 1916, including her own *John Baptist* and its reviews. In

---

[53] Rendel Harris, *The Ascent of Olympus* (Manchester: Manchester University Press), 1917.

[54] Sooner or later someone was bound to come out with this neat duality of worship and worshippers, but it has since been rejected. The ethnographic origins of the Greek people are unfortunately not so clear cut, and the decipherment of the Cretan script Linear B in 1953, revealing the names of Olympian gods in bronze-age Greece has further refuted the theory. It is to her credit that Harrison herself resisted the temptation to assign the different layers of cult in this way. It may have been for temperamental reasons that she preferred to keep the outlines blurry; in the event she has turned out to be right.

[55] Eugénie Sellers Strong, *Apotheosis and After-Life: Three Lectures on Certain Phases of Art and Religion in the Roman Empire* (London: Constable, 1915).

[56] 'Greek Religion and Mythology' (1917), 92.   [57] JEH to GM [764], 17 Feb. 1918.

summarizing the controversy she manages to articulate the clearest statement of her *eniautos-daimon* theory yet. The passage is so central to her distinctive view of Greek religion that it is worth quoting in full:

Prof. Ridgeway disposes of both the Eniautos-Daimon and John Barleycorn himself
by calling them 'abstract.' John Barley-corn he might perhaps be reconciled with
should he prove to be the lusty ghost of some bygone rollicking taverner, but with
the Eniautos-Daimon never. It has puzzled some of us why to Prof. Ridgeway a ghost
is always concrete, but in the narrow space of this chronicle I will not attempt to cross
swords (or is it bludgeons?) with my protagonist. My editor and my readers will
pardon me, I am sure, if instead I offer an explanation, and indeed something of an
apology, to two other most just and generous critics. Dr. Marett, quite content with
John Barley-corn, is a little uncomfortable with the Eniautos-Daimon, and feels that
he is 'something of a *philosopheme*, and smacks more of Cambridge than of Athens.'
I adore John Barely-corn—he is seasonal and periodic and daemonic, to my heart's
content—but may I remind Mr Marett that I was, as it happened, trying to make
a small contribution to science, not trolling out a folk-song. Therefore I invented a
class-name. As Mr Marett in his breezy, trenchant way says, 'The Eniautos-Daimon is
in another class—a class by himself.' My mistake has been—I see it plainly now—that
I did not clearly say at the outset, *I am using a new class-name, because I am grouping
together a new set of qualities which characterise a particular stage in divine development.*
I am not asserting the existence of a new false god.

I offer this apology especially to Mr Cook; he laments[58] that Prof. Murray should
not be 'content to speak of Dionysos with no new-fangled appellative' as the Greeks
spoke of him. 'New-fangled' is enough to rouse the demon in the meekest stylist, but
I think I see Mr Cook's point and thank him for a needed warning. As an expert
mythologist, he knows the magic in names and how easy it is to juggle with them; he
fears that a new generation getting up *Themis* for examination will carry away the
impression—never dreamt of by the writer—that there existed among the Greeks
the definite cult of a false god called Eniautos-Daimon. That would be indeed
lamentable and misleading. It might be safer to print the name without capitals.
I used capitals instinctively, not to turn a class-name into a proper name, but for pic-
turesque emphasis—to redeem my 'new-fangled', but I think necessary, 'appellation'
from its class-name dreariness. That the science of mythology can get on without a
class-name for the *periodic* stage in a daimon development, I do not believe. Year-spirit
is not wide enough; *eniautos* includes other periods. How the idea of the periodic
daimon grew up out of the festival repeated, I tried to show, at, I fear, tedious length,
in my *Art and Ritual*.

She had never before explained that her *eniautos-daimon* was not a new
spirit, but a *class-name*, expressing a stage in the development of the *daimon*.

---

[58] She notes at this point that Cook had suggested *eniausios* for *eniautos* (adjective for noun),
which would at least have made the phrase grammatical Greek. Inexplicably, she rejects his suggestion as 'less suggestive'.

Even A. B. Cook, with whom she had discussed her work[59] had not grasped this essential point. It took the excesses of her *John Baptist* article to make clear to Murray the confusion that surrounded her theory. In the light of this explanation of the *eniautos-daimon, John Baptist* is certainly less shocking. All she had meant to do was to show a pattern (invalid, maybe) in the workings of the mythological mind, one which later generations superimposed on the (historical, maybe) narrative of Salome's (ritual, maybe) dance.

She had heeded Murray's warning to be more careful. It is interesting that in this same article she applies to Rendel Harris the lesson she learned so painfully over *John Baptist*, the careful use of the 'desiccated' little verb 'is'. 'Dionysos is the ivy', Rendel Harris had written. 'Will Dr Rendel Harris pardon us', she responded, 'if we say that what he really means is, "the ivy was the one and perhaps the most primitive of the sanctities about which the complex conception we label *Dionysos* crystallized". Clumsy, but perhaps nearer the truth.' 'Words-of-one-syllableness' has its dangers.

---

[59] 'Greek Religion and Mythology' (1917), 80.

13. *Via crucis, via lucis*: Cambridge, France, and London 1916–1928

JANE HARRISON came back to Newnham in the middle of June 1916, fluent in Russian and with little reason to stay in Paris. Moutier, her 'magician doctor' had, himself, died of a heart attack looking after the wounded at the front. 'I'm afraid a great deal dies with him' was her terse comment. It was a sad homecoming. May Verrall was dying, and Harrison found her friend much iller than she had expected. It was a strange situation. For many years May had been interested in extra-sensory phenomena and was a committed member of the Society for Psychical Research which had been founded in 1882, making various contributions to the Proceedings of the society. When Murray had stayed with them on his first visit to Newnham in 1903 they had turned tables, and on other occasions had experimented with 'automatic writing'. After that Murray had engaged in literally hundreds of experiments, mostly of 'thought-transference', holding sessions at his home at 82 Woodstock Road, Oxford. In 1915 Murray became president of the society. May had been particularly interested in after-death experiences, and at the time of Harrison's surgery had been ready at her bedside to study the effects of recovery from ether. She had said that she looked forward to dying because she longed to find out what lay in worlds beyond. In the summer of 1916, when the spectre of death was real around her, she still seemed to welcome the prospect, with the expectation of reunion with her husband Arthur, who had died in 1912. Now she believed the end was soon to be upon her, and Harrison dared not leave her side.

'Here I am waiting for my known friend to die, & there you are waiting for an unknown kinsman to come into the world—what a queer world it is seen thro' one's ageing eyes, the race pushing on & the individual thrown off the wheel. What does it all mean?', Harrison wrote to Murray, who was awaiting the birth of a grandchild.[1] 'I think it is so hideous that the other life only

---

[1] JEH to GM [739], 16 June 1916. The grandchild was Philip Toynbee.

belongs to the individual—the bit of us that has to die that is spun off by the race-wheel', she had written to him on another occasion.[2] Two weeks later she reported that there was no change in May, who hung on the borderline of consciousness; there was no way of knowing how long she would go on. In spite of their close friendship Harrison had no sympathy for psychical research. All she could think of was how different things would be once May was gone. The house in Selwyn Gardens held memories of innumerable evenings of laughter, rich conversation and deep friendship, not only with the Verralls but also with Murray, who regularly stayed with them. Then, when symptoms of heart failure set in she wrote, 'how sad the waiting is, and how dazed one gets. She has wanted death so long one hopes almost for it now.'[3] May died on 2 July.

Cambridge grew increasingly dispiriting. Work went on, but how futile it all seemed! The colleges housed soldiers taking various types of courses. The food was appalling, consisting (in one student's memory at any rate) mainly of semolina and 'strange unidentifiable vegetarian dishes, of which the most revolting was the one known to us as a "mess of lentil pottage"'.[4] The only male undergraduates were those deemed unfit for military service. Newnham continued to take in women students, second-rate people they seemed to Harrison. The lack of scholarship was depressing. 'I contribute the bright modernity!' she laughed, wondering if she dared to hope that the day would come when 'we shall feel again that it is a good & pleasant thing to know Greek'.[5] However, she taught Russian to fifteen pupils, five of them members of staff. And she could still inspire students with her archaeology lectures. One student reading history recalled the first lecture that she attended at Newnham. It was 'one with slides, given by Jane Harrison in one of the rooms in the old Coaching Room Passage [now demolished]. It was on archaeology, and archaeology claimed me as her own for ever. I still go to view digs in which my great-nephew is working and wish I could take an active part in them myself.'[6]

Another Newnham student, M. G. Wallas, comments on a critical aspect of the change that swept Cambridge in the closing years of the war. Noting how easy it is to pile up instances of privation and bad food, she observed a more sinister trend, and one that would certainly have contributed to Jane Harrison's sense of ennui. A sense of strain began to grow between the dons, some of them intensely patriotic, and the students, who reacted

[2] JEH to GM [715], n.d.   [3] JEH to Jessie Stewart, 28 June 1916.
[4] D. C. Booth (Lawe), in Phillips (ed.), *A Newnham Anthology*, 120.
[5] JEH to GM [749], 16 Nov. 1916.
[6] Sister Phyllis, C.S.M.V. (E. P. Merryweather) in Phillips (ed.), *A Newnham Anthology*, 112.

against this fervour. It led to the criticism of authority, which took many different forms and varied in its intellectual and emotional seriousness. Paradoxically, a mild wave of anti-feminism could be felt among the students, perhaps reacting to the extreme feminist position that was prominent at the time. To everyone's astonishment a debate on the motion 'that woman's sphere is in the home' was passed; Wallas believes that this result was motivated by the sheer desire of students to shock the dons.[7] These developments must have disturbed and alienated Harrison.

Her letters of this period become more terse in style, and though they frequently refer to the people in her life, they do not reveal much: Fredegond and Gerald Shove (a conscientious objector whom she felt was harshly treated by the tribunal that examined him); the ascendant Greek scholar J. A. K. Thomson (a cousin to Jessie Stewart), who greatly admired Harrison's work and was beginning to publish his own; Winifred Lamb, whom Ridgeway shut out from his lectures because she was a member of the dissident Union of Democratic Control; various Stracheys, including Lytton, whom she admired for his bucking the trend towards Catholicism. She added to her collection of languages Old Slavonic, learned from a refugee Serb, and Polish ('to get the comparative side of things'),[8] Arabic ('it's good to find one's weak Hebrew verbs coming in useful'),[9] and especially Spanish ('I find Bulls very refreshing after the Bears').[10] Murray had suggested that Spain might hold interesting material on modern religious developments, and she had made plans for a visit in 1919. On the Russian Revolution she commented briefly, 'The Bears revolution had made me so happy—it is the best & biggest thing the War has brought & does justify our faith in them & it is splendid that there has been so little bloodshed.'[11]

If Harrison was discouraged by the change in Cambridge after the war, from the point of view of her students (former and current), she seemed to be in her heyday. Jessie Stewart writes that Harrison's work and college life 'had never been fuller or more appreciated than during her last three years at Cambridge', when her very presence was impressive. The anthropologist Audrey Richards remembered Jane Harrison's presence as she presided at the Literary Society, 'sunk in a large and rather dilapidated armchair and breathing fire'.[12]

She was also made a Justice of the Peace, selected, according to a candid friend, 'just to represent "Arts and Letters" ', with 'only an elegant indolence'

---

[7] M. G. Wallas in Phillips (ed.), *A Newnham Anthology*, 118.
[8] JEH to GM [777 (2)], 19 Apr. 1919.   [9] JEH to GM [779], 16 Oct. 1919.
[10] JEH to GM [756], 18 Mar. 1917.   [11] Stewart, *Harrison*, 176.
[12] Audrey Richards in Phillips (ed.), *A Newnham Anthology*, 132.

expected of her.[13] However, her own account of her experience on the Bench suggests that she took her responsibilities seriously, and no doubt her instinctive sympathy for victims of authoritarianism and officialdom made her a good arbiter. She was pleased to have rescued 'a poor Armenian' from a fine. ('I felt that all consideration was due to any one who could speak Armenian, perhaps the most difficult of all European languages.') He was in trouble over his identity card, 'but when the prefecture asks for the birth-place of your maternal grandfather, what are you to do? . . . The only sound policy is to write in the name of some obscure Yorkshire village. As the official will not be able to read, still less to pronounce it, his official soul will be satisfied.' But the fact remained that the Cambridge she knew and loved was gone.

Hope Mirrlees was at this time still working on a Diploma in Russian from the École des Langues Orientales, and she and Harrison spent from April to June 1919 back at the Hotel de l'Elysée, 'thankful to be out of Cambridge'.[14] Mirrlees received the diploma; Harrison did not bother with the credentials for herself.

A visit to Spain in the Lent term of 1920 brought some of her old spirit back. To Murray she sent a splendid postcard of two bulls resting face to face, on which she noted, 'Not as you might think and fear a bull-fight, they are conscientious objectors.'[15] They took daily Spanish lessons from a sculptor, 'sitting round a brazier in his studio. He is a brilliant irresponsible creature, a typical lordly generous bull, the best Andaluz', who also intro-duced them to Spanish *coplas* (traditional songs), 'wonderfully subtle and poignant'.

Spain 'almost suffocated' her with 'new & wondrous impressions' and made Italy seem 'pale & stale'. 'As to the Cathedral,' she wrote to Jessie Stewart, 'the beauty of it is amazing—one can't speak of it. I thought Chartres the most wonderful thing in the world but Seville is beyond even that & the Spanish cult seems somehow so infinitely more real & believing than anything in France or Italy, but how a people so kindly made the Inqui-sition I can't conceive.'[16] She witnessed the ritual dance of 'Los Seises' ('The Sixes'), which had been performed in Serville for at least five hundred years. Originally six (later ten) altar boys danced to celebrate the joy of the Eucharist. This ritual, performed before the altar, moved her 'as no sermon, no hymn, no picture, no poem has ever moved me'. The fading light, the

[13] Harrison, *Reminiscences*, 31. The following descriptions of her work as a JP are taken from pp. 31–5.

[14] JEH to Jessie Stewart, 31 May 1919.   [15] JEH to GM [783], Jan. 1920.

[16] JEH to JS, 23 Jan. 1920.

wondrous setting of the high altar and the golden grille, and the plangent sound of the singing which accompanied the ritual dance and procession with vestments and lights and banners combined to create an ecstatic experience. What also thrilled her was the raw paganism shining through the Roman Catholic veneer, of the prayer for light and healing addressed to the setting sun, of the stiff and decorous dance, its origin *'perdue dans la nuit des temps'* ('lost in the night of time'), a survival, she conjectured, of the dances of the Kouretes of Crete to the Mother and Son. 'Great Pan, indeed, is dead—his ghost still dances.'[17]

The experience rekindled her old passions and an interest in modern religious developments, which she finally wrote up in her *Reminiscences*:

The ritual dance is all but dead, but the ritual drama, the death and the resurrection of the Year-Spirit, still goes on. I realised this when I first heard Mass celebrated according to the Russian, that is substantially the Greek rite. There you have the real enacting of a mystery—the mystery of the death and resurrection of the Year-Spirit which preceded drama. It is hidden, out of sight; the priest comes out from behind the golden gate to announce the accomplishment. It is the coming out of the Messenger in a Greek play to announce the Death and the Resurrection. The Roman Church has sadly marred its mystery. The rite of consecration is performed in public before the altar and loses thereby half its significance.

I mention these ritual dances, this ritual drama, this bridge between art and life, because it is things like these that I was all my life blindly seeking. A thing has little charm for me unless it has on it the patina of age. Great things in literature, Greek plays, for example, I most enjoy when behind their bright splendours I see moving darker and older shapes. That must be my *apologia pro vita mea*.[18]

The visit to Spain was cut short suddenly when Hope Mirrlees fell ill. Of the details of the illness Harrison mentions only that she herself had to be inoculated for typhoid: was this what Mirrlees had? They continued to stay in the monastery at Seville with Harrison nursing Mirrlees night and day, but she grew worse and her parents were sent for. It was with great relief that she wrote on 24 February that the parents had arrived and that the danger of pneumonia was past. They moved to a comfortable hotel (with hot baths!) and by 6 March Hope was ready to travel home via Madrid.

Even the truncated visit was enough for Harrison to gather the material she wanted on bullfights, which she compared with Cretan bull festivals in a lecture at the Classical Association meeting in Cambridge in August. She had also mastered Spanish sufficiently to teach another language at Newnham. She was also ready to write her *Epilegomena to the Study of Greek Religion*.

---

[17] *Reminiscences*, 84.   [18] Ibid. 86–7.

Much shorter than *Prolegomena* or *Themis*, *Epilegomena* consists of a summary of all of her work on Greek religion, some of it repeated from her other works, restated in the light of the Freud and Jung she had been reading, and also of the Russian philosopher Vladimir Soloviov. Religion is now defined as the impulse to the life and preservation of the group. The final chapter, however, entitled 'The Religion of Today: Via crucis, via lucis', though adumbrated by her embrace of 'Unanimism' offers new material and differs in tone from anything she had previously published. For the first time one hears the voice of age and world-weariness. It was uncharacteristic of her to recapitulate earlier views; in times of greater energy she would abandon a theory once it was published and be off on the scent of some new trail. Now, perhaps conscious of her three-score years and ten, she produced a synthesis. The first chapter, 'Primitive Ritual' is subtitled with the Orphic saying 'ἔφυγον κακόν, εὗρον ἄμεινον' ('I have fled the evil, I have found the better'), and with the recognition that the better is the enemy of the good, she concludes with a plea to the young to be more ascetic.[19] What an ache of experience lies behind such words. Twenty years earlier, when urged by her doctor to cut down on alcohol and tobacco she had expostulated, 'I *hate* asceticism!'[20] Now it seems to her 'a very simple and obvious truth . . . the betterment of life involves asceticism—the expulsion of evil'. Just as in primitive societies tabu is imposed by the group in the interests of the group, so today asceticism is demanded of the individual in the interests of his own spiritual life, 'the setting out of the soul towards a higher value'.[21]

Epilegomena ends with a quotation from a letter of Keats to his sister-in-law, revealing that in preaching asceticism she was still seeking to come to terms with the loneliness of a life without marriage:

Notwithstanding your happiness and your recommendations I hope I shall never marry. Though the most beautiful creature were waiting for me at the end of a journey or walk, though the carpet were of silk, the curtain of the morning clouds, the chairs stuffed with cygnets' down, the food manna, the wine above claret, the windows opening on Winandermere [*sic*], I should not feel—or rather my happiness would not be so fine, as my solitude is sublime.

There, instead of what I have described, there is a sublimity to welcome me home. The roaring of the wind is my wife and the stars through my window-pane are my children. . . . I feel more and more every day, as my imagination strengthens, that I do not live in this world alone, but in a thousand worlds. No sooner am I alone than

[19] JEH to GM [801], n.d.   [20] JEH to GM [164], 8 Nov. 1903.

[21] *Epilegomena to the Study of Greek Religion* (Cambridge: Cambridge University Press, 1921), 38.

shapes of epic greatness are stationed around me and serve my spirit the office which is equivalent to a king's bodyguard.

Keats concludes, 'There is an awful warmth about my heart—like a load of immortality'. 'Yes', she echoes, 'and an awful light about his head.'[22]

Murray congratulated her on a 'wonderful achievement', though not without cavilling at her for underestimating evil, and jibbing at her habit of appealing to the 'very latest fashion' as a test of truth.[23] She had been despondent about *Epilegomena*, feeling that no-one wanted it and that the young no longer seemed to care about truth. Murray's approval restored her confidence.

One of the social changes that resulted from the war was the re-opening of the debate at both Oxford and Cambridge about the status of women. Oxford conferred its first degrees on women in May 1920, eliciting the comment from Harrison: 'I gnash my teeth when I think of all yr Somerville young women preening its in cap & gown—so like Oxford & so low to start after us & get in first!'[24] The debate at Cambridge had raged ever since the foundation of the women's colleges. In 1895[25] Harrison, as a Newnham Associate (one of an elected body of dons and former students) had signed a resolution 'that in the opinion of the Associates of Newnham College, the Senate should be asked to admit women to membership of the University and to University degrees'.[26] The motion to admit women to full membership of the university was put forward in 1920. The issue was a highly emotional one, its opponents citing their views on the place of women in the family, their fears that the experience of collegiate life of the men would be jeopardized by the presence of women at Cambridge, and a variety of other specious arguments. Vigorous lobbying of members of Senate was organized by the women, with Agnes Conway (Horsfield) co-ordinating the campaign. Harrison's view was that 'we have *no* chance. . . . I am sick of strife. Of course if we fail the Commission or Parliament will eventually step in but I hate to get it from the outside. . . . The mischief is all *local*, the country clergy come up thinking it is a foregone conclusion that Cambridge follows Oxford.'[27]

When the vote was taken on 8 December, the motion lost by 291 votes. After Christmas she reflected on it all: 'the old weary struggle about the vote

---

[22] *Epilegomena to the Study of Greek Religion*, 39–40. [23] GM to JEH [802], 30 July 1921.

[24] JEH to GM [789], 6 Aug. 1920.

[25] Jessie Stewart in referring to this incident gives the date as 1897, but that was the date of the Senate vote, not the Newnham resolution. See Stewart, *Harrison*, 184.

[26] Rita McWilliams-Tullberg, *Women at Cambridge: a Men's University, Though of a Mixed Type* (London: Victor Gollancz, 1975), 109–10. [27] JEH to GM [792], n.d.

begins again & all the fierce young disappointed ones come seething back & it is all as you say so "silly" & so small. Of course we shall get it & I think soon, but only now I fear thro' much bitterness, thro' outside compulsion.' 'A. B. Cook, she reported, was 'on the wrong side. St George fighting side by side with the old dragon Ridgeway'. There were consolations, though. 'Rendel Harris came & wrote me a beautiful letter after—reminding one of 1870. Give me a good Quaker for straight feeling.'[28]

The following year, 1921, the matter was voted on again, this time with a second, compromise proposal: to grant titular degrees by diploma to women (i.e. allowing them to put the letters BA after their name) without allowing them to graduate or become members of the university. A student of the time, M. E. Henn, recorded her impressions of the day, of men coming 'in their hundreds, from all corners of the United Kingdom: those aided by sticks and crutches being animated by a passion of anti-feminism in proportion to their years'.[29] While the vote was being held in the Senate house an enormous crowd gathered in the square outside (just as it had in 1897), chanting 'we won't have women'. Reporters described the crowd variously as either 'a howling mob' or 'a group of high-spirited undergraduates'. The voting and counting procedure was slow, and the results were not announced until 8.35 pm. 'Grace I' (to grant the women everything except full membership of the university) was counted first, and was defeated with 694 votes in favour, 908 against; 'Grace II' was then put forward (to grant the women titular degrees) and that passed, 1012 in favour, 370 against. When the results were announced, the mob, roused to frenzy reputedly by 'a mysterious grey haired clergyman', was incited to take the news to Newnham. They surged up Newnham Walk, seized on a long-handled, four-wheeled trolley which the porters used for coal, and used it as a battering ram to smash down the Clough Memorial Gates. The proctors took 'prompt and drastic action', forbidding anyone to leave the college while junior proctors and police 'scuttled from bush to bush while the Senior Proctor came and went inside the College with impressive speed and awful solemnity'

Next day the University was steeped in gloom and guilt, to an extent I imagine seen neither before nor since. Apart from the official and collective apolity of the University, Miss [Blanche Athena] Clough[30] was inundated with contrite statements from every conceivable group of undergraduates, athletic and otherwise. Certainly the

---

[28] JEH to GM [797], n.d.   [29] M. E. Henn in Phillips (ed.), *A Newnham Anthology*, 150.
[30] Principal of Newnham, 1920–3, niece of Anne Jemima Clough, and cousin of Florence Nightingale and Barbara Bodichon.

captain of the University rugger team rose to unprecedented heights of oratory in his plea for contributions to the fund to make good the damage and wipe out the stain.

So the gates were repaired and the hubbub died down—but the women of Newnham and Girton had to wait another twenty-six years before the Senate decreed in 1947 that they be given in person the degrees they had earned.[31]

. . . and until 1998 till degrees were granted retroactively to students who had been at Cambridge prior to 1948.

Harrison, at the age of 70, did not share the exhilaration of the students and could see the wider implications for Cambridge; 'It was comforting to get yr letter', she wrote to Murray.

It has been all so disgusting. I stood by & saw those young wild beasts break down the beautiful gates. I am glad tho that the other rightminded undergraduates have been really nice as you wld see in the papers. They are apologizing & raising a fund. Of course we refused any money from the guilty ones.

We go straight now to the Commission & by the end of Dec. we shall know. We hope that they will give us much more than the compromise scheme. . . . What outsiders seem unable to see is that unless we get membership *quickly* Newnham & Girton are doomed & parents naturally will not send their girls to Cambridge to be looked down on & even worse the best young women will not come here as lecturers. The position is too galling—we older ones have suffered enough but we were brought up to it—the young ones simply won't stand it. We have waited 50 years & the University hasn't done it. Parliament must. Already the pick of scholarship students some Head Mistresses tell us have chosen Oxford—small wonder—we are in real danger & the smashing of gates is a trifle to this . . .

No. Alas there is nothing that virtuous Oxford can do except pity us. FMC says he feels it his obvious duty to strangle his new born son as belonging to a sex unfit for civilized life![32]

The implications of the vote denying membership of the university to women were brought home to her personally when it affected the eligibility of Cambridge women for studentships at the British School at Athens. Women had first been admitted as students as early as 1890, but were not permitted to participate in excavation or to reside at the School, nor were they eligible for studentships until, in 1910, Newnham student Margaret Hardie was awarded a grant to work with William Ramsay in Anatolia. Two years later the committee reworded its criteria to restrict studentships to 'members of the University'. Perceiving that the new wording excluded women, Harrison had protested vigorously, and after a long debate won

---

[31] Henn in Phillips (ed.), *A Newnham Anthology*, 150–1.   [32] JEH to GM [794], n.d.

something of a compromise when the wording was adjusted to read 'while the Studentship was originally founded for members of the University, there is nothing on the side of the School to bar the admission of women, if the University in the exercise of its discretion thinks fit to interpret the offer in the wide sense.' Now on February 8 1922 a notice in the *University Reporter* stipulated that 'the student so nominated shld be either a duly qualified member of the University or a duly qualified student of Girton or Newnham, *preference being given to a duly qualified member of the University*' (italics hers). Now, Oxford women were preferred to Cambridge. She urged Murray to write to *The Times*.[33]

To add to her sense of just how the glory had departed from Cambridge came the 'praelections' or public lectures for a Chair, to fill the position of the Regius Professor of Greek after the death of Henry Jackson. With Murray as Oxford's counterpart she had a dream of what life might be like if someone like him were to be elected at Cambridge. The only candidate who would have satisfied her was Francis Cornford. However, she knew he had little chance. Of the other candidates: 'The field is a large but not a strong one. The old Monster[34] is in—it is absurd. . . . R. G. Bury is hopelessly dull. Edwards negligible. Edmonds I believe a learned scholar but his English— Lord! Glover just not first rate. Nobody *quite* first rate'[35] and the following a few weeks later, after the election of Pearson had been announced,

We are recovering from praelections or as they are now called Expositions. I am so relieved that we escaped Sheppard. I dread the actor-manager in Classics. Also I think he is barely sane. Pearson is quiet & kind & 'unexceptionable'. FMC gave a beautiful sermon quite over their heads—the row of old cabmen who were electors looked bothered.

It looks as if this wld be my last year in Cambridge. I retire forcibly the year after & I think it is better not to wait till one is hoofed out. Old Cambridge is gone. I felt that so at the praelections. . . . Write sometimes please.[36]

Leaving Cambridge meant saying goodbye to all that had made life rich and meaningful, and it was with 'measureless regret'[37] that she went. Her plans were to take a flat with Hope Mirrlees in Paris. Her terse 'Write sometimes please' to Murray indicates the degree to which she feared that this move would involve an irrevocable break with her dearest friends. Mirrlees

[33] JEH to GM [807], 19 Mar. 1922. For more information on the position of women at The British School at Athens see David Gill, 'The Passion of Hazard: Women at The British School at Athens before The First World War', *Annual of The British School at Athens, 2002* (forthcoming).

[34] William Ridgeway.   [35] JEH to GM [794], n.d.

[36] JEH to GM [796], n.d.   [37] *Reminiscences*, 90.

had no love for Murray.[38] Her one comfort was the 'flourishing little Russian school' she would leave to the university.[39]

On hearing of Harrison's plans to retire Victoria Buxton (de Bunsen) poured her heart out in a succinct but expressive letter:

To think you are going away from N.C. is very desolating. You *are* it—to me. And I do wish it was to be London, not far-off Paris. Still perhaps you will be able to do more there, there are greater possibilities, & I wonder what language it will be next?

Oh Jane it is hard to tell you what you were to so many of us. To me above all, surely, those 20 years ago. Each lot of students must have said the same but I cannot believe anybody ever realised it as I did & as I have all thro' the years.

You flashed into my world like some new planet. You stood for all the magic & mystery of the unknown & you lured us on to the quest, though you gave us no clue to it. You were very disturbing, but that was what we wanted. You never posed as an *authority*, as omniscient like most teachers do. You taught us the thrill & passion of intellectual things, the thrill that could be even stronger & *more* constraining than being in love! You *did* pull down our idols—you often made us afraid. I did not know *where* you were leading me. But oh how I blessed you. What sparks you struck out of our dull clay—I'd better not go on—this is only in answer to yours. Nobody but you makes me long & long for creative power of pen.

Yours ever, V.[40]

Meanwhile, Harrison was disastrously prevailed upon by Hope Mirrlees to make a bonfire of all the letters and papers she had saved over the years. These included not only all the correspondence she had received from Gilbert Murray, but also letters from Burne-Jones and others of her distinguished London friends. Perhaps Mirrlees's motive was simply to be unencumbered, but there lurks behind this event a more disturbing possibility, also indicated by Mirrlees's later behaviour in regard to Harrison: the desire to make a clean break with her past life and to embark on a new one where she, Hope Mirrlees, would be the central figure. Harrison also sold her Steer painting of the Yachts and a Conder which she had bought, like the Steer, on the advice of D. S. MacColl.

Harrison left Newnham in the summer of 1922. Her friends, led by Jessie Stewart, considered how best to pay her tribute. Part of their motivation was a genuine concern for her financial support. She continued to draw the private annuity she had had all her life from her mother's bequest, but that amounted to about £300 a year. Her pension from Newnham would amount

---

[38] JEH to GM [804], 12 Feb. 1922.   [39] JEH to GM [806], n.d.

[40] Victoria Buxton to JEH, 25 May 1922.

to no more than £50 a year. There was the possibility of a government pension, for which a person had to be nominated, and Agnes Conway took it upon herself to approach Murray to sponsor her application. In addition to this Agnes Conway spearheaded an approach to Harrison's many colleagues and friends to raise a financial gift. The signatories to her letter were Blanche Athena Clough, Arthur B. Cook, Francis Cornford, Francis Darwin, Sir Arthur Evans, James Frazer, Walter Leaf, D. S. MacColl, Gilbert Murray, Eleanor Mildred Sidgwick, and Katharine Stephen. They raised £325.

However, Harrison got wind of the scheme through a careless remark of Dörpfeld in a letter to her, and the thought of it made her 'go hot and cold with nervousness'. 'What are they up to at Cambridge?' she demanded of Murray. The university had let her retirement pass without recognition, although A. B. Cook had thought they ought to have done something for her. 'So like the University of Cambridge, isn't it?' she remarked bitterly. She was understandably embarrassed at the idea of the Murrays being asked to contribute:

If they write to you—they may have done so already—will you swear to give only 2/6—just that yr blessed name may appear. You will probably not escape as you are deeply tarred with the Eniautos-Daimon brush. No one ought to have money collected for them now-a-days who isn't a starving bear or even a starving Prussian eagle, & I am as rich as a Jew.[41]

Particularly embarrassing was the fact that she had just written to Lady Mary to ask permission to sell the lace shawl Mary had given her so that she could donate the money to an appeal for the 'Russian intellectuals'. 'The appeal is heart-rending & I have no money & no valuables & I long to help.'[42] She especially could not bear the thought of the Murrays giving money to her, 'because I know it goes all of it to good things & I am really a bad lot for in the depths of my heart I know I care for nothing except roots and daimons—about 3 people & a whole forest full of bears.'[43]

All the same, the fund went ahead. In 1923 Agnes Conway travelled to Paris with the gift and a list of donors inscribed in a white vellum book, with a fulsome tribute which ended with the words, 'The Year Spirit, born young again every spring, has entered into your soul and taught us all alike to feel ourselves the companions and sharers of your youthfulness. It is our earnest hope that he may long continue to find his embodiment in you and that in Paris no less than at Newnham his annual festival may still find you as young and ardent as we have ever known you.'

[41] JEH to GM [812], 1 Jan. 1923.   [42] JEH to MM, 9 July 1922.
[43] JEH to GM [812], 1 Jan. 1923.

Harrison was genuinely overwhelmed with the generosity of so many friends, and with the associations that came with their memories. Every name meant so much. As they had hoped, the part about the year spirit appealed to her enormously. The gift drew from her a fine letter of gratitude:

Dear Miss Conway

The gift you have brought and the beautiful letter that comes with it, fill me with wonder and delight that so many friends should so warmly remember me, wonder that they should feel me worthy of such remembrance. It is a special joy too, that you brought it yourself, you who are one of the earliest and dearest of my pupils, and in spirit always the youngest of my friends.

You are all much too kind. To accept such wealth might be *hybris* in one poor mortal, but since in your letter you count me kin to the Year Spirit, in his name and with tears in my eyes I accept.

To that Year Spirit I owe all. He brought me Cambridge on the eve of a great awakening. Classics were turning in their sleep. Old men began to see visions, young men to dream dreams. Henry Sidgwick and his band of friends had opened to women the gates of learning—gates still ajar. It was good to be young when Robertson Smith, exiled for heresy, saw the Star in the East and led us to the Bethleham [*sic*] of a newly understood faith. It was good to catch the first gleam of the Golden Bough lighting the dark wood of savage superstition. Who could grow old while Schliemann was digging up Troy? Who could stagnate into middle age when Arthur Evans set sail to his new Atlantis and telegraphed news of the Minotaur from his own labyrinth? We Hellenists were, it may be, a people who sat in darkness, but we had seen a great light. To live through a renouveau is to be perforce re-born.

My College and my Cambridge, Oxford, and London friends I leave with measureless regret. But a voice from within said 'Go.' A College to my mind is best ruled and taught by the young, though I have dreamed of a white-haired voteless consultative senate, influential because impotent. For myself I had long, perhaps too long, lived the strait Academic life with every faculty focussed on the solution of a few problems. I wanted before the end to see things more freely and more widely, and above all to get the new focus of another civilization. Russia, my Land of Heart's Desire, was closed to me: France and America in France have received me with a kindness I can neither repay nor ever forget.

You will smile, kindly I know, when I tell you that my head is already giddy with new impulses and new ideas! You have invoked the Spirit of Spring and it is with me to-day.

I thank you with all my heart.

Jane Ellen Harrison.[44]

Before settling in Paris, Harrison and Mirrlees went for a little tour in Burgundy, and then to Nancy, to attend lectures by Emile Coué (perhaps

---

[44] JEH to Agnes Conway, n.d.

Mirrlees's idea). They had heard him the previous year, after which Harrison had pronounced ' "I am dressing better every day"—that's the sort of fatuity that cheers me up somehow!'[45]

They then found accommodation at the Hotel de Londres, on the Rue Bonaparte, an 'exquisite clean sardine-box'[46] that was 'most unsatisfactory' according to Mirrlees.[47] Their rooms were on the fourth floor; there was no sitting-room and no dining-room, and they were reduced to 'seeking our omelettes, like Lear, in the storm'. There was the added problem of uncertainty whether they could stay on there permanently, as the proprietor preferred temporary guests. For a while it looked as if they would have to return to England; 'space to move and an occasional wash are all that I ask for'. They were rescued in November by Alys Russell, who obtained accommodation for them at the American University Women's Club, where they found themselves by contrast in 'veritable clover', the best bedrooms, room-service breakfast, unlimited hot baths, and admirable cooking 'of the best French kind (touched by American) and more than that a personal care and kindness that goes to one's heart'. Included with all this they were given at no extra cost a beautiful, large sitting-room, 'where I can breathe and work and even think, if the delights of Paris would leave me a free moment'.[48] For all this they paid the equivalent of 6/8d. a day. One wonders if Alys Russell in fact paid the extra cost of the sitting-room.

At the age of 72, in failing health, and heartbroken over the ethos of post-war Cambridge, Jane Harrison was still able to start a new life in France. She made new friends, learned new languages, and published three more books, two of them translations from the Russian. A great stimulus to her creativity was provided by her participation in the *entretiens* at Pontigny in the summers of 1923 and 1924.

Pontigny is a small town in Burgundy, where the Cistercians had built an abbey as part of their massive expansion in the twelfth century. In 1906 the abbey had been bought by the remarkable Paul Desjardins, Professor at the Collège de Sèvres, an intellectual who devoted his life to the promotion of his ideal, a secular spirituality. His idea was to found, on the basis of universal knowledge, a body of new doctrine. He dreamed of an ideal community of intellectuals who would spend their time, not in actual encounter with

---

[45] JEH to GM [805], n.d. Émile Coué was a French psychotherapist (1857–1926), who developed a psychological technique known as 'autosuggestion', best known for his recommendation that a person repeat every morning, 'Every day, in every way, I am getting better and better.' He was immensely popular in England in the 1920s.

[46] Quoted in Stewart, *Harrison*, 189.   [47] Mirrlees's draft biography.

[48] JEH to MM [GM 811], Xmas Day 1922.

one another, but who would work independently towards a common end while enjoying a fellowship in truth and justice.

In 1908, two years after Paul Desjardins had acquired the Abbey, his 8-year-old son was drowned in the millrace. Devastated by the accident, he felt that he could no longer live on the property unless he could find some way to devote it to the public good. Thus it was he established his '*décades*', or ten-day sessions, of disciplined reflection, discussion and exchange of ideas. Each *décade* was devoted to a specific topic of a literary, philosophic, or religious nature, nearly all with profound social significance. About fifty people were present at any one *décade* (thirty-five eminent international personalities, fifteen young people). At meal-times each young person was seated between two eminent ones, and changed place every three days. The mornings were devoted to private contemplation and study, the afternoons to exchange of ideas. In the evenings there was brilliant entertainment: charades, plays, and intellectual games. The *décades* were discontinued during the war, but resumed with fresh vigour afterwards, perhaps as the result of a second tragedy: Desjardins' second son was killed in action in 1915.

It is not clear how Jane Harrison received the invitation from Paul Desjardins to the *entretiens* in the summer of 1923. The April theme for meditation, 'Perpetual Youth', suggests that he had read *Themis*, which was being taught at French universities, or perhaps her name was suggested by Georges Raverat (whose daughter-in-law, Gwen, was a Darwin and cousin to Frances) who was a friend of Desjardins and had been a member of the Council of the 'Society of the Abbey of Pontigny' since 1912. Most probably he had made her acquaintance through both connections.

The Cistercian abbey, 'riding like a long ship over the rolling Burgundian corn-lands' is a monument to how architecture can express a philosophy. Just as the twelfth-century monks had taken a vow of poverty, and spurned elaborate and expensive decoration of their buildings, so they sought to express their love of beauty in proportion and simplicity. To enter one of these abbeys is a moving experience, for the architecture 'speaks'. The stones, even where they have been stripped of their explicitly Christian connotations, still testify to the ascetic lifestyle of the medieval monks; an asceticism of beauty, order, and peace. One of the participants of the 1923 *entretiens* described his impressions of the place:

Pontigny Abbey is situated in a region of poplar trees and winding streams. Grasses wave in the transparent water, swallows come to glance at their reflections, fly away, and come back. The countryside is gentle, without hills but not flat: a slight undulation is enough to hide the horizon. You can stroll comfortably through woods and meadows without ever being bored. But the walkers were absorbed in themselves. During the discussions, each strove to uphold a personal vocabulary to defend his inner world against an assault from other worlds present. At times, the spiritual life seemed to me like a jungle where you had to eat or be eaten. But the discussions begun in cells, continued learnedly in the salon, and pressed *ad absurdum* under the refectory vaults, were concluded in the calmness of nature. There these monks, consecrated to speech, revealed to one another the secret origins of the views which they had just exchanged.[49]

A feature of the grounds of the Abbey at Pontigny was its *charmilles*, or long, straight paths lined by trellised rows of hornbeams. There was a coded way of using the garden. Disappearing into these walks indicated an intention of engaging in a confidential tête-à-tête, which it would have been the height of rudeness to interrupt. You could have drawn a map of the parterre, à la Mme. de Staël, with the labels 'avenue of explanations', 'avenue of reconciliations', etc.

The theme of the *décade* which Harrison attended (23 Aug.–2 Sept. 1923) was '*Le trésor poétique réservé ou de l'intraduisible*'. The central question was 'Is there in the poetry of a people a private treasure, impenetrable to outsiders?' This general topic was broken down into five sections. In the first, some recent translations were compared with great, unfaithful, ones, and then with the text in the original language. Then, secondly, what makes poetry untranslatable? Thirdly, what makes a poet a 'national poet'? Are nations grouped around their national poets like tribes around their totems? Then, fourthly, is it possible that there is an invisible global family of those who find their world enlarged by the poetry of another people? Does the ability of great poetry to 'speak' to people come and go with different generations? Lastly, is not the notion of perfect comprehension itself a mirage? No doubt there have been a number of different Germano—French 'Goethes', Anglo–French 'Shakespeares', Italo–French 'Dantes'. 'This is all to the good! This is what keeps the great classics perpetually young, and us through them. Always seeking—that's the fate of humankind.'[50]

It is easy to see the appeal that all of this would have had for Harrison, though she had her reservations about going, claiming that she never liked Desjardins until she met him in this capacity: 'I thought him heavy & slightly

[49] Alfred Fabre-Luce, 'Les décades de Pontigny' in Anne Heurgon-Desjardins and Paul Desjardins, *Paul Desjardins et les décades de Pontigny: . . . études témoignages et documents inédits* (Paris: Presses universitaires de France, 1964), 173 (translation mine).

[50] See 'Extraits de quelques programmes des entretiens d'été de Pontigny, Août 1923, IIIe Décade: Arts et Lettres', in Heurgon-Desjardins and Desjardins, *Paul Desjardins et les décades de Pontigny*, 330–2 (translation mine).

gaseous, but here he is simply weighty, & always drops something that is worth while.'[51] The disciplined, ascetic, intellectual, free-thinking atmosphere restored for her the environment that she felt Cambridge had lost. The topic for discussion was surely dear to the heart of one who had written with such passion on the aspects of Russian being a key to Russian mentality. The place itself enthralled her:

This is an amazing place, exquisitely beautiful, & the spaciousness & peace are almost inconceivable after Paris where tho' we have a big house, this country mouse always feels like a rat in a trap. We feed in a huge refectory–on delicious food only marred by the fact that a ceaseless flow of converse is expected. I sit at present (we change every 3 days) between the Boche novelist Heinrich Mann who is a dear & very adored Russian philosopher Shestov, so I am content.[52]

Harrison loved the way the *entretiens* were run, with the mornings free to read and write. She loved the combination of freedom and discipline, the courtesy, and, be it said, the attention that was paid to her. She found herself admiring Desjardins for his intellectual strength, and Charles du Bos, who chaired the discussions, for the beautiful way he spoke French. The Frenchman's real passion for ideas was so refreshing after the Englishman's innate contempt. And then there was the stimulus of the other eminent participants, the 'magic' of their personalities. A group photo of this session includes (along with Paul Desjardins and Charles du Bos), Leon Shestov, Edith Wharton, André Maurois, Roger Martin du Gard, Jean Schlumberger, and André Gide.[53] In the midst of all this intellectual ferment Hope Mirrlees apparently staggered the French by remarking, 'Moi, je n'ai pas de vie intérieure!' ('Myself, I have no interior life!'). Perhaps she intended to shock, just as the Newnham students had in their debate on a woman's place, but it is conceivable that she meant it.

Virginia Woolf complained in 1925 about Hope Mirrlees and her writing, 'so full of affectations and precocities, that I lose my temper. But these things are mainly caused by being a spoilt prodigy . . . her father gives her motor cars for her birthday. . . . [S]he seems an odd mixture of rich conventional people, and highly sophisticated French poets and scholars. She can never make up her mind which she prefers.'

[51] JEH to GM [813], 29 Aug. 1923.   [52] Ibid.

[53] The others identified in the picture are: Mlle. H. Nordling, Mlle. Andreani, Walter Berry, Mlle. Jausseran, Boris de Schloezer, Pierre Vienot, Félix Bertaux, Albert-Marie Schmidt, M. Funck-Brentano, M. Andreani, Mlle. Marthe Bossavy, J. Heurgon, Jean Tardieu, Mlle. E. Fontaine, Alfred Fabrelace, Pierre Lancel, Germain d'Hangest, Mme. de Lanux, Mme Cahen, Miss Hope Mirrlees, Mme. Theo Van Rysselberghe, Miss Burns, Jacques de Lacretelle, and a 'Miss Strachey'.

For some time the 'Bloomsbury group' had gossiped innuendo about the nature of the relationship between Harrison and Mirrlees. In 1919 Virginia Woolf had received one of Hope Mirrlees's novels to review, and had written to Clive Bell that the task was even worse than Leonard's eczema, 'as every word will have to be picked over. It's all sapphism so far as I've got—Jane and herself.'[54] At the time of the 1923 *entretiens* Dora Carrington had urged Lytton Strachey to win the confidences of Harrison and Mirrlees, whose 'liaison' interested her. 'I'm sure they are a fascinating couple', she hinted.[55]

These snippets of correspondence raise again the question of the nature of the relationship between Harrison and Mirrlees. Carrington and Woolf both seemed to think that Mirrlees, at least, was a lesbian. Woolf's observation that they 'practically lived together' proves nothing. But Mirrlees certainly did have a 'passion' for Harrison. Was this sexual, and if so, in what sense? Given everything that we know about Harrison, it seems highly improbable that their relationship included physical sex, especially at this stage of Harrison's life, when she was in her seventies. The evidence for Mirrlees's sexuality is more ambiguous. Perhaps she fantasized. Most probable is that she encouraged rumours of this sort—perhaps even initiating them—as she grew addicted to her companionship with Harrison as her own claim to fame. Had it not been for Harrison she would never have gone to Pontigny or met the people she did. And emotionally, Hope's life revolved increasingly around Harrison. This is why she did not like Murray. Her own notes on Harrison's life contain several references to a dependence that seems psychologically unhealthy: 'Jane was amber—one of the life-giving substances. I . . . owe my whole picture of the universe to her, & everything about me that is not ignoble', with the ingenuous addendum '(I wrote this before I became a Catholic)'. In and of themselves these words would not amount to much, but they were accompanied by a behaviour towards Harrison that was possessive. She seems to have fed on the intimacy—whatever its nature—that existed between them. This would certainly have fascinated Carrington.[56]

---

[54] Hope Mirrlees, *Madeleine: One of Love's Jansenists* (London and Glasgow: W. Collins Sons & Co. Ltd, 1919). Mary Beard argues that 'Paris in the early years of the twentieth century was the lesbian capital of the Western world. . . . It was a city whose very name could be a shorthand for sapphism.' However, this proves nothing. It is also true to say that the Bloomsbury group also loved the intellectual climate of Paris, many of them becoming 'quasi-settlers', because of the French attitude to art and artists (*Invention*, 139). See Mary Ann Caws and Sarah Bird Wright, *Bloomsbury and France: Art and Friends* (Oxford: Oxford University Press, 2000), 9.

[55] Dora de Houghton Carrington, *Carrington: Letters and Extracts from Her Diaries*, ed. by David Garnett (London: Jonathan Cape, 1970), 258.

[56] For a thoughtful and well-informed discussion of this issue see Beard, *Invention*, 134–57.

Meanwhile Harrison was longing for Murray's presence at Pontigny, and ruminating on ways to persuade him to come the following year.

> Desjardins has practically promised me that next year we shall have a decade only true religion chiefly mysticism. He will try to get Unamino & Bergson & Shestov & you simply *must* come. I really think it wld do good & be enlightening. They manage the entretiens with marvellous skill. No one feels any mauvaise honte not even me when I expound about holophrases in frog—no easy matter. Everything goes so simply & easily, & yet one feels there are one or two master hands holding the thing together. It is a wonderful experience.

and, lest Lady Mary should raise objections about hygiene: 'So let us settle to meet here yearly—tell Mary the housekeeping is perfect. I don't think even she cld find anything to criticize except that baths are not!'[57]

She was back in England for the winter and realized how accustomed she had become to the standard of living at the American University Women's Club in Paris. She had already admitted to revising her opinion of Americans as a result of this splendid accommodation; now in London in the winter she confessed, 'I am getting quite Parisian & feel that London is a city of dreadful night & oh so cold with no "chauffage centrale" & "confort moderne" '.[58]

The following spring, 1924, Prince Mirsky was pressing her to undertake the translation from Old Russian into English of a seventeenth-century Russian manuscript narrating the persecution of an orthodox Archpriest, Avvakum (or Abbakum). On 24 April she wrote to him, 'How kind of you to try & get me the Abbakum text, but I fear it is difficult' and on 14 May, 'Yes I know full well there is another side to the Russian character but then that is a side that we English & the Germans & French possess too so it does not interest me. It gives me nothing fresh to live by. How kind of you to go on hunting for Avvakum. If you can get a copy from Russia I shall be more than glad to have it.' Then in July, 'I shall be quite alone. Miss Mirrlees is in England. We could get a little work done on Avvakum. I hope to finish it next Monday.'

Linguistically, the translation of *The Life of the Archpriest Avvakum, Written by Himself* is a phenomenal achievement, though it is impossible to know how much is Prince Mirsky and how much Jane Harrison. The story is that of an extraordinary life, a combination of thaumaturgy and unimaginable suffering as Avvakum was persecuted for his religious vocation. The *Life* was considered by Russians to be one of their finest literary works as well as being of great importance historically, chronicling some of the events of the

[57] JEH to GM [813], 29 Aug. 1923.   [58] JEH to GM, postcard n.d.

Russian Church's schism in the seventeenth century. But Dostoevsky had already pronounced: 'I think that if one were to translate a piece such as the narrative of the Archpriest Avvakum, the result would be nonsense; or better, nothing whatever would come of it'.[59] Harrison's *Avvakum* did not sell well; the story is very strange and perhaps Dostoevsky was right (it is certainly a hard read). Nevertheless, the narrative has sufficient interest that two more translations have been attempted since. The translation by Kenneth Brostrom for Michigan Slavic Translations complains about the 'numerous serious errors' and 'quaintly archaic, rather elevated manner' of Harrison's translation. That she attempted the task at all and completed it in so short a time is nothing short of amazing. And, after all, had she not herself been discussing at Pontigny the question of whether the ability of literature to speak to people comes and goes with different generations?

Mirsky paid Harrison a good deal of attention, which she enjoyed: 'My faithful and princely flirt is back & is coming to tea with me Sunday. If that flirt thinks he is going to do nothing but yawn he is a sadly mistaken flirt!'[60] Harrison confessed to Murray that she had lost her heart to a 'Bear Prince. . . . Why did I not meet him 50 years ago when I cld have clamoured to be his Princess?'[61] There seems every likelihood that he reciprocated these feelings.[62]

By November she had started, with Hope Mirrlees, on a second work of translation of a very different order, a small book entitled *The Book of the Bear*, a collection of stories from various countries. She wrote to Mirsky asking for Russian sources. 'I want of course bear stories that have some beauty or significance.'[63]

The Book of the Bear was published by the Nonesuch Press in 1926,[64] with illustrations by Ray Garnett. The stories are all Russian. They are also all inconsequential—imbecile, according to the preface—but that, say the authors, coupled with its dream-like character, is the sign of a true folk-tale.

[59] Quoted in Petrovich Avvakum, *Archpriest Avvakum, the Life Written by Himself: With the Study of V. V. Vinogradov /Translations, Annotations, Commentary, and Historical Introduction by Kenneth N. Brostrom*, Michigan Slavic Translations no. 4 (Ann Arbor: Michigan Slavic Publications c.1979.), p. vii.

[60] JEH to Hope Mirrlees, 19 June 1924.   [61] JEH to GM [814], n.d.

[62] This was told me unequivocally by Jean Pace, daughter of Jessie Stewart, who remembered Harrison and Mirsky.

[63] JEH to Prince Mirsky, 21 Nov. 1924.

[64] Jane Ellen Harrison and Hope Mirrlees, illus. by R. A. Garnett, *The Book of the Bear, Being Twenty-One Tales Newly Translated from the Russian* (London: Nonesuch Press, 1926).

A folk-tale has no moral. That, of course, is why she deemed them to 'have some significance'. By contrast, the epilogue consists of the Old Testament story of Elisha and the bears[65] and is entitled 'To Bad Children'. No comment is made. About the illustrations she had reservations, and wished that Jessie Stewart could have done them, as she had for her cousin Marion Harrison's *Byliny Book* of Russian hero-tales that had been published in 1915.[66] She felt that although the children in the illustrations were pretty in their own way, the Bear never rose to his real majesty. She suspected that the Nonesuch Press had accepted the book because of the illustrations by Ray Garnett, David Garnett being one of the firm. She conceded, however, that 'The Nonesuch do know how to get up a book & space it & print it.'[67]

During these years in Paris, Harrison and Mirrlees had many visitors to their flat. Jessie Stewart came and stayed with them, as did Mirrlees's mother, Lena, recently widowed—a difficult visit, since neither Mirrlees nor Harrison found it easy to get on with someone so restless. More welcome visitors were Leonard and Virginia Woolf. Leonard Woolf recalled that the first time he met Mirsky was in Harrison's flat, and described Harrison on that occasion as 'one of the most civilized persons I have ever known. She was also the most charming, humorous, witty, individual human being. When I knew her she was old and frail physically, but she had a mind which remained eternally young. She liked Mirsky and enjoyed talking to him, and he, I felt, sat at her feet.'[68] Virginia records in her letters a delightful anecdote, which reveals more than anything else of the period what was on Harrison's mind:

> On my way back from Spain I stayed a week in Paris and there met Hope Mirrlees and Jane Harrison. This gallant old lady, very white, hoary, and sublime in a lace mantilla, took my fancy greatly; partly for her superb high thinking agnostic ways, partly for her appearance. 'Alas,' she said, 'you and your sister and perhaps Lytton Strachey are the only ones of the younger generation I can respect. You alone carry on the traditions of our day.' This referred to the miserable defection of Fredegond [Shove] (mass; confession; absolution, and the rest of it.) 'There are thousands of Darwins' I said to cheer her up. 'Thousands of Darwins!' she shrieked, clasping her mittened hands, and raising her eyes to Heaven. 'The Darwins are the blackest traitors of them all! With that name!' she cried, 'that inheritance!' That magnificent record in the past!' 'Surely', I cried, 'our Gwen is secure?' 'Our Gwen,' she replied, 'goes to Church, (if not mass, still Church) every Sunday of her life. Her marriage, of course, may have

[65]   2 Kings 2: 23–4.

[66]   Marion Harrison, *Byliny Book: Hero Tales of Russia* (Cambridge: Heffer and Sons, 1915). 'Byliny' means 'what has been'.

[67]   JEH to Jessie Stewart, 30 Dec. 1926.   [68]   Woolf, *Downhill All the Way*, 26.

17. Jane Harrison, 1928, pastel drawing by Ralph Longstaff, 'hoary and sublime in a lace mantilla' (Virginia Woolf)

weakened her brain. Jacques is, unfortunately, French. A wave of Catholicism has invaded the young Frenchmen. Their children are baptised; their—' Here I stopped her. 'Good God', I said, 'I will never speak to them again! . . . Next week arrived your letter, which was the greatest relief in the world. Gwen is a militant atheist: the world renews itself: there is solid ground beneath my feet. I at once sent word to dear old Jane, who replied, a little inconsistently, 'Thank God'.[69]

Harrison returned to Pontigny in the summer of 1924, despite the fact that Desjardins's avowed intention of a *décade* devoted to the topic of mysticism never materialized, and that Murray did not attend. The first *décade* of 1924 was dedicated to the topic: '*La muse et la grace*', and Harrison gave a paper on 'The Well of Mnemosyne'. Earlier that day Desjardins had reminded the company of the Rule of St Bernard who founded the monastery, and who 'inspired the romance of the Holy Grail'. Du Bos read a passage from Nietzsche on inspiration. But this time she did not enjoy the event as much as the previous year, largely because Desjardins had delegated much of the leadership to Charles du Bos, whom she described as less 'nourri' than Desjardins. She also confessed to a feeling that she had 'sucked that orange' and would not go again. 'The habit of incessant *analyser*-ing palls after a time. Life is so much more than can be analysed.'[70]

She still found time and energy in 1925 to write her *Reminiscences of a Student's Life*, which was published by Leonard and Virginia Woolf at the Hogarth Press. This delightful volume is filled with just what the title promises, reminiscences: anecdotes of a woman looking back on seventy-five years with an eye always for the absurd, the witty, and for meaning in the trivial events of everyday life. Much has already been quoted from its ninety-two pages in this biography. But *Reminiscences* is not an autobiography, and in no way reflects the shape of the life of the woman who wrote it. She pleads deference for omitting any mention of 'the men and women who influenced me most—my real friends' because they were living still. Her Victorian demeanour allowed no reference to the most important episodes in her life, too intimate, too painful to share publicly. There is no mention of the Murrays or the Cornfords or Prince Mirsky to be found. Hope Mirrlees, to be sure, is there, her 'ghostly daughter, dearer than any child after the flesh'.[71] The Jane Harrison of *Reminiscences* comes across as a very different person from the Jane Harrison of the historical record. The wit and light-heartedness are there, but no indication of the periods of desolation and depression that struck her in the 1890s and in the years surrounding the Cornford marriage. The title speaks of a 'student's' life, yet there is no serious mention of her work on Greek religion. Why then did she write the *Reminiscences*? It was certainly not to put on record an account of her life,

[69] Virginia Woolf to Jacques Raverat, 30 July 1923, in *The Letters of Virginia Woolf*, iii. 58.
[70] JEH to Jessie Stewart 16 Sept. 1925.   [71] *Reminiscences* 90.

nor was it because she had any pretensions to 'greatness'. Was it to write a 'counter-account', an expurgated version of her life to supersede any different memories that others might have? Was she afraid of what Hope Mirrlees, with her pretensions, might write of her? Or was it rather a spiritual exercise of rewriting her memories as she prepared to make peace with herself and the world? These questions are explored in the introduction to this biography. She concludes,

At the close of one's reminiscences it is fitting that one should say something as to how life looks at the approach of Death. As to Death, when I was young, personal immortality seemed to me axiomatic. The mere thought of Death made me furious. I was so intensely alive I felt I could defy any one, anything—God, or demon, or Fate herself–to put me out. All that is changed now. If I think of Death at all it is merely as a negation of life, a close, a last and necessary chord. What I dread is disease, that is, bad, disordered life, not Death, and disease, so far, I have escaped. I have no hope whatever of personal immortality, no desire even for a future life. My consciousness began in a very humble fashion with my body; with my body, very quietly, I hope it will end. *Nox est perpetua una dormienda* [We must sleep a never-ending night].[72]

These reflections are followed by her thoughts on marriage and children, family, friendship, and community, which have been quoted elsewhere in this biography. She finishes with some well-edited thoughts on old age:

Old age, believe me, is a good and pleasant thing. It is true you are gently shouldered off the stage, but then you are given such a comfortable front stall as spectator, and, if you have really played your part, you are more than content to sit down and watch. All life has become a thing less strenuous, softer and warmer. You are allowed all sorts of comfortable little physical licences; you may doze through dull lectures, you may go to bed early when you are bored. The young all pay you a sort of tender deference to which you know you have no real claim. Every one is solicitous to help you; it seems the whole world offers you a kind, protecting arm. Life does not cease when you are old, it only suffers a rich change. You go on loving, only your love, instead of a burning, fiery furnace, is the mellow glow of an autumn sun. You even go on falling in love, and for the same foolish reasons—the tone of a voice, the glint of a strangely set eye—only you fall every so gently; and in old age you may even show a man that you like to be with him without his wanting to marry you or thinking you want to marry him.

But then 'old age is lonely.' Not if you follow my example! My friends, men and women, are most of them some twenty years younger than I am . . . And I admit, Fate has been very kind to me.[73]

[72] Ibid. 87. The quotation is from Catullus 5. 6.   [73] Ibid. 89–90.

By 1925, when it became uncertain whether they could continue to stay at the American University Women's Club, and Harrison's health began to deteriorate further, they began to think about returning to England, but not before spending a couple of months in the South of France, staying with friends at Aix-en-Provence and Menton from November to January. From Sainte Maxime-sur-Mer she wrote to Mirsky, who had read a paper to the Heretics Society, 'But oh don't get like Eliot. Under compulsion of Hope I have been reading him but my mind is too stiff & old. Of course I admire his gift of language but I can't understand even the headings of his chapters tho of course I know Miss Weston's work well.'[74] The following May she wrote a poignant letter of condolence to Mirsky on his mother's death: 'I expect you were & always have been thro those last troublous years her mainstay & comfort. That is something to remember in yr great loss. I have always wondered what it was like to have a mother for I sent mine out of the world—but one has to pay the price in losing her.'[75]

On the way back to England they broke their journey at Beaune in Burgundy, 'a lovely little walled town' and visited the famous hospice,

where everything goes on just as when it was first built. It is really the nave of a huge Church—the doors at the East end open into a chapel whre Mass is said & the patients can assist[76] in their beds. Everything down to the smallest cup & basin is renewed on the old models & the 'pharmacie' is still used. You will see [on the postcard] the patients lying in their cabin beds. I did not dare to ask about the sanitation! probably that too still is of the 15th century.[77]

In the spring of 1926 Hope Mirrlees found a 'tiny mousetrap of a house' in London for them at 11 Mecklenburgh Street, so as to be close to the Nonesuch Press who were publishing *The Book of the Bear*.[78] The move, with the need to attend to things like 'carpets and chairs', irked her. On the other hand she discovered, on Murray's recommendation, the Swedish author Selma Lagerlof ('How often have I blessed yr Holy Name for telling me of Selma. I adore her & read her in Swedish. She is really big & unselfconscious & imaginative.')[79] and with Mirrlees started to learn Icelandic in order to read the Icelandic Eddas ('after the Latin tongues it is to me like the joy of bathing in my native sea').[80] She continued, with the help of a new friend, Guy le Strange, to work on Persian. If she could have her life all over again, she maintained, she would devote it to languages.

[74] JEH to Mirsky, 6 Jan. 1926.   [75] JEH to Mirsky, 6 May 1926.
[76] Presumably with the sense of the French *assister*, 'to be present'.
[77] JEH to Ella Lane, 6 May 1925. The letter is in the possession of the author.
[78] JEH to GM [831], n.d.   [79] Ibid.   [80] JEH to Jessie Stewart, 30 Dec. 1926.

She still had the energy to complete revisions for a new edition of *Themis*, which came out later that year. There are not many changes from the first edition, except that Murray found new evidence in Herodotus that added weight to his view of Dionysos as a *daimon*. Harrison wrote a new preface, welcoming the fact that now Walter Leaf incorporated her theory of the 'eniautos-daimon' into his *Homer and History*,[81] and writing a palinode on the Olympians, claiming that

the psychology of Freud has taught me that the full-blown god, the Olympian, has a biological function which could never be adequately filled by the *daimon*. . . . Disciple as I am in this matter of Nietzsche, I ought never to have forgotten that humanity needs not only the intoxication of Dionysos the daimon, but also, and perhaps even more, that 'appeasement of form' which is Apollo the Olympian.[82]

She ends by expressing her intention to re-examine the subject of Orphism. The ten years between the first edition of *Themis* and her leaving Cambridge, during which time she claims (perhaps with some exaggeration) that she 'never opened a Greek book', cleared her mind of the 'old and obsolete' controversies that had surrounded her first venture into Orphic doctrines. Now, and with the experience of Pontigny behind her, and with fresh insight shed by what she calls the 'diffusionist' school,[83] she hoped to devote whatever energies were left to her to the Orphic mysteries and Orphic eschatology. 'Some soundings in these perilous waters I have already made. But for the most part I must set sail in seas as yet for me uncharted. "It may be that the gulfs will wash us down." '[84]

They did. A doctor diagnosed leukaemia. In the summer of 1927 she experienced some kind of attack, and suffered 'many strange and terrible things' which she described to Murray:

Down by the sea at Camber I was smitten with phlebitis, they got me back to London in an ambulance. Think of a Ker in an ambulance! Wasn't it grand! Then at the end of August your Ker went right down to the gates of Hades & there she stayed fluttering to & fro, & it seemed that the gates must clang behind her. But after many long weary weeks with the help of two doctors, two nurses & a lusty masseur of Herculean build, the Younger Erinys dragged her reluctant back to the upper air. And

[81] Walter Leaf, *Homer and History* (London: Macmillan, 1915).

[82] *Themis: A Study of the Social Origins of Greek Religion* (2nd edn., Cambridge: Cambridge University Press, 1927), p. viii.

[83] Those who hold that all or most cultural similarities are due to diffusion, as opposed to those who believe in parallel and independent evolution of cultural patterns (*Oxford English Dictionary*).

[84] *Themis*, p. x.

here I am now in bed, just able to put two feet to the ground if heraldically supported, but to think of standing alone is like some wild dream.

And here comes your birthday book to tell me there are pleasant things in the world—I shall not be able to read it for a long time properly, but I cut a page here and there and catch sight of Ther-like things which fill my inner spirit with laughter and delight.

Thank you for sending it. Come soon yourself.

Yours ever,

K.[85]

It was her last letter to Gilbert Murray. She recovered enough to attend Thomas Hardy's funeral on 17 January 1928 in Westminster Abbey before relapsing. She never seems to have lost her interest in life, even when her own was ebbing, and there is a sad note to the events at the end. Her dear friend Victoria (Buxton) de Bunsen came to visit her, and described to Jessie Stewart what happened:

My dearest Jessie

I have just been to JEH. Hope was of course *most* ungracious & very overwrought I thought. She said it was out of the question for anyone to see her, it wd. kill her. There was a nice nurse but she had terribly missed her nurse cousin Miss Lane who left on 4 just before she was so desperately ill. . . . I *left*. Then Hope went up to Jane who said she must see me, so H. had to run after me into the street. I went up for one moment. She is in the tiny back drawing room. She doesn't look washed—& very thin, just a [illegible] passive. She said, '*All* the life's gone out of me,' her voice fairly strong. Hope reads to her & the last 2 days she's better, temp. down each morn[?] a better night. I gave her all yr messages, love & sympathy. She looked so pleased. It *is* difficult. Obviously Hope *wishes* to keep everybody away—& said she would *not* write to Jane's friends or even answer the phone! but the man servant 'could do it!' Yet she is very anxious & *very* devoted. They have a very nice lady doctor now & *close* by. H. said her nieces call. I wonder who else of her friends are looking after her? I shall phone every other day or so—& I will let you know & will *go* again before long. . . . They say sort of pneumonia, lung and heart, & phlebitis.[86]

Was Mirrlees genuinely trying to do the right thing for her dying friend? Or do we see once again the possessiveness that seems to overshadow all of her care for her famous friend?

Jane Harrison died at 11 Mecklenburgh Street on 15 April 1928. Her will, a final clue to her relationship with Mirrlees, left everything to her niece, Marion Harrison.

Two days later Virginia Woolf met a distraught Hope Mirrlees crossing the graveyard behind Mecklenburg Street in the bitter windy rain, and recorded,

---

[85] JEH to GM [838], 8 Jan. 1928.   [86] Victoria de Bunsen to Jessie Stewart.

'We kissed by Cromwell's daughter's grave, where Shelley used to walk, for Jane's death.'[87]

Virginia and Leonard Woolf attended the funeral at St Marylebone Cemetery, Finchley on 19 April,

> getting 'there' . . . just as the service ended; marching into the church clamorously; but it was only barely full of the dingiest people; cousins I fancy from the North, very drab: the only male relation afflicted with a bubbly chin, a stubbly beard, & goggly eyes. Distinguished people drag up such queer chains of family when they die. They had hired Daimlers too, which succeeded the coffin at a foots [sic] pace. We walked to the grave; the clergyman, a friend, waited for the dismal company to collect; then read some of the lovelier, more rational parts of the Bible; & said, by heart, Abide with me. The gravedigger had given him, surreptitiously, a handful of clay, which he divided into three parts and dropped at the right moments. A bird sang most opportunely; with a gay indifference, & if one liked, hope, that Jane would have enjoyed. Then the incredibly drab female cousins advanced, each with a fat bunch of primroses & dropped them in; & we also advanced & looked down at the coffin at the bottom of a very steep brazen looking grave—But tho' L. almost cried, I felt very little—only the beauty of the Come unto me all ye that are weary; but as usual the obstacle of not believing dulled & bothered me. Who is 'God' & what the Grace of Christ? & what did they mean to Jane?[88]

The following October Virginia Woolf read at Newnham the lecture that was later published as *A Room of One's Own*, with its thesis that a woman must have money and a room of her own if she is to write fiction. Explicitly, with its shadowy figure of J—H—walking in the gardens of Fernham, the idea of the importance of 'a room of one's own', and the reference to Harrison's books on her shelves, and implicitly in its whole thesis that 'great poets do not die, they are continuing presences, they need only the opportunity to walk among us in the flesh',[89] the book is a memorial to her dead friend.

That the lecture was intended as a tribute to Harrison is borne out by the last words of Virginia Woolf's letter to Pernel Strachey, Principal of Newnham, thanking her for the invitation to lecture:

And now you must pull yourself together, . . . and bury Jane.[90]

---

[87] *The Letters of Virginia Woolf*, iii. 180. Cromwell's granddaughter is meant. The graveyard, that of St George the Martyr's Church on Queen Street, was just behind the house on Mecklenburg Street. The area, including 11 Mecklenburg Street, was bombed during the Second World War.

[88] Ibid. 181.   [89] Ibid. 171.   [90] *The Letters of Virginia Woolf*, iii. 551.

Bibliography

A complete bibliography of Jane Harrison's publications can be found in Shelley Arlen, *The Cambridge Ritualists: an Annotated Bibliography*, but those referred to in the text are included in the list below.

AARON, D. (ed.), *Studies in Biography*, Harvard English Studies (Cambridge, Mass.: Harvard University Press, 1978).

ACKERMAN, ROBERT, 'Some Letters of the Cambridge Ritualists', *Greek, Roman, and Byzantine Studies*, 12 (1971), 113–36.

—— 'Jane Ellen Harrison: the Early Work', *Greek, Roman, and Byzantine Studies* 13 (1972), 209–30.

—— *J. G. Frazer: His Life and Work* (Cambridge: Cambridge University Press, 1987).

—— 'The Cambridge Group: Origins and Composition' in Calder (ed.), *The Cambridge Ritualists Reconsidered*, 1–19.

—— Introduction in Harrison, *Prolegomena*, Mythos edn., pp. xii–xxx.

—— *The Myth and Ritual School: J. G. Frazer and the Cambridge Ritualists*, Theorists of Myth (New York: Garland Publishing, 1991).

ANNAN, NOEL, *The Dons: Mentors, Eccentrics and Geniuses* (London: HarperCollins, 1999).

ARLEN, SHELLEY, *The Cambridge Ritualists: an Annotated Bibliography of the Works by and About Jane Ellen Harrison, Gilbert Murray, Francis M. Cornford, and Arthur Bernard Cook* (Metuchen, NJ and London: Scarecrow Press, 1990).

ARNOLD, MATTHEW, *Culture and Anarchy* (London: Macmillan, 1903).

ASLIN, ELIZABETH, *The Aesthetic Movement* (New York: Excalibur Books, 1969).

AVVAKUM, PETROVICH, *The Life of the Archpriest Avvakum Written by Himself*, trans. Jane Ellen Harrison, ed. Hope Mirrlees and D. S. Mirsky (London: Hogarth Press, 1924).

—— *Archpriest Avvakum, the Life Written by Himself: With the Study of V. V. Vinogradov / Translations, Annotations, Commentary, and Historical Introduction by Kenneth N. Brostrom*, Michigan Slavic Translations no. 4 (Ann Arbor: Michigan Slavic Publications, c. 1979).

AYER, A. J. (ed.), *The Humanist Outlook* (London: Pemberton, 1968).

BEARD, MARY, *The Invention of Jane Harrison* (Cambridge, Mass.: Harvard University Press, 2000).

BEARD, MARY, 'Pausanias in Petticoats or *The Blue Jane*', in *Pausanias: Travel and Memory in Roman Greece*, ed. Susan E. Alcock, John F. Cherry, and Jaś Elsner (New York: Oxford University Press, 2001), 224–39.

BELL, CLIVE, *Art* (London: Chatto & Windus, 1914).

BENT, JAMES, THEODORE, *The Cyclades, or, Life Among the Insular Greeks* (London: Longmans, Green and Co., 1885).

—— *Aegean Islands: The Cyclades, or; Life Among the Insular Greeks* (Chicago: Argonaut, 1965; 1st pub. 1885 under subtitle).

BERARD, CLAUDE, et al., *City of Images: Iconography and Society in Ancient Greece* (Princeton: Princeton University Press, 1988).

BERGSON, HENRI, *Creative Evolution*, trans. Arthur Mitchell (London: Macmillan, 1960).

BORLAND, MAUREEN, *D. S. MacColl: Painter, Poet, Art Critic* (Harpenden: Lennard Publishing, 1995).

BREAY, C., 'Women and the Classical Tripos 1869–1914', in *Curriculum, Culture and Community*, suppl. 24 (Cambridge: Cambridge Philological Society, 1999), 49–70.

BRIGGS, WARD W., and CALDER, WILLIAM M. (eds.), *Classical Scholarship: a Biographical Encyclopedia*, Garland Reference Library of the Humanities (New York: Garland Publishing, 1990).

BROOKE, RUPERT, *The Letters of Rupert Brooke*, ed. Sir Geoffrey Keynes (London: Faber, 1968).

BRUNN, HEINRICH VON, *Geschichte der griechischen Kunstler* (Braunschweig, 1853).

—— *I rilievi delle urne estrusche* (Berlin: Deutsches archäologisches Institut, 1870).

—— and Flasch, Adam, *Griechische Kunstgeschichte* (Munich: Verlangsanstalt für Kunst und Wissenschaft, 1893).

BUCHAN, J. *The Dancing Floor*, ed. Marilyn Deegan (Oxford: Oxford University Press, 1997).

BURKERT, W., *Homo Necans: the Anthropology of Ancient Greek Sacrificial Ritual and Myth* (Berkeley: University of California Press, 1983).

—— *Greek Religion* (Cambridge, Mass.: Harvard University Press, 1985).

BUTCHER, S. H., *Some Aspects of the Greek Genius* (London: Macmillan, 1891).

CALDER, WILLIAM M., III (ed.) *The Cambridge Ritualists Reconsidered*, Illinois Classical Studies, Suppl. 2 (Atlanta: Scholars Press, 1991).

CARPENTER, HUMPHREY, *OUDS: a Centenary History of the Oxford University Dramatic Society 1885–1985* (Oxford: Oxford University Press, 1985).

CARPENTIER, MARTHA CELESTE, *Ritual, Myth, and the Modernist Text: the Influence of Jane Ellen Harrison on Joyce, Eliot, and Woolf*, Library of Anthropology (Amsterdam: Gordon and Breach, 1998).

CARRINGTON, DORA DE HOUGHTON, *Carrington: Letters and Extracts from Her Diaries*, ed. David Garnett (London: Jonathan Cape, 1970).

CAWS, MARY ANNE and WRIGHT, SARAH BIRD, *Bloomsbury and France: Art and Friends* (Oxford: Oxford University Press, 2000).

CLARK, RONALD WILLIAM, *The Life of Bertrand Russell* (London: Jonathan Cape, 1975).

CLARKE, A. K., *A History of the Cheltenham Ladies' College, 1853–1979* (3rd edn. London: Faber and Faber, 1979; 1st pub. 1953).

CLOUGH, BLANCHE ATHENA, *A Memoir of Anne Jemima Clough* (London: Arnold, 1897).

COLLIGNON, MAXIME, *A Manual of Mythology in Relation to Greek Art*, trans. and enlarged by Jane E. Harrison (London: Grevel, 1890).

COLVIN, SIDNEY, *Memories and Notes of Persons and Places* (London: Arnold, 1921).

COOK, A. B., 'Descriptive Animal Names in Greece', *Classical Review*, 8 (1894), 381–5.

——*Zeus: A Study in Ancient Religion*, 3 vols. (Cambridge: Cambridge University Press, 1914–40).

CORNFORD, FRANCIS MACDONALD, *Thucydides Mythistoricus* (London: Arnold, 1907).

——*From Religion to Philosophy: a Study in the Origins of Western Speculation* (New York: Longmans, Green and Co., 1912).

——*The Origin of Attic Comedy* (London: Arnold, 1914).

CRAWFORD, R., *The Savage and the City in the Work of T. S. Eliot*, Oxford English Monographs (Oxford: Oxford University Press, 1987).

CUDDY-KEANE, MELBA, 'The Politics of Comic Modes in Virginia Woolf's *Between the Acts*', *Publications of the Modern Language Association of America*, 105/2 (March 1990), 273–85.

DELANY, P., *The Neo-Pagans: Rupert Brooke and the Ordeal of Youth* (New York: Free Press, 1987).

DODDS, E. R., *The Greeks and the Irrational*, Sather Classical Lectures. (Berkeley: University of California Press, 1951).

DUNCAN, ISADORA, *My Life* (New York: Liveright, 1927).

EASTERLING, PATRICIA E., 'Gilbert Murray's Reading of Euripides', *Colby Quarterly*, 33/2 (June 1997), 113–27.

EDEL, LEON, *et al.*, *Telling Lives: the Biographer's Art*, ed. Marc Pachter (Washington DC: New Republic Books, 1979).

EDMUNDS, LOWELL (ed.), *Approaches to Greek Myth* (Baltimore: Johns Hopkins University Press, 1990).

ELIOT, GEORGE, *The Mill on the Floss* (Harmondsworth: Penguin Books, 1979).

EMERSON, ALFRED, 'Heinrich von Brunn', *American Journal of Archaeology*, 9/3 (1894), 367.

EURIPIDES *Hippolytus*, trans. Gilbert Murray (London: G. Allen & Sons, 1902).

EVANS, A. J., 'Mycenaean Tree and Pillar Cult and its Mediterranean Relations', *Journal of Hellenic Studies*, 21 (1901), 99–204.

EVANS, JOAN, *Time and Chance* (London: Longmans, Green and Co., 1943).

FARNELL, LEWIS RICHARD, *The Cults of the Greek States*, 5 vols. (Oxford: Clarendon Press, 1896–1909).

——*An Oxonian Looks Back* (London: Martin Hopkinson Ltd, 1934).

FRAZER, J. G., *Pausanias' Description of Greece*, 6 vols. (London: Macmillan, 1898).

FREUD, S., *Totem and Taboo: Resemblances Between the Psychic Lives of Savages and Neurotics*, trans. A. A. Brill (London: G. Routledge & Sons, 1919).

FRY, ROGER, *Letters of Roger Fry*, ed. Denys Sutton (London: Chatto & Windus, 1972).

GARDNER, ALICE, *A Short History of Newnham College, Cambridge* (Cambridge: Bowes & Bowes, 1921).

GARDNER, ERNEST, *Ancient Athens* (London: Macmillan, 1902).

GODDARD, H. C., 'Language and the New Philosophy', *Hibbert Journal*, 9 (1910–11), 247–62.

GRIERSON, H. J. C., *Swinburne* (rev. edn. London: Longmans, Green and Co., 1959).

GUTHRIE, W. K. C. (ed.), *The Unwritten Philosophy and Other Essays* (Cambridge: Cambridge University Press, 1950).

HARRIS, RENDELL, *The Ascent of Olympos* (Manchester: Manchester University Press, 1917).

HARRISON, JANE ELLEN, 'Archaeology and School Teaching', *Journal of Education*, 2 (1880), 105–6.

—— *Myths of the Odyssey in Art and Literature* (London: Rivingtons, 1882).

—— 'The Judgment of Paris', *Magazine of Art*, 5 (1882), 502–10.

—— 'Hellas at Cambridge', *Magazine of Art*, 7 (1884), 510–11.

—— *Introductory Studies in Greek Art* (London: T. Fisher Unwin, 1885).

—— 'Archaeology in Greece, 1887–1888', *Journal of Hellenic Studies*, 9 (1888), 118–33.

—— 'The Festival of the Aiora', *Classical Studies*, 3 (1889), 378–9.

—— 'Two Cyclices Relating to the Exploits of Theseus', *Journal of Hellenic Studies*, 10 (1889), 231–42.

—— 'On the Meaning of the Term Arrephori', *Classical Review*, 3 (1889), 187.

—— 'The Sculptured Tombs of Hellas', *Edinburgh Review*, 185 (1897), 441–64.

—— 'Delphika', *Journal of Hellenic Studies*, 19 (1899), 205–51.

—— 'The Dawn of Greece', *Quarterly Review*, 194 (1901), 218–43.

—— *Prolegomena to the Study of Greek Religion* (Cambridge: Cambridge University Press, 1903).

—— 'The E at Delphi', summary in *Proceedings of the Cambidge Philological Society*, 70 (1905), 1–3.

—— *The Religion of Ancient Greece*, Religions, Ancient and Modern (London: Constable, 1905).

—— *Primitive Athens as Described by Thucydides* (Cambridge: Cambridge University Press, 1906).

—— 'The Pillar and the Maiden', *Proceedings of the Classical Association*, 5 (1907), 1–13.

—— 'The Kouretes and Zeus Kouros', *Annual of the British School at Athens*, 15 (1908–9), 308–38.

—— 'The Influence of Darwinism on the Study of Religions', *Darwin and Modern Science: Essays in Commemoration of the Centenary of the Birth of Charles Darwin and of the Fiftieth Anniversary of the Publication of The Origin of Species*, ed. A. C. Seward (Cambridge: Cambridge University Press, 1909).

—— *Themis: a Study of the Social Origins of Greek Religion. With an Excursus on the Ritual Forms Preserved in Greek Tragedy by Gilbert Murray and a Chapter on the Origin of the Olympic Games* by F.M. *Cornford* (2nd edn. Cambridge: Cambridge University Press, 1927; 1st pub. 1912).

—— *Ancient Art and Ritual*, Home University Library of Modern Knowledge (London: Williams and Norgate, 1913).

—— *The Religion of Ancient Greece* (London: Constable, 1913).

—— *Alpha and Omega* (London: Sidgwick and Jackson, 1915).

—— *Russia and the Russian Verb: a Contribution to the Psychology of the Russian People* (Cambridge: Heffer and Sons, 1915).

—— 'The Head of John Baptist', *Classical Review*, 30/8 (1916), 216–19.

—— *Aspects, Aorists and the Classical Tripos* (Cambridge: Cambridge University Press, 1919).

—— *Epilegomena to the Study of Greek Religion* (Cambridge: Cambridge University Press, 1921).

—— *Mythology* (Boston: Marshall Jones, 1924).

—— *Reminiscences of a Student's Life* (London: Hogarth Press, 1925).

—— *Myths of Greece and Rome*, Benn's Sixpenny Library (London: Benn, 1927).

—— and MacColl, D. S., *Greek Vase Paintings: a Selection of Examples* (London: T. Fisher Unwin, 1894).

—— and Mirrlees, Hope, *The Book of the Bear, Being Twenty-One Tales Newly Translated from the Russian*, illus. R. A. Garnett (London: Nonesuch Press, 1926).

—— and Stewart, Jessie G., *Jane Ellen Harrison: a Portrait from Letters* (London: Merlin Press, 1959).

—— and Verrall, Margaret de G., *Mythology and Monuments of Ancient Athens: Being a Translation of a Portion of the 'Attica' of Pausanias, with an Introductory Essay and Archaeological Commentary* (London: Macmillan, 1890).

Harrison, J. F. C., *Learning and Living, 1790–1960: a Study in the History of the English Adult Education Movement* (London: Routledge & Kegan Paul, 1961).

Harrison, Marion, *Byliny Book: Hero Tales of Russia* (Cambridge: Heffer and Sons, 1915).

Henderson, John, *Juvenal's Mayor: The Professor who Lived on 2^d a Day*, Suppl. 20 (Cambridge: Cambridge Philological Society, 1988).

Heurgon-Desjardins, Anne and Desjardins, Paul, *Paul Desjardins et les décades de Pontigny: études témoignages et documents inédits* (Paris: Presses universitaires de France, 1964).

Holroyd, Michael, *Lytton Strachey: a Biography* (Harmondsworth: Penguin Books, 1971).

Hunt, Violet, *The Wife of Rossetti: Her Life and Death* (London: John Lane, The Bodley Head, 1932).

Hurwit, J. M., *The Athenian Acropolis: History, Mythology, and Archaeology from the Neolithic Era to the Present* (Cambridge: Cambridge University Press, 1999).

Huxley, Julian, *The Individual in the Animal Kingdom*, Cambridge Manuals of Science and Literature (Cambridge: Cambridge University Press, 1912).

HYDER, CLYDE K. (ed.), *Swinburne: the Critical Heritage*, Critical Heritage Series (London: Routledge & Kegan Paul, 1970).

HYMAN, STANLEY EDGAR, *The Armed Vision: a Study in the Methods of Modern Literary Criticism* (New York: Vintage Books, 1955).

——*The Tangled Bank: Darwin, Marx, Frazer and Freud as Imaginative Writers* (New York: Atheneum, 1974).

JAMES, WILLIAM, *The Varieties of Religious Experience: a Study in Human Nature: Being the Gifford Lectures on Natural Religion Delivered at Edinburgh in 1901–1902*, Modern Library of the World's Best Books (New York: Modern Library, 1902; repr. London: Longmans, Green and Co., 1908).

JENKINS, IAN, *Archaeologists & Aesthetes in the Sculpture Galleries of the British Museum 1800–1939* (London: British Museum Press, 1992).

——WAYWELL, GEOFFREY B. (eds.), *Sculptors and Sculpture of Caria and the Dodecanese* (London: British Museum Press, 1997).

JENKYNS, RICHARD, *The Victorians and Ancient Greece* (Oxford: Blackwell, 1980).

JOHN, AUGUSTUS EDWIN, *Chiaroscuro: Fragments of Autobiography* (New York: Pellegrini & Cudahy, 1952).

KENNEDY, DENNIS, *Granville Barker and the Dream of Theatre* (Cambridge: Cambridge University Press, 1985).

KLUCKHOHN, CLYDE, *Anthropology and the Classics* (Providence, RI: Brown University Press, 1961).

KUNZE, MAX, *Die Antikensammlung im Pergamonmuseum und in Charlottenburg* (Mainz: Philipp von Zabern, 1992).

LANG, ANDREW, *Myth, Ritual and Religion*, 2 vols. (2nd edn. London: Longmans, Green and Co., 1913; 1st pub. 1887).

LAWSON, JOHN CUTHBERT, *Modern Greek Folklore and Ancient Greek Religion: a Study in Survivals* (Cambridge: Cambridge University Press, 1910).

——*Walter Leaf, 1852–1927, Some Chapters of Autobiography, with a Memoir by Charlotte M. Leaf* (London: John Murray, 1932).

LEVY, PAUL, *Moore: G. E. Moore and the Cambridge Apostles* (London: Weidenfeld and Nicolson, 1979).

LLOYD-JONES, HUGH, *Blood for the Ghosts: Classical Influences in the Nineteenth and Twentieth Centuries* (London: Duckworth, 1982).

——'Artemis and Iphigenia'. *Journal of Hellenic Studies*, 103 (1983), 92–3.

——'Jane Ellen Harrison, 1850–1928' in Shils and Blacker (eds.), *Cambridge Women: Twelve Portraits*, 29–72.

MACCARTHY, DESMOND, *The Court Theatre* (London: A. H. Bullen, 1907).

MACCOLL, D. S., 'A Year of Post-Impressionism', *Nineteenth Century* (1912), 29.

——*Poems* (Oxford: Blackwell, 1940).

McDOUGALL, W., *Psychology, the Study of Behaviour*, Home University Library (London: Williams and Norgate, *c.* 1912).

McGINTY, P., *Interpretation and Dionysos: Method in the Study of a God* (The Hague: Mouton, 1978).

MACINTOSH, F., 'Greek Tragedy in Performance: Nineteenth- and Twentieth-Century Productions' in *The Cambridge Companion to Greek Tragedy*, ed. P. E. Easterling (Cambridge: Cambridge University Press, 1997), 284–323.

McNEES, ELEANOR JANE (ed.), *Virginia Woolf: Critical Assessments*, Helm Information Critical Assessments of Writers in English, 4 vols. (Mountfield: Helm Information Ltd., 1994).

McWILLIAMS-TULLBERG, RITA, *Women at Cambridge: a Men's University, Though of a Mixed Type* (London: Victor Gollancz, 1975).

MAHAFFY, JOHN PENTLAND, *Greek Pictures Drawn with Pen and Pencil* (London: Religious Tract Society, 1890).

MAIKA, PATRICIA, *Virginia Woolf's Between the Acts and Jane Harrison's Con/spiracy* (Ann Arbor: UMI Research Press, c. 1987).

MAINE, HENRY JAMES SUMNER, *Ancient Law: Its Connection with the Early History of Society and Its Relation to Modern Ideas* (London: John Murray, 1861).

MALLESON, ELIZABETH, *Autobiographical Notes and Letters, with a Memoir by Hope Malleson* (Guildford: privately printed, 1926).

MANNHARDT, WILHELM, *Wald- und Feldkulte* (Berlin: Gebrüder Borntraeger, 1875–7).

MARETT, R. R., *The Threshold of Religion* (2nd edn. London: Methuen, 1914; 1st pub. 1909).

MARSHALL, MARY PALEY, *What I Remember* (Cambridge: Cambridge University Press, 1947).

MIRRLEES, HOPE, *Madeleine: One of Love's Jansenists* (London and Glasgow: W. Collins Sons & Co. Ltd., 1919).

MIRSKY, D. S., *Jane Ellen Harrison and Russia* (Cambridge: Heffer and Sons, 1930).

MONK, RAY, *Bertrand Russell: the Spirit of Solitude* (London: Jonathan Cape, 1996).

MURRAY, GILBERT, *A History of Ancient Greek Literature*, Short Histories of the Literatures of the World (London: Heinemann, 1897; repr. New York: Appleton, 1932).

—— *The Rise of the Greek Epic; Being a Course of Lectures Delivered at Harvard University* (Oxford: Clarendon Press, 1907).

—— *Four Stages of Greek Religion: Studies Based on a Course of Lectures Delivered in April 1912 at Columbia University* (New York: Columbia University Press, 1912); repr. *Five Stages of Greek Religion* (London: Watts and Co., 1935).

—— *Euripides and His Age*, Home University Library of Modern Knowledge (London: Williams and Norgate Wm. Briggs, 1913).

—— 'The Conception of Another Life', *Edinburgh Review*, 221 (1915), 122–39.

—— 'Herd Instinct and the War', *Atlantic Monthly*, 115 (1915), 830–9.

—— *Faith, War and Policy, Lectures and Essays* (Boston: Houghton Mifflin Company; London: Oxford University Press, 1918).

—— *Jane Ellen Harrison: an Address Delivered at Newnham College, October 27th, 1928* (Cambridge: Heffer and Sons, 1928).

—— *Gilbert Murray: an Unfinished Autobiography, with Contributions by His Friends* (London: Allen and Unwin, 1960).

NEWTON, C. T., *Essays on Art and Archaeology* (London: Macmillan, 1880).

NEWTON, C. T., *C. K. Ogden: A Collective Memoir*, ed. J. R. L. Anderson and Florence, P. S. (London: Elek, 1977).

—— *The Oxford Book of Greek Verse in Translation*, ed. T. F. Higham and C. M. Bowra (Oxford: Clarendon Press, 1938).

PARIS, PIERRE, *Manual of Ancient Sculpture*, ed. and augmented by Jane Ellen Harrison (London: Grevel, 1890).

PEACOCK, SANDRA J., *Jane Ellen Harrison: the Mask and the Self* (New Haven: Yale University Press, 1988).

PETISCUS, A. H., *The Gods of Olympos: Or Mythology of the Greeks and Romans*, trans. Katherine A. Raleigh, (London: T. Fisher Unwin, 1892).

PETSAS, PHOTIOS, *Delphi: Monuments and Museum* (Athens: Krene Editions, 1981).

PHILLIPS, ANN, *A Newnham Anthology* (Cambridge: Cambridge University Press, 1979).

PHILLIPS, K. J., 'Jane Harrison and Modernism', *Journal of Modern Literature*, 17/4 (Spring 1991), 465–76.

PICKERING, W. S. F. (ed.), *Durkheim on Religion* (London: Routledge and Kegan Paul, 1975).

RABY, PETER, *Samuel Butler: a Biography* (London: Hogarth Press, 1991).

RAIKES, ELIZABETH, *Dorothea Beale of Cheltenham* (London: Archibald Constable and Co., 1908).

RAVERAT, GWEN, *Period Piece: a Cambridge Childhood* (London: Faber and Faber, 1952).

REINACH, A., 'Themis: Un nouveau livre sur les origines socials de la religion greque', *Revue de l'Histoire des Religions*, 69 (1914), 323–71.

RICHARDS, I., *The Meaning of Meaning* (London: Kegan Paul, 1936).

RIDGEWAY, WILLIAM, 'What People Produced the Objects Called Mycenean?', *Journal of the Hellenic Studies*, 16 (1896), 77–119.

—— *The Early Age of Greece* (Cambridge: Cambridge University Press, 1901).

—— *The Origin of Tragedy* (Cambridge: Cambridge University Press, 1910).

ROBINSON, ANNABEL, 'A New Light our Elders had not Seen: Deconstructing the "Cambridge Ritualists"', *Echos du Monde Classique/Classical Views*, 42, NS 17.3 (1988), 471–87.

—— 'Something Odd at Work: the Presence of Jane Harrison in *A Room of One's Own*' in McNees (ed.), *Virginia Woolf: Critical Assessments*, ii. 215–20.

ROHDE, ERWIN, *Psyche: Seelenculte und Unsterblichkeitsglaube der Griechen*, 2 vols. (Freiburg: Mohr, vol. i, 1890; vol. ii, 1894), trans. W. B. Hillis from the 8th edn., *Psyche: the Cult of Souls and Belief in Immortality Among the Greeks* (London: Routledge & Kegan Paul, 1950).

ROSSITER, STUART, *Blue Guide, Greece*, 4th edn. (London: Ernest Benn, 1981).

RUSSELL, BERTRAND, *The Principles of Mathematics* (Cambridge: Cambridge University Press, 1903).

—— *The Autobiography of Bertrand Russell*, 2 vols. (London: Unwin Brothers, 1967).

RUTKOWSKI, BOGDAN, *The Cult Places of the Aegean*, (New Haven: Yale University Press, 1985).

SCHLESIER, RENATE, 'Jane Ellen Harrison' in Briggs and Calder (eds.), *Classical Scholarship, a Biographical Encyclopedia*, 127–41.

—— 'Prolegomena to Jane Harrison's Interpretation of Ancient Greek Religion' in Calder (ed.), *The Cambridge Ritualists Reconsidered*, 185–226.

SHATTUCK, SANDRA, 'The Stage of Scholarship: Crossing the Bridge from Harrison to Woolf' in Jane Marcus (ed.), *Virginia Woolf and Bloomsbury: a Centenary Celebration* (London: Macmillan, 1987), 278–98.

SHILS, EDWARD, and BLACKER, CARMEN (eds.), *Cambridge Women: Twelve Portraits* (Cambridge: Cambridge University Press, 1996).

SIDNEY, SAMUEL, *Railways and Agriculture in North Lincolnshire* (London: W. Pickering, 1848).

SKAFF, WILLIAM, *The Philosophy of T. S. Eliot: from Skepticism to a Surrealist Poetic, 1909–1927* (Philadelphia: University of Pennsylvania Press, 1986).

SMITH, JEAN, and TOYNBEE, ARNOLD, *Gilbert Murray: an Unfinished Autobiography* (London: Allen and Unwin, 1960).

SMITH, LOGAN PEARSALL, *The English Language* (London: Williams and Norgate, 1912).

SMITH, W. ROBERTSON, *Lectures on the Religion of the Semites. First Series: The Fundamental Institutions* (Edinburgh: Adam & Charles Black, 1889).

SNODGRASS, ANTHONY M., *Homer and the Artists: Text and Picture in Early Greek Art* (Cambridge: Cambridge University Press, 1998).

SOURVINOU-INWOOD, CHRISTIANE, 'Myth as History: the Previous Owners of the Delphic Oracle' in Jan Bremmer (ed.), *Interpretations of Greek Mythology* (London: Routledge, 1987), 215–241.

STEVENSON, R. A. M., 'Greek Vase Painting', *The Art Journal* NS 57 (1894), 208–9.

STEWART, JESSIE G., *Jane Ellen Harrison: a Portrait from Letters* (London: Merlin Press, 1959).

STEWART, JOHN ALEXANDER, *Plato's Doctrine of Ideas* (Oxford: Clarendon Press, 1909; repr. New York: Russell and Russell, 1964).

STOCKING, GEORGE W., *After Tylor: British Social Anthropology, 1888–1951* (Madison: University of Wisconsin Press, 1995).

STRACHEY, BARBARA, *Remarkable Relations: the Story of the Pearsall Smith Family* (London: Gollancz, 1980).

STRACHEY, RAY, *The Cause: a Short History of the Women's Movement in Great Britain*, 2nd edn. with an new preface by Barbara Strachey (London: Virago, 1979).

STRAUSS, DAVID FRIEDRICH, *The Life of Jesus, Critically Examined*, trans. Marian Evans (New York: C. Blanchard, 1860).

STRAY, CHRISTOPHER, 'Digs and Degrees', *Classics Ireland*, 2 (1995), 121–31.

—— *Classics Transformed: Schools, Universities, and Society in England, 1830–1960* (Oxford: Clarendon Press, 1998).

—— (ed.), *Classics in 19th and 20th Century Cambridge: Curriculum, Culture and Community* (Cambridge: Cambridge Philological Society, 1999).

STRONG, EUGÉNIE SELLERS, *Apotheosis and After-Life: Three Lectures on Certain Phases of Art and Religion in the Roman Empire* (London: Constable, 1915).

STRONG, EUGÉNIE SELLERS, *Letters to a Tutor: the Tennyson Family Letters to Henry Graham Dakyns (1861–1911), with the Audrey Tennyson Death-Bed Diary*, ed. Henry Graham Dakyns (Metuchen, NJ: Scarecrow Press, 1988).

THOMAS, DONALD, *Swinburne: the Poet in His World* (London: Weidenfeld and Nicolson, 1979).

THOMSON, GLADYS SCOTT, *Mrs. Arthur Strong: a Memoir* (London: Cohen & West, 1949).

TORGOVNICK, MARIANNA, 'Discovering Jane Harrison' in Carola M. Kaplan and Anne B. Simpson (eds.), *Seeing Double: Revisioning Edwardian and Modernist Literature* (New York: St. Martin's Press, 1996), 131–48.

TROTTER, WILFRID, *Instincts of the Herd in Peace and War* (3rd edn. Oxford: Oxford University Press, 1953; 1st pub. 1915).

TURNER, FRANK, *The Greek Heritage in Victorian Britain* (New Haven: Yale University Press, 1981).

TYLOR, EDWARD B., *Primitive Culture: Researches into the Development of Mythology, Philosophy, Religion, Art, and Custom* (London: J. Murray, 1871).

VERRALL, ARTHUR WOOLLGAR, *Euripides the Rationalist* (Cambridge: Cambridge University Press, 1985).

VICINUS, MARTHA, *Independent Women: Work and Community for Single Women, 1850–1920* (London: Virago, 1985).

VICKERY, J. B., *The Literary Impact of the Golden Bough* (Princeton: Princeton University Press, 1973).

VILDRAC, C., *Livre d'Amour* (Paris: Éditions de la nouvelle revue française, 1919).

WATERHOUSE, HELEN, *The British School at Athens: The First Hundred Years* (London: The British School at Athens, 1986).

WEST, FRANCIS, *Gilbert Murray: a Life* (Beckenham: Croom Helm, 1984).

WILSON, DUNCAN, *Gilbert Murray, OM, 1866–1957* (Oxford: Clarendon Press, 1987).

WOOLF, LEONARD S., *Downhill All the Way: an Autobiography of the Years 1919–1939* (London: Hogarth Press, 1967).

WOOLF, VIRGINIA, *A Room of One's Own* (London: Hogarth Press, 1929; repr. Toronto: Clarke, Irwin & Co., 1978).

——*The Letters of Virginia Woolf*, iii. *A Change of Perspective*, ed. Nigel Nicolson (London: Hogarth Press, 1977).

——*The Diary of Virginia Woolf*, ed. Anne Olivier Bell (Harmondsworth: Penguin Books, 1981).

Credits

The author and publishers are grateful for permission to include the following copyright material and apologize for any errors or omissions:

Unpublished material from the diary of A. C. Benson is reproduced by kind permission of the Master and Fellows, Magdalene College, Cambridge.

Unpublished material from Frances Crofts Cornford's letters is reproduced by kind permission of Professor J. P. Cornford.

Unpublished material in the Jane Harrison archives is reproduced by kind permission of the Principal and Fellows, Newnham College, Cambridge.

Unpublished material from the archives of D. S. MacColl is reproduced by permission of Robert A. Elton and Glasgow University Library, Department of Special Collections.

Unpublished material of Hope Mirrlees is reproduced with permission of the Literary Executors of her Estate.

Unpublished material of Gilbert Murray is reproduced by kind permission of Alexander Murray.

Unpublished material of Harry Payne is reproduced with his permission.

Unpublished material by Bertrand Russell is reproduced by kind permission of the Betrand Russell archives, William Ready Division of Archives and Research Collections, McMaster University Library, Hamilton, Canada.

Unpublished material of Jessie Stewart is reproduced by kind permission of K. Claire Pace and Judy Dunn.

Frontispiece: Reproduced courtesy of the Principal and Fellows, Newnham College, Cambridge.
Fig. 2 Photograph by the author.
Fig. 9 Reproduced courtesy of Andrée MacColl.

Index